SHAKESPEARE STUDIES

SHAKESPEARE STUDIES
Volume XXXIII

EDITOR
SUSAN ZIMMERMAN

Queens College
The City University of New York

ASSOCIATE EDITOR
GARRETT SULLIVAN

Pennsylvania State University

Madison • Teaneck
Fairleigh Dickinson University Press

PR
2885
.552
v.33

Associated University Presses
2010 Eastpark Boulevard
Cranbury, NJ 08512

The paper used in this publication meets the requirements
of the American National Standard for Permanence of Paper
for Printed Library Materials Z39.48-1984.

International Standard Book Number: 0-8386-4075-3 (vol. XXXIII)
International Standard Serial Number: 0-0582-9399

All editorial correspondence concerning *Shakespeare Studies* should be addressed to the Editorial Office, *Shakespeare Studies,* English Dept., Queens College, CUNY, Flushing, NY 11367. Orders and subscriptions should be directed to Associated University Presses, 2010 Eastpark Boulevard, Cranbury, New Jersey 08512.

Shakespeare Studies disclaims responsibility for statements,
either of fact or opinion, made by contributors.

PRINTED IN THE UNITED STATES OF AMERICA

Contents

6 Contents

8 *Contents*

Foreword

V<small>OLUME</small> XXXIII of *Shakespeare Studies* is pleased to continue its tradition of Forums on theoretical, historical, and critical issues of importance to Shakespearean scholars with a series of commentaries on "Extra-mural Psychoanalysis," organized and edited by Cynthia Marshall. Contributions to the Forum consider collectively the current relevance of psychoanalytical theory to literary criticism, featuring the work of Lynn Enterline and David Hillman (working in tandem), Lisa Freinkel, Graham Hammill, Elizabeth D. Harvey, Heather Hirschfeld, Kristen Poole, Douglas Trevor, and Susan Zimmerman, with an introduction by Cynthia Marshall.

Volume XXXIII also presents the third in another of its series, essays on "Early Modern Drama Around the World: The State of Study," initiated in Volume XXXI by former Editor Leeds Barroll. Previous essays in this series have discussed theatrical practices during the time of Shakespeare in Japan, China, France, and Spain. In a departure from its predecessors, Part III of this series features only one essay, an extensive and timely analysis of "The Architecture of Italian Theaters" by Eugene J. Johnson.

The three articles in this volume represent an interesting diversity of topic. Gina Bloom's "Words Made of Breath: Gender and Vocal Agency in *King John*" examines the tensions between spiritual and material meanings of breath in the early modern period; and Leeds Barroll's "Shakespeare and the Second Blackfriars Theater" urges a reconsideration of the historical documents dealing with the King's Servants at the Blackfriars. A review article by Paul Cohen on Timothy Hampton's work on Renaissance France focuses on the role of nationalism in the development of the nation-state, an issue that engages many cultural and political historians of early modern England as well.

Finally, Volume XXXIII offers its customary collection of wide-ranging reviews, including (among others) studies of Shakespeare as literary dramatist, of London civic theater, of Shakespeare and the Victorians, of Shakespeare and the Lacanian gaze, of early modern uses of script and print, of English attitudes toward ethnicity and race, of English mercantilism and disease, and of theaters and encyclopedias in early modern Europe.

SUSAN ZIMMERMAN, Editor

Contributors

JONATHAN BALDO is Associate Professor of English at the Eastern School of Music of the University of Rochester. He is currently completing a book on rationalism and historical memory in Shakespeare.

GINA BLOOM is Assistant Professor of English at Lawrence University. She is currently completing a book concerned with the representation and performance of voice on the early modern English stage.

A. R. BRAUNMULLER has recently served as co-editor of *The Complete Pelican Shakespeare* and in 2004 lectured at events marking the four hundredth anniversary of the Treaty of London (King's College, London).

MICHAEL D. BRISTOL is Greenshields Professor of English at McGill University. He is author of *Big-Time Shakespeare, Shakespeare's America/America's Shakespeare*, and *Carnival and Theatre.*

DOUGLAS A. BROOKS is Associate Professor of English at Texas A&M University and editor of *Shakespeare Yearbook.* He is currently completing a book that examines the conceptual links between printing and parenting in early modern English literature.

PALMIRA BRUMMETT is Professor of History at the University of Tennessee. She is currently writing a book on early modern European mapping of the Ottoman empire.

PAUL COHEN is Maître de conférences at the University of Paris-VIII (Vincennes-Saint Denis). He is currently completing a book on the emergence of French as a national language in early modern France.

HOLLY A. CROCKER is Assistant Professor of English and Comparative Literature at the University of Cincinnati. She is currently editing a collection of essays entitled *Comic Provocations: Exposing the Corpus of the Old French Fabliaux*, and is completing a book entitled *Seeing Chaucer's Manhood*.

LARS ENGLE is Associate Professor of English and Chair of the English Deparment at the University of Tulsa. He is the author of *Shakespearean Pragmatism* (1993), and a co-editor of *English Renaissance Drama: A Norton Anthology* (2002).

LYNN ENTERLINE is Professor of English at Vanderbilt University. She is author of *The Rhetoric of the Body from Ovid to Shakespeare* (2000), and *The Tears of Narcissus: Melancholia and Masculinity in Early Modern Writing* (1995). She is currently writing *Shakespeare's Schoolroom*, a book that examines archival and literary reactions to rhetorical training and disciplinary practices in Elizabethan grammar schools.

LUKAS ERNE is Professor of English at the University of Neuchâtel, Switzerland. He is the author of *Shakespeare as Literary Dramatist* (2003), and the editor, with M.J. Kidnie, of *Textual Performances: The Modern Reproduction of Shakespeare's Drama* (2004).

LISA FREINKEL is Associate Professor of English and Director of the Program in Comparative Literature at the University of Oregon. Her current project, *Shakespeare's God*, examines the interrelated questions of money, language, and the sacred in Shakespeare's work.

GRAHAM HAMMILL is Associate Professor of English at the University of Notre Dame. He is the author of *Sexuality and Form: Caravaggio, Marlowe, and Bacon*, and is currently completing a project on Moses and political theology from Machiavelli to Freud.

ELIZABETH D. HARVEY is the author of *Ventriloquized Voices: Feminist Theory and Renaissance Texts*, editor of *Sensible Flesh:*

On Touch in Early Modern Culture, and co-editor of *Luce Irigaray and Premodern Culture: Thresholds of History*. She is currently completing a book on early modern literature and medicine that is entitled *Inscrutable Organs*.

DAVID HILLMAN is a Lecturer in English at the University of Cambridge and Fellow of King's College, Cambridge. He is currently completing a book, *Shakespeare's Entrails: Belief, Scepticism & the Interior of the Body*, and co-editing (with Adam Phillips) *The Book of Interruptions*.

HEATHER HIRSCHFELD, Assistant Professor of English at the University of Tennessee, Knoxville, is the author of *Joint Enterprises: Collaborative Drama and the Institutionalization of the English Renaissance Theater*. She is currently working on early modern revenge tragedy and religious change.

PETER HULME is Professor in Literature at the University of Essex. He is the co-editor (with William H. Sherman) of the recent Norton edition of *The Tempest*.

EUGENE J. JOHNSON is Class of 1955 Memorial Professor of Art at Williams College. He is working on a book on the architecture of theaters in Italy in the sixteenth and seventeenth centuries.

M. LINDSAY KAPLAN is Associate Professor of English at Georgetown University. She is the editor of a contextual edition of *The Merchant of Venice* and is currently researching a book on changing attitudes towards marital sexuality in post-Reformation English culture.

ROSEMARY KEGL is Associate Professor of English at the University of Rochester. She is currently completing a book on the staging of death in English Renaissance drama.

CAROLE LEVIN is Willa Cather Professor and Graduate Chair of the Department of History at the University of Nebraska, Lincoln. She is the author of *The Heart and Stomach of a King: Elizabeth I and the Politics of Sex and Power* (1994), *The Reign of Elizabeth I* (2002), and, most recently, the co-edited collections *High and*

Mighty Queens of Early Modern England (2003) and *Elizabeth I: Always Her Own Free Woman* (2003).

CYNTHIA MARSHALL is Professor of English at Rhodes College. She is author of *The Shattering of the Self: Violence, Subjectivity, and Early Modern Texts* (2002), and editor of *Shakespeare's Production:* As You Like It (2004).

NABIL MATAR is Professor of English and Department Head at Florida Institute of Technology. His *Britain and Barbary, 1589–1689* is forthcoming in 2005.

KRISTEN POOLE is Associate Professor of English at the University of Delaware. She is currently working on a book about eschatology and physics in early modern England.

CHRISTOPHER PYE is Professor of English at Williams College. Author of *The Vanishing: Shakespeare, the Subject and Early Modern Culture*, he is completing a book on Shakespeare and the history of distraction.

KATHERINE ROWE is Professor of English at Bryn Mawr. She is the author of *Dead Hands: Fictions of Agency, Renaissance to Modern* (1999), and co-editor of *Reading the Early Modern Passions: Essays in the Cultural History of Emotion* (2004) with Gail Kern Paster and Mary Floyd-Wilson.

MICHAEL SCHOENFELDT is Professor of English and Associate Dean for the Humanities at the University of Michigan. He is currently editing the *Companion to Shakespeare's Sonnets* and is at work on a book-length study of the ethics of emotion in early modern culture.

PAUL STEVENS is Professor and Canada Research Chair in English Literature at the University of Toronto. He is currently editing a collection of essays with David Loewenstein on *Early Modern Nationalism and Milton's England.*

ALAN STEWART is Professor of English and Comparative Literature at Columbia University. He is currently completing a book on Dr. Lopez and the Portingales of Elizabethan London.

JULIA THOMAS is a lecturer at the Centre for Critical and Cultural Theory, Cardiff University, UK. She is author of *Pictorial Victorians* (2006) and *Victorian Narrative Painting* (2000). She is currently writing a book on Shakespeare and illustration.

DOUGLAS TREVOR is Assistant Professor of English at the University of Iowa. He is the author of *The Poetics of Melancholy in Early Modern England* (2004), and is currently working on a book about theology and love in seventeenth-century England.

EVELYN B. TRIBBLE is Professor of English at the University of Otago. She is working on two book projects: one on Shakespeare, film, and sound, and the other on distributed cognition in the theater and in print culture.

SUZANNE VERDERBER is Assistant Professor of English and Humanities at Pratt Institute and is currently working on a book examining the construction of the fiction of the individual in the medieval period.

JULIAN YATES teaches in the Department of English at the University of Delaware. He is the author of *Error, Misuse, Failure: Object Lessons and the English Renaissance* (2003).

SUSAN ZIMMERMAN is Professor of English at Queens College, CUNY, and Editor of *Shakespeare Studies*. She is most recently the author of *The Early Modern Corpse and Shakespeare's Theatre* (2005).

SHAKESPEARE
STUDIES

EARLY MODERN DRAMA
AROUND THE WORLD

The State of Study: 3

Preface

The Editor

THE SERIES "Early Modern Drama Around the World," begun in Volume 31 by Founding Editor Leeds Barroll, focuses on non-British theatrical traditions that are roughly contemporaneous with the life of Shakespeare. Volume 31 featured articles by Grant Shen on late Ming drama and Richard Pym on drama in Golden Age Spain; Volume 32 on Japanese and French theaters, by Mitsuru Kamachi and Stephanie O'Hara, respectively. In the current volume, Eugene J. Johnson has contributed an essay from his authoritative study of the architecture of Renaissance Italian theaters and its relationship to theatrical practices of the time.

The Architecture of Italian Theaters Around the Time of William Shakespeare

Eugene J. Johnson

In italy during Shakespeare's lifetime (1564–1616) two of the most important architectural innovations in the history of modern theater took place: the invention of the proscenium arch and the invention of the theater with boxes. Together, these innovations redefined the way the audience viewed the action of the play and the audience was accommodated. In the decades before Shakespeare's birth, the modern notion of an illusionistic setting for the action had been developed by Italian painters and architects. The purpose of this series in *Shakespeare Studies* on drama outside England is to situate early modern English theater in a larger global context. Continental Europe in the sixteenth century saw the simultaneous growth of several centers of new dramatic expression, each with its own distinct characteristics. English drama was uniquely splendid as literature, for instance, but it was Italy that largely gave Western theater its modern visual and spatial forms.

The Italian contributions came into being through a rich series of experimentations with possible architectural forms for theaters: from literal reconstructions of ancient Roman theaters, driven by humanist interest in antiquity, to the construction of large rectangular rooms with their own stages to house court spectacles, to the building of commercial theaters for the performances of *commedia dell'arte* troupes. The situation was extremely complex, and so these three categories were quite fluid and often bled into each other. Further complicating the story was the political situation on the Italian peninsula, divided into a number of separate small states, each with its own peculiar form of government and its own cultural traditions. These states watched each other carefully, sometimes emulating and always striving to outdo whatever their rivals may have ventured in the way of theater. Out of this stew of political, cultural, and economic interests rose the architecture of the modern theater. Sadly, the visual and physical evidence for this remarkable moment is almost entirely gone. All the theaters built in Italy during this period, with three exceptions, have vanished, as has most other visual evidence. As a consequence, the study of Italian theater architecture of early modern times has to be based almost entirely on written documentary sources. Only from these documents, which scholars continue to unearth, can we reconstruct in our imaginations what once stood.

A standard way to define the theater focuses on three elements: the text, the actors, and the audience. For an architectural historian, this definition is inadequate, because it fails to take into account the physical setting that brings these three elements together—that allows the audience to hear the actors recite the text, to see their movements and expressions, and to be carried visually to another time and place by the illusions created by the scenery. This essay, then, focuses on spaces that were constructed or adapted to contain theatrical performances rather than on the performances themselves.

Although a few plays were given in private settings a bit earlier, modern theater history in Italy, in the sense of performances presented to a more or less public audience, seems to begin in 1486, when Ercole d'Este, Duke of Ferrara, ordered a production of Plautus's *Menaechmi* in the courtyard of his palace and when the production of a tragedy by Seneca, *Ippolitus*, was offered by Cardinal Raffaele Riario, nephew of Pope Sixtus IV, in front of his palace in Rome.[1] In both cases ancient Roman plays were deliberately revived, in line with the general interest in revivifying the culture of antiquity in fifteenth-century Italy. Very quickly modern plays began to be written and performed at courts around the peninsula, alongside revivals of Roman works, which were given sometimes in Latin and sometimes in new translations into Italian. In these early years no one built theaters. Plays were performed on temporary stages erected in the courtyards or large halls of palaces. To maintain decorum, men and women were accommodated in different parts of the theater, and princely personages became as important a part of the show as what appeared onstage.

Artists of the caliber of Leonardo da Vinci, in Milan, and Raphael, in Rome, designed sets for courtly theatrical events. For one set by Leonardo, who was a mechanical as well as an artistic genius, a few quick sketches are preserved. The set consisted of a mountain that, to the amazement of the audience, opened to reveal another scene inside. All visual traces of Raphael's set for a performance of the great playwright and poet Lodovico Ariosto's *I suppositi* in 1519[2] have vanished, but perhaps one may be able to imagine something of what they looked like from the architectural settings of his last frescoes in the Vatican Stanze. The play was given under the patronage of Pope Leo X, who had it performed in the palace of a friendly cardinal rather than in the Vatican itself. The political import of the gathering of the audience into a palatial hall can be grasped from a couple of details. After the audience (all male) had arranged itself on steps at one end of the room, the pope, followed by cardinals and foreign ambassadors, entered. Leo settled himself in a chair raised on a podium five steps above the floor, while the cardinals and ambassadors arranged themselves in lines to either side of the elevated papal throne. The audience literally watched the play over the shoulders of Leo, who was symbolically placed at the center of the Christian world. The room was lit by a series of newly made candelabra in the form of letters that spelled out LEO X PON. MAXIMUS—a dazzling early moment of having one's name up in lights. Presumably Leo sat directly opposite the vanishing point of Raphael's one-point perspective set. As the ruler, Leo was uniquely privileged to have that view—the only point from which the perspectival illusion worked perfectly. After the performance the theater was dismantled. Raphael's set was never seen again, and the blazing papal name went to who-knows-what reward. This Roman theater, in its temporary nature, was utterly typical of what happened in the late fifteenth and early sixteenth centuries.

Not too long before Shakespeare was born, however, permanent court and commercial theaters began to be erected in Italy. The earliest evidence we have for a permanent theater was one built in 1531 in Ferrara, the architect apparently none other than Lodovico Ariosto himself.[3] The theater was not erected in the ducal palace, as one might expect since it was under ducal patronage, but rather in a space above an apothecary shop. There is no known description of the seating, but we do know that the set was a permanently installed generic view of a city (how constructed we are not told) that could be, as a contemporary source put it, "Cremona one night and Ferrara the next." As such, it could serve year after year for a succession of plays. Sadly, the theater only lasted one year, burning down in December of 1532 just before the scheduled performance of one of Ariosto's own plays. We are told—who knows how reliably—that Ariosto died shortly thereafter, grief-stricken by the loss of his design.

The earliest permanent court theater for which we have an actual description was built in Mantua by the court architect Giovanni Battista Bertani, an artist of considerable inventive powers whose work is unfortunately not very well known outside Italy. Mantua since the late fifteenth century had been a city with a rich theatrical life, even if its Gonzaga rulers could never quite afford everything their voracious appetites for the arts led them to desire. The theater was commissioned from Bertani by Cardinal Ercole Gonzaga, regent during the minority of the heir, Francesco. The building was well under way in 1549, but it may not have been completed until 1551.[4]

The only trace we have of this theater is a short passage in a longer poem written by one Raffaello Toscano to celebrate the wonders of Mantua. The poem was published in 1586, two years before the theater was destroyed by fire and replaced by one designed by Antonio Maria Viani, court painter and architect at the end of the sixteenth century.

Toscano devotes a mere sixteen lines to the theater, but from that brief notice quite a clear general picture of the theater emerges.

> Rich is the scene: where the actors intent
> On the beautiful works gather often,
> Whose proud and noble ornaments
> Show how much art Art has placed here.
> And there quickly follows a city of hewn beams
> and of wood painted, or carved in relief,
> Which seems to be filled with as many arts
> And virtues as once had Athens.
>
> Against the great Stage which gracefully slopes
> Bertani the architect places a thousand steps
> That a half-circle make, and there one ascends
> With great ease to the roof;
> Below is a field, where often the fiery Mars
> Lights the breasts of his followers:
> Temples, Towers, Palaces and Perspectives
> There are; and figures that appear live.

The poet's opening blast, "Rich is the scene," sets the stage for telling us that the scenery was made of wood, painted, and covered in relief. The forms came together to make a city "which appears to be filled with as many arts and virtues as once had Athens." Although this claim must be taken with a tablespoon of salt, it tells us of the ambition to rival the ancients that stands behind the theater's design. The last two lines of the next stanza make clear that all the arts were used for the scenery: the architecture of the stage buildings, the sculptural figures that appeared to be alive, and the perspective paintings that presumably suggested depth behind the three-dimensional structures. Whatever was performed in Mantua in the court theater during the second half of the sixteenth century took place before that unchanging city of arts and virtues.

Opposite the gracefully sloping stage (surely raised) Bertani placed "a thousand steps," easily ascended to the roof. That number of steps seems unlikely, but surely several rows rose toward the ceiling. The steps were arranged in a half-circle—a crucial point. Greek and Roman theaters, avidly studied by humanist scholars, had semicircular seating, and Bertani's theater deliberately imitated that aspect of ancient theater design. At the base of the steps lay an open area, like the orchestra of an ancient theater, on which the actors also performed. The poet's image of Mars, the god of war, often inflaming the breasts of his followers from here makes one wonder if the theater might have been put to other, more obviously political uses—the rallying of troops when Mantua was threatened, for instance. All in all, the poet describes a theater whose auditorium could have been taken almost literally from the text of the Roman architect, Vitruvius, whose *de architectura* is the only architectural treatise to come down to us from antiquity. But the set was not derived from antiquity. Rather, it was the generic, illusionistic city set that had been developed in the first half of the sixteenth century. Ariosto's set that burned in Ferrara in 1531 is but one in a line of illusionistic city sets that goes back to Ferrara in 1509, when Pellegrino da Udine painted an illusionistic backdrop of a view of that city.

Bertani's theater followed by only a decade the theater that Sebastiano Serlio had erected in a palace in Vicenza in 1539. Like Bertani's, Serlio's theater had curved seating (albeit not in a semicircle, but in a segmental curve) and a scene of a city onstage. Serlio's publication in 1545 of woodcuts of his Vicentine theater in the first volume of his multivolume illustrated book on architecture probably served as an important contemporary source for Bertani.[5] Serlio's theater is very famous, because he left us visual traces in his book, but one must be careful not to put too much emphasis on it—to take it as too completely typical—just because we are lucky enough to have an actual record of what it looked like. Serlio's theater, like almost all theaters that preceded Bertani's, was temporary. The Mantuan theater was permanent. Theater architecture was no longer just for the moment; if it was not for the ages, at least it was for the foreseeable future.

What Bertani's theater stood inside is not clear. Some scholars believe that instead of constructing the theater in one of the cavernous rooms of the extensive and ever-expanding Gonzaga palace, Bertani built a new shell to contain it outside the walls of the palace, along an important street of the city. If that were indeed the case, then Bertani's was surely one of the very earliest freestanding buildings in Italy erected to house a permanent theater. It makes sense that such a development might have taken place in Mantua. Unfortunately, we just can't be sure that it did. By the middle of the sixteenth century going to regularly staged theatrical performances, sponsored by ruling princes, had become part of normal life in some court cities, especially during carnival season. Putting a new theater between the palace and the town would keep the crowds out of the palace, while the prince and his party could enter and leave with ease. A visible theater outside the palace would be yet another example of princely largesse—of that duty of good princes to patronize the arts, embellish their realms, and entertain their citizens.

No other city in Italy in the second half of the sixteenth century had a more vigorous development of court theater than Florence under the Medici.[6] Particularly to celebrate dynastic weddings, but also to honor important visitors, the Medici produced a series of spectacular theatrical events. In 1565, for instance, the enormous Salone dei Cinquecento in Palazzo Vecchio was fitted out by Giorgio Vasari for a performance of *La Cofanaria* by Francesco d'Ambra to mark the marriage of the heir to the duchy, Francesco, to a Hapsburg princess, Giovanna d'Austria.[7] This was a signal event in Medici history. Francesco's mother, Eleanora of Toledo, was not a princess, but only the noble daughter of the Spanish viceroy of Naples. Francesco's father, Duke Cosimo I, later the first Grand Duke, had not been able to command a consort of royal blood, but he could provide one for his heir.

Vasari arranged the rectangular Salone dei Cinquecento so that seats were placed along three walls, atop a raised terrace protected by a balustrade, to accommodate some 360 women. In the middle of the hall rose a dais on which the duke and duchess and the royal newlyweds sat, the center of attention. The men of the audience occupied benches placed around the dais The raised stage, placed on one of the short sides of the room at the same level as the terrace of the women's seats, was framed by a pair of Corinthian columns that formed what seems to have been the very first proscenium arch. Between the columns hung a curtain painted by Federico Zuccaro to show a ducal hunt taking place in a landscape with the city of Florence in the background. This first proscenium arch, then, literally acted as a picture frame. When the curtain disappeared, another picture was revealed—a set that represented an actual quarter of Florence. In the middle of the set the Via Maggio, a major thoroughfare south of the Arno, seemed to stretch into the distance, because Vasari had painted it according to the principles of one-point perspective. To either side of the receding street, and at right angles to it, were shown the houses that bordered the Arno a the entrance to the street. Via Maggio was one of the major urban developments of the reign of Cosimo I, and so the set represented modern Florence prospering under Medici rule. There was also a triumphal arch depicting the Arno and the Danube, now in symbolic confluence through the Medici-Hapsburg union. Over the architrave that spanned the distance between the columns of the proscenium to form the top of the picture frame rose the Medici coat of arms, borne by putti. The walls of the room had already been decorated by Vasari with important scenes from Florentine history. The whole was a celebration of Florentine and Medici power, with the rulers at the center of the show. The room did not serve only as a theater, however. After the play, the audience withdrew and then returned to find the space set up as a banquet hall. After eating, the guests again withdrew and returned to find the room converted to dancing, which lasted till dawn.

The Medici continued to use views of their city and its cultural heritage as the sets for important theatrical performances that served dynastic purposes. In 1569, to honor the visit of the Archduke Karl of Austria, the Medici produced Giambattista Cini's play *La Vedova*, with a set by Baldassare Lanci that showed the political heart of Florence. The audience looked at a representation of Palazzo Vecchio, the medieval town hall that the Medici now occupied as their residence. In the distance rose Filippo Brunelleschi's dome of Florence Cathedral, moved for the occasion a bit to the east so that that staggering achievement of Florentine architecture would be visible onstage. In front of Palazzo Vecchio appeared the three sixteenth-century statues that grace the Piazza Signoria, including Michelangelo's famous *David*. To stage right one made out the arcade of the Loggia dei Lanzi, while to stage left appeared the northernmost bays of the Palazzo degli Uffizi, under construction at the time. Vasari, the favored architect of Cosimo I, designed the Uffizi to house the bureaucracy of Cosimo's newly created autocratic state. Lanci's set represented the past and present achievements of Florence and the symbols of Medici control. According to a contemporary observer, Ignazio Danti, Lanci used periaktoi, rotating vertical triangular prisms with different scenes painted on each side, to make possible quick set changes. The scene of Palazzo Vecchio gave way to the Ponte Santa Trinità, another site in Florence, and that in turn to the nearby village of Arcetri. In this production, the unity of place established by the single city set earlier in the century was abandoned for a far more fluid movement of the action from place to place.

Vasari's Uffizi was to serve several other purposes, however, one being as the site of a new permanent court theater to replace the Salone dei Cinquecento. The Salone did not easily lend itself to the increasingly lavish court spectacles the Medici wished to put on, because there was no room for the deep stage such spectacles required to house multiple sets and the machinery to make flights of gods and goddesses appear onstage. Lanci's periaktoi took the shallow stage of the Salone about as far as it could go. Vasari designed the new theater in the Uffizi with a stage almost as deep as the length of the long, rectangular auditorium, to which he gave a sloping floor to enhance the audience's ability to see the fabulous things happening on stage. The theater was not completed until it was used for the celebration of the wedding in 1586 of Cosimo I's daughter, Virginia, to the Duke of Modena, Cesare d'Este. At that time the architect Bernardo Buontalenti decorated the interior of Vasari's auditorium so that it seemed to be a vast garden, with trellises containing fruits, rabbits, and deer overhead. Live birds were released after the audience entered. Here the auditorium space itself became a means to transport that audience to another place, long before the curtain went up to reveal a view of a part of Florence in which the theater was not actually located. Women sat on carpeted steps arranged against three walls of the auditorium. Men again sat on benches surrounding the dais placed in the center of the hall to show off the royal personages.

In 1589, for the wedding of Grand Duke Ferdinando de' Medici to a French princess, Christine of Lorraine, the Medici put on what was probably the most sumptuous theatrical performance of the entire sixteenth century in Italy, and maybe in Europe. Buontalenti remodeled the theater a second time, turning it into a monumental hall with a giant order of pilasters along the sides. Three stage curtains played havoc with the audience's sense of place. A red house curtain dropped to reveal a second curtain, painted to look like a continuation of the architecture of the rest of the room to create what a contemporary called a "perfect amphitheater." This curtain, in turn, dropped to reveal a depiction of the city of Rome. Then Rome fell to uncover a set of the city of Pisa, a Medici possession, which was the location of the action of the play, a comedy, *La Pellegrina*, written some years earlier by Girolamo Bargagli for Ferdinando, but never performed. For this wedding, however, the dusted-off play was not the thing. Instead, all the stops were pulled out for the *intermedi*, six musical interludes performed before the play began and after each of its five acts. Each *intermedio* had its own elaborate set, often with moving parts. Figures in lavish costumes designed by Buontalenti, whose drawings are preserved, floated down to the stage on clouds, or dove into what appeared to be ocean waves. There was a hellish grotto with flames. At the end all the Olympian gods descended from the skies to bless the happy couple and augur a new golden age for Florence. The poetry of Giovanni Bardi for the intermedi was learned and elegant—if not perhaps up to Shakespearean standards—and the music required remarkable vocal agility from the singers. The whole was designed for political purposes; the libretto of the *intermedi* was published so that it could carry praise of the new couple and their realm throughout the courts of Europe.

Commercial theaters for paying audiences enjoyed a development parallel to that of court theaters. Around 1549, the year the permanent court theater in Mantua was begun, a commercial theater was constructed in Rome in Palazzo Santi Apostoli, a large residence next to the church of the same name. Giorgio Vasari tells us that a man named Giovanni Andrea dell'Anguillara, "a truly rare man in every sort of poetry," put together a company of people of various talents and erected an "apparatus" for playing comedies to "gentle-men, lords and great personages."[8] The seating area consisted of steps ordered to accommodate people of different ranks. Unfortunately Vasari doesn't get more specific about the structure, but he at least tells us that architectural consideration was given to the several classes of spectators who paid to see the performances. The audience in Serlio's theater in Vicenza in 1539 had also been arranged according to rank. In this Roman theater cardinals and other high prelates, who might not want to be seen at a public performance of a comedy, got quite special treatment. Unique to Roman society, this group was provided with "some rooms" where they could see the comedies through shutters without themselves being seen. This detail of the theater in Santi Apostoli is remarkable, because it seems to be the earliest of its kind of which we have notice. Here the highest class had the privilege of being in the theater, a public place, without anyone seeing them. In court theaters, the rulers wanted to be the center of the show. In Rome, the cardinals wanted not to be part of the secular show at all.

This theater, Vasari tells us, was quite beautifully decorated by two members of the troupe, the painter Battista Franco and the sculptor Bartolomeo Ammannati, the latter about to be employed on the lavish villa constructed between 1550 and 1555 by a new pope, Julius III. Each artist contributed works of his own specialty to the theater in Palazzo Santi Apostoli. The troupe spent so much money on it that they could not collect sufficient receipts to cover their expenses—presumably because the space was too small. So the whole apparatus was moved into a recently completed church, San Biagio della Pagnotta in the Strada Giulia, into which the scenery, paintings, sculptures, seats, and the rooms for cardinals were made to fit. San Biagio had been designed in the second decade of the sixteenth century by Donato Bramante as part of the vast Palazzo dei Tribunali, commissioned by Julius II to house all the ecclesiastic and civil courts of Rome. The palace was never completed, and so the church was an orphaned building that could be converted to the purposes of a theater. It must, however, have taken friends in high places to obtain permission to use the church that way. The plan of San Biagio, known from a contemporary drawing,[9] was that of a Latin cross, with three equal arms ending in shallow apses and a longer fourth arm for the nave. Semicircular seating, if the theater had such seating, could have been fit into the crossing area, with the stage placed in the arm where the high altar would have stood. But the seating could also have been arranged to form three sides of a square or rectangle.

In the theater in San Biagio, says Vasari, many comedies were presented "to the incredible satisfaction of the people and courtiers of Rome." Vasari closes this passage by mistakenly telling us that it was in the theater in the church of San Biagio that *commedia dell'arte* was invented. We know that not to have been the case, but Vasari's calling the performers "Zanni,"—the name of a stock character in *commedia dell'arte*—does mean that such a troupe or troupes performed here. We have no idea how long the theater in San Biagio remained open, but at least for a while it permanently housed performances of comedies before a paying audience rigorously separated by class.

The rise of *commedia dell'arte*, a popular form of entertainment performed by troupes of what Cole Porter dubbed "strolling players," was one of the crucial developments in the history of the theater in Italy during the sixteenth century.[10] The earliest document we have for the creation of a *commedia dell'arte* troupe dates from 1545—a contract signed by a small group of men in Padua. They performed in Venice in 1546 and 1549; in the latter year they left Venice for Rome to play that city for carnival. They may have appeared in the theater in the palace of Santi Apostoli or in the church of S. Biagio that Vasari described. The dates are certainly right. According to the remarkably reliable Venetian chronicler Marin Sanudo, a troupe of players from Rovigo had appeared even earlier, in 1533, in a private palace on the island of Murano, where Venetians made their famous glass. The audience had to pay to see the performance. Because these troupes were composed of professionals who made their living on the stage, they were often looked down on by upper-class Italians.

Comedies were immensely popular all over the peninsula, and each city or state seems to have accommodated them in its own way. In Naples in 1536 the Prince of Salerno had a comedy performed in his palace in honor of the Emperor Charles V. The prince footed the bill; the audience did not have to pay. Apparently the prince stood at the door of his palace and welcomed the citizens of the city to the performance. They went home, we are told, "full of love and affection for him." Theater as political bribery, one might say. He and his wife continued to support the performance of comedies in their palace into the next decade. It's not clear if the prince hired professional players or made use of the talents of local nobles for this effort. The earliest known contract among comedians in Naples comes from 1575, but Benedetto Croce, the author of the major work on theater in Naples in the Renaissance,[11] believes they must have been present far earlier. In 1581, in an act of counter-Reformatory zeal typical of the day, comedies in Naples were banned, just as they were banned in that decade in Milan and Venice, but in Naples the comedies rather quickly came back. In 1583 Philip II of Spain, who ruled the city, gave the Hospital for Incurables the right to the income from comedies.[12] In 1592 the papal nuncio lamented that even the clergy went to comedies, which were surely being performed at that point in rented spaces and also in a building dedicated to theatrical performances. In the early seventeenth century the church of the Genoese colony in Naples was called *San Giorgio alla commedia vecchia*. In 1595 the Genoese had acquired the property where the "commedia vecchia" stood to erect a new church—thus the name.

In the early years of *commedia dell'arte*—roughly the 1530s through the 1550s—the players had to play wherever they could find space. Sometimes it would be a hall in a palace; sometimes it would be a rented space in a much less distinguished building. They used only the simplest of sets, which they carried with them, and their costumes also came along in the baggage. The sets consisted mostly of a painted backdrop, perhaps with a view of a town, and two houses, placed to either side of the stage, through which they made their exits and entrances. The audience was accommodated in a casual manner. Perhaps the hall would contain stools to rent. Perhaps not. Women certainly could not have been in the audience unless separate seating was provided for them. In many cases the audience may have been all male.

The description of a rather modest theater in Venice that the English traveler Thomas Coryat set down during his visit to the city in 1608[13] probably gives us a good idea of what many of these theaters were like. Coryat found the theater quite inelegant by English standards, and he was not impressed by the quality of the scenery and the costumes either. Much of his description is devoted to the lavish dress of the courtesans who sat apart from and above the male members of the audience, who occupied rented stools on the ground floor. From the scraps of information Coryat supplies, it would seem that the theater consisted of a single rather shabby room, with a stage at one end and some balcony or balconies for the courtesans. Coryat seems to have been unaware that this theater could hardly have been open more than a year, that it must have been hastily cobbled together after the expulsion of the Jesuits from Venetian territory in 1607 as part of the settlement of a bitter feud between Venice and the papacy. Essentially no theaters had operated in Venice between 1585 and 1607, as we shall see. What most amazed Coryat was the presence of women onstage. They charmed him; he felt that they performed quite as well as the men.

During the second half of the sixteenth century in the principal Italian cities theatrical spaces were set up to accommodate the traveling players, either by princes or by private citizens on the lookout for profit. For instance, a Mantuan Jew, Leone de Sommi (identified in documents as "Leone hebreo"), in 1567 petitioned Duke Guglielmo Gonzaga for permission to set up a "stanza" for the presentation of comedies "by those who go about performing for a price." He requested a monopoly on such an enterprise for ten years. In return, he offered to give two sacks of wheat annually to the poor. Leone was supported in his request by a ducal cousin, Francesco Gonzaga, count of Novellara, who found the proposal useful for the poor and for the pleasure of the city. The count seems to have consulted with Leone about his plans, for he believed that Leone intended to provide a commodious room where ladies and gentlemen could attend plays decently. That suggests something like the segregated seating universally employed in court theaters. There is no record of the duke's reply to the request for permission.

Comedy was a hot commodity in Mantua in 1567. Two companies were playing simultaneously, and the city was split in its allegiances to the two principal actresses, Flaminia and Vicenza. One of the troupes performed in the court theater, presumably the one designed by Bertani almost twenty years earlier—a fact that tells us that court theaters could serve popular as well as dynastic purposes. The other troupe worked in a private house fitted out to accommodate the plays. Both theaters were filled. At one point a performance was also given in the Palazzo della Ragione, or town hall. Even monks were going to the theater, as many as twenty-five at a time; the bishop was driven to issue an order prohibiting clergy from going near such sinful doings. In one theater members of the audience could stand on the stage and block the view of the action of the rest of those in attendance. This situation led to loud protests and even a near riot.

In Genoa, also in 1567, a group of professional actors drew up a contract to work together from Lent through the carnival of 1568.

That year permission was given for the performance of a comedy in the *hostaria del Falcone*, an inn. Inns and taverns became the favored sites for theatrical events in Genoa. In 1572 the Gelosi, one of the most avidly sought-after troupes of the day, petitioned the government of Genoa for permission to perform for the entire month of November, something, the Gelosi pointed out, "universally desired by all the nobility." The government granted permission. The room the Gelosi planned to use, they said, had a capacity of only one hundred to one hundred fifty gentlemen (no gentlewomen, apparently). Such a size might well accord with the capacity of a large room at an urban hostelry. In 1575, according to a notarial act, a group of Genoese from leading families, such as the Spinola, Grimaldi, Doria, and Pallavicino, joined together to have a carpenter construct a stage and scenery for performances during the last week of carnival. The whole was to cost the not inconsiderable sum of eighty gold scudi, and the carpenter was provided with a painter to execute the scenery. Genoa found itself in an extremely prosperous state in the middle of the sixteenth century, in good part thanks to the very successful efforts of the city's aristocrat-bankers.

In Bologna as early as 1547 the great hall on the *piano nobile* of the Palazzo del Podestà was given over to housing entertainments. The palace had been built in the late thirteenth century as the seat of the administration of justice in the city. Remodeled in the late fifteenth century, the building continued to play its role as one of the city's principal governmental structures until Pope Julius II occupied Bologna and took over the governmental functions. The old oligarchical government of the city by its leading citizens was replaced by the rule of a single man, the papal legate. The Palazzo del Podestà became an immense relic of a past political situation, its great hall lit by nine enormous windows a white elephant of a space. The legate, however, allowed the old aristocracy of the city to run Bologna's cultural affairs, and so they took over the palace as the site of the entertainments they offered themselves and their city. In 1598, for instance, the papal legate allowed a certain Giuseppe Guidetto to fit the room out for the performance of comedies, to sell fruit, and even to schedule ball games in the hall. Such a conversion of a building of immense importance to a civic polity into a place of entertainment was not unique to Bologna. In Siena, after the Medici took control of the city in 1555 following a gruesome siege, they converted into a theater the room in the town hall in which the nobles of the city had met to vote on the laws of the land. The ancient seat of representative government became the showplace of the largesse of the conquering despot. Good government was usurped by good entertainment.

In Florence comedies became as popular as they were in other Italian cities. The Medici dukes, however, wanted to keep them under their control, and so they constructed a theater for comedies, the Baldracca, literally parallel to the court theater of the Uffizi. Located just east of the eastern wing of the Uffizi, the Baldracca consisted of a large rectangular room with a relatively shallow stage at one end. Although clearly inferior in status to the court theater in the Uffizi, it was directly connected to that part of the Medici architectural domain, so that the grand duke and his party could attend the comedies unseen. Along one side of the theater there were one or more rooms, screened from the view of the audience, that members of the court could enter directly from the Uffizi. While ordinary citizens enjoyed the raucous fun of the comedies in public, the grand duke and company could enjoy the coarse jokes in private and thereby maintain the air of superiority on which their increasingly autocratic rule in part depended. This theater appears to have been in operation by 1576–78, although its form may have been modified later. There are documents from the end of the century that speak of two tiers of "stanzini," or little rooms, controlled by private citizens of means, that acted like theater boxes, but it is not clear that these little rooms were part of the original design of the 1570s.[14] On at least one occasion, the *commedia dell'arte* folk were invited to play the big theater in the Uffizi itself. During the wedding festivities of 1589, comedies were given there to entertain the large wedding party, which probably could not have fit into the Baldracca. One of the great comic actresses of the day improvised a mad scene in fractured French that particularly delighted the French bride, Christine of Lorraine.

The Baldracca was not alone in being a separate theater for comedies directly connected to a princely palace. In Mantua a separate theater for comedies, connected to the Gonzaga palace by a long corridor that allowed the duke and his party to reach the theater directly, was constructed by the court architect, Antonio Maria Viani, probably in the 1590s. Duke Vincenzo Gonzaga had married a Medici, and so he was certainly well informed about theaters in Florence. Such theaters adjoining princely residences were the forerunners of the great opera houses that later came to be constructed next to royal palaces, such as the Teatro San Carlo in Naples, inaugurated in 1737.

Permanent commercial theaters for the performance of comedies, then, had been constructed by the 1570s, and perhaps even a decade earlier. In some ways the most important of these for the subsequent history of theater architecture opened in Venice for the carnival of 1580. There were two such, built not far from each other in the parish of San Cassiano by noble families, the Michiel and the Tron, for profit.[15] The two most famous *commedia dell'arte* troupes of the day played them, the Gelosi in the Michiel theater, the Confidenti in the Tron. Of both theaters we have no visual trace, but we can reconstruct at least something of their appearance from the considerable documentation preserved in the records of the Council of Ten, the powerful governing body that had decreed in 1508 that it had to approve all theatrical performances in Venice and its territories.

Venice was devastated by plague in 1576. As the city slowly got back on its feet, entertainment seems to have been crucial to its citizens' recovery of a sense of well-being. In the last years of the 1570s, the Council of Ten approved theatrical events for carnival with numbingly similar provisos: that the performances had to be decent and had to conclude at a reasonable hour of the night. Suddenly, in 1580, the language of approval shifted. The Ten ordered that the places where comedies were to be performed had to be inspected by competent architects to make sure that they were safe. The new language signals a new architectural situation, and that situation was the construction of theaters with rows of superimposed boxes. We know from other documents that there were boxes surrounded by corridors and entered by doors. In the next few years decrees of the Ten insisted that lights be kept lit in the corridors throughout the performances, and there were promises to the Ten from owners of the theaters and troupes of actors that the doors to the boxes would be kept open, so that nothing scandalous could occur inside. Such promises were surely the result of what had happened in the boxes during the first season these two theaters were open. Venetians seem quickly to have figured out how to use the boxes as if they were modern motel rooms. It is even possible that some of Venice's famous courtesans set up shop in a box or two. No such private space in a public place had ever existed before in the city, or indeed on the Italian peninsula. Meetings between men and women of the upper classes, the people who rented the boxes, were tightly regulated in Venice, as indeed in the whole of Europe, in the sixteenth century. The boxes provided private space where it was possible for clandestine encounters to occur.

We know that patrician families rented the boxes, which became extensions of the family's private space. Men and women of the same family could attend performances together, sitting side by side. We know this happened because of the comments of at least one prudish writer who strenuously condemned the patricians who took their daughters to comedies, where they heard the foulest possible language spoken onstage. The bawdiness of some of these plays was undeniable, and Venetians, who still have a taste for earthy humor, enjoyed them immensely.

The economic incentive for the construction of these theaters is clear. Venetian nobles were always out to make a ducat, and they saw a chance to profit from the great popularity of comedies at carnival, just as Leone de Sommi had hoped to do in Mantua a decade or so earlier. Their new type of theater with boxes took advantage of the unusual structure of Venetian society, dominated not by a ruling prince but by an oligarchy of rich noble families. Those families could afford to rent boxes that provided comfortable, private spaces at the theater, and which also provided small stages from which the nobles could display themselves to the rest of the audience. The theater owners and the actors split the income from the rents and ticket sales. The theaters seem to have started off as a great economic success. We don't know how large they were, or how many boxes each contained. They seem to have been constructed inside already existing spaces, perhaps warehouses or something similar, and to have been made of wood. One can imagine a system of wooden beams supporting wooden floors, with thin partitions between the boxes. There is no indication that they made any visual impact on the surrounding city. Both were next to canals, so that they could be reached by gondola. Many of the streets in Venice were not paved in the sixteenth century, and noblewomen would not have wanted to slog through mud in their lavish dresses to get to a performance.

The scandalous behavior in the boxes and onstage created a very strong reaction against these theaters among the elderly patricians who ran the city, whose thinking about public morality had come to be dominated by the Jesuits. The French ambassador informed Henry III in 1583 that the Jesuits had such influence over leading members of the Venetian government that they could get the government to do whatever they wanted. While this statement may have been an exaggeration—the government did not allow the Jesuits to build their church wherever they wanted in the city—it contained a large grain of truth. The Jesuits were said to have mounted a very Jesuitical argument against the theaters, claiming that much of the Venetian patriciate would be burned up, were the theaters to catch fire.

In 1585 the Council of Ten struck a mortal blow against the two theaters, ordering their demolition within fifteen days. Rarely indeed did the Venetian government bring an end to the business ventures of the patricians who dominated it. The threat of the theaters to public morality and even, perhaps, to the safety of the ruling class caused this highly unusual move. As far as we know, the theaters were immediately dismantled, and there is just one further mention of a theatrical performance in the records of the Ten for the rest of the century. Only in 1607, when the Jesuits were banished from Venetian territory, did comedies return. They did so with amazing rapidity; there is a report of the performance of a comedy within a month of the Jesuits' expulsion. Within a few years, the Tron family had built a theater on the site occupied by their theater of 1580, perhaps even out of the original materials of that structure. When the first public performance of an opera for a paying audience, anywhere, took place in Venice during the carnival of 1637, it took place in the theater with boxes of the Tron family (although by then the theater was in its third or fourth incarnation).

From Shakespeare's lifetime come the only two Italian theaters of the sixteenth century to survive: the Teatro Olimpico in Vicenza and the ducal theater in Sabbioneta. The third remaining early Italian theater, the Teatro Farnese at Parma, was built in 1618, only two years after Shakespeare's death. Not much alike, these theaters point to the highly experimental nature of theater architecture toward the end of the cinquecento and the beginning of the seicento.

The Teatro Olimpico was designed by Andrea Palladio in 1580, the year of his death.[16] It was completed by his son and by the architect Vincenzo Scamozzi in time to open during the carnival of 1585 with a production of Sophocles' *Oedipus Rex* in a new Italian translation. Like Bertani's court theater in Mantua, which Palladio had probably seen, the Olimpico was a deliberate "copy" of an ancient Roman theater, except for the fact that it was an indoor rather than an outdoor space. The audience sat on curved rows of steps, laid out in an oval instead of a semicircle to fit the theater onto the piece of land that the Accademia Olimpica had purchased. At the opening performance, the wives of the members of the Accademia sat in chairs placed in the orchestra for them.

The Teatro Olimpico was not a court theater, however. The Accademia Olimpica was an association of Vicentine aristocrats passionately interested in antiquity. Palladio, an aristocrat only of talent, had been invited to join their ranks. He had spent much of his career studying the ruins of Roman architecture, and he had made drawings of the Roman theaters at Verona, Vicenza, and Pola. In addition, he had drawn the illustrations that graced the pages of Daniele Barbaro's learned commentary on Vitruvius, published in Venice in 1558. He probably knew more about Roman theaters than almost anyone else living at the time. He had even built temporary wooden theaters, designed in the ancient manner, in the main room of the town hall of Vicenza and in a still unknown site in Venice. No one else at the time could have brought so much experience to such a commission.

The stage of the Olimpico consists of a long, narrow rectangle raised above the adjoining orchestra. Surrounding the rectangle are tall walls articulated by ancient architectural forms and encrusted with statues of local worthies in ancient garb. Five doors lead offstage, two at the sides and three in the back wall. From these doors extend in forced perspective remarkable sets of buildings supposed to represent ancient Thebes—although they could also, to recall what was said of Ariosto's city scene of the 1530s, double as Cremona or Ferrara if needed. Designed by Scamozzi, these perspectives fuse to Palladio's archaeological concept of a Roman stage wall a type of perspective scenery that had been current in Italy from at least the second decade of the sixteenth century. (Actors could not walk down the streets of this perspective city, because an actor at the far end of a street would tower over the flanking palazzi.) This kind of scenery, developed out of the interest of Italian painters of the fifteenth and sixteenth centuries in one-point perspective, had generally been applied across one entire wall of a space used for a dramatic performance. As such, it formed an illusionistic backdrop that could create the sense of an enveloping cityscape. Here the cityscape has been reduced to five streets that seem only tenuously connected to the *all'antica* architecture of the stage wall: two separate theatrical traditions in a forced, but very beautiful marriage.

The Olimpico, at least in the parts that are deliberately *all'antica*, is the fulfillment of more than a century of humanist study of the theaters of the ancients, going back at least to Leon Battista Alberti's *de re aedificatoria*, the first modern treatise on architecture composed around 1450. Basically, the Olimpico is the only built record we have of the antiquarian interest of humanists in the theatrical architecture of antiquity. The Olimpico is also a dead end. One can only pretend to be an ancient Greek or Roman in modern dress for so long before contemporary needs begin to take precedence.

In 1588 a member of a cadet branch of the Gonzaga family, Vespasiano, carved out for himself the tiny duchy of Sabbioneta, which is close enough to Parma almost to be a modern suburb. Vespasiano laid out the city as an example of the idealized urban planning that characterized Italian architectural thought of the time. Among the buildings he erected in his small capital was a freestanding theater, the earliest one to survive in Italy.[17] Vespasiano's architect was none other than Vincenzo Scamozzi, author of the perspective sets at Vicenza. Located halfway between the city square and the ducal Palazzo del Giardino, the theater is clearly a civic monument detached from the duke's residence, yet close enough to that residence to recall his control. Scamozzi may have had no precedents to which he could turn for the exterior architecture of a modern theater, and so he designed something that looked a bit like a palace, but with fewer stories. The pedimented windows, the niches, and the rather learnedly mannered play of their rhythms, mark this as a building of importance in the city, but they do not quite convey the notion that it is a theater. Scamozzi seems deliberately not to have recalled Roman theater architecture in this building, in that he did not employ superimposed arched orders of the kind found on the exterior of the Theater of Marcellus in Rome (illustrated in Serlio's books) or the Colosseum. In the 1530s that system had been employed in Venice by Jacopo Sansovino on the Libreria di San Marco, a building that Scamozzi knew well because he was about to complete it. One suspects that Scamozzi deliberately avoided superimposed arched orders so that he would not be seen as a follower of Sansovino, whose Libreria Scamozzi criticized for its "incorrect" use of the ancient orders.

Inside the theater at Sabbioneta is a rectangular space typical of the shape of court theaters in Italy throughout the sixteenth century. Most theaters at court had been temporarily erected in the largest room of the palace—invariably a rectangular hall—with a stage at one end and with seats at the other end and along the sides.[18] The great permanent Medici theater in the Uffizi, probably designed by Vasari in the 1560s but only completed and opened for business in the 1580s, had maintained just this form. At Sabbioneta, Scamozzi provided Vespasiano with a certain architectural grandeur. The steps for the audience are curved in a U shape, and at the top of the steps rises a row of monumental columns, among which Vespasiano and his courtiers sat. The seats, reminiscent of the steps in an ancient theater, literally had a novel twist toward the stage, where they curved outward so that the audience seated nearest the stage would have a head-on view of it. This curve allowed them to enjoy, without getting cricks in their necks, the permanent perspectival city scene that Scamozzi erected across the entire stage. A sketch by Scamozzi, now in the Uffizi in Florence, gives us an idea of the appearance of the set. It is not entirely clear how men and women were separately accommodated in this house.

The walls of the theater were decorated with frescoes. At the tops of the walls along three sides are painted balconies containing a painted audience whose members are frozen in eternal responses to the action onstage or in the auditorium, however that might change. On the broad walls that flank the space between the seating and the stage are depictions of scenes of ancient Rome, so that the theater not only provides the illusion of looking at an action in another time and place, but even of being in another place while enjoying the play. The Roman landscapes are framed by painted triumphal arches, through one of which Vespasiano would enter the theater to the acclaim of his subjects already gathered inside.

In 1618 the Duke of Parma, in order to impress the Grand Duke of Tuscany who was planning to pass through Parma on his way to Milan, ordered the construction of an immense theater in the ducal palace. Designed by an architect and hydraulic engineer from Ferrara, Giovanni Battista Aleotti, the theater occupied a huge existing space in the palace that had served as the armory.[19] Although the room is not on the ground floor, but rather on the *piano nobile*, Aleotti arranged for it to be flooded for mock naval battles. Like the nearby theater in Sabbioneta, which Aleotti must have gone to see, the Farnese theater in Parma has ties to several different theatrical traditions. The seating is on steps arranged in an elongated U, like the seating in a Roman arena rather than a Roman theater. The flat space surrounded by the seats could be used for mock naval battles, or for jousts and tourneys of the sort that Renaissance aristocrats enjoyed by donning fake medieval finery. Toward the stage, on the side walls, are triumphal arches surmounted by equestrian portraits of Farnese dukes. These portraits suggest the tourneys on horseback that could take place in the theater, but they also make clear that one purpose of the theater was dynastic celebration, which indeed had always been the purpose of court theaters. One imagines the the Farnese dukes used them for entrances, emulating Vespasiano Gonzaga at nearby Sabbioneta. At the far end of the theater is a truly modern deep stage, framed by a richly encrusted proscenium arch. Behind that arch was all the stage machinery a scene designer of the period could desire for fantastic effects of flying figures and quick scene shifts from one exotic locale to another. Such dual purpose theaters were sometimes erected as temporary outdoor structures. A particularly spectacular one was built in Bologna a few years later. But they were not common as permanent installations in a ruler's palace.

Perhaps the most remarkable detail of the Teatro Farnese is the wall of two levels of superimposed columns and arches that surrounds the arena seating. The architecture represents an almost line-for-line quotation of the exterior that Andrea Palladio had designed for the Basilica, or town hall, in Vicenza in the middle of the sixteenth century. In the Farnese palace the two rows of real columns and arches were continued by an illusionistic ceiling painting, now lost, into a third level thronged with enthusiastic painted spectators. In the center of the ceiling figures of ancient gods soared through the sky over the heads of the audience below. The illusion that one was outside must have been quite overwhelming. One approached the theater up a grand staircase in the palace and then entered a splendid architectural inversion of interior and exterior that foreshadowed the kinds of illusions of time and place that would occur onstage. Why Aleotti would choose to use the exterior architecture of a building constructed to house the oligarchical government of Vicenza (which was ruled by Venice at this point anyway) as the frame for a ducal arena *cum* modern proscenium stage is not an easy question to answer. In part the fame of Palladio's Basilica would have made the allusion to outdoor architecture clear. Ancient theaters were outdoor spaces. Modern Italian theaters, for reasons of climate, were indoor spaces, but they often tried to maintain a tie to the *al fresco* theaters of antiquity by masquerading, or indeed by transvesting. We know from a contemporary print of Vicenza that the space in front of the Basilica was used for processions, tourneys and other types of theatrical events.[20] The citizens of the city watched from Palladio's porticoes, just as the illusionistic audience watched from the top portico painted on the ceiling in Parma.

Shakespeare died, then, before the experimental stage of Italian theater architecture had run its course. The Teatro Farnese, with its roots in Roman arenas, in the theaters constructed for tourneys and in those constructed for performances at court, offered little that would prove useful for commercial theater in the future, although the future of theater would be commercial. At the same time the Farnese theater was built, Venetian aristocrats were busily opening new theaters with boxes for commedia dell'arte, theaters modeled on those built in Venice in 1580. Sadly, we still know all too little about Venetian theaters of the years 1607–1637—the years between the return of comedy to the city and the first public performance of an opera for a paying audience. Someday, one hopes, someone working in the vast Venetian archives will come across the material to tell that crucial part of the story of the development of the modern theater. The Venetian theaters are the origin of the *teatro all'italiana*, with boxes stacked in several levels around the auditorium. As Italian opera began to spread around Europe in the second half of the seventeenth century, this type accompanied the new theatrical art form, much as the sea turtle carries its own house, its shell, to become the most prevalent form of theater architecture in the Western world for at least two centuries.

Bibliographic Note

The study of these theaters and their architecture has been carried out almost exclusively by Italians, although in French we have an important series of essays by an international group of scholars: *Le lieu théâtral a la renaissance*, Jean Jacquot, ed. (Paris: Éditions du Centre National de la Recherche Scientifique, 1964). There is almost nothing by English-speaking scholars except the passages in Allardyce Nicoll's *The development of the theatre*, first published in 1927 and then revised four times.[21] Partly to remedy the lack of a comprehensive study of this material in English, I am in the process of writing a book about the architecture of Italian theaters from the late fifteenth to the late seventeenth centuries. This article may be seen as something like an outline of part of that book.

Italian scholarship on this subject has been prolific and often of very high quality. The fundamental work on the history of the Italian theater is Alessandro D'Ancona's *Origini del teatro italiano* of 1891 (Rome: Bardi Editore, 1971, reprint) a remarkable achievement of late nineteenth-century scholarship. Graced with copious quotations of original documents, D'Ancona's work takes the reader from the earliest public performance of a Roman comedy since ancient times, in the courtyard of the ducal palace of Ferrara in 1486, through a range of developments in the seventeenth century. Although the two volumes of the book are out of date in many ways, it is always a pleasure to go back to see what D'Ancona had to say. He almost never lets you down.

In 1968 Simon Towneley Worsthorne issued a second printing of his musicological study, *Venetian Opera in the Seventeenth Century* (Oxford: Clarendon Press, 1954), with an updated bibliography that included only one new item on theater architecture, Licisco Magagnato's slim volume, *Teatri italiani del Cinquecento* (Venice: Neri Pozza, 1954). (Worsthorne missed *Le lieu théatrale a la Renaissance*.) Since 1968 there has been a flood of new scholarship in Italian. The most accessible to an English-speaking audience is the excellent volume by Nino Pirrotta and Elena Povoledo, *Music and Theater from Poliziano to Monteverdi* (Cambridge and New York: Cambridge University Press, 1982), an English translation of their *Li due Orfei: da Poliziano a Monteverdi* (Turin: Einadui, 1975). Pirrotta, one of the most distinguished musicologists of his day, focused on music history in his half of the book. Povoledo, on the other hand, is one of the leading Italian historians of the visual aspects of theater: the house, the scenery, the costumes. Those are the subjects of her part. Povoledo was responsible for the publication of the *Enciclopedia dello spettacolo*, 9 vols. (Rome: Le Maschere, 1954–62), the marvelous compendium that has formed the basis for the flowering of Italian scholarship on the history of the theater during the post–World War II period. The encyclopedia gathered together, with commendable accuracy for the Italian entries (I hesitate to judge in other fields), what was known about the history of the theater in the mostly Western world at that time. The very scholarship that the encyclopedia encouraged, of course, has made it in some ways out of date.

Of the Italians who have contributed particularly important studies I would like to single out a few. Lodovico Zorzi's *Il teatro e la città* (Turin: Einaudi, 1977) consists of three long chapters devoted to the history of the theater in Ferrara, Florence, and Venice, three of the principal centers of theatrical life in early modern times. In his introduction Zorzi wrestles with poststructuralist methods coming out of France, feeling the need to explain them to an Italian audience and to adapt his own work to them—which he proceeds to do in blessedly clear prose. Each of the three cities had a unique theatrical culture, just as Ferrarese, Florentine, and Venetian painting all look very different. Zorzi makes the history of theater an integral part of the history of urbanism and the history of ideas. If one has time for no other book mentioned here, then one should treat oneself to Zorzi (an English translation of which is as much to be desired as it is unlikely). Another particularly noteworthy volume is Siro Ferrone, *Attori mercanti corsari: La Commedia dell'Arte in Europa tra Cinque e Seicento* (Turin: Einaudi, 1993). And one needs also point out a quite recent volume, with entries by many experts, that surveys the theater in Italy, Spain, France, Germany, and England in the sixteenth and seventeenth centuries: *Storia del teatro moderno*, vol. 1, *La nascità del teatro moderno: Cinquecento-Seicento*, Roberto Alonge and Guido Davico Bonino, ed. (Turin: Einaudi, 2000). A particularly useful, up-to-date bibliography can be found in Emmanuelle Hénin, *Ut pictura theatrum: théatre et peinture de la Renaissance italienne au classicisme français* (Geneva: Librairie Droz, 2003).

Much of the work done by Italians has been on theater in specific cities. Fabrizio Cruciani has produced two very fine volumes on Rome: *Il Teatro del Campidoglio e le feste romane del 1513, con la ricostruzione architettonica del teatro di Arnaldo Bruschi* (Milan: Il Polifilo, 1968) and *Teatro nel Rinascimento: Roma 1450–1550* (Rome: Bulzoni, 1983). The first deals with what may have been the earliest purpose-built theater of the Renaissance (albeit a temporary one) for the induction into Roman citizenship of two members of the Medici family, kinsmen of the recently elected Pope Leo X. The second takes us from the early revivals of Roman drama under the patronage of Cardinal Raffaele Riario, a rare devotee of the theater, to the beginning of pay-as-you-enter theater for *commedia dell'arte* around 1550.

Venice has been the focus of the work of Nicola Mangini, whose volume, *I Teatri di Venezia* (Milan: Mursia, 1974), was the first serious attempt to write the very complex history of theaters in Venice.

His essays, including the crucial "Alle origini del teatro moderno: lo spettacolo pubblico nel Veneto tra Cinquecento e Seicento," were collected in *Alle origini del teatro moderno e altri saggi*, (Modena: Mucchi, 1989). Venetian theaters are now much more fully covered in Franco Mancini, Maria Teresa Muraro, and Elena Povoledo, *I teatri di Venezia e il suo territorio*, 2 vols. (Venice: Corbo e Fiore, 1995–96), with ample bibliography. Forthcoming from Oxford University Press is a volume by two musicologists, Jonathan and Beth Glixon, with the working title of *Inventing the Business of Opera: The Production of Musical Theater in Seventeenth-Century Venice.* The Glixons are well-practiced sleuths in the Venetian archives, and so we can look forward to a richly documented account of how Venetian opera houses functioned in the seventeenth century.

For Florence two works in English are available: A. M. Nagler, *Theatre Festivals of the Medici 1539–1637* (New Haven and London: Yale University Press, 1964); and James M. Saslow, *The Medici Wedding of 1589: Florentine Festival as Theatrum Mundi* (New Haven and London: Yale University Press, 1996). There are several recent works on Renaissance theaters in Florence, many being exhibition catalogs produced by the cooperative efforts of Italian scholars: *Il luogo teatrale a Firenze*, ex. cat. (Milan: Electa, 1975); Sara Mamone, *Il teatro nella Firenze medicea* (Milan: Mursia, 1981); *Il potere e lo spazio: la scena del principe*, ex. cat. (Milan: Electa, 1990); Paolo Lucchesini, *I teatri di Firenze* (Rome: Newton Compton, 1991); *I teatri storici della Toscana,* vol. 8, *Firenze* (Venice: Marsilio, 2000); *Teatro e spettacolo nella Firenze dei Medici,* ex. cat. (Florence: Olschki, 2001). The theaters of other cities are less well studied, and much of the literature thereon is the work of local antiquarians.

Notes

1. Fabrizio Cruciani, *Teatro nel Rinascimento. Roma 1450–1550* (Rome: Bulzoni, 1983), 219–27. The play was given three times, in three different places: in front of the cardinal's palace near Campo de' Fiori, in the Castel Sant'Angelo for Pope Innocent VIII, and in the courtyard of the cardinal's palace, which was shaded with a curtain for the occasion. The version in front of the palace would have been visible to the public, whereas those given inside were for invited audiences.

2. Ibid., 449–69.

3. Egidio Scoglio, *Il teatro alla corte estense* (Lodi: Biancardi, 1965), 91–93.

4. Ercolano Marani and Chiara Perina, *Mantova: Le Arti*, vol. 3, part 1 (Mantua: Istituto Carlo D'Arco, 1965), 15; Licisco Magagnato, *I teatri italiani del cinquecento*, ex. cat. (Mantua: Palazzo Ducale, 1980), 47.

5. For the recent translation of Serlio, see *Sebastiano Serlio on Architecture*, 2 vols., trans., intro. and commentary by Vaughan Hart and Peter Hicks (New Haven and London: Yale University Press, 1996–2001). Serlio's theater has been analyzed to excellent effect by John Orrell, *Human Stage: English Theater Design, 1567–1640* (Cambridge: Cambridge University Press, 1988), 130–49.

6. The standard account in English of Florentine theater under the Medici is A. M. Nagler, *Theatre Festivals of the Medici 1539–1637* (New Haven and London: Yale University Press, 1964), to which one can add the more specialized James M. Saslow, *The Medici Wedding of 1589: Florentine Festival as Theatrum Mundi* (New Haven and London: Yale University Press, 1996).

7. Vasari's accounts of theatrical activities, sprinkled throughout his *Lives*, have been collected by Thomas A. Pallen, *Vasari on Theater* (Carbondale: Southern Illinois University Press, 1999).

8. Ibid., 83; Cruciani, 620–33.

9. Arnaldo Bruschi, *Bramante* (London: Thames and Hudson, 1973), fig. 180. Andrea Palladio drew a section (ibid., fig. 179) that shows the interior vaulted and thus usable. The church was much altered in the eighteenth century.

10. Siro Ferrone, *Attori mercanti corsari La Commedia dell'Arte in Europa tra Cinque e Seicento* (Turin: Einaudi, 1993) is a particularly rich study of the phenomenon, on which there is a considerable bibliography in English. Also see Roberto Tessari, "Il mercato delle Maschere," in *Storia del teatro moderno e contemporaneo*, vol. 1, *La nascità del teatro moderno Cinquecento-Seicento*, Roberto Alonge and Guido Davico Bonino, eds. (Turin: Einaudi, 2000), 119–91.

11. Benedetto Croce, *I teatri di Napoli dal rinascimento alla fine del secolo decimottavo*, Giuseppe Galasso, ed. (Milan: Adelphi, 1992). Reprint of fourth ed. of 1947.

12. Under Philip II two public theaters had opened in Madrid in 1580 and 1581. See Charles Davis and J. E. Varey, *Los corrales de comedias y los hospitales de Madrid: 1574–1615. Estudio y documentos* (Madrid: Tamesis, 1997).

13. Thomas Coryat, *Coryat's Crudities*, 2 vols. Glasgow: James MacLehose and Sons, 1905), 386–87, reprint of edition of 1611.

14. What we know about the Baldracca comes from two articles by Annamaria Evangelista: "Il teatro dei comici dell'Arte a Firenze," *Biblioteca teatrale* 23–24 (1979): 70–86, and "Le compagnie dei Comici dell'Arte nel teatrino di Baldracca a Firenze: notizie dagli epistolari (1576–1653)," *Quaderni di Teatro* no. 24 (1984): 50–72.

15. For an account of these theaters, see Eugene J. Johnson, "The Short, Lascivious Lives of Two Venetian Theaters, 1580–1585," *Renaissance Quarterly* 50, no 3 (2002): 936–68.

16. Recent works on the Teatro Olimpico include: J. Thomas Oosting, *Andrea Palladio's Teatro Olimpico* (Ann Arbor: UMI Research Press, 1981); Andreas Beyer, *Andrea Palladio Teatro Olimpico: Triumpharchitektur für eine humanistische Gesellschaft* (Frankfurt am Main: Fischer Taschenbuch, 1987), and Stefano Mazzoni, *L'Olimpico di Vicenza: Un teatro e la sua "perpetua memoria"* (Flor-

ence: Le lettere, 1998). Scamozzi's sets have most recently been treated in Valeria Cafà, "Interventi sul Teatro Olimpico," in *Vincenzo Scamozzi 1548–1616*, ed. Franco Barbieri and Guido Beltrami (Venice: Marsilio, 2003), 251–59.

17. For the theater in Sabbioneta see Stefano Mazzoni, *Il teatro di Sabbioneta*, (Florence: Olschki, 1985), and Kurt W. Forster, "Stagecraft and Statecraft: The Architectural Integration of Public Life and Spectacle in Scamozzi's Theater in Sabbioneta," *Oppositions* 9 (1977): 63–87. Also Stefano Mazzoni, "Vincenzo Scamozzi architetto-scenografo," in *Vincenzo Scamozzi 1548–1616*, ed. Franco Barbieri and Guido Beltrami (Venice: Marsilio, 2003), 71–87; and Valeria Cafà and Sandra Vendramin, "Il Teatro Ducale a Sabbioneta," in ibid., 176–282.

18. There are exceptions to this practice: for instance, the theater in Ferrara set up to celebrate the wedding of Alfonso d'Este to Lucrezia Borgia in 1502. There the audience, seated against one long wall, faced a stage arrayed along the other long wall.

19. The most extensive treatment of the history of this theater is in Irving Lavin, "Lettres de Parmes (1618, 1627–28) et débuts du théâtre Baroque," *Le lieu théâtral a la renaissance*, Jean Jacquot, ed. (Paris: Éditions du Centre National de la Rechereche Scientifique, 1964), 107–58. The entire text was republished in English in *"All the world's a stage . . .": Art and Pageantry in the Renaissance and Baroque*, ed. Barbara Witsch and Susan Scott Munshower, 2 vols. (University Park: Pennsylvania State University Press, 1990), 2: 518–79.

20. Illustrated in Howard Burns et al., *Andrea Palladio, 1508–1580: The Portico and the Farmyard* (London: Arts Council of Great Britain: 1975), cat. 28.

21. Allardyce Nicholl, *The development of the theatre*, 5th rev. ed. (New York: Harcourt Brace & World, 1967; orig. ed. London: Harrap, 1927). Another general work in English, Margarete Baur-Heinhold, *The Baroque Theatre: A Cultural History of the 17th and 18th Centuries*, trans. Mary Whitall (New York: McGraw-Hill, 1967) has nice illustrations but an untrustworthy text.

FORUM

Extra-mural Psychoanalysis

Extra-mural Psychoanalysis

Cynthia Marshall

Introduction

Historical study is generally thought of as reliable and down-to-earth, so Walter Benjamin's fanciful mention of a "puppet called 'historical materialism'" seems a bit shocking. The surprise is not so much the puppet's "Turkish attire" or the "hookah in its mouth" as its purpose-built role—to win philosophical disputes by dealing out empirical facts while secretly relying on theology. Benjamin is critiquing a historicist practice lacking "theoretical armature"; he advocates instead engagements capable of "brush[ing] history against the grain"—the sort of approach New Historicism subsequently adopted.[1] Still, the image of an automaton carries unsettling implications of a mechanical, manipulable, and, at worst, potentially deceptive capacity in historicist study. Because historical materialism may mystify its own theoretical principles, Benjamin calls for a methodology bolstered and tempered by philosophical consideration.

Benjamin's puppet serves as a reminder of the ongoing critical dispute, especially visible in early modern studies, between historicist practice and transhistorical theory. The long dominance in literary study of historicism, the recent advent and development of cultural studies, and inflated rumors of the "death of theory" have given license in some camps to avoidance of hermeneutic or methodological questions, and even to a disdain for theory, particularly psychoanalytic theory. Of course, attacks on theory are not new; in Paul de Man's famous take, "the resistance to theory is a resistance to the use of language about language," so that "theory *is* itself . . . resistance."[2] Theoretical engagements with historicism are, and aim to be, disruptive, for the acknowledgment that facts themselves are subject to ideological shaping complicates the narratives history can tell—with the damage to de Man's own reception after the revelation of his wartime involvements offering a case in point. Psychoanalysis, a theory altogether concerned with stories told about the past, has its own developed historiography, which is skeptical of certainties, alert to layered and redoubled meanings, and interested in the implications of transference, while accepting of the unfolding nature of discourse.[3] Thus Jacques Derrida can characterize resistance to psychoanalysis as "one of the cards dealt to our time" and suggest not only the self-resisting tendency embedded in the system of thought "like an auto-immune process" but also the inventiveness of resistance itself.[4] In recent years, the continued evolution of psychoanalytic thought, together with creative forms of resistance and what Derrida called the "invagination of borders" by other discourses, has resulted in work wedding analytic methods and principles with other lines of inquiry, including historicism.[5] Such cross-fertilization is clearly visible in Carla Mazzio and Douglas Trevor's influential *Historicism, Psychoanalysis, and Early Modern Culture*, as well as in recent publications by Harry Berger, Jr., Marshall Grossman, Julia Lupton, Tracey Sedinger, and others, including those whose work follows.[6] The unanticipated appearance of psychoanalytic theory in all three papers of a plenary session devoted to "postmodern theory/early modern belief" at a recent meeting of the Shakespeare Association of America was the genesis for this forum, which offers a sample of the work being done at the juncture of psychoanalytic theory and other discourses, especially historicism, in the study of early modern literature.

These developments do not herald a new synthesis of historicism and psychoanalysis, for the two discourses are typically combined in contestatory or dialectical ways, in scholarship that exploits as well as explores the tension between empiricist and theoretical models. Yet the new sense of flexible borders suggests that we can identify the arrival in early modern studies of what Jean Laplanche called "extra-mural psychoanalysis" (*le psychanalyse hors-les-murs*).[7] Unlike mechanical applications of a set of concepts, or a clinical process apt to become an "excuse for not thinking," psychoanalysis in this broader sense is a process of speculation and experiment, merging with "theory as experience." While maintaining a distinctive character, the "self-confident psychoanalysis" Laplanche describes needn't reject other discourses out of hand; instead it can "adopt the approach of all great thinkers" in engaging with alien concepts.[8] This marks a refreshing departure from the history of a discourse marked by defensiveness and its obverse, a wish to dominate. Let me be clear: I am not speaking for all versions of psychoanalytic theory, some of which would take issue with Laplanche's formulations, but characterizing a practice growing in early modern studies.

Psychoanalysis has long been understood to hold special relevance for the early modern period, most simply because of Freud's reliance on Shakespeare in formulating key concepts, more generally because the period saw the emergence of modern forms of subjectivity. The historiography of early modernity—the redoubled nature of Renaissance knowledge, the self-conscious reversion to the past in developing cultural precepts—resembles Freud's idea that knowledge of the past is layered like an archaeological site, and it anticipates his complexly theorized concepts of memory (repression, screen memory, *Nachträglichkeit*). Because of its temporal remoteness, early modernity occupies for us the position of desired other, or object of knowledge (Lacan's *objet petit a*), yet because of its decisive influence, it also serves as shaping force, or Other (*Autre*). Our discoveries about the early modern period confirm our own belatedness or exclusion, yet in powerful and sometimes illusive ways we are constituted by the culture we would investigate. As a result, in transactions with early modern texts we may have less in common with the confident early Freud than with James's Maisie—condemned to a flickering knowledge that no access to fact can ever altogether remedy, since she is herself the evolving effect whose cause she would discover.

In the papers assembled here, almost every contributor writes of matters of inside and outside, suggesting the centrality of questions of boundaries for early modern culture, for psychoanalytic theory, and for contemporary concerns. Relevant boundaries may define historical eras, disciplines, groups, or individuals; the issues range from the personal and interpersonal (human anatomy, sexuality), to the political and religious, to the metaphysical, or what Susan Zimmerman calls "the ultimate border problem," the body's eventual decay. This generalized concern with boundaries, with the psychic other, prompts the question: what use is psychoanalysis in relation to the problem of social and historical otherness? More explicitly political discourses rightly claim greater effectiveness in direct social intervention, yet psychoanalysis provides tools for explicating, and potentially undoing, psychical and cultural constructions supporting alterity. Freud's disappointment was palpable when he wrote, in 1915, "it might have been supposed . . . that 'foreigner' and 'enemy' could no longer be merged."[9] Attempting to account for this merger, and drawing on Freud's meditations on the demands and compromises of civilized life, Julia Kristeva describes how internal alienation is projected onto the world.[10] Lacan, identifying a gap between the subject and language, suggests how self-definitions are inevitably false; under the sway of the Other, we most identity with what we block ourselves from ever seeing. The Lacanian sense of the self as extrinsically molded has been further developed by Slavoj Žižek, who offers insights for cracking the code of ideological formations. For psychoanalysis, otherness is a necessary constituent of selfhood. Therefore, while it is crucially important to gather the data of cultural studies and history that allows understanding of the experiences of those who are remote from us temporally, spatially, and culturally, factual information alone proves inadequate. Also necessary are analytic tools for understanding our relation to others, lest they be permanently inscribed in the position of alterity. As Anthony Easthope argues, the celebration of diversity in radical work loses its edge when positions become fixed.[11] Attention to the unfixed relation of signifier to subject—most simply put, to textual complexities—holds open the gaps in meaning, and hence can enable resistance to inscribed formulations.

This poststructuralist concern with alterity and with multilayered, sometimes contradictory, knowledge indicates the distance between the work I am describing and the structural, individualist, sexist, and often homophobic conceptual apparatus that made a certain strain of Freudian thought a redoubt of socially conservative humanism. Under the influence of Lacan, Laplanche, Kristeva, Irigaray, Butler, Felman, and others, psychoanalytic critics have recently been concerned with social rather than individualist readings, intent on dispelling abjecting discourses about otherness, and devoted to rooting out tendencies that collapse innovation. That psychoanalysis cannot offer a solution to the problem of transference, or close the gap between the subject and the signifier, or dispel subjective limitations, does not signal its failure but its contribution, its way of keeping questions alive and resisting interpretive closure. Psychoanalysis may always be at risk of turning in on itself, as a discourse and in its particular, problematizing arguments. Yet historicism may too readily turn outward in search of new or additional facts without taking adequate measure of its own positionality and argumentative practices. To create a complexity of argument and design capable of accounting for the work of language across time, what's needed is mutually influencing dialogue between the two discourses, one introverted, one extroverted—and that's what the following papers offer.

In their jointly authored contribution, Lynn Enterline and David Hillman discuss the usefulness and value of psychoanalysis for the study of early modern culture. Together they lay the theoretical groundwork for the forum, considering models of historiography, the methodological question of transference (particularly in connection with a sense of the past's alterity), and the issues of the speaking body and the riddle of sexuality. Playing ideas productively off one another, they construct a dialogue that itself resembles the Möbius strip Hillman invokes to describe our relation to early modernity, which exists "paradoxically both inside *and* outside the present." Hillman sees evidence in the early modern period of crisis in the "relation between selfhood and corporeality," as the notion of the body as sealed and contained (Elias's *homo clausus*), produced a twofold sense of alienation—the body ceased to be the site of connection with others, and became alien itself. Enterline is more skeptical about tracking changes in subjectivity, for she hears evidence of "alienation of self from body" in early modern texts, as in Ovid and in Lacan. She notes as well how the shadow of the ego may occlude the observer's view and how formations we share with the earlier period may be least visible to us. Because psychoanalysis persistently requires that we pay attention to sexuality, it helps bring to the surface intractable assumptions about identity and power that are bound up in the discourse of sexuality and gender. Neither Enterline nor Hillman embraces psychoanalysis as a blueprint; instead, they describe a "critical practice in which psychoanalytic theory and historical/textual evidence are 'mutually implicated.'" For both, psychoanalysis has value for its resistance to easy closure of questions about the body, identity, and sexuality.

Graham Hammill differentiates between the study of historical constructions of sexuality, which depend on Foucault for theoretical support, and the study of sexuality itself, which requires engagement with psychoanalysis. As Hammill shows, the record of psychoanalytic explanations of sexuality (post-Freudian ones, in particular) is marked by imprecision if not outright failure, so one finds little of immediate methodological utility. Echoing Enterline and Hillman on the value of open questions, Hammill finds the murkiness about sexuality in psychoanalytic writing to be productive in itself. For instance, Lacan's sense of sexuality as "an effect of representation," "the inability of any system of meaning to give full meaning to the subject," returns readers to early modern texts with the idea of sexuality as a physical affair unsettled and perhaps dislodged. For Hammill, the real challenge for psychoanalytic study of premodern sexuality involves unpacking the metaphorical and mythic structures that sustain it.

The myths propping up sexuality interest Elizabeth Harvey as well; her essay traces the history of anatomical knowledge underlying Freud's constructions of sexuality, especially female sexuality. Following Luce Irigaray in charging Freud with irresponsible historicism, Harvey uses his archeological method against his theory of sexuality, excavating the ideas and beliefs—originally from Galen, but fostered by Helkiah Crooke and other early modern writers—that subtend his knowledge. The genealogical project, implicitly indebted to Foucault, shows Freud to draw on a long cultural tradition, a past Harvey calls "psychoanalysis's unconscious," since it is both his source and his blind spot; the anatomical knowledge itself she calls "imaginary," evoking a psychoanalytic sense of unwilled accession to cultural forces.

Doug Trevor puts humoralism into dialogue with psychoanalytic thought, suggesting the limitation of both systems when it comes to explaining love. Trevor shows how Galenic notions of love melancholy infuse *Romeo and Juliet,* yet are also resisted and even treated as something of a joke. Juliet's willful idealization of her lover, the mystification of the moment of mutual attraction, and the sheer excessiveness of the play's language of love accord more closely with psychoanalytic (especially Lacanian) than with humoralist accounts of passion, so that Shakespeare might be seen as getting traction from Galenic thought as he makes contributions to an emergent humanism. Ficino's notion of lovers exchanging souls, for instance, finds a psychoanalytic counterpart in the concept of introjection—after passing through the discourse of love, which proclaims itself outside any system of explanation.

Such poetic mediation was necessary because, as Kristen Poole points out, psychoanalysis was originally posited on a bounded, modern subject (*homo clausus* again), while the early modern period assumed permeable boundaries between self and world—the human body was in constant interaction with its environment, individuals could intermingle, and "demons were an integral part of the natural world." Moving beyond the critique of Freud's historical contingency, Poole challenges us to consider how fundamental notions of time, space, and matter determine self-understanding and shape experience in the world. Although Freud himself compares the evolving field of psychoanalysis to physics—"the basic notions of [physics] as regards matter, centers of force, attraction, etc., are scarcely less debatable than the corresponding notions in psycho-analysis"—he was poorly positioned to see how his own ideas rely on distinct assumptions about the physical universe.[12] Indeed, Laplanche points out that his theory assumes a mechanistic model of the universe already "out of date at the very moment when Freud tried to press it into service."[13] Following Poole's challenge, then, perhaps we can see the Freudian problematic of memory, and even the whole dynamic of the unconscious, as an attempted compromise with the alienating nature of the modern physical world, as well as adopting her caution about applying the ideas of one conceptual universe—a term she uses with bracing literalness—to another.

Acknowledgment of psychoanalysis as a materialist discourse is likewise important in Susan Zimmerman's essay on the anxious fascination provoked by dead bodies, or representations of dead bodies, in early modern culture. Located at the border between human and inhuman, symbolic and organic, the putrefying corpse undermines logical distinctions. It presents a conundrum that Zimmerman illuminates by means of Julia Kristeva's concepts of abjection and the semiotic. The problem of dead bodies exists across time, but Zimmerman locates a particular tension in early modern religious ideology between the psychosomatic unity of medieval Christianity and an emergent body-soul dualism; one result of transition in theological and ontological systems was a heightened anxiety about the fate of the dead, including the status of the dead body. Zimmerman reads the horror provoked by the ghost in *Hamlet* as evidence of early modern concern about the status of the newly dead—a reading that overturns the traditional oedipal understanding of the ghost ("Old Hamlet," as it/he is renamed in such accounts) and substitutes a differently realized psychoanalytic encounter, one that is attentive to historical context while also accounting for ongoing fascination with the play.

Heather Hirschfeld employs "the psychoanalytic vocabulary of compulsion" not to symptomatize religious beliefs and behaviors but "to account for the very tenacity of certain religious convictions" in the early modern period. For psychoanalysis, compulsive behavior testifies to a conflict between contradictory wishes, a conflict the subject finds easier to reproduce than to resolve. Hirschfeld proposes that post-Reformation theology laid the path for compulsiveness by paradoxically requiring believers to exercise their free will in submitting to God's will. For the Christians in *The Merchant of Venice*, a wish to force Shylock to convert to Christianity exactly balances a commitment to seeing him continue to occupy the place of Jewish Other; they are locked in the paradoxical desire that the Jew be both saved *and* damned. Hirschfeld astutely suggests how a psychotheological inquiry can illuminate the religious politics of the early modern period.

Psychoanalysis can enable inquiry into textual puzzles of the past, and historical contextualization and background-checking can enrich understanding of psychoanalysis itself, yet it would be a mistake to see these discourses as happily symbiotic. As a striking instance, Lisa Freinkel shows that neither history nor theory can provide firm ground for understanding the fetish, for in both its Marxian, economic sense of commodity fetishism and its Freudian, sexual one, the word names a misuse, an inappropriate investment. Aligning the fetish with *catachresis*, the rhetorical figure for abuse of metaphor, Freinkel documents the suspicion with which linguistic inventiveness was met by early modern rhetoricians. Generation of babies, generation of capital—these were "natural" returns on investment of love or money, while *catachresis*, by producing only more words, was (and is) like fetishism in perpetuating an always-unsatisfied desire. Psychoanalysis can aid our understanding of culture, including early modern culture, by probing self-defeating efforts at certainty, raveling historical assertions into threads of words. Whether psychoanalysis is inside or outside the walls, it keeps pointing out how language loops through reason, unreason, the body, and desire, effecting our links with each other and with the past, though not always in exactly the ways we think.

Notes

1. Walter Benjamin, "Theses on the Philosophy of History," *Illuminations: Essays and Reflections*, ed. Hannah Arendt (New York: Random House-Schocken, 1969), 253, 262, 257.

2. Paul de Man, *The Resistance to Theory* (Minneapolis: University of Minnesota Press, 1986), 12, 19.

3. See Cynthia Marshall, "Psychoanalyzing the Prepsychoanalytic Subject," *PMLA* 117, no. 5 (2002): 1207–16.

4. Jacques Derrida, *Resistances of Psychoanalysis*, trans. Peggy Kamuf, Pascale-Anne Brault, and Michael Naas (Stanford: Stanford University Press, 1998), viii.

5. Ibid., 62.

6. Carla Mazzio and Douglas Trevor, eds., *Historicism, Psychoanalysis, and Early Modern Culture* (New York: Routledge, 2000). See also Valeria Finucci and Regina Schwartz, eds., *Desire in the Renaissance: Psychoanalysis and Literature* (Princeton: Princeton University Press, 1994).

7. Jean Laplanche, *New Foundations for Psychoanalysis*, trans. David Macey (Cambridge, MA: Basil Blackwell, 1989), 11; *Nouveaux fondements pour la psychanalyse* (Paris: Quadrige, 1987).

8. Laplanche, *New Foundations*, 8, 92.

9. Sigmund Freud, "Thoughts for the Time on War and Death," *The Standard Edition of the Complete Psychological Works of Sigmund Freud*, ed. James Strachey (London: Hogarth Press and Institute of Psychoanalysis, 1953–74), 14:277.

10. Julia Kristeva, *Strangers to Ourselves*, trans. Leon S. Roudiez (New York: Columbia University Press, 1991).

11. Antony Easthope, *Privileging Difference*, ed. Catherine Belsey (New York: Palgrave, 2002).

12. Sigmund Freud, "On Narcissism," *Standard Edition*, 14:77.

13. Laplanche, 40. See also Freud's related reference to physics in "Instincts and Their Vicissitudes": "Physics furnish an excellent illustration of the way in which even 'basic concepts' that have been established in the form of definitions are constantly being altered in their content" (*Standard Edition*, 14:117).

Other Selves, Other Bodies

Lynn Enterline and David Hillman

*T*HE FOLLOWING DIALOGUE *grew out of conversations we had about current methodologies in Renaissance studies. Our initial discussions explored the intersection between psychoanalysis and historicism. From those, specific questions emerged about where to go from here, particularly with respect to early modern experiences of embodiment. We would like to thank Cynthia Marshall for giving us the opportunity to investigate our shared concerns.*

LE: The longer I've thought about early modern subjectivity, the more I've understood how fundamental determinations of sameness and difference are to contemporary critical accounts of the period—and at the same time, how important it is to address the reasons for the choices we make, however intractable the theoretical and historical problem may be. Corollary questions about the power and limitations of genealogical explanation, moreover, become especially acute when critics pursue psychoanalytic modes of inquiry. With respect to the current turn toward emphasizing the strangeness of early modern literature and culture to our own— something of a reaction against earlier, Burckhardian recognitions of similarity between modern and early modern—I remain something of a skeptic. Both claims are plagued by a shared problem: these claims, whether about the early modern period's difference from our own or its resemblance, cannot but be influenced by what Lacan might call the "wandering shadow" of the observer's "own ego."[1] A crucial psychoanalytic premise is that with respect to the question of "the subject," no one occupies an uncompromised position of observation. This premise need not lead, however, to a dead end. It is accompanied by an equally important axiom: our entanglement in the stories of others can, in fact, be productive for both the observer and the observed. From this perspective, the work of historians like Dominick LaCapra and Joan Scott suggest that a crucial task for critics interrogating the experiences of subjects from other cultures and moments in history is to inquire into the transferential basis of their own investments in those stories.[2] And as Freud and Lacan were quite aware, the transference is not simply a critique of absolute claims to knowledge derived from the positivist tradition. It is also a revealing relationship—a mutual involvement of one in the other that constitutes the condition of the possibility of unexpected insight into both subjects at hand. New meanings, texts, and materials emerge from the pressure of our critical, theoretical, and historical inquiry; and these, in turn, stand the chance of altering, however slightly, the "early modern" frame through which many critics have tried to see our "modern" condition (whether in likeness or in difference). This, at any rate, is the ongoing dialogic movement that allows me to understand Lacan's cryptic but tantalizing observation that provides the epigram for LaCapra's essay, "History and Psychoanalysis": "[l]e transfert c'est le concept même de l'analyse, parce que c'est le temps de l'analyse."[3]

So, we are in a moment where the idea of difference, of rendering the past strange, appeals. Several decades of New Historicist scholarship have pointed out the dangers of assimilating the early modern too closely to the modern; and that modern discourses run the risk of distorting or disguising what in the early modern period does not resemble our own. It often occurs to the feminist in me, however, that the danger in starting from the premise of the early modern period's strangeness is that we risk losing a sense of the inequities and violences that *persist* over time and cultural/historical difference, particularly in the realms of gender and sexuality. It makes me notice yet again that we have only just begun to uncover how such asymmetrical relations of power shape our own critical assumptions, never mind received accounts of literary and cultural history based on those assumptions. One distinct advantage to psychoanalytic inquiry, it seems to me, is that it keeps requiring us to put the question of sexuality on the table. More important, it does by suggesting that "sexuality" is not a phenomenon we can delimit, define, and know (not to mention designate as "normal" or "abnormal"). Rather, psychoanalysis insists that sexuality remains an obdurate *question*—one that upsets historically based divisions of knowledge. It is a question that nonetheless is central to early modern culture, to our own, and to our evident, long-standing investment in discovering something about ourselves in relation to that past.

When it comes to critical reflection on our own transferential relation to the early modern period, the tools of literary criticism offer distinct advantages. In literary criticism as in Freud, Lacan, and the best contemporary psychoanalytic theory, investigations of subjectivity require close, careful, dialogic reading of rhetorical and narrative detail carried out from a position of modesty—i.e., with the full admission that no one reader fully recovers a text's final significance. It is this shared attention, in both literary and psychoanalytic theory, to what the screen of language has to tell us about the forms and effects of self-representation that seems to me to offer a revealing, though not final, index of what our own transferential investments have to tell us about continuities and disjunctions between early modern subjectivities and our own.

DH: You've hinted at a kind of oscillation in critical trends, between a making-similar and a making-strange of early modernity, and indeed I agree that it is high time to move beyond this dichotomy; to accept that "we" (moderns) are—and are not—"them" (early moderns). Renaissance culture *is* other—separate from our own and in crucial ways inaccessible to us; but at the same time, since we have intimate affective and intellectual connections with early modernity, these continuities should lead to "productive entanglements" as you aptly put it. Hans-Georg Gadamer has expressed it like this: "Temporal distance is not something that must be overcome . . . The important thing is to recognise the distance in time as a positive and productive possibility of understanding. It is not a yawning abyss, but is filled with the continuity of custom and tradition, in the light of which all that is handed down presents itself to us."[4] Our subjection to time can thus be both a potential limitation *and* a potential source of insight.

Revealing analogies might be drawn between the philosopher Stanley Cavell's views of our relation to otherness and these critical and methodological questions. I propose that we understand these critical trends as an unnecessary choice between the refusal to recognize separateness and the refusal to acknowledge connection: two kinds of skepticism, which we can understand as denials of forms of knowledge. The rather woolly idea that the great authors of the Renaissance are "our contemporaries" can be seen as something like a denial of the truth of separateness, of our ultimate isolation as members of a particular historical period (for better or worse). On the other hand, the insistence on contingency and difference seems to me to overemphasize the gap between past and present, self and other. This perception of "our" externality to the Renaissance can itself be understood as a form of skepticism, a denial of a mutual complicity and interanimation; for the idea of the inaccessibility of the other needn't entail giving up the attempt to know the other—only the renunciation of the kind of epistemological knowing that demands certifiable evidence or proof. This type of knowing has affinities with much of the empirical historicism that has dominated early modern studies in recent years. We might redescribe the issue as one of whether the assumption is of one culture being inside the other or outside it—a paradigmatically skeptical dichotomy. It would be more accurate, and fruitful, to think of the relation on the model of a Möbius strip, hence of early modernity as paradoxically both inside *and* outside the present.

I think the Renaissance itself was deeply concerned with these issues of otherness and (in)accessibility—that the great flourishing of the culture of the period can hardly be separated from them. Psychoanalysis is similarly preoccupied with these same issues, and psychoanalytic interpretations of early modern culture gain much of their power precisely from the fact that so much of this culture appears to have anticipated the kinds of engagement and questions psychoanalysis addresses. I find it useful to think of the matter in these terms, and of the solution (such as it is) as a kind of productive balance: of, on the one hand, empirical historicist scholarship subject to skeptical scrutiny and a sense of the strangeness of the Renaissance, and, on the other, a more intuitive grasp allied to the belief that we can after all empathize with early modern modes of subjectivity. Psychoanalysis can be helpful in this endeavor in its attempts to come to terms with the ways in which we influence and are influenced by each other, and at the same time in reminding us that we are never at one—even with ourselves; it reveals the instabilities and misrecognitions in the relations between selves and others—as it can, at its best, reveal the vertiginously unstable and transferential qualities of the relation between past and present.

Psychoanalytic interpretation of early modern culture makes me think of Kafka's well-known half-joke about his Jewish heritage: "What have I in common with Jews? I have hardly anything in common with myself!" Over the past two decades, literary critics and historians have been preoccupied with the question, "What have we in common with early moderns?" Psychoanalysis responds, in the time-honored Jewish manner of answering a question with a question—productively, I believe: "What have we in common with ourselves?"

LE: This balancing act between otherness and sameness becomes most pressing with respect to contemporary investigations of early modern bodies. At once a site of connection (we all have one) and of inaccessibility (we have no unmediated access to the sensations felt by another), the body demands immense critical discretion, a shuttling back and forth between what you've described as a kind of balance between skepticism and empathy. What psychoanalytic theory contributes to this investigation, it seems to me, is a kind of critical edge for one's intuition by way of a theory of the body's relation to language—one that usefully reminds us that concentrating exclusively on the difference between historical periods may lead us to lose sight of the difference *within* any speaking subject's relation to his or her body. Historicist descriptions of early modern bodies, insofar as they rely on the assumptions of reference and empiricism, comfort because the difference is be located out there, in an earlier period, *and not in us.* Perhaps I am trying to describe something Cavell would call a denied knowledge—that we are "strangers to ourselves," that such strangeness is something all too easily displaced and misrecognized as someone else's.

DH: For me too, these matters come to a head, so to speak, through thinking about the body. Human finitude appears to find its most direct, obvious, apt expression in the finitude of the human body in relation to other bodies, in relation to the external world, in relation to the past (and the future). Here is where psychoanalysis and early modernity seem to me to embrace "as it were from the ends of opposed winds": both can be seen to be relentlessly grappling with the problem of the relation between selfhood and corporeality; but whereas—to put the matter rather too tidily—early moderns were coming to the problem through a process of loss (of presence, or of immediacy—of, let's say, a relative psycho-somatic oneness), psychoanalysis has been at pains to come to terms with the already lost, to *re*connect body and (say) mind after centuries of increasing disjunction. Modern subjectivity emerged out of the intense pressure placed upon the unity of body and self, inner and outer.

I agree with you that the problem of the relation of the body to language is indeed a version of the problem of (in)accessibility; but this matter seems to me precisely to pinpoint the space of difference (insofar as such pinpointing can ever be valid) between pre- and post-Renaissance modes of thought. The body in the early modern period is at a point of crisis and profound transition; and one way of defining this transition is to say that early modernity is the period during which the human body changed from being understood first and foremost as a site of connection to being conceived of as *the* indubitable locus of inaccessibility—at first, of the other, eventually, of one's own body *as* other. It is largely because of the growing abyss between somatic inner and outer that these questions (of the relation of mind to body, and of self to other) were becoming such urgent problems during the sixteenth and seventeenth centuries.

Psychoanalysis thus emerges at the other end of the Cartesian tunnel of psycho-somatic inaccessibility. Psychoanalytic thinking seems to allow a return to the body—to the somatic roots of psychic life—in a nonreductive manner, which is to say, without recourse to mere biologism or materialism. Psychoanalysis is *not* helpful in this endeavor insofar as one regards it as providing some kind of key or blueprint for interpretation; it does however seem to me interesting and useful when placed in apposition to early modernity—what Shoshana Felman calls a relation of implication, rather than application. Then we can begin to think in a mutually productive manner about the ways in which both psychoanalysis and early modernity struggle to come to grips with the relations of body and language, or wrestle with the relation between affect and physiology, embodied self and other. In my work I try to use psychoanalysis as, among other things, an archeological tool, a method of unearthing the genealogies of the structures of subjectivity that were in the process of being formed in the early modern period; and at the same time to trace the roots of psychoanalysis at the point of their emergence in the early modern notion of disembodied and fractured interiority.

LE: I particularly like your word, "apposition," for the relationship between psychoanalysis and early modern literature and culture. I also agree that we have inherited a pressing early modern question: the nature, degree, and affective texture of the connection between subjectivity and corporeality. With respect to current critical practice, both applied psychoanalysis and empiricist historicism (or for that matter, simple notions of "materialism" uninflected by either Marxist or psychoanalytic theory) evade the truly complex problems posed by our attempt to investigate the conditions of embodied subjectivity in the early modern period. But your suggestion that in the early modern period, in contrast to our own, the human body was "conceived as a site of connection"—or that the Renaissance was a moment with an emergent sense of losing a "relative oneness of body and soul"—strikes me as at once an intriguing idea and as the kind of narrative with which I opened this discussion: one made possible in retrospect, as a kind of symptom or aftereffect of contemporary discourses of alienation. Rather like Lacan's mirror stage, it is a story of "before" made possible only by the after— only in this case, nostalgia attaches to the earlier rather than the later moment.

What is perhaps more interesting than my generalized caution about historical genealogy, however, is that I hear rather different testimony in the texts of the period—testimony of a sense of profound and disturbing alienation of self from body. And, as you will not be surprised to hear, I have as yet to find an indubitable historical "moment," text, or author from which this predicament seems to be a dramatic departure. I suppose I tend to think of historical periods as I do speaking subjects—entities riddled with conflict and dissension; which means that they resist genealogical narratives of transition (never mind the meliorist stories of progress sometimes told by our predecessors). In our current critical moment, one's sense of early modern experience, of course, will vary a great deal depending on the particular discourse or discourses—literary, popular, medical, educational, legal, political—under investigation. (Variation between these discourses, of course, contributes to internal contradiction rather than consensus.)

Let me be specific: part of my reason for writing my book on Ovidian rhetoric was to demonstrate that in the *Metamorphoses*, the story of a speaking subject's distance from his or her own "tongue" (at once body and language) pervades Ovid's poem, shapes the narrator's self-representation as *"auctor,"* and is a crucial reason for the text's extraordinary popularity among Renaissance poets. Ovid lingers on the moment of self-estrangement—Philomela's severed tongue, Actaeon's changing form and voice, the song that emerges from Orpheus's severed head—as figures for authorship. And it is precisely these stories that most attract Shakespeare. With respect to the tradition of rhetorical training inherited from Rome (and given impetus in early modern grammar schools and universities), poets like Shakespeare were fascinated by Ovid's tendency to represent what it means to occupy a speaking body as a violent scene of alienation from one's own tongue. To take the example that conveys what I argued about the Ovidian tradition most succinctly: Lucrece's traumatic induction into a sense of the social/sexual meaning of her own body (as "chaste") leads, in *The Rape of Lucrece*, to "more woe than words" and thus her identification with two mute Ovidian women: Philomela and Hecuba. More important still, it is precisely Lucrece's alienation from her own body and tongue that allows Shakespeare to explore the dynamics of publication and authorship.[5] Here I believe I'm talking about what you aptly pointed out earlier—that psychoanalytic explanations derive their power because "so much of [early modern] culture appears to have anticipated the kinds of engagement and questions psychoanalysis addresses." Ovidian figures that appealed most strongly to early modern authors seem to insist on the subject's estrangement from his or her body, his or her voice.

In a different approach to the same question about Shakespeare's Lucrece, Katherine Maus writes that in contrast to Augustine, Lucrece does not believe her soul and body are one. She therefore refuses the absolute judgment of guilt with which Augustine burdens her suicide.[6] Put telegraphically, my reading of Shakespeare's Ovidianism is that it takes place by means of cross-voicing as well as cross-dressing, a hallmark displacement of language from embodied experience that defines his career-long interrogation of what it means to say "I," to occupy a body, and to understand the significance of that body's meaning and value in one's own culture. The question raised with such relentless focus in *Lucrece*—that of a body's social value as well as the affective consequences attending the subject's ability to live with it (or not)—reminds me of a further methodological point. While I agree with Gadamer's notion of the "positive and productive condition of understanding" raised by "the continuity of custom and tradition" across gaps of time, I first turned to feminist and queer versions of psychoanalysis in order to remain alert, as Walter Benjamin famously cautioned, to the way in which "tradition" involves inherited forms of inequity, barbarism, and violence.

Clearly my reading of Ovid's popularity in the period (and specific attraction for Shakespeare) is just as subject to the "pre-posterous" effects of historical narration and theorizing as your own. As I said at the beginning of our exchange, it seems to me to come down to the details of a reading as well as a critic's (historically, socially, personally inflected) investments and transferences. The question of how early modern subjects experienced their own bodies remains intractable at the general level: too many particular histories are involved and implicated (both early modern and modern). But I do think it *can* be addressed at the level of individual readings, particularly those in which the question of a subject's affective relation to his or her own embodiment remains an open question. The kind of reading I am talking about—a kind that I do believe will push our understanding of early modern subjectivity further still—will address what you call the "somatic roots" of social and psychic life or what I call the subject's linguistic and fantasmatic relation to the material and social conditions of her own body. This fantasmatic relationship to the material conditions of existence, it seems to me, most benefits from Felman's notion of a critical practice in which psychoanalytic theory and historical/textual evidence are "mutually implicated."

DH: It's hard to disagree that generalizing about something as complex and multifarious as early modern ideas of embodiment is an enterprise fraught with perils, and that eras are at least as "riddled with conflict and dissention" as individuals. Caution is certainly in order—and yet perhaps we should be cautious about being *too* cautious. Unless we treat individuals *as if* we can come to know them, as if they cohere in some significant manner, we run the risk of denying their individuality—of refusing to acknowledge them in all their fully embodied, separate existence; and I want to suggest that much the same may be said of historical periods. We cannot of course know what "the" early modern experience of embodiment was like—no more than could the men and women of early modernity; but the fact of its being an enigma does not mean that it is inaccessible. Any narrative about history will be subject to the mechanism of *Nachträglichkeit* or "deferred action"—but this "after effect" complicates rather than invalidates it. I do accept that a degree of skepticism is in order in relation to genealogical narratives; perhaps it would have been better to suggest that one story early moderns appear to have been telling *themselves* was of a loss of body-soul at-oneness, as the story Freud and many later psychoanalysts invoke is one of re-linking body and mind or affect. Wary of our pretensions to mastery, we still have to keep coming up with narratives.

I'd like to pick up on your reference to Lacan's mirror stage, partly because it will allow me to indicate briefly what kinds of questions might arise from the interweaving of psychoanalysis and early modernity. In his essay on the mirror stage, Lacan pictures identity as a kind of self-alienating armoring, of an originally corporeal nature.[6] (Freud too, famously—and somewhat opaquely—speaks of the ego as "first and foremost a bodily ego; it is not merely a surface entity, but is itself the projection of a surface";[7] meaning, presumably, that the ego is constructed around—as a projection of—the boundary between the interior and the exterior of the body.) Psychoanalysis has a good deal to say about this picture of the body and its relation to the newfound "alienation of self from body" that you point to. But there are interesting affinities between such notions of the body-ego and early modern sociohistorical and philosophical developments that emphasized bodily closure and self-control, and that contributed to an image of the human that Norbert Elias has dubbed *homo clausus*: a being "severed from all other people and things 'outside' by the "wall" of the body."[8] And while this notion was of course not shared by all early moderns, the fantasmatic notion of the body as a sealed container does seem to have taken on a life of its own over the course of the Renaissance.

So questions arise: to what extent were these psychoanalytic formulations of the emergence of the subject arrived at under the influence of a historically specific episteme? And: if picturing the body as if it consists of an impenetrable integument is a standing possibility (even temptation) for the human being, and if psychoanalysis proffers reasons why this fantasy or nightmare becomes more active or urgent at certain moments (often of crisis) in an individual's life: can psychoanalytic thinking help us, by extension, to understand something about the historical conditions that were tied to these changes in notions of the body in the sixteenth and seventeenth centuries? Can we find ways to examine these matters side by side, mutually implicating each without privileging either methodology? And most importantly: how are we to avoid, or at least to take into account, the possibility that our interpretation of these ideas will end up being circular (rather than Möbius-like)?

Historical moments of radical departure from the past are indeed notoriously hard to pin down. And yet, let me end with a signal moment from a signal play—a moment that seems to me inseparable from the problematics of bodily closure and subjectivity I've just been addressing: "O God, I could be bounded in a nutshell and count myself a king of infinite space—were it not that I have bad dreams" (*Hamlet*, 2.2.254–56): a choice between historicist and psychoanalytic approaches to comprehending this sentiment can only be detrimental to a fuller kind of apprehension of either.

Notes

1. "All the objects of [the subject's] world are always structured around the wandering shadow of the subject's own ego. They will all have a fundamentally anthropomorphic character, even an egomorphic we could say. Man's [*sic*] ideal unity, which is never attained as such and escapes him at every moment, is evoked at every moment of his perception" (Jacques Lacan, *The Seminar of Jacques Lacan Book II: The Ego in Freud's Theory and in the Technique of Psychoanalysis 1954–55*, trans. Sylvana Tomaselli [New York: Norton, 1988], 166).

2. LaCapra discusses several ways in which "the historian is implicated in a twofold 'dialogic' relation that involves transference" in "History and Psychoanalysis," *Critical Inquiry* 12, no. 2 (Winter 1987): 222–51. Of particular relevance here is his observation that "transference . . . would highlight the issue of the historian's voice in narration and analysis—an issue prematurely foreclosed when one assumes full unity not only of narrative but of narrative and authorial voice," 229. On questions arising specifically from attempts to interpret the texture of past experience, see Joan Scott, "Experience," in Judith Butler and Joan Scott, *Feminists Theorize the Political* (New York: Routledge, 1992).

3. As quoted in LaCapra, ibid., p. 222.

4. Hans-Georg Gadamer, *Truth and Method* (New York: Crossroad, 1984), 338.

5. *The Rhetoric of the Body from Ovid to Shakespeare* (Cambridge: Cambridge University Press, 2000).

6. "Taking Tropes Seriously: Language and Violence in Shakespeare's *Rape of Lucrece*," *Shakespeare Quarterly* 31(1986): 66–84.

7. Jacques Lacan, "The mirror stage as formative of the function of the I," in *Écrits: A Selection*, trans. Alan Sheridan (London: Norton, 1977), 1–7.

8. Sigmund Freud, *The Ego and the Id* (1923), quoted from the Standard Edition, vol. 19, p. 26.

9. Norbert Elias, *The History of Manners*, vol. 1 of *The Civilizing Process*, trans. Edmund Jephcott (New York: Pantheon Books, 1978), 257.

Psychoanalysis and Sexuality

Graham Hammill

Of what use is psychoanalysis for the study of sexuality? By this question, one could mean the following. Of what use is psychoanalysis for uncovering the historically specific legal and theological categories of norms and deviations by which individuals experienced themselves as sexed, gendered beings and their pleasures as sexual pleasure? If that is the question, then the answer is easy to give. Psychoanalysis is of almost no use whatsoever. The kind of psychoanalysis read, studied, and defended by current literary studies (e.g., Freud and Lacan) is burdened by a specialized vocabulary and a tricky logic, so that the insights it tends to produce are legitimately difficult for others to understand. Among psychoanalysts sexuality is at best an inconsistent concept. At worst, the concept is incomprehensible. Throughout his career, Freud unwaveringly insisted that sexuality must accompany the theory of the unconscious. While the unconscious works according to specifiable laws (such as condensation and displacement), it always expresses a wish that is fundamentally sexual. However, it is quite clear that Freud also had a very difficult time explaining what he actually meant. It seems entirely appropriate, in fact most likely necessary, that when in the late 1980s the history of sexuality was instituted as a field of academic study, the main practitioners within this field defined themselves against Freud, Lacan, and that version of psychoanalysis. Anyone who is working on the historical construction of sexuality—on the legal, ethical, theological, scientific, and social organizations of erotic pleasures and especially the ways in which those organizations change over time, across a variety of groups—and is also searching for theoretical support would do better to follow Foucault, who accepted the radical nature of the unconscious but worked very hard to dissociate it from sexuality, or—if inclined to use psychoanalysis—to follow Jung, who argued that the libido is a nonsexualized psychical intensity, akin to Nietzsche's will to power, and that sexuality is to be found in individuals' relations to culturally constructed archetypes.[1]

If instead, in asking about the usefulness of psychoanalysis, one means to ask about the value of the study of sexuality itself, then psychoanalysis is of use. However, this assertion needs qualification. Psychoanalysis is not particularly useful because its assertions about sexuality are obviously true. While Freud and Lacan are both very sure of what sexuality is not, neither is very sure at all of what it is. What makes psychoanalysis of great interest to the study of sexuality is this uncertainty. Freud tends to attribute his uncertainty to the newness of psychoanalysis. Ever the scientist, he believes that further concrete research will produce firmer concepts that better grasp reality. Positing language as the site of that uncertainty, and not incomplete research, Lacan attributes Freud's uncertainty to his not developing fully enough the implications of his insights about speaking and representation. By focusing on language, Lacan can describe both uncertainty and sexuality in some detail. But when sexuality concerns the historical and political, Lacan falters as much as Freud. The fact of this faltering says as much about the limits of sexuality as a topic of study as it does about the limits of psychoanalysis. That is, the difficulty that psychoanalytic thought has with sexuality is symptomatic of sexuality itself as an object of critical knowledge and historical analysis.

Central to this difficulty is the concept of libido. The term, Latin for lust or desire, is of course not at all new to Freud. According to the *OED*, the term is in use in English as early as the fifteenth century. However, before Freud the term does not have the kind of totalizing force that he gives it. When Milton uses the word "libidinous" in *The Reason of Church Government* to describe poetasters, to take a well-known example, the term describes an overly powerful attachment to the erotic that not all humans share.[2] Freud's innovation is to use libido to describe a sexual drive found in everyone at all times in human history. In order to place some limits on this broad claim, in his early writings Freud defines the human as split between an extremely malleable and mobile sexual drive, oriented toward objects, and an ego drive, serving mainly self-preservation. The thesis gets attacked by Jung who seizes on the opposition between sexual and ego drives in order to argue that neurosis is caused by a conflict between them, when the individual feels self-reproach for not fulfilling what Jung thinks of as that individual's "life-task." Rather than serving as the stuff of libido, in Jung's account sexuality becomes a kind of blockage that prevents libido, which Jung understands to be general psychical intensity, from continuing down its right path. Freud sees this theory as nothing less than "a new religio-ethical system" that bears little resemblance to his understanding of psychoanalytic practice.[3] Jung drains libido of its sexual substance in order to define sexuality through morality. In response, Freud elaborates his complex theory of the drives. Jettisoning his initial opposition between sexual and ego drives, Freud argues for an already sexualized primary narcissism.[4] He salvages his central thesis that the reality of the unconscious is sexual, but on the condition that sexuality becomes increasingly unfamiliar and its domain increasingly expansive. Defined neither by an object of attraction nor by a particular activity, sexuality becomes synonymous with excitation, but not quite. In the 1915 edition of *The Three Essays on Sexuality*, Freud lays out the problem most clearly. Libido has "a *qualitative* character to it," in that it differs from hunger, and is also "a quantitatively variable force . . . derived not from the so-called sexual parts alone, but from all the bodily organs."[5] That is, sexuality is an excitation that differs from other excitations in some imprecise way; the difference is not defined by specific body parts.

Lacan fully exploits the cunning of this imprecision. Freud suggests that sexual excitation cannot be satisfied by physical means mainly because it takes a mental representation as its object. For Freud, this is true for every form of excitation but is especially true of sexual excitation. Following Freud's logic, Lacan proposes that sexuality is an effect of representation. When you are hungry, you think about what you would like to eat, and your hunger is in part motivated by that mental representation. Once the desire for what you think you want to eat exceeds the satisfaction of actually eating, there is a kind of leftover excitation that is the sexual drive. According to this understanding, sexuality is always "deduced from something other than sexuality itself," as Lacan puts it.[6] Raising the problem of mental representation to the problem of representation *tout court*, Lacan argues that sexuality emerges from the inability of any system of meaning to give full meaning to the subject—an understanding of sexuality extremely familiar to readers of Shakespeare. Rather than proposing Freud's version of sexuality as a psychoanalytic problem to be resolved, Lacan makes that problem into the definition of sexuality. Sexuality emerges precisely where one's desire becomes a problem to oneself. On the one hand, this move totalizes a Freudian understanding of sexuality, while on the other hand, it comes quite close to the understanding of sexuality Foucault proposes in his later work. Foucault proposed sexuality as a form of "problematicization" in which an experience concerning truth and falsehood is formed "where the relation to self and to others is linked."[7] To be sure, from Foucault's point of view Freud and Lacan on libido are part of that history of problematicization, but in a way that is not unfriendly to his own project.[8] In Lacan's revision, the concept of libido is itself a kind of problematicization of sexuality, albeit from a non-Foucauldian and relatively ahistorical point of view.

Can psychoanalytic thought move beyond this understanding of sexuality? In his later writings, Freud begins to suggest an answer to this problem. After World War I, Freud most famously begins to write about war neurosis, which leads him to propose the theory of the death drive, but also he begins to work more seriously on applying psychoanalytic concepts to collective forms of life. This is especially the case with the concept of libido. Addressing political formations that emerged after the war, Freud begins to argue for reconceiving libido so that it can account for what he calls mass psychology, what we might nowadays call the psychology of the multitude. In a rare topical reference, he proposes that "if the importance of the libido's claims on [the internal organization of armies] had been better appreciated, the fantastic promises of the American President's Fourteen Points would probably not have been believed so easily, and the splendid instrument would not have been broken in the hands of the German leaders [*Kriegskünstlern*, or learners of the art of war]."[9] Freud's reference is to the Kapp Putsch, when German Free Corps (militias that were precursors to the National Socialists) successfully marched on Berlin in violent reaction to the Versailles Treaty's demand that these paramilitary groups disband.[10] He claims that libido is the key to understanding this new form of collective life and its organization of violence and leadership, and he is also quite clear that he is incapable of fully explaining what he means. At best, Freud explains, he understands that normative understandings of sexual differentiation are not relevant. "There is scarcely any sense in asking whether the libido which keeps groups together is of a homosexual or of a heterosexual nature, for it is not differentiated according to the sexes, and particularly shows a complete disregard for the aims of the genital organization of the libido."[11] This sentence can stand for the general problem that Freud faces after World War I. He recognizes the need for de-subjectivizing psychoanalytic concepts, the concept of libido in particular, but at the same time his terms and habits of thought so thoroughly assume subjectivity that he has great difficulty thinking beyond them.

When dealing with this articulation, Lacan again tries to make Freud's problem into a general solution. Describing the sexual drive as "a subjectification without subject," Lacan proposes that libido is the myth of an "unreal" organ.[12] This proposition has two main components. First, libido is an organ, as Lacan puts it, of "immortal life, irrepressible life." Second, he continues, this is a version of life "that has need of no organ."[13] That is, libido is absolute life, life that has no need to be embodied because it is life itself. Such a version of life does not exist in reality, but it does exists in myth. And as myth, Lacan argues, libido "articulates itself on the real in a way that eludes us."[14] Lacan tries to grasp the same kind of problem that Freud does in his later works. Sexuality is most significant as an aspect of collective life, not as the physical reproduction of the collective but its metaphorical and mythic endurance. Lacan suggests that collective life assumes an absolute reflection of itself (the folk as the ideal content of the state, for example) which is somehow sustained in erotic practices. Most striking, though, is the difficulty he has explaining the problem. His frustratingly paradoxical formation—libido as an organ which is not one—shows his own lack of precision in explaining what he thinks Freud is on to. Like Freud, Lacan ends his discussion of libido and mass psychology with a topic reference that is as mystifying as it is suggestive. "There is something profoundly masked in the critique of history that we have experienced. This, re-enacting the most monstrous and supposedly superceded forms of the holocaust, the drama of Nazism." For Lacan, all other forms of critique have failed to understand that in such forms of violence, "we try to find evidence for the presence of the desire of this Other that I call here *the dark God*."[15]

Over the past fifteen years, the study of sexuality in sixteenth- and seventeenth-century literary England has focused almost exclusively on varieties of deviancy. And for very good reason: to dismantle the inadequate notion that married, heterosexual love was the unquestioned norm of the time. Recent scholarship has more than demonstrated that the idealization of heterosexuality is a product of Victorian and cold war habits of thought that reveals more about the nineteenth and twentieth centuries than about the sixteenth or seventeenth. While psychoanalytic work on premodern and early modern sexuality should be in no way opposed to these findings, nevertheless the problem of sexuality would have to take psychoanalytically informed criticism in a different direction. More is at stake for psychoanalysis in the concept of sexuality than showing the supposed norm to be in fact defined by the deviant. The question about the use of psychoanalysis for the study of premodern or early modern sexuality is really whether or not, even as it insists on the centrality of the concept, psychoanalysis offers terms or a critical logic by which to think beyond sexuality. Freud and Lacan both underscore the urgency of this problem, but neither is able to resolve it. By insisting on and utterly defamiliarizing the concept of sexuality, both stumble across the problem of collective life, the fantasies, myths, and violent acts that sustain it. At stake now for a psychoanalytic engagement with sexuality, after Freud and Lacan, is dismantling the myth of absolute life, the violent and erotic means by which that myth is promulgated and sustained. To be sure, engaging in such a project further defamiliarizes what we understand to be sexuality, but that should be no problem at all.

Notes

1. For Jung's critique of Freud on the libido, see "On the Psychology of the Unconscious," in *Two Essays on Analytical Psychology*, ed. Gerhard Adler, trans. R. F. C. Hull (New York: Bollingen, 1953; rpt. 1967), 3–117.

2. John Milton, *Reason of Church Government*, in *John Milton: Complete Poems and Major Prose*, ed. Merritt Y. Hughes (Indianapolis: Bobbs-Merrill, 1984), 670.

3. Freud, *On the History of the Psychoanalytic Movement*, trans. Joan Riviere, revised and ed. James Strachey (New York: Norton, 1966), 62.

4. "On Narcissism," in *General Psychological Theory*, ed. Philip Rieff (New York: Collier, 1963), 80–82.

5. Freud gives his clearest version of this definition of libido in additions he made in 1915 to *Three Essays on Sexuality*, trans. James Strachey (New York: Basic Books, 1972), 83–84.

6. Jacques Lacan, *Four Fundamental Concepts of Psychoanalysis*, ed. Jacques-Alain Miller, trans. Alan Sheridan (New York: Norton, 1981), 204.

7. Michel Foucault, "The Concern for Truth," in *Foucault Live*, ed. Sylvère Lotringer, trans. John Johnston (New York: Semiotext(e), 1989), 296. I discuss this point at greater length in *Sexuality and Form: Caravaggio, Marlowe, and Bacon* (Chicago: University of Chicago Press, 2001), 128–30.

8. Arnold Davidson argues this point in *The Emergence of Sexuality: Historical Epistemology and the Formation of Concepts* (Cambridge: Harvard University Press, 2001), 66–92, 209–15.

9. Freud, *Group Psychology and an Analysis of the Ego*, trans. and ed. James Strachey (New York: Norton, 1959), 27.

10. The classic historian of the Free Corps is Robert Waite, *Vanguard of Nazism: The Free Corps Movement in Post-War Germany* (Cambridge: Harvard University Press, 1952). Klaus Theweleit's *Male Fantasies* is an exemplary study of sexuality in the Free Corps movement. He shows the extent to which Freud's insight about libido was accurate and inadequate. *Male Fantasies*, trans. Stephen Conway, Erica Carter, and Chris Turner, 2 vols. (Minneapolis: University of Minnesota Press, 1987–89).

11. Freud, *Group Psychology*, 73.

12. Lacan, *Four Fundamental Concepts*, 184, 205.

13. Ibid., 198.

14. Ibid., 205.

15. Ibid., 274–75, emphasis Lacan's.

Imaginary Anatomies

Elizabeth D. Harvey

In the "Aetiology of Hysteria," the paper that he read to the Viennese Society for Psychiatry and Neurology in 1896, Freud inaugurated a system of archeological metaphors that was to subtend his subsequent elaboration of psychoanalysis:

> Imagine that an explorer arrives in a little-known region where his interest is aroused by an expanse of ruins, with remains of walls, fragments of columns, and tablets with half-effaced and unreadable inscriptions. . . . he may start upon the ruins, clear away the rubbish, and, beginning from the visible remains, uncover what is buried. If his work is crowned with success, the discoveries are self-explanatory . . . the fragments of columns can be filled out into a temple; the numerous inscriptions, which, by good luck, may be bilingual, reveal an alphabet and a language, and when they have been deciphered and translated, yield undreamed-of information about the events of the remote past, to commemorate which the monuments were built. *Saxa loquunter!*[1]

The trope functioned as a recurrent analogy for the excavation of psychic life, as well as a reference to Freud's precise and learned conversancy with the science of archeology.[2] His vivid evocation of ruins, obliterated inscriptions, and the possibility of rendering an indecipherable language intelligible depicts a relationship with past cultures—ancient and early modern—that is foundational to psychoanalysis itself, although sometimes in ways that Freud did not fully recognize. He figured the archeological site as the analysand's unconscious and the analyst as an archeologist, but the cultural past, synecdochized as ruins, is also psychoanalysis's unconscious, a prehistory to which Freud himself had only limited and intermittent access. One of Freud's most brilliant readers and critics, the French feminist philosopher, linguist, and psychoanalyst Luce Irigaray recognized this oblivousness; she charged him with neglecting history, with failing "to investigate the historical factors governing the data with which he is dealing."[3] Irigaray's insight (influenced partly by Cornelius Castoriadis's idea of a radical imaginary)[4] extends the Freudian definition of the unconscious beyond the bounds of the individual to encompass a culture that is as resonant with memory as childhood is for the subject. Even as Freud continually summons the past as an analogy for the sedimentation of psychic life, the historical layering of the psychic and anatomical concepts he "discovers" is continually elided. History is at once Freud's obsession, evinced in his web of archeological metaphors and in his reference to the material civilizations that were being unearthed, and his blind spot, as Irigaray would say, the lacuna in the anatomical observations that underlie his psychoanalytic theories.

The Renaissance was itself structured by its disinterral of a forgotten and buried past, and just as early modern subjects were literally exhuming statues, monuments, and texts, so were they also engaged in translations, transcriptions, and recreations of a lost antiquity. I am suggesting, then, a particular appropriateness to the coupling of psychoanalysis and early modern culture though their mutual preoccupation with recovery and unearthing, an investigation of what Sir Thomas Browne called in *Urne-Burial* "the deep discovery of the Subterranean world."[5] That Freud's invention of psychoanalysis is based on and intertwined with hysteria situates the body and female sexuality at the center of the psychoanalytic enterprise. That his theorization of this new method had persistent recourse to archeological metaphors suggests that the so-called objective anatomical facts upon which his ideas rested were made possible by a historical discourse that we might call the anatomical unconscious, a corpus of cultural attitudes and interpretations of bodily organs and systems that sustained and made possible anatomical knowledge. I will argue here that both for Freud and early modern subjects, the human body was as archeologically layered as the body of the earth. Indeed, Helkiah Crooke, the English physician and author of the vernacular anatomical treatise *Mikrokosmographia,* used a metaphor similar to Freud's in his evocation of anatomical history, suggesting in his prefatory defense of human dissection that the history of anatomy is marked by ruins. Although a foundation for the medical arts was laid in antiquity, he says, it was lost and "worne out by length of time, for want of Letters and meanes to preserve them."[6] Where Crooke refers to a lost textual archive, I will claim that human corporeality is the palimpsested record of its anatomical discoveries, its cultural habits, and the historically specific understanding of its functions. In this sense, the body is a kind of a precipitate of medical history and cultural practices. Luce Irigaray claimed that a symptom of the profoundly unanalyzed nature of Freud's discourse derives from his belief in anatomy "as an irrefutable criterion of truth." She goes on to argue that "science too has its history"; [7] her critique suggests that psychoanalysis's universalizing tendencies—those transhistorical assumptions to which many scholars of early modern culture have objected—can be countered by making manifest the obscured anatomical history upon which Freud's claims depend.

The benefit of this historicizing approach both situates Freud's anatomical pronouncements in a specifically late nineteenth-century context and also reveals how they emerge from a much longer Western cultural tradition. In turn, it allows us to consider the temporally distant and often strange early modern medical descriptions of the human body through a present that has been permeated by psychoanalytic interpretations of anatomical knowledge. Judith Butler, who reads Freud through Lacan and Irigaray, among others, explores the implications of Freud's idea of a bodily ego, a notion that, prefiguring Lacan, links the formation of a psychical concept (the ego) with the externalized sense of the body. [8] The coincidence of the physiological and the psychical produces what Butler calls an "imaginary investiture," a process through which body parts become epistemologically accessible. Anatomical descriptions, in other words, are produced by joining the psychic and the corporeal, so that descriptions of the body are always "psychically and phantasmatically" informed, taking place as they do within an imaginative schema. [9] While Freud's idea of the bodily ego generates a theory that, starting with hysteria, maps the intimate linkage between the somatic and psychical registers, he nevertheless continues to assert the apparent transparency and indisputability of anatomical principles. The idea of imaginative investiture nevertheless offers important ways of understanding Renaissance anatomy, particularly the operations of the sexual and reproductive organs and the various faculties that mediated between the early modern soma and psyche: the passions, memory, imagination, and the senses.

Freud's theories of sexual "difference" (what Irigaray calls "in-difference") are culturally anticipated by the Galenic homology, the notion that male and female bodies are isomorphic and that their difference lies in the positioning of the reproductive organs, with the female parts of generation cloistered within the body, and the male organs lying outside. Galen's now well-known image of the mole's eyes, which was frequently repeated by early modern anatomists, including Crooke, drew on two discussions of the sense of sight in *Historia Animalium*, where Aristotle singles out the mole as the only viviparous animal that does not have eyes.[10] Aristotle refines his assertion by suggesting that the mole has eyes of a sort; although they are not visible, they exist as undeveloped parts, hidden under a covering of skin. Galen's use of the mole as analogy for the female reproductive organs influenced a scientific way of thinking about the relationship between male and female bodies that had extraordinary subsequent currency and longevity, setting up as it did a value-laden distinction in a scopic economy. The same linkage of sight with epistemological truth in an anatomical description of the reproductive and sexual organs underpins Freud's account in "Some Psychical Consequences of the Anatomical Distinction Between the Sexes." In both cases, female sexuality is rendered dependent on and subservient to male sexual structure and function. The Greek word for uterus in its neuter form is cognate with *hysteron*, what comes after or behind, signaling the assignment of the female organs to secondary place,[11] a relegation that is consolidated through the order in which the sexual and reproductive organs are described in anatomy treatises. The effect of this anatomical and philosophical subordination is simultaneously to construct a homology and to disavow it.

That is, just as moles burrow blindly beneath the earth, the encrypting of the female organs within the body relegates them to darkness and invisibility. Freud's often-cited description of female sexuality as a dark continent and his comparison of the pre-Oedipal phase in girls to the discovery of the Minoan-Mycenean civilizations draw on a similar sense of occultation.[12] The anatomical homology between the sexes and the conjugation of female sexuality with darkness and interiority are early modern inheritances, which are themselves legacies of antiquity. Far from negating the power of female sexuality, this medical description consigned the female sexual and reproductive organs to an imaginary register, whose operations continually escape the logic of the symbolic. In his anatomical description of the uterus, for instance, Helkiah Crooke, argues against the idea of a uterus that ranged throughout the body (it "is not like a gadding creature that moveth out of one place into another" [224]), asserting instead that it is tethered "as a moored Ship in a Tempest betweene her Anchors" (223) by ligaments that permit the matrix to rise and fall in the body. This movement may, he tells us, produce the disorder known as suffocation of the mother, or early modern hysteria. While he is at pains to refute the idea of the matrix possessing motion, he nevertheless attributes to it certain kinds of agency: "by muscles the voluntary motion of the Womb," for instance, draws "the seede into his cavity (as a Hart draweth a Snake out of the holes of the earth by drawing in his breath at his Nosethrils) and embrac[es] it afterward" (230). The womb is susceptible to odors, he says, and because sweet smells have vapors that rise to the brain and affect its membranes, "the membranous wombe is presently drawne into consent with the Brayne" (252). The sympathy between the brain and matrix is also a feature of the womb's relation with almost all the other organs and faculties in the body. Although Crooke explicitly denies the matrix's ability to wander in the body, he converts its influence from physical motion to "consent," an empathetic bond that gives the womb a sympathetic power throughout the body, capable of disrupting or creating with a kind of unruly abandon.

Psychoanalysis, the talking cure, is founded on a body that speaks through its somatic symptoms, and these coded corporeal signs are then interpreted by the psychoanalyst in much the same way as the archeologist reads the fragments of a buried civilization. If Freudian hysteria accentuated the fundamental unknowability of female sexuality, it also made apparent the equally enigmatic relationship between the body and the psyche through its conversion of psychic disruption into somatic symptoms. It is in this last respect that psychoanalysis may have the most value for early modern studies. As recent works on the passions, the humors, and memory demonstrate,[13] it is the subtle, invisible ligatures between the body and its faculties that are providing the most fertile ground for studies of early modern subjectivity. Descartes and his followers posited a body and mind more firmly cordoned off from one another than their earlier modern predecessors imagined. The vapors, subtle spirits, humors, souls, and sympathetic mediators between bodily organs and mental processes had a well-articulated existence in early modern medicine and in treatises on memory and the passions, and the tools of psychoanalysis that Freud provided can help us understand how complex a commerce there was for early modern subjects between the body and the psychic elements that vitalized it.

Notes

1. *The Standard Edition of the Complete Psychological Works of Sigmund Freud,* Vol. III: *Early Psycho-Analytic Publications,* ed. James Strachey (1962; London: Vintage, 2001), 192.

2. Diane O'Donoghue, "Sites of Dispacement: Visualities of the Freudian Unconscious," paper delivered at the CIHA, Montreal, Canada, August 2004.

3. Luce Irigaray, *This Sex Which Is Not One (Ce Sexe qui n'en est pas un,* Paris: Minuit, 1977), trans. Catherine Porter and Carolyn Burke (Ithaca: Cornell University Press, 1985), p. 70.

4. Cornelius Castoriadis, *The Imaginary Institution of Society,* trans. Kathleen Blamey (*Institution imaginaire de la société,* Editions de Seuil, 1975). (Cambridge: Polity Press, 1987). In his 1964–65 essay "Marxism and Revolutionary Theory" Castoriadis introduced the "imaginary" as a term that expanded Lacan's definition into the social and political realms (*World in Fragments: Writings on Politics, Society, Psychoanalysis, and the Imagination,* ed. and trans. David Ames Curtis [Stanford, CA: Stanford University Press], 1997], xv). The radical imagination for Castoriadis has both an individual psychic and a social dimension, and for him, the social is always historical; indeed, he asserts that history "is impossible and inconceivable . . . outside of . . . the *radical imaginary*" (Castoriadis, *The Imaginary Institution,* 1987: 146)

5. Sir Thomas Browne, *Religio Medici* in *Selected Writings,* ed. Sir Geoffrey Keynes. (Chicago: University of Chicago Press, 1968, rpt. 1970), 119.

6. Helkiah Crooke, *Mikrokosmagraphia. A Description of the Body of Man. Together with the Controversies thereto Belonging. Collected and Translated out of all the Best Authors of Anatomy, Especially out of Gasper Bauhinus and Andreas Laurentius.* (London: William Jaggard, 1615), p. 36. All subsequent references are to the 1615 edition. I have silently modernized i, j, u, v, and long s, and expanded contractions.

7. Luce Irigaray, *This Sex Which Is Not One (Ce Sexe qui n'en est pas un,* Paris: Minuit, 1977), trans. Catherine Porter and Carolyn Burke (Ithaca: Cornell University Press, 1985), 71.

8. Judith Butler, *Bodies That Matter: On the Discursive Limits of "Sex"* (New York: Routledge, 1993), 59.

9. Ibid., 60, 66.

10. Crooke, 216; Aristotle, *Historia Animalium* 1.9, 4.8.

11. Martha Noel Evans, *Fits & Starts: A Genealogy of Hysteria in Modern France* (Ithaca: Cornell University Press, 1991), 4.

12. "Female Sexuality" in *The Standard Edition of the Complete Psychological Works of Sigmund Freud,* Vol. XXI: *The Future of an Illusion, Civilization and Its Discontents and Other Works,* ed. James Strachey (1964; London: Vintage, 2001), 226.

13. *Forgetting in Early Modern English Literature and Culture: Lethe's Legacies*, ed. Christopher Ivic and Grant Williams (London and New York: Routledge, 2004) and *Reading the Early Modern Passions*, ed. Gail Kern Paster, Katherine Rowe, and Mary Floyd-Wilson (Philadelphia: University of Pennslvania Press, 2004) are two of the most recent additions to this body of work.

Love, Humoralism, and "Soft" Psychoanalysis

Douglas Trevor

Like humoral theory, psychoanalysis has been largely hesitant to appraise the most esteemed of human passions, love, in any terms other than symptomatic ones. That is, both discourses might be characterized as treating love somewhat suspiciously, in almost wholly affective terms. In *A Treatise on Lovesickness* (first ed. 1610), for example, Jacques Ferrand follows Galen in naming "the temperature of the humor as the principal cause" of love, and describes its caloric dimensions and melancholic quality by citing André du Laurens, a French physician whose Galenic credentials were impeccable.[1] Lacan's Seventh Seminar (1959–60) is also devoted to analyzing the "ideal of human love," and in particular the high estimation of "genital love" and interpersonal attachment, and its phobic relation to feminine sexuality.[2] "Analysis," according to Lacan, "has brought a very important change of perspective on love by placing it at the center of ethical experience."[3] But love also changes Lacan's attitude toward analysis, for what is demanded at the end of analysis, he asks at the conclusion of this seminar, if not "*bonheur* or 'happiness'"?[4] Love is not containable by the praxis of Lacanian psychoanalysis, even if love is somehow what psychoanalysis is about.

I think that a theoretical reappraisal of love, not to mention the other passions performed and solicited in Shakespearean dramaturgy, would benefit from a critical approach that balances an awareness of the period's theories for understanding the passions with a psychoanalytic perspective on human agency. Coupling these discourses means critiquing their distinct, and shared, limitations, which is probably not very unsettling for scholars interested in Galenism, since humoral theory has been safely relegated by sci-

ence to the category of metaphor or associative—rather than diagnostic—understanding.[5] For psychoanalytic critics, however, a
version of what I will term "soft" psychoanalysis is potentially
controversial. By "soft" psychoanalysis, I mean to designate the
use of psychoanalytic concepts, and the consideration of the kinds
of questions that psychoanalytic inquiry typically provokes: questions regarding agency, subjectivity, self-awareness, and of course
self-delusion. Such questions abound in Shakespeare, but when
psychoanalytic readings of their manifestations are developed ho-
listically, they often produce jargon-filled interpretations deemed
persuasive only by those readers who are already "in the know."

By juxtaposing the limitations of humoral theory and psychoanalysis, it is my belief that we might produce more nuanced readings of the emotional contours of Shakespearean characters than
would be possible if we restricted ourselves to a single critical approach, be it psychoanalytic or historicist. To give an example of
the kind of interpretation I have in mind, I would like to turn to a
work that revolves around issues of love, selfhood, and passionate
outbursts: *Romeo and Juliet* (1595?). As the play opens, we as readers and spectators are led to believe that Romeo is suffering through
an extreme bout of love melancholy, brought about by his rejection
at the hands of Rosaline. If we come to the play prepared to insert
a humoral analysis, we find much fodder with which to work, and
yet also some points of resistance. Ferrand's *Treatise on Lovesickness* postdates *Romeo and Juliet* by more than a decade, but Ferrand draws amply from materials available to Shakespeare's
generation, materials that help to make love melancholy the most
celebrated kind of sadness in the literature of the sixteenth century.
Romeo displays the expected symptoms of this sadness perfectly.
As described by his father, the young man is said to spend his time
thus:

> Many a morning hath he there been seen,
> With tears augmenting the fresh morning's dew,
> Adding to clouds more clouds with his deep sighs.
> But all so soon as the all-cheering sun
> Should in the farthest east begin to draw
> The shady curtains from Aurora's bed,
> Away from light steals home my heavy son,
> And private in his chamber pens himself,
> Shuts up his windows, locks fair daylight out,

And makes himself an artificial night.
Black and portentous must thus humour prove,
Unless good counsel may the cause remove.[6]

When he appears onstage immediately thereafter, the young Montague confirms his father's description, in effect mourning his own demise as a lover, such that he is no longer himself: "This is not Romeo," he says to Benvolio, "he's some other where" (1.1.191).

If we turn now to the pseudomedical and philosophical texts available in the period from which Romeo and our understanding of him might emanate, we find a wide range of materials that would interpret the condition of love melancholy with the utmost, diagnostic seriousness. To find one's death by love unreciprocated is the worst of imaginable calamities, Marsilio Ficino argues, for "[e]ach man by loving gives up his own soul, and by loving in return restores the foreign soul through his own. Therefore, out of justice itself, whoever is loved ought to love in return."[7] Without the benefit of reciprocal love, the figurative death of the soul risks becoming the literal death of the body, as the superabundance of the melancholic humor produced by the overheated blood makes the victim susceptible to all other infirmities, physical and mental alike.[8] Thus does the melancholic heart, in the words of Timothy Bright, author of *A Treatise of Melancholie* (1586) "ouercome with inward heauines, and skared with inward feares . . . withdraweth it selfe, and shroudeth it as secrete and closse."[9] In order to avert such isolation, Bright recommends that melancholic lovers be aided by the "comfort of their friends," who may distract them from meditating on their pitiable state by "other delights brought in in steed, and more highly commended" than the scornful woman.[10] Even more to the point, Bright suggests that if the "melancholick is to be perswaded [that] the subiect of that he liketh is not so louely," he will find his blood cooled as a result, and a more serious melancholic bout potentially averted.[11]

Benvolio adopts this exact cure for Romeo's love melancholy, offering to attend the Capulet's feast with his cousin so that he may "Compare her [Rosaline's] face with some that I shall show, / And I will make thee think thy swan a crow" (1.2.86–87). While Romeo's cousin hardly would have needed a primer course in humoral theory to devise this strategy for improving Romeo's mood, nonetheless, the playwright's identification of one of his titular characters with a "Black and portentous . . . humour" invites a Galenic analysis (1.1.134). Likewise, the play itself pays dividends for readers knowledgeable of at least some of the dimensions of sixteenth-century, European medical practice and beliefs. For example, the hasty consummation of Romeo and Juliet's marriage serves not only to validate a bond forged without the permission of the lovers' parents, but also—less romantically—the evacuation of Romeo's pent-up seed, which, unreleased, would continue to overheat his body and mind.[12]

Nonetheless, to pursue a strictly Galenic reading of the play here is problematic for a number of reasons. For starters, the play itself offers its own resistance to a full-on, "humoral" interpretation. That is, while every medical authority that one may cite from this period or earlier ones views the condition of love melancholy with the utmost gravity, Romeo's friends and relatives do not. Rather, they see Romeo's mood as at least partly affected. Benvolio's reaction to his cousin's mournful self-description (1.1.166–76), for example, causes Romeo to ask if he laughs at his state of mind: "No, coz," comes the sarcastic reply, "I rather weep" (1.1.176). Mercutio is also in on the joke. Asked by Benvolio to summon Romeo, he replies, "Nay, I'll conjure too. / Romeo! Humors! Madman! Passion! Lover!" (2.1.7).

That a distance exists between the status of humoral theory as a viable means by which to explain the passions and its incorporation in *Romeo and Juliet*, that the latter in other words is not *interpolated by* but rather *in play with* the former, is made abundantly clear in a number of other ways, most notably through the character Juliet. Critics who have noticed Juliet's levelheadedness in comparison to Romeo's emotional immaturity, including her desire for the physical consummation of her love for reasons of imagined enjoyment (3.2.26–31), are noticing something else: her body does not seem to obey the same fluid dynamics as does her young husband's. She is in control of what she is thinking, and her passionate outbursts appear appropriate in relation to the objects and events that cause them. At the very least, others do not laugh at her for feeling what she does. On the contrary, her refusal to have her emotions scripted for her—"I'll look to like, if looking liking move;" she says to her mother when she proposes a match with Paris, "But no more deep will I endart mine eye / Than your consent gives strength to make it fly"—sets her apart from the more volatile model of human agency that not just Romeo but the entire irrational conflict between the Capulets and Montagues represents (1.3.99–101). Juliet not only stands outside of a certain kind of historicist analysis, she invalidates it as irrelevant to her psychological situation.

If love melancholy is something of a joke in *Romeo and Juliet*, and humoral theory cannot see where this "humor" lies since it is inside of it, psychoanalysis can, but only to a point. Of course, there is not *a* psychoanalytic reading of *Romeo and Juliet*, nor a single kind humoral one for that matter, but unlike Freud, who emphasizes issues of debasement and neuroses when he writes of love attachment,[13] Lacan, in his Seventh Seminar, focuses on the dialectical impulses to idealize: both the love object and one's own self-presentation before this object. In her reading of this seminar, Kaja Silverman emphasizes the importance of idealization in Lacan's understanding of love, "without which there is no love, and no pleasurable identification,"[14] and the manner in which this idealization occurs within the subject and between the subject and his or her love object. This means that narcissism is a fundamental attribute of love, insofar as lovers project their own images and wants onto the objects they love, rather than erasing or supplanting their own identities with that of the other.[15]

Shakespeare is not only aware of this feature of the love bond, he exploits it for dramatic effect by having Juliet learn that Romeo has slain Tybalt *before* she consummates her love with her husband. In effect, what this scene (3.2) witnesses is that Romeo's murder makes Juliet's idealization of him *stronger*, not weaker: the "Beautiful tyrant, fiend angelical! / Dove-feathered raven, wolvish-ravening lamb!" becomes, just a few lines later worth the lives of "ten thousand Tybalts" (3.2.75–76, 114), precisely because the initial impediment to loving Romeo in this scene, the fact that he has been revealed as a murderer, forces Juliet to love him that much more in order to justify her desire for him as both a lover *and* an idealized love object. Thus asked by her nurse if she will weep over Tybalt's body, Juliet opts instead to mourn her presumed death as a "maiden-widowèd" (3.2.135), mourn in other words that Romeo's banishment might cost her the opportunity to consummate her marriage.

One temptation afforded by a psychoanalytically inflected understanding of this scene, however, is to deconstruct Juliet's love as mere desire. In fact, the play sustains, in opposition to both Ficino and Freud, the notion that love and desire can mutually reinforce, rather than degrade, one another.[16] Moreover, and more problematically—although also, I think, more intriguingly—the play leaves unscripted the precise manner in which Romeo and Juliet become attached as mutual love objects. Directors have typically filled in this lacuna by staging the young lovers looking into one another's eyes during the Capulet feast, although nothing in the text, other than logical inference, scripts this mutual gaze for us. What Shakespeare gives us instead is commentary on the life-changing encounter, first by Romeo—"O she doth teach the torches to burn bright!" (1.5.41)—and, only after their shared sonnet, by Juliet.

Romeo and Juliet's passions indeed constitute the heart of this play; Shakespeare is less interested in how the two meet than in the depths of what they both feel shortly thereafter, less interested in what the two lovers say to one another than in how they describe the way they feel about the other to various confidants (the Nurse, Friar Laurence, and so on), and less interested in establishing an airtight *raison d'être* for their deaths than in making sure they die passionately, with drug overdoses and daggers. Regardless of the form one's psychoanalytic account of this love takes, it will lead one inevitably back to these passions, which themselves invite a historicist account outside of the purview of psychoanalysis itself, although this account also is bound to frustrate, since the precise reason why these two end up together is as much a matter for the stars to have decided than for their bodies, or their families.[17]

Lacan's Seventh Seminar situates amorous attachment within a tradition that *Romeo and Juliet* both avows and disavows. Examining courtly love as the cultural code by which the high idealization of the love object was permanently established in Western culture, Lacan insists that this idealization requires that the feminine object be "introduced oddly enough through the door of privation or of inaccessibility."[18] *Romeo and Juliet* does not offer quite the same message. If he began his composition not with a characterological approach but a situational one, Shakespeare could have hardly selected a better scenario in which both to refute the supposition that the virgin can only become a whore by making Juliet's introduction to wedded bliss exactly that, while transforming the relationship between Romeo and Juliet into that which cannot be held as real, even as it signifies, through emotional torment and death, the kernel of the real, Heidegger's *das Ding*. And yet, the tragic trajectory of this love does not invalidate the love of Romeo and Juliet as something slight and immature; on the contrary, the two lovers give everything they can to substantiate their feelings, except a reason for their feelings, which—the play argues—is beneath the dignity of love in the first place. It is around the proclaimed power of these feelings, rather than what motivates them, that Shakespeare has the entire drama of the play rest. *Romeo and Juliet* is made "excellent" and "lamentable," as its full title in the Second Quarto proclaims, precisely because the young lovers refuse to compromise what they somehow forge between them by linking it with the corrupted cultural values of Verona, within the city limits of which it cannot function anyway. Humoralism can no more explain such love than the Montagues and Capulets can identify the source of their dispute. Limitless anger is appeased, in *Romeo and Juliet*, only through the sacrifice of love, but not even grieving parents can fully substantiate the loss of their children, and the statues to be erected in their honor will decay over time, not just because they lack the appropriate organs and fluids that might or might not attest to love in this period, but rather because they are missing something that cannot be named but only felt.

The kind of love toward which Shakespeare gestures in *Romeo and Juliet* defies the discursive range of language itself, even as it is constituted—not wholly but largely—by words on the page, so perhaps we should not be surprised to see it wiggle so persistently out of the grasp of both psychoanalytic and humoralist interpretations. Nonetheless, a love that proclaims its effects above and beyond its causes can be circled around, its paradoxical features enumerated and puzzled over most fully when looked at from the inside and outside at once. The aim of the kind of work I have attempted to describe, and perform a truncated version of, is at the very best only softly psychoanalytic, but such "soft" psychoanalysis is in my mind the most effective means by which to conjoin our historicist sensibilities with our post-modern perspective on the psychological.

Notes

1. Jacques Ferrand, *A Treatise on Lovesickness*, ed. Donald A. Beecher and Massimo Ciavolella (Syracuse: Syracuse University Press, 1990), 240.

2. Jacques Lacan, *The Ethics of Psychoanalysis* (Seminar 7), ed. Jacques-Alain Miller, trans. by Dennis Porter (1986; New York: Norton, 1992, rpt. 1997), 8.

3. Ibid., 8.

4. Ibid., 292.

5. Jerome Kagan, for example, finds the Galenic understanding of inborn temperaments highly useful, even as he rejects the humoral basis for this understand-

ing. See *Galen's Prophecy: Temperament in Human Nature* (New York: Westview Press, 1994).

6. William Shakespeare, *The Most Excellent and Lamentable Tragedy of Romeo and Juliet*, in *The Norton Shakespeare*, ed. Stephen Greenblatt, Walter Cohen, Jean E. Howard, Katharine Eisaman Maus (New York: W. W. Norton, 1997), act 1, scene 1, lines 124–35. Subsequent citations will be made parenthetically.

7. Marsilio Ficino, *Commentary on Plato's "Symposium" on Love (De Amore)*, trans. by Sears Jayne (Woodstock, CT: Spring Publications, 1985), 56.

8. See André du Laurens. *A Discourse of the Preservation of Sight: of Melancholike Diseases; of Rheumes, and of Old Age*, trans. Richard Surphlet (1597; London: Ralph Iacson, 1599), 120.

9. Timothy Bright, *A Treatise of Melancholie*, facs. of the 1586 edition (New York: Columbia University Press, 1940), 107.

10. Ibid., 255.

11. Ibid.

12. See Ferrand, *A Treatise on Lovesickness*, 334. Ferrand does not sanction the Arabic cure for love melancholy, attributed to Avicenna and Haly Abbas, which approves of purchasing "'young girls and sleep[ing] with them frequently'" (ibid.).

13. See Sigmund Freud, "A Special Type of Choice of Object Made by Men" (1910), in *The Standard Edition of the Complete Psychological Works of Sigmund Freud*, trans. by James Strachey (London: Hogarth Press, 1953–74), 11: 165–75; "On the Universal Tendency to Debasement in the Sphere of Love" (1912), 179–90; "The Taboo of Virginity" (1918), 193–208.

14. Kaja Silverman, *The Threshold of the Visible World* (New York: Routledge, 1996), 43.

15. As screenwriter, Lacan would have therefore rewritten the "you complete me" line in *Jerry Maguire* (1996) to, "you provide me with the opportunity to imagine my own self-completion, and therefore I love you."

16. For Ficino, "the desire for coitus (that is, for copulation) and love are shown to be not only not the same motions but opposite." *Commentary on Plato's "Symposium,"* 41.

17. Lacan terms the criterion of the "ethically, culturally, and socially valorized" as "external to psychoanalysis," although their operation of course permeates the psyche. *The Ethics of Psychoanalysis*, 144.

18. Ibid., 149.

Psychologizing Physics

KRISTEN POOLE

In his essay "The Uncanny," Freud describes *unheimlich* "forms of ego-disturbance" as a "harking-back . . . to a time when the ego had not yet marked itself off sharply from the external world and from other people" (236). This process of demarcation and differentiation—of the self from others, of the self from the greater environment—is of course central to psychoanalysis as a mode of therapy and critique. Freud, Lacan, and the multitude of scholars in their wake are invested in theorizing the various processes by which this differentiation takes place, and the manifold psychological consequences of this division of internal and external, self and world.

For Freud, "harking back to a time" of the undifferentiated self means retracing the line of an individual's developmental chronology, working backward until one reaches a state of infantile unity with the mother, or at least the naïve fantasy of such unity. But if we hark back along a different type of chronology (remaining sensitive to the risks of transposing a developmental paradigm onto historical progression), we also find ourselves arriving at "a time when the ego had not yet marked itself off sharply from the external world and from other people." Early modern England was a place of competing and often contradictory models of subjectivity. To be sure, one model was indeed that of the differentiated self. This self was given imaginative expression in the idea of the *homo clausus*; it was also taking form in the emerging meaning of "individual" as a unique and separate person. This particular self has received extensive critical attention, in large part because we identify here the origins of the "modern" subject. This subject has been approached largely through a study of the classical body, a form that is self-contained and whose functions are carefully regulated. The focus on the body is an intuitive one for studying the state of the

95

psyche, given that psychic experiences are often caused by and registered through bodily experiences. The body provides a particularly salient site of analysis for literary scholars, as it operates in both material and metaphoric registers; it brings together a study of material culture and representation.

The classical body has been positioned in relation to other bodies, or other models of subjectivity. First, it was pitted against the grotesque, a mode of corporeality that is the antithesis of the closed and regulated classical body. Building upon Bakhtin's seminal study of Rabelais, scholars focused on ways in which the body could be portrayed as porous, uncontrolled, indulgent, and leaky, and examined how this portrayal of the body registered social and political concerns. If the classical body can be figured as a model of Freud's modern psyche and the differentiated self, the grotesque body could be said to represent a more primordial, pre-Oedipal moment in which bodies and selves were merged together through unregulated gastronomic and sexual pleasures. Out of this interest in the grotesque body grew an intense examination of the humoral body (spurred by the groundbreaking work of Gail Kern Paster). This body can also be porous and leaky, but the intent of early modern medical practice was to carefully regulate the balance and flow of the four humoral fluids. As Michael Schoenfeldt has recently argued, this attention to corporeal regulation, especially of ingestion and excretion, renders the humoral body closer in spirit to the classical than to the grotesque.

The extensive scholarship on the body in the last decade or so has been richly rewarding, and has offered new avenues for psychoanalytic study. But the focus on the body has largely overlooked the environment in which that body moves and operates. While scholars have noted, for instance, that humoral theory connected the body to the larger cosmos, the implications of this connection have remained largely unexamined. (An important exception to this tendency is the work of Mary Floyd-Wilson, who demonstrates how early modern conceptions of race depended upon an understanding of the humoral body's links with the environment.) This nearly exclusive focus on the subject—if not dis-embodied then dis-located—follows Freud's own interests and logic. Insofar as his concern is with the ego that has "marked itself off sharply from the external world," that external world drops away as a field of exploration.

Freud's lack of overt attention to the subject's environment is intriguing, since his essay on the uncanny is in fundamental ways predicated upon a certain understanding of the physical world. More precisely, his notion depends upon a normative understanding of physics, upon an expectation that time, space, and matter behave according to universal standards. In "The Uncanny," Freud articulates the mechanisms of psychic repression, as moments too overwhelming for the psyche to process enter the unconscious, there to play out a drama of repetition that is triggered by particular events. The sensation of the uncanny is expressed through a perceived destabilization in time and space. Freud's model implicitly relies upon a linear sense of time, a temporality that is always moving inevitably forward. Thus the sense that one is reexperiencing an event—that is, the notion that time is operating in a circular or repetitive fashion—is perceived as deeply irregular and therefore disturbing. Likewise, Freud's model depends on an understanding of space as stable and discrete. The *unheimlich*, that which is simultaneously home and not-home, is a sense that one inhabits competing, collapsing, or contradictory spaces. Neuroses are thus experienced as the wounded psyche projecting itself onto the world and distorting the subject's experience of time and space. The normative operations of time and space are so self-evident that they are not even addressed by Freud, but simply assumed as a given, as an unquestioned, transcendent, organic norm. So too the operations of matter are assigned a latent but normative role in figuring the uncanny. The molecules that make up one person, place, or thing cannot be in two places, cannot transform themselves from one thing to another. Thus only the neurotic perceives doubling and physical transformations.

The laws of physics are, however, a modern invention. This is a fact that is rarely acknowledged in critical discourse, in spite of the recent focus on the historicity of cultural epistemes. With the past viewed through the lens of contingency, many aspects of experience that were once considered transhistorical and transcultural— say, the emotion of love, or even the physical experience of the body—are now considered to be shaped by social discourse and practice. But the experience of space, time, and matter has been largely omitted from this inquiry, and is still often tacitly presumed to be governed by transhistorical (or perhaps better yet, ahistorical) laws. For us, Newtonian physics have become so naturalized as to become inevitable and invisible.

So too we take as a given that the physical world has certain immutable properties, and that any perceived distortion in the operations of matter are purely in the mind of the beholder. Such was not the case in early modern England. Throughout the sixteenth and into the seventeenth century, it was widely understood that human beings shared the world with demonic agents, and that this world was mutable, fungible, and porous. Recent work on demonology, especially the research of Stuart Clark, causes us to rethink our understanding of the place of demons in early modern culture. For starters, we need to recognize that demonology itself was not an isolated, arcane, or purely academic subject; rather, demons infiltrated a range of discourses—their actions were rationally accepted as evidence in courts of law, and they were studied as a means to comprehend the boundaries and operations of nature, for example. To think of early modern demons in terms of the "supernatural," Clark argues, is a fundamental anachronism, since it was widely agreed at the time that demons were an integral part of the natural world and had to abide by the laws of physics (168). This, Clark observes, "ma[d]e demonology as much an exercise in epistemology and ontology as in theology and morality" (166). What demons reveal is not so much the strangeness of early modern conceptions of the "supernatural," as the strangeness (to us) of their understanding of the natural. Otto Casmann, in *Angelographia* (Frankfurt, 1597), parsed eight areas in which demons could act within the natural world, which Clark summarizes as follows: "in producing disorders of the weather, moving objects from place to place (often so quickly that they appeared to become invisible), making statues move and animals speak like men, distorting the ordinary motions of things, assuming various shapes, disturbing bodily humours and vital spirits, presenting objects to the imagination in dreams, and affecting human senses and emotions" (163).

As this list illustrates, nearly every aspect of human life was vulnerable, in theory, to demonic manipulation. The weather, matter, health, and emotions—elements on the outside as well as the inside—could be altered through demonic agency. The self itself was open to demonic intervention; the subject was subject to demonic meddling. This understanding of demonic power and the natural conditions which enabled it led to what Katherine Eisaman Maus has identified as three "permeabilities" present in early modern discussions of witchcraft—the permeability between one individual and another, between minds or spirits and bodies, and between illusion and reality (328–29). In a permeable world, how can the ego become sharply differentiated from the external world and other persons? In a world where mutability is the norm—where time, space, and matter are understood to be flexible and metamorphic—how can one experience the disturbance of the uncanny? The early modern understanding of the relationship of self and environment differed so radically from our own that the conditions for the uncanny were, by and large, absent: the physics did not always allow for the psychic response Freud presents.

Freud's notion of the uncanny (and by extension, his notion of the mechanisms of repression) thus depends upon the friction of the modern self confronting the modern world. This self, differentiated and even closed off from the world around it, contains a swirling psychic motion of repetition and transformation, as various unconscious urges and desires undergo shape-shifting in order to surface into the realm of the conscious and the social. By contrast, the world around it is governed by the absolutes of modern physics, of an immutable order to time, space, and matter. What models might emerge if we consider the engagement of the early modern subject with the environment? If we demonize the individual? That is to say, what happens when we put the individual subject in an environment that operates according to demonic logic?

We might begin by working schematically with two models of the bodied subject. Putting the classical self/body in the context of the demonic universe, we meet the inverse, or the negative image, or perhaps the *Doppelgänger* of Freud's uncanny. Here we find an ideally stable self in a physical environment of profound instability. We might imagine that the friction of this encounter produced a variety of the sensation of the uncanny, threatening the sense of self by recalling the tenuousness of a presumed stability. Putting the humoral body in this demonic world, by contrast, we might perceive a lack of friction, as the logic of the humoral is strikingly akin to the logic of the demonic. The demonic world can be perceived as the fluidity of the humoral body writ large. Just as this body is an ever-shifting composite of fluids that can morph into one another—blood can become semen or milk, for example—so too the demonic body, and by extension the demonic universe, is one of ever-shifting relations. This is the body, and the self, that cannot be differentiated from the world or others; the individual becomes truly indivisible from the world. Without the sharp distinction of stability/instability present in the encounter between the modern subject and modern world, or the classical self and the demonic world, the meeting of the humoral body with the demonic world doesn't allow for sharp differentiation. Thus while this early modern self could experience fear, anxiety, and even horror in the face of the demonic, the uncanny might be an alien sensation.

I present these scenarios as hypothesis, not thesis. The point is to think about what happens when we historicize the understanding and experience of physics, and to consider how deeply the sense of self is contingent upon these variable physics. Psychoanalytic models of repression, trauma, and alienation (to suggest just a few) often rely upon a particular understanding of the operations of time, space, and matter; this understanding, even if it remains at the level of the intuitive, thus shapes our discussion of the psyche. The available physics may well shape the psyche itself. What is in order, then, is to extend the study of the self beyond the bounds of the body and into the world, to examine more fully the mutability of the environment over time (or the understanding and experience of that environment) and how this environment affects the formation and perception of the subject.

Works Cited

Clark, Stuart. *Thinking with Demons: The Idea of Witchcraft in Early Modern Europe.* Oxford: Oxford University Press, 1997.

Floyd-Wilson, Mary. *English Ethnicity and Race in Early Modern Drama.* Cambridge: Cambridge University Press, 2003.

Freud, Sigmund. "The Uncanny." *The Standard Edition of the Complete Psychological Works of Sigmund Freud*, ed. James Strachey. London: The Hogarth Press, 1955; 1981.

Maus, Katharine Eisaman. "Sorcery and Subjectivity in Early Modern Discourses of Witchcraft." In *Historicism, Psychoanalysis, and Early Modern Culture*, ed. Carla Mazzio and Douglas Trevor, 325–48. New York: Routledge, 2000.

Paster, Gail Kern. *The Body Embarrassed: Drama and the Disciplines of Shame in Early Modern England.* Ithaca: Cornell University Press, 1993.

Schoenfeldt, Michael C. *Bodies and Selves in Early Modern England: Physiology and Inwardness in Spenser, Shakespeare, Herbert, and Milton.* Cambridge: Cambridge University Press, 1999.

Psychoanalysis and the Corpse

SUSAN ZIMMERMAN

PSYCHOANALYTIC THEORY assumes that in "recovering" the past we recast it so as to collapse the temporal distinctions between past, present, and future. The concept of chronology is itself a construction that falters under scrutiny: in the practice of psychoanalysis, this is both a working assumption and a felt experience. For the analysand, the past is reconstructed as an exercise in the future anterior, that is, the hermeneutic act retrospectively alters the future of the past, conjoining it reciprocally and unsequentially to the present.[1] From a poststructuralist perspective, language itself is slippery, precluding the possibility that "reality," however it may be fantasized, can be captured in temporally fixed and unitary representations. In both its therapeutic practices and critical applications, then, psychoanalytical theory negotiates the multilayered, protean dimensions of time and language, resisting—partially and imperfectly to be sure—the categorical boundaries of the symbolic order.

My own recent book, conducted in accordance with these assumptions, focused on representations of the corpse in the religious discourse of medieval and early modern England, and on "impersonations" of the corpse on the English public stage.[2] I chose to study the corpse because of its visible, material challenge, in any epoch, to concepts of unitary fixity. If the body itself can be said to serve as hermeneutic matrix for the subject's construction of borders (outer and inner, visible and invisible, determinant and indeterminate), then the putrefying corpse constitutes a direct and apprehensible challenge to such constructions. As an entity that slips between categorical signifiers, the putrefying corpse represents the ultimate border problem.

What I would like to do here is explore the status of the corpse in early modern Christianity in terms of Julia Kristeva's theory of abjection—a linkage that heretofore I have considered only briefly. I will end with a speculation about how Kristeva's reconfiguration of the Freudian death-drive—and in particular her triangulation of sex, leprosy, and death—resonates tellingly with the indeterminate ghost in Shakespeare's *Hamlet*.

In *Powers of Horror*, Kristeva addresses the signification of the corpse as part of a larger speculation concerning pre-symbolic, "semiotic" experience in the development of the subject.[3] Kristeva's revisionist project has a double action: in making her case for the bio-psychical forces at work in the infant prior to Lacan's Imaginary, or mirror stage, Kristeva simultaneously collapses the binaries in Freud's discussion of the death drive (organic/inorganic, animate/inanimate).[4] As I see it, Kristeva's venture into the "semiotic" is an attempt to reconfigure the properties and potentialities of the material body, or, stated more broadly, to address the conundrum of materiality itself. I would suggest that a similar conundrum is inscribed in the anthropomorphism of medieval Christianity, and that the Reformation condemnation of the material idol (and by direct and indirect inference, of the material corpse), represents an intensely focused attempt to dissociate materiality and generative power. To state the issue somewhat differently, it might be said that the ontological status of the material body, its status as determinate (dead) or indeterminate (generative) roils the ideological foundations of both psychoanalysis and Christianity.

The linchpin of Christianity is, of course, the mystery of an incarnated deity, a man/god, who undergoes bodily sacrifice in order to earn for ordinary beings the right to transcend mortality, that is, death and putrefaction. The body of the dead Christ does not putrefy: Christ himself resurrects and trans*figures* his body as a model for that of the redeemed believer, whose own putrefied remains will undergo a lesser kind of metamorphosis into an eternally changeless state. Further, at least for medieval Christians, it was (literally) the body and blood of Christ, re-sacrificed throughout time in the sacrament of the Eucharist, that enabled an inversion, as it were, of the Incarnation: the ingestion (or "sacramental cannibalism")[5] of the god/man, the divine corporeal, in the corruptible bodies of the faithful. Thus, as Caroline Walker Bynum demonstrates, medieval Christianity was profoundly anti-dualistic; bodily process was inseparable from spiritual transformation.[6] The conundrum of the corpse was that it generated new forms of material life through a process of disintegration or *unbecoming at the same time* that it served as the raw material for the transformation of the believer into a changeless, eternally static state. The spiritually realized self was, in Bynum's phrase, a "psychosomatic unity,"[7] the corpse serving as disturbing if compelling evidence of the generative power of fragmentation.

The danger that reformists astutely identified in the Catholic hypostatization of the body was its implicit affirmation of this generative power as a constituent property of materiality. For iconoclasts, such an affirmation diminished the antecedent, *dis*embodied, *im*material being of God the Father, whose identify *as* God proceeded from his unique status as pure spirit. The proto-dualistic revisions of reformist theology thus insisted on dividing body and spirit, material and immaterial, inanimate and animate, while subordinating or discounting the problematic relationship of putrefaction to redemption. Significantly, reformist tracts prepared for public consumption, such as the homily on idolatry (1563), attacked the supposed perversity of Catholic anthropomorphism by singling out the corpse as the only material entity that could fully demonstrate what *dead* means. The corpse, *axiomatically* dead ("dead as stocks and stones"), became the transparent signifier for the deadness of materiality.[8] However, it is noteworthy that in the English cultural imagination, the corpse refused to be "quiescent" (to borrow one of Freud's adjectives for inorganic matter). Long-standing beliefs in the power of the corpse to generate life from its putrefying liquids, to kill by contagion, to bleed, to walk, even to attack the living, remained manifest in resistance to reformist funerary and burial rituals, in local reports of appearances of the un-dead, and in fictional representations of corpses and ghosts, including those on the public stage.

In short, what I am outlining here is a tension in early modern religious ideology between, on one hand, an incipient dualism, an effort to reconceptualize the body in terms of boundaries that served to demarcate differences, and on the other, a continuing insistence on body boundaries as fluid, or subject to destabilization. This contestation centered on the proper interpretation of the material principle in the Christian system and ultimately on the signification of the corpse—specifically, the relationship of fragmentation to reconstitution (redemption) in a changeless state. For me, the issues at stake in this argument resonate strikingly with Kristeva's probing of the semiotic.

For Kristeva, abjection, experienced in the human subject as "a conglomerate of fear, deprivation and nameless frustration" (15), originates in *pre*-discursive experience ("these 'operations' are *pre-meaning* and *pre-sign*," "analogous to vocal or kinetic rhythm").[9] It is as if there is a later eruption in the speaking subject of a trans-linguistic "spoor of a pre-object" (*PH,* 73). This nameless "spoor" signals the "recognition of the *want* on which any being, meaning, language, or desire is founded" (5); it "stake[s] out the transition from a state of indifferentiation to one of discretion (subject/object)" (32):

> There would be a "beginning" preceding the word . . . In that anteriority to language, the outside is elaborated by means of a projection from within, of which the only experience we have is one of pleasure and pain. The non-distinctiveness of inside and outside would thus be unnamable, a border passable in both directions by pleasure and pain. (61)

This unnameable border evokes the originary "processes of division in *the living matter* of an organism"; further, these "bio-physiological processes" are "themselves already inescapably part of signifying processes, what Freud labeled "drives" (*KR,* 28). Thus the undifferentiated "spoor" of a "pre-object" resonates "back" to organic division while simultaneously anticipating symbolic differentiation.

But it is the corpse, a material entity inhabiting the symbolic order yet unamenable to categorization, that effectively *collapses* the border between the symbolic and the organic:

> decay does not *signify* death . . . refuse and corpses *show me* what I permanently thrust aside in order to live . . . the corpse, the most sickening of wastes, is a border that has encroached upon everything . . . The corpse . . . is the utmost of abjection. It is death infecting life . . . The in-between, the ambiguous, the composite. (*PH,* 3–4)

According to Kristeva, the danger of the corpse, of abjection, is that it threatens to engulf the totality of the subject's identity as constructed by the symbolic order, drawing one "toward the [semiotic] place where meaning collapses" (2), where the subject, "fluctuating between inside and outside, pleasure and pain, would find death, along with nirvana" (63–64).

Thus Kristeva situates the simultaneous death of the symbolic order and the subject at a bio-psychical border whose fluctuations, originary source of the subject's experience of pleasure and pain, end in "nirvana." The corpse serves as material witness to the ambiguous relationship between fragmentation and "nirvana" in the structure of human life; abjection enables the subject to comprehend the corpse in the self. Ultimately, of course, Kristeva's argument ends with a paradox rather than a resolution. On one hand, "nirvana" suggests an ecstasy of oneness, a complete fusion that gives the lie to symbolic differentiation as well as to the indeterminacy of putrefaction. But "nirvana" simultaneously suggests incorporation, ingestion, a (further) tearing apart of the "fragment" that is the self, the individual. The paradox lies in the simultaneous ecstasy/terror of obliteration.

It should already be clear that Kristeva's theory connects in provocative ways with that medieval orientation toward the Christian body that the Reformation was so keen to eradicate. If the medieval Christian is a "psychosomatic unity," then the body must not only be redeemed, it must also be a part of the redemptive process. Thus the reciprocity of body/spirit metaphors; the preoccupation with suffering as sacrifice, mutilation, and dismemberment; the centrality of the Eucharist as the literal ingestion of the god/man; the fascination with states of transition, preeminently that of corpse; and the transformative concept of redemption as fragmentation enabling immortality. At bottom what is common to Kristeva's system and the *gestalt* of medieval Christianity is a nondualistic approach to psychic/religious phenomena that eschews categorical clarifications for the suggestive irresolutions of paradox. I find such conjunctions provocative and illuminating, although presumably unrelated in historical terms. Thus my analysis of these temporally discrete discourses provides a particular kind of nonlinear linkage in which insights are a function of unintended reciprocations.

Such linkages help, I would argue, in understanding the horror/attraction of the ghost in *Hamlet*. When the ghost first appears, he comes encased in armor, a "portentous figure," a "fair and warlike form" (1.1.112, 50).[9] He is, emphatically, a material revenant, a "thing" and a "nothing," a "fantasy . . . *in complete steel*" (1.1.24, 25, 26; 1.4.52, my emphasis). As armored warrior, the ghost replicates the living King Hamlet, but this eerie if familiar image evokes an unsettling question: who/what inhabits this dead-Hamlet-armor? Or, to put it another way: what does the impregnable-looking casing *hide*?

What lies behind the armor is of course a corpse: if what makes Hamlet Sr. seem alive is his battle-ready fierceness, then what makes him an "illusion" is the mystery within. The singularity of *this* revenant is that its indeterminate status *as* revenant, its half-life/half-death, is literally figured as a contradiction: steel exterior vs. "no/thing," an apprehensible outside enclosing and containing an unviewable interior.

When Hamlet first sees the "questionable shape" (1.4.43), he wants to believe that it signifies an invincible, avenging power that defies the dictates of nature, but he soon becomes aware that the ghost is *his* dependent, that the ghost's exhortation creates a symbiotic relationship in which the son as avenger must prove the father's invincibility. These reciprocal claims are threatening, forbidden, unknowable: if the animated warrior king belongs to the Prince, so also does the corpse within the armor, the "no/thing" behind the mask.

Significantly, the ghost itself, in language echoing Hamlet's own, repeatedly references corrupt and corrupting bodies—the "garbage" (1.5.42) of Claudius's body preyed upon by Gertrude's lust, the "leprous distilment" (64) of the poison that renders the living body of the King "lazar-like," barked about "with vile and loathsome crust" (72). This image of leprosy would have a special horror for Hamlet: it is Hyperion the sun god horribly metamorphosed, his once idealized body seized by a kind of anticipatory putrefaction. "O horrible! O horrible! Most horrible!" (80): certainly the disfiguring death of the sun king, but also the idea of *this* "dead corse" (1.4.52) resurrected "in complete steel."

Hamlet's deeply ambivalent response to the ghost resides, I would suggest, in his inability to reconcile its implicit contradictions: the seeming vitality of its determinate form (the ghost as idol), with the materiality of its unbecoming—the mindlessly generative rot within, the undiscriminating deliquescence. Thus the apparition emblematizes an unfixable margin between life/death, process/stasis, partition/unity. Although it fully exploits the paradoxes of Christian belief *and* the tensions in the controversy over idolatry, the ghost is nonetheless not reducible to any sectarian status (Catholic/Protestant). It is a mystery in material form, a palpable impalpable, or, as Kristeva would say, "death infecting life . . . a border that has encroached upon everything" (*PH*, 3–4).

Interestingly, Kristeva's theory of abjection also comments (although never explicitly) on the function of the ghost in the representation of Hamlet's sexual imagination. Kristeva's vocabulary for abjection is of course itself sexual—the ecstasy of death ("nirvana") as an obliterating fusion/incorporation. But Kristeva speculates further that the abject originates in the violent separation of the infant from the womb, an explusion which leaves a trace or memory in the subject of "the archaic mother," originary site of terror and desire. Significantly for *Hamlet*, Kristeva argues that the biblical abomination of leprosy "becomes inscribed within the logical conception of impurity . . . [as] intermixture, erasing of differences, threat to identity": and that ultimately, "the fantasy of the born body, tightly held in a placenta that is no longer nourishing but devastating, converges with the reality of leprosy" (101). Thus Kristeva's identification of leprosy with originary defilement makes it possible to triangulate the ghost/corpse, Gertrude, and Hamlet: that is, the "leprous distilment" that disintegrates the sun-king is analogous to Gertrude's lust, which transforms (in the ghost's furious words) a "radiant angel," to a creature who "prey[s] on garbage" (1.5.55, 57). By reinforcing Hamlet's own rage at his mother's unfathomable desire ("To post / With such dexterity to incestuous sheets" [1.2.156–57]), the ghost thereby links leprosy, garbage, lust, and death—the component parts, as it were, of Hamlet's sexual imagination, inextricably linked throughout the play with his desire for his own obliteration.

But if the contours of Hamlet's dilemma are more sharply defined by Kristeva's conjunction of leprosy with birth/death, and I think they are, in the end the paradox of Shakespeare's material/indeterminate ghost eludes captivation. The brilliance of Shakespeare's creation—and, I would argue, of Kristeva's theory in an altogether different mode—is their power to probe the inexpressible, to bring us closer to the kind of intuition that fractures symbolic constraints. In this instance, improbably, Shakespeare and Kristeva enhance each other's expressive power, and thereby demonstrate the reciprocally illuminating relationship of art and psychoanalysis. At the same time, however, this very relationship underscores the slipperiness of all representation, as well as the impossibility of resolving those psychic phenomena that most persistently compel us—the mystery of sex and death, the conundrum of the corpse.

Notes

1. Lacan puts it best: "What is realized in my history is not the past definite of what was, since it is no more, or even the present perfect of what has been in what

I am, but the future anterior of what I shall have been for what I am in the process of becoming." See "The Function of Language in Psychoanalysis," in Anthony Wilden, ed., *The Language of the Self: The Function of Language in Psychoanalysis* (Baltimore: The Johns Hopkins University Press, 1968), 63.

2. See *The Early Modern Corpse and Shakespeare's Theatre* (Edinburgh: Edinburgh University Press, 2005).

3. *Powers of Horror: An Essay on Abjection*, trans. Leon S. Roudiez (New York: Columbia University Press, 1982). This essay represents the fullest elaboration of Kristeva's theory but it appears in other publications as well (see below).

4. See "Beyond the Pleasure Principle," in Peter Gay, ed., *The Freud Reader* (New York and London: Norton, 1989), 594–626. For a helpful commentary on Lacan's notion of the subject's relationship to a "partial object" anterior to the Imaginary (developed, in part, in response to the work of Melanie Klein), see Wilden, 160–65.

5. See Caroline Walker Bynum, *Fragmentation and Redemption: Essays on Gender and the Human Body in Medieval Religion* (New York: Zone Books, 1996), 185.

6. The paradox of fragmentation and fusion pervades medieval ritual and iconography, as seen, for example, in the mutilation and miraculous reassembly of martyrs, the worship of relics as spiritually invested body parts, the representation of post-death purgation as bodily burning, the metaphors of bodily wasting and orgasmic transport in the writings of the mystics, and the representation of Christ's redemptive fluids as bi-gendered (the blood of circumcision and crucifixion, the milk of lactating breasts). See Bynum, *Fragmentation and Redemption*, and *The Resurrection of the Body in Western Christianity, 200–1336* (New York: Columbia University Press, 1995).

7. *Resurrection of the Body*, 11.

8. See "Agaynste parell of Idolatry and superfluous decking of churches" in *The seconde tome of homelyes*, 1563 (STC 136663).

9. See Toril Moi, ed., *The Kristeva Reader* (New York: Columbia University Press, 1986), 29, 94.

10. Quotations from the play are taken from the Arden edition, ed. Harold Jenkins (London: Methuen, 1982).

Compulsions of the Renaissance

HEATHER HIRSCHFELD

IN FREUD'S *History of an Obsessional Neurosis*, the case history that develops most explicitly his theory of compulsion, Freud compares the behavior of his patient, the Rat Man, to the biblical Balaam who, employed by the Moabites to curse the Jews, could only bless them. The Rat Man, Freud explains, would remove stones from his beloved's walking path in order to protect her; he would then reconsider his work, would worry that the clearing itself might cause her harm rather than good, and would replace the stones. The Rat Man insisted that this self-canceling activity was a labor of love; Freud agreed but also interpreted it as an expression of hate, so that the replacement of the stones was not—or at least not only—part of a continued effort to protect the beloved but rather an attempt to injure her. Such activity made the Rat Man not simply a Balaam figure—a character who operated against his conscious intent—but an *"inverted* Balaam": a character who operated against his conscious intent to the detriment, rather than the benefit, of others, his beloved, and himself.[1]

Balaam's behavior, of course, was governed by God's intervention—"the Lord thy God would not harken unto Balaam; but the Lord thy God turned the curse into a blessing" (Deuteronomy 23:5)—and Freud does not attribute psychic motives to the Old Testament figure as he did to characters such as Hamlet, Macbeth, or Goethe's Werther. Rather, he takes Balaam's experience as exemplary, using the divine causality inscribed in the biblical account as a model for his notion of the psychic causality driving his patient. Such use of the model or example, a practice championed by early modern texts for its resistance to the scholastic regime of the syllogism, marks the possibility for a specific engagement of psychoanalytic theory with the English literary Renaissance—an engagement organized around logics of religious belief and practice.

Recent scholarship by critics such as Elizabeth Bellamy, Lynn Enterline, Graham Hammill, and Cynthia Marshall have demonstrated, despite the qualms of some New Historicist challengers, the relevance of psychoanalytic approaches to the political and aesthetic designs of early modern texts. But, with a few exceptions, there has been much less work bringing together the theological structuring of early modern literature and the principles of psychoanalysis.[2] Rather, psychoanalytic critics seem to have ceded interpretive rights to scholars such as Deborah Shuger, whose compelling assertion that "religion during this period supplies the primary language of analysis" could be seen to preempt the use of other hermeneutic systems in understanding Reformation and post-Reformation spiritual commitments.[3] It is a mistake, however, to believe that the only or the best way to appreciate a culture's texts is through that culture's own interpretive paradigms *tout court*. For the Renaissance the case is especially acute, since the period is heavily invested in refuting older and establishing fresh hermeneutic approaches. In what follows I want to suggest the usefulness of psychoanalytic theory for "coming to terms" with early modern belief, for using Freudian and post-Freudian theoretical schemas not in order to discredit or "unmask" religiosity as a symptom but in order to account for the very tenacity of certain religious convictions in this time period and their translation into fictive works.

The psychoanalytic vocabulary of compulsion is particularly appropriate for this purpose. Compulsive activity, a "form of behaviour to which the subject is obliged by an internal constraint," was explained by Freud as a representation and an accommodation of a "conflict between two opposing impulses of approximately equal strength."[4] In seeking to allay the conflict, however, compulsive behavior ironically reproduces or reinforces it, keeping the conflict as well as its compulsive activity alive. The logic of Freudian compulsion or *Zwang* is thus premised on a particularly sensitive understanding of the overdetermination of contradictory behavior, one that privileges or credits the obligations driving that behavior rather than one that critiques its inconsistencies. It is precisely this kind of sensitivity that is required for literature dealing with the paradoxical demands of post-Reformation theology, which committed the believer to a fundamental distrust of human choice and agency in the face of God's inscrutable providence. To treat certain literary performances as compulsive, then, is to address—using terms that are both consonant with and analytical of doctrinal obligations—the literary effects of theological structuring. It is to pursue the possibility of what Eric Santner has called "psychotheology": a hermeneutic approach predicated on the idea that "at the core of both psychoanalysis and the Judeo-Christian tradition . . . is an ethics pertaining to my *answerability to my neighbor-with-an-unconscious.*"[5] The goal is not, in other words, to diagnose the neighbor—in this case, the literary form or character—as compulsive; the goal is to describe the contours of the compulsive behavior and to understand the spiritual conflict that drives it. In so doing, we understand more fully the reach of religious formulas into this period's theatrical display.

Of the compulsive behaviors that dominate the Renaissance stage, two of the most striking involve conversion and confession, practices that call attention themselves to Reform notions of the limits of human agency in matters of the soul and its salvation. For a Calvinist such as William Perkins, for instance, true conversion was by definition *not* compelled; forced conversion was suspect, the work of human will rather than God's grace. "When any man is converted this worke of God is not done by compulsion . . . man willeth not his owne conuersion of himselfe by nature, but by grace wholly and alone," Perkins explains.[6] Perkins's understanding of the operation of divine election could be seen as the condition that produces the very activity it opposes; the negation of human choice in salvation, that is, leads to efforts to test or prove one's chosenness. This irony of compulsive Protestant self-scrutiny has been documented, of course, by literary critics and historians looking at figures from Luther to Nicholas of Spira to John Bunyan. Less attention has been given, however, to a different compulsion that ensues from the logic of predestination that Perkins is advancing: the compulsion to convert *the other.* To see the investment in the conversion of the other as a psychological compulsion is to open up new interpretations of conversion plays and of the religious convictions these plays dramatize.

The Merchant of Venice provides a particularly rich example: the complicated interplay of insistence and suspicion that characterizes the Christians' treatment of Shylock can be seen as a symptomatic response to the potentially paralyzing logic of post-Reformation soteriology and the way its precepts invited the Christian to look to the figure of the Jew in order to evaluate or measure the prospect of his own salvation. In a theological world dominated by credos of predestination and divine decree (however divided that world was by rival interpretations of those credos), the figure of the Jew served as the Protestant's gauge of his own election, and in *Merchant* Shakespeare dramatizes the way this figuration generated both the desire that Shylock convert *and* the desire that he *not* convert, the desire that be saved *and* the desire that he be damned. The rhythm of the entire play, and in particular the trial scene of act 4, are thus governed by the compulsively self-canceling efforts of the Christians to demand that Shylock in ways that ensure he does not.

To see the Christians' activity as compulsive is to complicate interpretations that see the play either as an endorsement of the triumph of the new dispensation over the old or as testimony to the corruption of Christian charity in the face of a Jewish adversary. It is also to complicate the traditional account of Christian suspicion of Jewish conversion in the earlier periods, which was heightened in Renaissance England in the wake of the forced baptisms of the Iberian Inquisitions and the spread of a small but measurable Marrano community to a few English port cities. In his seminal work *Shakespeare and the Jews* James Shapiro suggests that an "increasing sense of the impossibility of sincere Jewish conversion in the late sixteenth and early seventeenth centuries occur[ed] at precisely the same time that apocalyptic belief in the imminent conversion of the Jews was on the rise, creating a sharp and disturbing division between the two positions."[7] What Shakespeare demonstrates in *Merchant* is that these positions—like the arenas of Venice and Belmont—seem mutually exclusive but are really mutually enabling. The vocabulary of Freudian compulsion provides the terms by which we can recognize that suspicion in *Merchant* is not the opposite—nor even the causal consequence—of Jewish conversion but its very condition, a condition that continues to fuel, even as it undermines, apocalyptic hope.

The compulsion to confess on the English Renaissance stage is also driven by religious conflict, only here that conflict concerns the structure of Christian repentance in the aftermath of the Reformation abandonment of the sacrament of penance and yearly auricular confession. By the end of the 1540s, the sacrament of penance and the rite of private confession were essentially written out of liturgical and devotional practice, and by the time of the Elizabethan Book of Common Prayer Holy Communion "no longer . . . require[d] an individualized act of auricular confession."[8] It is possible that the Renaissance theater filled the gap left by the loss of these practices, and that the accountings of stage sinners such as Faustus, Barabas, or Bosola provided audiences with a vicarious experience of recantation and the possibilities for absolution it afforded. It is also possible that the Renaissance theater satirized these practices, and that the pleadings of these same sinners testified to the futility or inefficacy of confession. What I would suggest is that we consider how the of the loss of auricular confession, despite its replacement by a number of spiritual forms such as catechisms and handbooks, was dramatized in the elaborate and potentially destructive designs of characters who pursue mortal sin precisely so that they can admit to their crimes. Despite the Foucauldian overtones here, this approach is a psychoanalytic effort: to understand this paradox as the psychical result of a change in religious practice.

Vindice of *The Revenger's Tragedy* is a particularly vibrant example of the compulsion to confess. After each successful trick or murder, the protagonist announces either to the victim or to a cohort his responsibility in the deed. So although his revenge is conducted on behalf of his former fiancee and father, his elaborate programs for exacting vengeance—all exaggerated parodies of traditional revenge conventions—seem to be less about obtaining an impossible justice and more about orchestrating scenes that allow him to proclaim his own sinfulness. What makes his relentless program of self-disclosure compulsive is the way his efforts, designed to efface a sinful self and give rise to someone new and pure, only mire him more deeply in his sinful origins. Vindice's revenge plots are strewn with moments of self-revelation that shipwreck him on the very sinful self that confession is meant to overcome.

This miring may be part of an anti-Catholic diatribe, a critique of the hollowness and vulnerability of the sacrament of penance. It may also be a critique of the loss of auricular confession: Vindice's revenge ploys may be the almost Antinomian result of human depravity unalleviated by the possibility of ecclesiastical absolution. But to see this miring as the effects of a compulsion would be to see it as part of a more complex psychic conflict created by a religious predicament: a lingering attachment to the possible rewards of confession combined with a commitment to a Calvinist fundamentalism that would deny confession's efficacy.

Merchant and *Revenger's Tragedy* provide two examples of the way compulsive activity drives characters and the narratives in which they participate. The compulsive activity represents, I have argued, the unconscious effects of theological positions that place tremendous pressure on notions of human agency and that reconfigure the way the individual understands his or her relation to sin and salvation. The early modern theater was capable, in other words, of weaving into its plots and conventions a set of psychic responses to religious issues. Freudian and post-Freudian interpretive paradigms allow us to appreciate this ability and the complex understanding of early modern belief it underwrites.

Notes

1. Sigmund Freud, *Notes upon a Case of Obsessional Neurosis.* In *The Standard Edition of the Complete Psychological Works* (London: Hogarth Press, 1955), X: 189–93.

2. For such an exception see Julia Lupton, *After-lives of the Saints: Hagiography, Typology, and Renaissance Literature* (Stanford, Calif.: Stanford University Press, 1996).

3. Debora Kuller Shuger, *Habits of Thought in the English Renaissance: Religion, Politics, and the Dominant Culture* (Toronto: Renaissance Society of America, 1997), 6.

4. J. Laplanche and J.-B. Pontalis, *The Language of Psychoanalysis,* trans. Donald Nicholson-Smith (New York: W. W. Norton and Co., 1983), 77; Freud, *Obsessional Neurosis,* 192.

5. Eric Santner, *On the Psycho-theology of Everyday Life: Reflections on Freud and Rosenzweig* (Chicago: University of Chicago Press, 2001), 9.

6. William Perkins, *A Reformed Catholike* (Cambridge, 1597), A8.

7. James Shapiro, *Shakespeare and the Jews* (New York: Columbia University Press, 1994), 20.

8. Ramie Targoff, *Common Prayer: The Language of Public Devotion in Early Modern England* (Chicago: University of Chicago Press, 2001), 33.

The Use of the Fetish

Lisa Freinkel

That use is not forbidden usury,
Which happies those that pay the willing loan. . . .

(Sonnet 6, lines 5–6)

W HATEVER "fetishism" is in practice, cultural critics have increasingly come to the conclusion that, *in theory*, the concept—relevant at once for psychoanalysis, economics, anthropology and aesthetics—tends to redound upon itself vertiginously. "If today's critical theorists have a fetish," writes one bemused critic, "it is probably *fetishism* itself" (Wray 1998). Fetishism as theory collapses into the terms of its own analysis. It enacts what it describes. As Baudrillard puts it: "Instead of functioning as a metalanguage for the magical thinking of others, [the theory of fetishism] turns against those who use it, and surreptitiously exposes their own magical thinking" (90).

The kind of "magical thinking" that Baudrillard has in mind, entails nevertheless two eminently *rational* activities: abstraction and quantification. If we can speak generally about the concept (a big "if" for Baudrillard and others): *fetishism* describes a certain decontextualization of the world of things. It describes the movement of abstraction away from material contexts—a movement that transforms *uses* into *values*, and *means* into *ends*. What once was savored in a specific circumstance and for a discrete purpose, is now delivered from that context, and savored in and of itself. Released from the specificity of use and purpose, the fetishized object can be valued, seemingly, on its own terms. The materially useful object thus becomes the immaterially precious subject. Qualitative diversity becomes quantitative intensity. In short, *fetishism* describes the fungibility of the world of things.

At the same time—and this is the pathos of fetishism that is increasingly detailed today, by critics as diverse as Peter Stallybrass and Slavoj Žižek—the theory of fetishism itself has proved to be supremely fungible. The theory describes the abstraction of the world of things, but at the same time, it itself becomes an abstract theory. *Fetish* is a fetish. "It seems the word's usage is always somewhat 'indiscriminate,'" writes cultural critic William Pietz, citing another theorist's dismay at the fungibility of the term. As Pietz points out, *fetishism* always threatens to slide "into an impossibly general theory" (Pietz 1985, 5). Pietz's response to this dilemma is a familiar one: *Historicize. Contextualize. Particularize.* As we shall see, however, the use of *fetish* provides a singular challenge to this familiar strategy—a singular challenge that has, nonetheless, much to teach us about the general difficulties we encounter whenever we seek to historicize our psychoanalytic terms of art.

At the start of his triptych of essays on "The Problem of the Fetish," Pietz explains that he intends to explore the history of *fetishism* as a general theoretical term, and that he must begin accordingly "with a study of the origin of the fetish as a word and as a historically significant object" (ibid.). Pietz knows, as every good critic knows, that *history* is the proper critical corrective to critical misappropriations. We can correct the misprisions of our present critical usage by tracing the origins and history of our language. The strategy is as old as the Academy itself: as basic as Plato's etymologies, or the philologies of Renaissance humanists; as methodologically acute and self-aware as Derridean deconstruction or—on the other side of the postmodern coin—the genealogies produced within contemporary cultural studies. The fundamental impetus remains the same: at stake is an effort to correct sloppy thought through an attention to linguistic decorum. In rhetorical terms at issue here is the effort to purge one's discourse of **catachreses**.

The *OED* defines *catachresis* (*abusio* in Latin) as an "abuse or perversion of a trope or metaphor." Since metaphor—or *translatio* as the Latin rhetors called it (from *trans* + *fero*)—entails a transfer of proper names, catachresis can thus be understood as an *improper* transfer. According to one influential modern handbook, catachresis "improperly" applies a term to that thing "which it does not properly denote." Its terms violently "wrenched from common usage," catachresis is hence often glossed as a "mixed" or "implied" metaphor; its language is "extravagant," "far-fetched" (see Lanham 1991, 31). The dictionary built into my word processing program is even more straightforward: catachresis is "the incorrect use of words, for example, by mixing metaphors or applying terminology wrongly."

Understood as mixed metaphor or as the misapplication of terminology, catachresis is simply *wrong*. Its abusive use constitutes an entirely avoidable breach in linguistic propriety. It is in such terms that the author of the first-century treatise *Rhetorica ad Herennium*, distinguishes catachresis as wrongful abuse (*abusio*) from the appropriate appropriations of *translatio*. "Metaphor occurs when a word applying to one thing is transferred to another, because the similarity seems to justify this transference." Catachresis on the other hand entails a transfer based not on justifiable similitude, but on mere proximity. "Catachresis is the inexact use of a like and kindred word in place of the precise and proper one" (*Ad Herennium* 4.33.45, 4.34.45).

William Pietz addresses just this catachrestic indecorum in his history of the "discursively promiscuous" *fetish*. The word, he claims, has "always" been a problem for those who would contain and control its sense; its use has "always" amounted to something like abuse (Pietz 1985, 5). To demonstrate Pietz's point, we need only examine the two most influential uses of the fetish: Marx's and Freud's. As W. J. T. Mitchell has pointed out, Marx's notion of commodity fetishism (*der Fetischcharacter der Ware*) acquires its force as a "kind of catachresis"—violently yoking together connotations of primitivity and rationality (Mitchell 1986, 191). For Mitchell it is indeed the very impropriety of the trope, however, that gives Marx's critique its bite. One could make a similar argument for Freud's use of the term in his discussions of sexual perversion. Inappropriate substitutes for properly sexual objects, he writes, "are with some justice likened to the fetishes in which savages believe that their gods are embodied" (Freud [1905] 1975, 19). Again the simile gathers impact thanks not to its "justice" but instead to the violent torsion with which it joins opposing terms. Sex and religion, savage and civilized are brought together in the notion of a "sexual fetish" through "a kind of catachresis."

According to Pietz, such catachreses may, however, be impossible to avoid. If *fetish* has, as Pietz puts it, "always" been a problem for theory, if it has "always" been feared improper in its use, it is because the problem of use is inscribed in the term's historical origin itself. As Pietz persuasively demonstrates, the early modern history of the fetish is written across languages and lineages, unfolding within the cross-cultural spaces of the West African coast during the sixteenth and seventeenth centuries. As both a conceptual category and a novel material object, the fetish is thus "not proper to any prior discrete society" (ibid.). Instead, both concept and object originate interstitially, in the context of cultural and economic exchange.

Specifically, Pietz traces the evolution of the pidgin term *fetisso* from the Portuguese characterization of West African religion as witchcraft, or *feitiçaria* . However, as Pietz argues, the complex of usages comprised by the pidgin term cannot be simply derived from its nearest etymological root: "the basic components of the idea of the fetish were not present in the medieval notion [of *feitiçaria*]" (Pietz 1987, 35). Instead, the *fetisso* only evolves in the course of translation and transaction across competing cultural practices and discursive fields. "[I]n this complex intercultural world, crossed by many different African and European languages but with no language of its own," the *fetisso* helped mediate between perspectives ranging from Portuguese Catholic, to Iberian Jew, to Islamicized as well as non-Islamicized African (Pietz 1987, 39). And, increasingly, after the formation of the Dutch West Indies Company in 1621, *fetisso* also mediated the worldview of the Calvinist Dutch, who finally usurped the Portuguese hold over the Gold and Slave Coasts.

According to Pietz, then, what defined the early modern fetish was the very movement of cultural and economic exchange that, to some degree, the fetish also mediated. *Fetish* is thus a term originating not only in but also *as* translation: a term with no "prior discrete society" to call its linguistic home. Thanks to such migratory origins, the objects that *fetish* denotes are in this way named by a term that is *always already* a translation: there is no "proper" name for the fetish object. Nonetheless, there *is* a proper name for this sort of improper act of naming: namely, *catachresis*.

To understand catachresis as an "abuse" or "impropriety" that is radically originary, and hence at once necessary and even commendable, we have to turn from the first-century *Ad Herennium* to a source that would have been equally authoritative for an Elizabethan reader: namely, Quntilian. For Quintilian, catachresis is ultimately unavoidable: it names the "practice of adapting the nearest available term to describe something for which no actual term exists" (*Institutio Oratoria* 8.6.34). Catachresis fills in the gaps in a lacking lexicon, troping linguistic deficiency into neologism. For example, in lieu of a *proper* proper name, "*acetabula* quidquid habent": certain flasks are always called vinegar (*acetum*) flasks, no matter what liquid they literally contain. No other name can name them. In this way, for Quintilian catachresis comprises not a perversion or misuse of metaphor, but rather something like its limiting case. If all metaphor "adds to the copiousness of language by the interchange [*permutando*] of words and by borrowing [*mutuando*]," catachresis is metaphor that we cannot do without. "A noun or a verb is transferred from the place to which it properly belongs to another *where there is either no literal term* or the transferred is better than the literal" (8.6. 4; emphasis added). With catachresis the literal name is already a figure.

It's not difficult to see the economic logic implicit in Quintilian's account: metaphor entails a transfer of property—a loan or an exchange of the proper name. Yet herein lies the difficulty of catachresis. Because catachresis borrows a name where none previously existed, the transfer it enacts is strictly speaking unilateral. No "interchange" is possible; this is one loan that cannot be repaid. We cannot give back the vinegar and still retain the flask. Our flasky vehicle can never be separated from its vinegary tenor; catachresis provides a "proper" name that is irreducibly figurative: *acetabulum*. Yet at the same time, this irrecuperable loan enriches language in previously incalcuable ways. Like conventional metaphor, catachresis "adds to the copiousness of language," as Quintilian would say. Yet unlike conventional metaphor, this copia is produced from nothing. From lack itself. Our catachrestic investment thus yields rich returns indeed.

It is here that we begin to see the potential early modern import of the trope. At the heart of catachresis—*abusio* as the Latins call it—lies the *problem of proper use.* Small wonder then that Quintilian's most astute Elizabethan reader, George Puttenham, illustrates the trope by reference to those two discourses that his culture most closely identified with the problem of use: the discourses of *money* and *love.*

[I]f for lacke of naturall and proper terme or worde we take another, neither naturall nor proper and do vntruly applie it to the thing which we would seeme to expresse, and without any iust inconuenience, it is not then spoken by this figure *Metaphore* or of *inuersion* as before, but by plaine abuse, ... as one said very pretily in this verse.
   I lent my loue to losse, and gaged my life in vaine.

Whereas this worde *lent* is properly of mony or some such thing, as men do commonly borrow, for vse to be repayed againe, and being applied to loue is vtterly abused, and yet very commendably spoken by vertue of this figure. For he that loueth and is not beloued againe, hath no lesse wrong, than he that lendeth and is neuer repayde.

(3.17.9–10)

Quintilian's definition of catachresis as a linguistic loan that adds riches, although it cannot be repaid, is here illustrated "prettily" in words that are, simultaneously and oxymoronically, "utterly abused." Just as money is borrowed "for *use* to be repaid again" so is the speaker's love lent with an idea of future return. And yet, of course, the investment of the speaker's love is in vain; it has been lent at a loss, because lent where love was absolutely lacking. Lent to a beloved who loves not. The speaker lent his love to loss.

But let's go one step further. Puttenham's choice of examples handily invokes a broader social logic of *use*—one that dates back at least as far as Aristotle. The equation of money and love is, after all, that figure classically invoked to define proper economic relations in terms of proper (i.e., procreative) sexual relations. As Aristotle famously argues in the *Politics*, usury generates an improper form of wealth because it creates interest *unnaturally*. Undergirding his argument is the metaphorical link between the art of making money, and the act of making love. "And this term *interest*, which means the birth of money from money, is applied to the breeding of money because the offspring resembles the parent. Wherefore of all modes of getting wealth this is the most unnatural" (1.10). For Aristotle, the metaphor that joins money and love—that joins biological offspring to the metaphorical offspring of money—enables a clear line of critique. Making money is just like making babies, albeit *unnaturally* so. In one broad sweep the metaphor defines the proper use of both money and love, both coin and body.

And yet, what else is this "metaphor" but a catachresis? Money is *not* like love at all, right? Isn't that the punch line of the classical critique? The metaphor is entirely inappropriate. And yet, as Puttenham's analysis of catachresis suggests, perhaps such tropes, for all their impropriety, are necessary. Without the figure of abuse, the discourse of proper use cannot be spoken so "prettily" (as Puttenham might say). At the same time, another Tudor writer, Thomas Wilson, will argue in his *Arte of Rhetorique* against catachresis, as quickly as Puttenham argues in its favor. It would seem, indeed, that like the divergent positions on catachresis available in the first century CE (the anonymous *Ad Herennium* condemning the trope, while Quintilian celebrates it), in the sixteenth century there is also room for considerable debate about the function and legitimacy of "abuse." It is in the sixteenth-century version of this debate, however, that the modern battle lines are drawn: that the contours of the modern discourses of money and love, wealth and eros, are first ambivalently drawn. Unsurprisingly, then, the same Thomas Wilson who defines catachresis as improper in his 1560 *Arte of Rhetorique* will replay Aristotle's arguments against money-lending in his 1569 *Discourse Upon Usury*. And it is this same Wilson whose *Arte of Rhetorique* will supply a young playwright named William Shakespeare with "The Epistle to Persuade a Young Gentleman to Marriage": a text which puts forward the arguments deployed in Shakespeare's procreation sonnets. The challenge which these early modern texts present is, I'd like to argue, the challenge of rhetoric. For it is in rhetoric, *as* rhetoric, that the early modern period does its "best" (most rigorous, most nuanced, and most paradoxical) thinking about both money and love.

In other words: the catachreses of Marx and Freud—of the modern discourses of capital and desire respectively—find, as it were, their origin both in and as Puttenham's figure of abuse.

Works Cited

Aristotle. *Politics*. Trans. Benjamin Jowett (1905). Oxford: Clarendon Press.

Baudrillard, Jean. 1981. *For a Critique of the Political Economy of the Sign*. Trans. Charles Levin. St Louis: Telos Press.

[Cicero]. *Ad c. Herennium De Ratione Dicendi Libri IV*. Trans. Harry Caplan (rpt. 1954). Cambridge, MA: Harvard University Press.

Freud, Sigmund ([1905] 1975). *Three Essays on the Theory of Sexuality*. Tr. James Strachey. New York: Basic Books.

Lanham, Richard A (1991). *A Handlist of Rhetorical Terms*. 2nd ed. Berkeley : University of California Press.

Mitchell, W. J. T. (1986). *Iconology: Image, Text, Ideology*. Chicago: University of Chicago Press.

Pietz, William (1985). "The Problem of the Fetish, I." In *Res* 9: 5–17.

—— (1987). "The Problem of the Fetish, II." In *Res* 13: 23–45.

—— (1988). "The Problem of the Fetish, IIIa." In *Res* 16: 105–23.

Puttenham, George (1589). *The Arte of English Poesie*. London: Richard Field. STC 20519.

Quintilian. *Institutio Oratoria*. Trans. H. E. Butler (rpt. 1959). Cambridge, MA: Harvard University Press.

Wray, Matt (1998). "Fetishizing the Fetish." *Bad Subjects* 41 (Dec.) *http://eserver .org/bs/41/wray.html*.

ARTICLES

Words Made of Breath:
Gender and Vocal Agency in *King John*

Gina Bloom

Wʜᴇɴ ᴘʜɪʟɪᴘ, the conflicted French monarch of Shakespeare's *King John*, swears to a peace agreement with England, he gives weight to his words by emphasizing that they are made of breath. Standing beside England's monarch, he declares:

> This royal hand and mine are newly knit,
> And the conjunction of our inward souls
> Married in league, coupled and linked together
> With all religious strength of sacred vows;
> The latest breath that gave the sound of words
> Was deep-sworn faith, peace, amity, true love
> Between our kingdoms and our royal selves.
>
> (3.1.226–32)[1]

In his recollection that breath enables words to be sounded and promises to be kept, Philip presents his vocal expression as, at once, a physical and a spiritual act. On the one hand, breath is the airy matter that, from a physical perspective, must be released in order for vocal sounds to be produced and heard. The actor who plays Philip on the stage cannot help but recognize this material reality, as he would need to decipher the best places to pause and breathe while delivering this key speech. Yet as Philip insists upon the inviolability of the vow of peace he has sworn to his new ally, he emphasizes less the physical properties of breath than its spiritual significance. In claiming that his breath carries "deep-sworn faith, peace, amity, true love," Philip thematizes his breath as the guarantor of steadfastness. While the joining of hands may be symbolic of an agreement, the exchange and coupling of breath enacts a deeper commitment, a "conjunction of . . . souls."[2]

As Philip's lines invoke the notion that speech is breath—a trope prevalent throughout Shakespeare's plays and in early modern writing more generally—they suggest a tension between Philip's thematization of speech (breath being a metaphor for voice) and his performance of speech (breath being the physical substance that enables the actor playing Philip to be heard). On a thematic level, the trope of breath represents to Philip's audiences the depth of his promise, but from a material, performance perspective, where Philip's words are in essence mere ephemeral air, Philip's promises seem far more uncertain. Such promises, as the audience will soon learn, are only as staunch as the actual breath Philip, and the actor playing him, use to communicate.

In its simultaneous acceptance and suspicion of the agency of the breath, *King John* stands in good historical company. Early modern anatomists and natural philosophers embrace similarly ambivalent positions on the nature of breath—an ambivalence, I would argue, that is animated by their uneasy divergence from Aristotelian theories of vocal sound.[3] Aristotle establishes that the human voice acquires its capacity to create meaning when the soul stirs the air within the body, causing that air to strike the vocal organs and the speaker to emit the breath that carries words; soul is effectively contained in the breath expelled during voiced speech.[4] Early seventeenth-century anatomists like Helkiah Crooke and natural philosophers like Frances Bacon diverge from Aristotle in their emphasis on the physical properties of breath and the environment through which it moves. Using tools like dissection, observation, and experiment, they move beyond abstract theorizing of the soul to describe, for instance, how changes in the temperature and moisture of the air delay the reception of a voice. Yet, as many have pointed out about the seventeenth century "revolution" in science, such practical, materialist explanations by no means point to a clear break with ancient thought. For one thing, even anti-scholastic explanations of vocal sound are grounded in ancient theories of matter.[5] Moreover, as Bruce R. Smith notes, many early modern writers try to reconcile Aristotelean views of voice as soul with their own observations about the voice's physical properties.[6] Aristotelean and "new" scientific perspectives did not always coexist without friction, however. When writers turn to the role of breath in vocal communication, a fascinating tension arises between spiritual and physical explanations. Crooke's and Bacon's studies of vocal sound lead them to imply that, in some cases, the physical attributes of breath and its environment can compromise the successful transport of sound, and, concurrently, of soul.

Philip's speech, like *King John* as a whole, gains dramatic energy by capturing this tension between spiritual and material meanings of breath. The result is almost comical in Philip's case, for moments after reciting his solemn lines, Philip breaks his vow of peace and renews a conflict with England that will rage and subside repeatedly for the rest of the play. Like the promises of other rulers in the play, Philip's sworn oaths turn out to be, in the words of *King John's* Constance, "vain breath" (3.1.8), mere puffs of air that have no value because they lack secure form.[7] While Philip deploys the metaphor of speech as breath in order to shore up his vocal authority, he learns quickly that he cannot disavow what Constance recognizes as a material fact of vocal performance. Breath may be a vehicle for the soul and thereby a guarantor of communicative power, but it is also, as Bacon and Crooke reiterate, "vain," ephemeral air and is thus an untrustworthy medium for expression. With its inherent unmanageability, physical breath can undermine even the most heartfelt of men's vows.

It is no surprise that Constance, rather than Philip, underscores this sobering perspective on vocal authority, for the tension I have cited between spiritual and material meanings of breath takes on gendered significance in *King John*. As I shall argue, the play's central authoritative characters, all of whom are men, tend to ignore, displace, or misread the precarious materiality of their voices, often invoking the trope of breath as soul to cement their vocal power. By contrast, the play's more marginalized characters, women and children, recognize and call attention to breath's ephemeral material form. Their appeals to breath's material attributes, rather than signifying these characters' complete disempowerment, as one might expect, point instead to the characters' surprising influence in the play's political arena. Constance, Eleanor, and Arthur demonstrate the ways the unpredictable physical form of the voice can be constitutive of vocal power. In doing so they prompt an interrogation of modern assumptions about the relationship between voice and agency. Where a traditional view of potent, transgressive speech might emphasize a bond between voice and body—the speaking agent having "a voice of her own"—I maintain that in *King John* it is the *disarticulation* of voice from body that generates vocal power. Through the trope of breath, the play presents this more capacious model of agency as especially available to, and practiced by, women and youths.[8]

As I have begun to suggest, the play's perspective on vocal authority is intimately tied to the material circumstances of its performance. This is particularly true on account of its use of boys to play the parts of Constance, Eleanor, and Arthur. Using boys to enact women's parts, Shakespeare's stage disrupted any assumed unity of voice and body, dissociating male anatomy and female voice. Yet whatever roles they played, boy actors were ideally positioned to interrogate through their performances the material conditions for vocal agency because of their liminal physical state. With their physiologically and acoustically unsteady pubescent voices, boy actors exposed the material realities of vocalization, showing, much like Crooke's and Bacon's writings, the work involved in directing ephemeral breath. As the play's marginalized characters underscore the precarious materiality of their utterances, they establish a parallel between the challenges of vocal agency that face them as characters in the fiction of the play and the challenges that face actors in theatrical performance of the play. Thus, I will argue in closing, *King John* throws into relief the interconnectedness between the projects of "theatrical" and "literary" analysis.

The Windy Breath of Soft Petitions

King John is certainly not unique among Shakespeare's plays in its use of tropes of breath to thematize problems of vocal agency. A range of plays invoke the voice's evanescent physical form as emblematic of vocal inadequacy. For instance, Falstaff, shirking his obligation to be honorable, mocks the word "honor" as but "Air," and thus not worth his trouble (*1Henry IV*, 5.1.133–40). Longaville appeals to a commonplace syllogism involving breath to excuse his practice of oath-breaking: "vows are but breath, and breath a vapour is . . . If broken then, it is no fault of mine" (*Love's Labours Lost*, 4.3.66; 70).[9] A vow composed of breath, a mere vapor, is fragile by its material nature; that it cannot be upheld, Longaville submits, is a logical conclusion. Beatrice appeals to the same syllogism involving breath to reprimand Benedick for attacking Claudio with mere "foul words" (*Much Ado About Nothing*, 5.2.51): "Foul words is but foul wind, and foul wind is but foul breath, and foul breath is noisome; therefore I will depart unkiss'd" (5.2.52–54). No matter how vehement Benedick's words may have been, their physical na-ture—mere wind—betrays their impotence. For all these charac-ters, if "words be made of breath" (*Hamlet*, 3.4.197), then spoken promises are, by their very nature, untrustworthy. Insofar as the actors playing the parts of Falstaff, Longaville, and Beatrice use their own breath to sound out these statements, the very perform-ance of these lines helps convey suspicion about vocal authority. Since breath is a crucial part of any vocal performance, it serves as a particularly fitting trope for accenting concerns about vocal agency that are a frequent subject of investigation in Shakespeare's dramatic fictions.

The trope of breath serves this function to particularly compel-ling effect in *King John*, the history play that employs imagery of breath more pervasively than any other. Jane Donawerth notes, in fact, that *King John* ranks second among Shakespeare's plays for oral speech imagery (including tongue, mouth, throat, ear, air, and breath). Moreover, she shows that the play's descriptions of lan-guage tend to be more physical than in other plays that emphasize linguistic imagery, with "breath" being the most frequent metaphor for language.[10] Indeed, it is partly through meditations on the phys-icality of breath, I would suggest, that *King John* grapples with an issue that has dominated criticism of the play since the late twenti-eth century: language and authority.[11] Language in *King John* has been described as an "agent of dissolution" in a world devoid of a single external source of authority and a "manifestation of the cor-ruption in political ambition."[12] For most critics who address lin-guistic instability in *King John*, speech in the play is interesting insofar as it intersects with a range of historical practices and cul-tural ideologies that were the site of early modern debates about authority, including patrilineal descent, historiographic methodol-ogy, patriotic values, religious providentialism, and Machiavellian individualism.[13]

Although the relationship between the play's speech and the forces generating early modern culture has received extensive treat-ment, scholarship has devoted less attention to the central material practice that the speech of the play addresses: the practice of vocal performance itself. Moreover, despite extensive work on the play's verbal style, no one has investigated the materiality of the spoken word as it relates to the play's treatment of gender differences. Yet in *King John* imagery of breath reveals a crucial difference between

the vocal authority of men and that of women and children. Indeed,
the play imagines an expanded political role for its marginalized
characters and a more circumscribed role for its most powerful
male characters by underscoring that breath is not only a metaphor
for confident, soul-filled speech, but also the ephemeral material
form the spoken word assumes when it conveys thought. *King
John*'s women and children affect the play's political landscape by
harnessing the unpredictable theatricality of breath.

Eleanor models such vocal agency in her first utterance of the
play: a whisper. When the play opens, Eleanor's son, King John,
learns that France will support, with military force if necessary, another claimant to England's throne, Constance's son Arthur. At the
conclusion of this public political showdown, Eleanor quietly rep-
rimands her son for not listening to her when she had cautioned
him to take Constance's complaints about Arthur's right to the
throne more seriously. In effect, it is because he would not listen to
either woman that he now must engage in military action. To John's
rejoinder that England is his by right as well as by "strong possession" (1.1.39), Eleanor corrects him:

> Your strong possession much more than your right,
> Or else it must go wrong with you and me;
> So much my conscience whispers in your ear,
> Which none but heaven and you and I shall hear.
>
> (1.1.40–43)

The lines set up a generative conflict between the role of breath in
vocal performance and the figure of breath as a metaphor for voice.
As Juliet Dusinberre argues, Eleanor's whispered rebuke of John
may be construed within the fiction as a private utterance, but the
speech actually appeals strategically to the theater audience, who
clearly are also party to Eleanor's remark. Dusinberre notes that Eleanor's whisper, as it solicits the audience's recognition of her "superior intelligence" and control over political events of the play,
advances her theatrical power.[14] I would add that the whisper is an
ideal mode of utterance for defining the theatrical nature of Eleanor's agency insofar as it reflects on the role of breath in crafting
sound. More than any other form of vocal utterance, whispers foreground that the one action essential to any vocalization is the production of breath, for the whisper communicates without using the
critical organ early modern writers associated with speech, the lar-

ynx.[15] In Shakespeare's theater, the dramatized whisper is an especially efficient theatrical device for displaying actors' engagement of their breath. Actors cannot speak in genuine whispers if they wish for the audience to hear their words. Whereas the character Eleanor uses only breath in her whispered remarks to John, the actor playing Eleanor must engage both breath and larynx to project these lines—and must incorporate visual markers of the *aside* to indicate private speech. As Eleanor's whisper sets up a tension between theatrical and fictional uses of voice, it exposes Eleanor's power as rooted more in her public theatrical presence than her domestic role as John's mother. Eleanor's vocal agency is a function of her ability to use the theatrical medium to distance her voice from her person. While she *figures* her critical maternal voice as breath—gentle in its tone and inaudible to anyone but John—she *performs* her voice loudly to the theater audience, wryly reminding them that she holds the royal reigns.

Eleanor's recognition of the material attributes of the voice, and especially the role of breath in crafting sound, enables her to exercise a softer, more subtle, and less easily circumscribed kind of power than has been recognized by critics of the play. Critics who discuss female speech in *King John* have generally emphasized the outspokenness of Eleanor as the source of her vocal power. Noting in particular the quarrel between Eleanor and Constance that dominates the play's plot and commands much stage time, critics comment on the sheer quantity of lines given over to female voices and the "irreverent" nature of these contributions.[16] Women, Phyllis Rackin writes, "set the subversive keynote" in this particular history play, but only until the second half when, killed off, they are reduced to "the silent objects of male narration."[17] Nonetheless, if we examine the ways Eleanor and Constance gesture when they speak toward the material form of their voices, we discover that their vocal agency also can involve less overtly aggressive, and thus less easily circumscribed, forms of theatrical verbal display.

For instance, later in the play when Eleanor watches Philip and Lewis whispering about whether they will accept Angier's peace proposal, a plan that would enable John to keep the crown without further bloodshed, she says to John:

> Mark how they whisper. Urge them while their souls
> Are capable of this ambition
> Lest zeal now melted by the windy breath

Of soft petitions, pity, and remorse,
Cool and congeal again to what it was.

(2.1.475–79)

Eleanor's shift from noting the whispers to considering the state of
the souls of the French is a logical one in terms of early modern
understandings of the signification of breath. Followers of Aristotle
would see breath as a vehicle for the speaker's soul, thus imbuing
an utterance with sense and conviction. As whispers corroborate
the role of breath in creating vocal sound, a conversation performed
in whispers represents communication as a transmission of souls.[18]
But, unlike Philip, whose imagery of breath we examined at the beginning of this essay, Eleanor does not dwell on the spiritual significance of breath; she immediately recalls how its material form
shapes the soul's adoption of new convictions: "Lest zeal now
melted by the windy breath . . . cool and congeal." Because the
Folio of *King John* does not punctuate the phrase "Lest zeal now
melted by the windy breath," there is much disagreement among
editors about to whom the "windy breath" belongs and whether
zeal refers to France's eagerness for the peace plan or for Arthur's
cause. The disagreement has implications, I would argue, for how
we comprehend the agency of breath, and thus of female vocal
power. Most editors argue that the speech refers to France's support
for Arthur's cause (placing the comma after *zeal*) and, by implication, the "windy breath" would belong to Hubert and his "soft petitions" for peace.[19] Braunmuller argues persuasively, however, that
since Hubert's speech has been anything but "soft" (the Bastard has
just referred to Hubert's declamatory rant in favor of the peace settlement as "cannon-fire" [2.1.462]), the "windy breath" belongs to
Arthur's mother Constance and *zeal* is support for the peace offer.[20]
To paraphrase: Constance's future pleas against the peace proposal
(which would leave her cause for Arthur unsupported by removing
France as her advocate) might, with their appeals to pity and remorse, lead the French to change course. The reading makes more
sense of the description of "windy" speech as that which is filled
with "pity and remorse." Significantly for my purposes, the reading also gestures toward the peculiar power of "windy breath,"
which can shape the play's political landscape perhaps even more
effectively than the "cannon-fire" that characterizes Hubert's
speech.

The agency of Constance's speech, and more broadly of "windy breath," becomes even more pronounced if one recognizes how Eleanor's lines draw on breath's material attributes. However "windy" Constance's pleas might be, they are still able, Eleanor suggests, to "cool and congeal" France's zealous commitment to Arthur, returning France's "melted zeal" to the level at which it was in the beginning of the play. Editors have not suggested this particular reading of "zeal" in conjunction with my reading of "windy breath" above, but the reading makes sense in light of early modern understandings of the material properties of the breath.[21] Many liquefied substances congeal and harden when they cool, and the breath was observed in the early modern period to be capable of altering the temperature of the substance with which it comes into contact. Indeed the breath's ability to act as an agent of both warming and cooling is a source of amazement to Thomas Wright, who writes, "Some men wonder (and not without reason) how it commeth to passe, that out of the same mouth should issue a cold wind to coole the hot pottage, and a hot breath to warme the cold hands."[22] If we account for this larger scope of capability for windy breath, Constance's potential pleas have even more extensive agency: her voice can not only change France's mind about peace (the current issue at stake), but also restore France to its original ardent level of support for Arthur's cause (the much bigger issue at stake). Calling Constance's speech "windy breath" would seem to mock her expressive capacities: Constance will not blow anything down; hers is not the voice of "cannon-fire," but the circuitous, undirected sound of pleading. Nevertheless, the play suggests that vocal power need not be direct, commanding, and intense in order to work. Constance's breath is imagined to be capable of turning a debilitated, melted substance into a hardy, solid one, reconstituting France's enfeebled determination. And like the breath Wright describes, which has contrasting effects on the substance with which it comes into contact—cooling the porridge and warming the hands—Constance's breath need not even be directed toward a particular goal in order to work. She may wish only to change France's mind about a peace with England, but because breath's effects are not determined solely by the intentions of the speaking individual, Constance's windy petition may accomplish much more than is planned.

For both Constance and Eleanor, the potency of breathed sounds stems, surprisingly, from breath's ephemeral form and from its resistance to being controlled by its producer—the very qualities that would seem to threaten vocal agency by undermining the link between voice and body. For Constance and Eleanor, the relation of speech and body proves "scandalous," to borrow the term Shoshana Felman uses in her feminist psychoanalytic account of J. L. Austin's speech act theory.[23] Insofar as speaking is a bodily act, Felman argues, speech exposes the speaking subject as never in full control of its articulations: "the [speech] act cannot know what it is doing."[24] In Judith Butler's reading of Felman, "the speaking body signifies in ways that are not reducible to what a body 'says.'"[25] A similar disjunction between voice and body helps explain the peculiar agency of Constance's windy breath and Eleanor's powerful whispers. Because of the material attributes of their voices, of their breath, Constance and Eleanor's utterances may exceed the meanings intended by the speakers—saying more, doing more than these speakers and their audiences expect.

Poststructuralist feminist accounts of language resonate suggestively with early modern scientific writings on vocal sound. For early modern theorists of acoustics, a dissociation between voice and body is essential to communication, for breath must be transitory in order to work as a conveyer of sound. Explaining the physiology of speech, Helkiah Crooke notes that sound is produced when two bodies collide, emitting an audible "species." In the case of voice, a rush of air—the breath motivated by the lungs—hits the vocal organs, causing the air to break and for an audible species to be emitted.[26] The *Oxford English Dictionary* provides a useful definition of what Crooke means by "species": "a supposed emission or emanation from outward things, forming the direct object of cognition for the various senses or for the understanding."[27] The "species audible" emitted when two objects collide acts, in effect, as an ambassador for or translator of the original collision, transforming that message into a language that the senses can understand. The sound we hear, then, is not the original sound produced by the collision of objects but rather a re-presentation of that sound, what Francis Bacon calls an "image" of the sound. Bacon explains this important distinction: "After that *Sound* is created, (which is in a moment,) wee finde it continueth some small time, melting by little and little. In this there is a wonderfull Errour among Men, who take this to be a *Continuance* of the First *Sound*; whereas (in truth) it is a *Renovation*, and not a *Continuance*."[28] In effect, early modern acoustic theory problematizes the "metaphysics of presence"[29] that *King John*'s Philip espouses in the passage with which we began. Bacon and Crooke treat the voice not as the smooth continuance of a speaker's mind and intentions, but as a re-presentation of the speaker's original thoughts, made audible through technologies of sound propagation. Considered from this scientific perspective, the agency of a voice is contingent on its difference and distance from its site of production.[30]

This is not to say that Crooke and Bacon overlook the problems such a theory of vocal agency presents, and the way these writers frame such problems sheds light on *King John*'s interrogation of vocal agency. In particular, as Bacon and Crooke explore the technologies of sound propagation, they note ways that the medium through which sound moves—most commonly air—can often compromise the vocalized message. The quality of the air (e.g., density, temperature, motion) can affect the temporal and spatial life of a sound. Explains Crooke, "Pure-thin and cleere ayre" will "sooner receive the sound" than "Ayre which is contained in a concavous or hollow place."[31] Bacon goes on to write that although thin air accepts the sound well, being "better pierced," "Thinner or Drier *Aire*, carrieth not the *Sound* so well, as more Dense."[32] The time of day or year matter because these variables determine the heaviness and moisture of the medium. Bacon claims we hear better at night as well as when the southern winds are blowing, because the thickness of the air at these times "preserveth the *Sound* better from Wast[e]." The quality of the air not only affects the progress of a sound, but can destroy it completely. Bacon explains this "*Sudden . . . Perishing* of *Sounds*" as resulting from the active influence of the environment through which sound moves:

> The *Aire* doth willingly imbibe the *Sound* as gratefull, but cannot maintaine it; For that the *Aire* hath (as it should seeme) a secret and hidden Appetite of Receiving the *Sound* at the first; But then other Grosse and more Materiate Qualities of the Aire straightwaies suffocate it.[33]

Bacon ascribes human attributes of will and appetite to the air, depicting the space between speakers and listeners as a battleground of competing tendencies; whether a sound reaches its destination will depend on which side wins out—the "appetite" of reception or the "materiate" quality of suffocation.[34] Thus, the fact that vocal sound both is composed of air and relies upon an airy medium for transport means that any utterance is vulnerable to environmental conditions beyond the speaker's control.

It is no wonder that so many of *King John*'s characters turn to metaphors of breath to express their distrust in vows. Even Constance does so early in the play, before she realizes breath's agentive potential. When she receives news that the French king has sacrificed Arthur's cause to secure his own dynasty, she is dumbfounded, unable to believe that a monarch's oath is violable. To Salisbury, who delivers the news, she retorts:

> I trust I may not trust thee, for thy word
> Is but the vain breath of a common man.
> Believe me, I do not believe thee, man;
> I have a king's oath to the contrary.
>
> (3.1.7–10)

The matching meter at the beginnings of lines 8 and 10 accentuates the contrast between the spondees "vain breath" and "king's oath." Constance envisions a clear hierarchy between the inherently potent word of a king and the futile word of comparatively "common" men. Underlying her disbelief is her inability to recognize at this point that while a king might represent divine authority, and embody that authority in his voice, the breath that creates that voice is composed of human stuff and thus can be just as "vain" as the breath of ordinary men.

Yet unlike the kings and common men about whom Constance speaks—and to whom we will turn in the second part of this essay—Constance soon follows Eleanor in recognizing and exploiting dramatically the unpredictable material attributes of the breath. When she learns later in this act that Arthur has been captured and infers (correctly) that his life must be in danger, she falls into a vocal rage that the male characters of the play find unbearable and label a symptom of her mad "affliction" (3.4.36).[35] Insisting on her sanity, Constance stands by her right to grieve vocally and to denounce the world around her. Ignoring Philip's pleas that she be silent and at peace, she declares:

> No, no, I will not, having breath to cry.
> O that my tongue were in the thunder's mouth;
> Then with a passion would I shake the world,
> And rouse from sleep that fell anatomy
> Which cannot hear a lady's feeble voice
> Which scorns a modern invocation.
>
> (3.4.37–42)

Reading this passage too quickly, we might conclude that Constance expresses only frustration about the ineffectiveness of her "lady's feeble voice." Yet like Eleanor's whisper, Constance's lament works on multiple levels. For while she rhetorically declares herself vocally powerless, in the theater she is a dominant presence, her pathos the center of attention in this scene. Constance subtly corrects King Philip's assessment of her moments before: "A grave unto a soul, / Holding th'eternal spirit against her will, / In the vile prison of afflicted breath" (3.4.18–20). Constance's "afflicted breath" is not merely a sign of a deteriorating body and mind, but an efficient instrument through which she criticizes men of power: she penetrates Pandulph's lofty spiritual guise, declaring him "too holy" (3.4.44); and she calls King Philip out on his purported sympathy for her plight, arguing that if he truly cared, he would hasten "To England" (line 268) and rescue Arthur.[36] Constance uses her "afflicted breath" to mourn for her son while at the same time exposing the hypocrisy around her. When she refuses to be "gentle Constance" and proclaims she will continue to rant as long as she has "breath to cry," Constance figures her vocal exclamations—whether they be heartbroken sobs or furious exclamations—as motivated by her breath. Since, she argues, breath is an indicator of both speech and life, she need only live in order to speak. Simply by breathing, she has tools to express her grief and anger against the men who betrayed her and are responsible for her son's imminent death.

In her use of breath to circumvent restrictions on her speech, Constance resembles some of Shakespeare's similarly constrained female heroines who are able to exploit the breath's precarious form when they seem least able to control expression. We might think here of the sleeping Desdemona in *Othello*, with her "balmy breath that dost almost persuade" Othello not to murder her (5.2.16). The uncontrollable flow of breath similarly grants an eerie form of vocal power to Lavinia in *Titus Andronicus*. When Marcus inquires about her ravaged appearance, Lavinia parts her lips as if to speak and "like to a bubbling fountain stirr'd with wind" blood pours from her mouth, "[c]oming and going with [her] honeyed breath" (2.4.23–25). As her breath pushes forth the blood from her mouth, it communicates to Marcus that she has been raped, her tongue removed to prevent her from informing on her assailants. With gruesome literalism, *Titus Andronicus* points to breath as a medium for speech, one that need not be controlled by the speaking subject in order to be effective. Indeed, Lavinia and Desdemona need not even intend to speak—to direct breath—in order to communicate, albeit in limited ways.[37] Like Constance, they perform surprising acts of vocal agency precisely at the moments that they have the least control over their voices. Notably, this agency, a function of the "scandalous" relationship between voice and body, is made possible by the association of these women's voices with the material form of breath.

Constance affirms the expanded agency of the material breath when she goes on to articulate her wish that her cries could be made more forceful if they were even further detached from her person: if her "tongue were in the thunder's mouth," her "lady's feeble voice" might be able to "shake the world." Constance follows Bacon and Crooke in representing vocal agency as a function of the distance of the voice from the speaking body. Indeed Constance imagines her voice to be not less but *more* potent when it enters its erratic natural environment: like the laments of Lavinia, which can be heard when the natural forces of the wind carry forward her "honeyed breath," Constance's cries would become more effective were they to leave her "lady's" body and be delivered by thunder.[38] The speech bears an interesting resemblance to Emilia's insistent refusals to be silent at the end of *Othello*. Locating her vocal agency in the potent movements of another unpredictable force of the air, the northern winds, Emilia responds to Iago: "'Twill out, 'twill out! I peace? / No, I will speak as liberal as the north" (5.2.217–19).[39] Emilia daws on an early modern understanding of winds as among the most vigorous forces of nature, their agency in part a function of their mysterious and independent workings. Bacon's *The Naturall and Experimentall History of Winds* (trans. 1653) figures winds as potent agents of change, affecting human appetite and inflicting any number of diseases, all "without help of man."[40] The aptness of wind as a metaphor for Emilia's voice becomes further evident when we see how Bacon compares winds to human breath:

> The breath in mans *Microcosmos*, and in other Animals, doe very well agree with the windes in the greater world: For they are engendered by humours, and alter with moisture as winde and rain doth, and are dispersed and blow freer by a greater heat. And from them that observation is to be transferred to the winds, namely, that breaths are engendered of matter and yields a tenacious vapour, not easie to be dissolved; as Beanes, Pulse, and fruits; which is so likewise in greater windes.[41]

Unpredictable, fleeting, ungovernable, yet "tenacious" in its power, breath, like "greater winds," is a compelling trope for female voice. And as Emilia bolsters her confidence to speak by comparing her voice to the northern winds, so Constance denounces corrupt male power by entrusting her windy breath to the unpredictable capacities of the environment, a forum well outside the scope of human direction.

Holy Vows and Hot Air

Recognizing that Constance's breath thrives beyond the "grave" of her body is crucial if we want to appreciate the vocal agency Constance exhibits even when she is no longer present mentally and physically. Since Constance's body disappears from the stage and from the fiction of the play in 4.2 (when her death is reported), critics often assume that erased with Constance's body is her poignant interrogation of the play's dysfunctional, masculine political culture.[42] However, as some recent critics and directors of the play have suggested, the absence of women's bodies does not inevitably preclude their ability to serve as a subversive force in the play.[43] Constance's "afflicted breath," hardly reducible to being an "attribute"[44] of her body, seems to linger on as an agent of critique even when, perhaps especially when, her body is absent.

Indeed, throughout the second half of *King John*, the model of vocal agency enacted by Constance (with her self-distanced, "windy" petitions) and Eleanor (with her subtly theatrical whispers) haunts the play's adult male characters, who grapple repeatedly with the implications of this model for their political authority. As these male characters dominate vocally the second half of the play, they are incapable of recognizing how the unpredictable and detachable material form of the voice enables vocal power. Even when they affirm the materiality of their speech, they refuse to interpret breath's agency as a function of its uncontrollable form. An investment in guiding the unguidable material breath is evident in John's first confrontation with the pope's legate Pandulph. Pandulph demands that John answer to charges of slighting one of the pope's chosen archbishops: "This in our foresaid Holy Father's name, / Pope Innocent, I do demand of thee" (3.1.145–46). Pandulph has not (yet) asserted John's inferiority to the pope, but John interprets this demand for answers as a challenge to his su-

premacy: "What earthy name to interrogatories / Can task the free
breath of a sacred king?" (3.1.147–48). Although the folio version
of this line employs in place of *task* the word "tast"—an older
spelling for *taste*, meaning also to put to trial—most modern editors
steer clear of the sensual significance of *tast*, usually substituting a
range of alternatives, including *task*, *tax*, and *test*.[45] However, the
sensual significance of *tast* is crucial to the passage, which invokes
as it disavows, the materiality of speech. Pandulph's command that
John use his voice to explain his actions is, in John's formulation,
tantamount to forcing John to offer up his breath—"the free breath
of a sacred king"—for tasting, thus possibly for consumption and
possession.[46] John bristles at the implication that his "free breath"
will, once it enters the space beyond his body, be acted upon (i.e.,
tasted) by Pandulph.

To authorize his words, John thus collapses the distance between
his voice and his body, maintaining that even once his voice as
breath leaves his body, it remains securely linked to that sacred origin. The claim has validity in terms of early modern understandings of breath as a conveyer of soul. Balthazar Gerbier presents this
perspective elegantly in his lecture *The Art of Well Speaking* (published in 1650), which describes the "Spirituall soule" of the
voice—"its sence"—as clothed in a "corporeal robe," and "enter[-
ing] into the pores by permission of the corporall ayre." When this
"spirit . . . of humane speech" arrives at its destination, the listener's ears, it "bereaves its selfe of the Corporeall robe, and is conveyed unto our intelectuall parts, and there manifests it selfe, as in
a true draught, the very being, thoughts, conceptions, desires, inclinations, and the other Spirituall passions of him that speaketh."[47]
During the final moment of communication, the "spiritualle soule"
is transmitted to an auditor virtually intact ("as in a true draught"),
enabling a voice to affect listeners in the way its speaker intends
("the *very* being, thoughts, conceptions, desires, inclinations" of
the speaker). We can see why Philip and *King John*'s other confidently powerful male characters would so frequently summon the
metaphor of breath as soul, for according to this perspective, the
effectiveness of a speech act is virtually entirely dependent on the
intentions of its speaker, which can be efficiently conveyed to another through the vehicle of breath.

These male characters can maintain overconfidence about their
vocal authority, however, only at the cost of neglecting the messy
and unpredictable nature of what Gerbier calls the voice's "corpo-

real robe." Disavowing the volatile physicality of breath thus prevents the play's male characters from taking advantage of breath's expanded capacities. Pandulph is a case in point. Like John, he insists upon his breath's freedom of movement and his own capacity to direct that movement. In an effort to convince Philip's son Lewis to continue his father's fight against England, Pandulph blusters that his breath will remove obstacles to the dauphin's ascension to England's throne:

> Now hear me speak with a prophetic spirit;
> For even the breath of what I mean to speak
> Shall blow each dust, each straw, each little rub,
> Out of the path which shall directly lead
> Thy foot to England's throne.
>
> (3.4.126–30)

Although Pandulph's voice is compared to a wind, it is imagined, unlike Constance's "windy . . . soft petitions," as targeted in its force and certain in its outcome. Pandulph believes he has complete dominion not just over world events, but over the material form of his voice; indeed, the breath he uses to articulate his plan will, through its local motion, clear the path for Lewis's political future. Pandulph considers his breath so potent that when John finally apologizes to Rome and asks the legate to pressure France into surrendering, Pandulph confidently declares that his material voice will work upon Lewis: "It was my breath that blew this tempest up . . . My tongue shall hush again this storm of war" (5.1.17–20).

Lewis, however, swiftly challenges Pandulph's vocal authority by seizing on and deconstructing the very metaphors of breath that Pandulph has so arrogantly deployed. When Pandulph instructs Lewis, in the name of the pope, to lay down his arms, Lewis refuses, reinterpreting Pandulph's "holy breath" (5.2.68) as hot air:

> Your breath first kindled the dead coal of wars
> Between this chastis'd kingdom and myself,
> And brought in matter that should feed this fire;
> And now 'tis far too huge to be blown out
> With that same weak wind which enkindled it.
>
> (5.2.83–87)

Rather than disavowing the unpredictable material nature of breath, Lewis embraces it. Adapting the early modern proverb "a little wind kindles, much puts out the fire,"[48] Lewis counters that the words Pandulph spoke to reignite tensions between England and France will hardly dissipate the full-fledged, blazing fire already in progress. Such fires (as audiences who attended the Globe's eventful 1613 performance of *Henry VIII* would have observed) respond to climatic winds, not to human breath; they obey laws of nature that exist beyond even the most steady and controlled human action.

Despite his rhetorically effective recognition that no human subject has the capacity to direct natural phenomena, Lewis shares Pandulph's audacious belief that he can keep the flames of war moving to his own advantage. In the same breath that he challenges Pandulph's agency, he flaunts his own. Using the personal pronoun "I" almost a dozen times in his thirty-line riposte, he claims the victories of war to be his own, the progress of this "fire" to be a consequence of his actions—self-guided work of one who is "too high-born to be . . . [an] instrument" (5.2.79–81) of Rome. Nevertheless, as recollections of the material world teach Pandulph his lesson about the contingency of voice, so they show Lewis the limits of personal agency in a tumultuous world. As the next scene unfolds, we learn that the ships Lewis assumes will clinch his victory against England crash to pieces, falling victim to unpredictable weather patterns that endanger the travel not only of ships, but, as Crooke and Bacon note, of words.

The voices and egos of other male characters in *King John* follow a similar trajectory. Salisbury's breath, which he uses to swear sacred oaths, proves to be just as "vain" as Constance had once supposed. When he and the other noblemen discover Arthur's dead body and, believing this to be King John's work, vow revenge, Salisbury appeals to his breath as the source for the steadfastness of his oath: "Kneeling before this ruin of sweet life [the dead body of Arthur], / And breathing to his breathless excellence / The incense of a vow, a holy vow" (4.3.65–67). Echoing Salisbury's sentiment that the breathing of a vow is equivalent to spiritual commitment to the matter at stake, Pembroke and Bigot solemnly recite together, "Our souls religiously confirm thy words" (4.3.73). Similar oaths are reiterated again when the nobles pledge their allegiance to Lewis and join the French fight. But, as throughout the play, the material conditions of speaking seem to undermine the spiritual authority of men's oaths. However passionate their commitments, the lords are just as incapable of keeping these breathed vows as they were in keeping their initial oaths of loyalty to the English king. As soon as they hear that Lewis has secretly vowed to execute them after they help him win the war, they return to John, swearing their allegiance.

Significantly, Lewis's oath regarding their execution, communicated by the dying Melun, plays on the imagery of breath the nobles had used when they first articulated their oaths. According to Melun, Lewis has sworn that

> Even this night, whose black contagious breath
> Already smokes about the burning crest
> Of the old, feeble, and day-wearied sun—
> Even this ill night, your breathing shall expire.
>
> (5.4.33–36)

The night's approach is imagined as rapidly spreading black air, here metaphorically described as "contagious breath" surrounding the men whose breathing, or life, shall expire. Once we note that the nobles highlight breath in their original swearing of oaths against John—"breathing to [Arthur's] breathless excellence / The incense of a vow, a holy vow" (4.3.66–67)—we can more easily observe the pun on *expire*. The figurative description of dying as losing one's breath or becoming "breathless" is analogous with the physical act of speaking—both involve the *expiration* of breath. The pun effectively mocks the solemnity of the noble's earlier oath-swearing ceremony, recalling, in contrast, the fragile material form of even the most heartfelt and sacred utterances.

Whereas movements of air—the "night's . . . breath"—endanger the lives of the nobles, they save, at least temporarily, the life of Arthur. Moments before Arthur accidentally kills himself during his escape from the palace, the youth miraculously manages to save his life by convincing his murderer, Hubert, of the unpredictability of breath. Arthur's opportunity to remind Hubert of the unstable nature of his breath arises when, as a consequence of the time expended by Arthur's "innocent prate" (4.1.25), the hot iron Hubert plans to use to excise Arthur's eyes cools and the coals that could be used to reheat the iron burn out. To Arthur's argument that this is nature's support for his cause—"The breath of heaven hath blown his [the coal's] spirit out (lines 109–10)—Hubert responds, "with my breath I can revive it [the coal]" (line 111). According to early modern terminology concerning agency, Hubert imagines his breath as the *instrument* that, as it acts upon the *patient* (the coal), will enable the *patient* to become an *instrument* again.[49]

By this point in the play, such optimism regarding the instrumentality of breath should give the reader and listener pause. It certainly gives Arthur an opening to deliver his most convincing argument yet: breath is the kind of instrument that must leave the body of the speaker to work, thus its effect on the patient is particularly difficult to predict. Instead of rekindling the fire, Hubert's breath may cause the fire to "sparkle. . . . / And like a dog that is compelled to fight, / Snatch at his master that doth tarre him on" (lines 114–16). Arthur suggests that when Hubert uses his breath to enable the agency of the instrument of torture, he may unintentionally surrender his own agency, turning the coals against himself instead. Whatever the intentions of the principle who uses it, breath may not have its anticipated effects—fire might respond to the breath differently. No doubt, as critics have observed, Hubert wavers in carrying out the torture largely as a consequence of his growing compassion for Arthur.[50] Yet Hubert's decision seems to be informed, at least in part, by his recognition of the limits of his control over breath. For it is Arthur's demonstration of the dispersal of human agency in a mercurial material world that immediately precedes Hubert's capitulation.

Choreographing Breath in the Theater

Although Hubert's breath in this scene is imagined to be used only for the purposes of blowing air on coals, the significance of Arthur's comments to the representation of vocal agency in *King John* cannot be ignored, especially given the frequency with which the play associates breath with speech. Insofar as Arthur takes comfort in the surrender of breath to the vagaries of the air, he can be differentiated from *King John*'s adult male characters, who either disavow the materiality of breath completely, insisting upon its figurative, spiritual significance, or deny the precariousness of breath's material form in their claims that they can command the uncommandable movements of this airy substance. Arthur, by contrast, articulates a view of breath that resembles Constance's and Eleanor's. As we have seen, Constance and Eleanor not only foreground breath as the matter that causes words to resound, but they also demonstrate the agency of breath as "scandalous," a function of its transience and detachability from the speaker. "Windy breath," for Constance and Eleanor, is effective not in spite, but *because* of its mobile, unpredictable form.

Similarities between Arthur, Constance, and Eleanor seem to have been observed and emphasized throughout the history of the play's performance. In the nineteenth century directors cast a female actor for the part of Arthur, a practice that, as Dusinberre argues, resolves the problem of finding a male child talented enough to perform this exacting role.[51] Whatever the intended reasons for this gender switch, it approaches the effect of Shakespeare's all-male company, insofar as it links Arthur to the play's female characters through the sex of the actors playing these roles. In Shakespeare's period, however, the casting of apprentice boys for these parts would have served the additional purpose of helping define the play's meditations on the issue of vocal agency: boys already represented a scandalous relationship between voice and body. And as they experienced the voice changes that were believed to accompany puberty, they were often viewed as incapable of controlling their voices.

The challenges of vocal control present for any actor would have been particularly acute where boy actors were concerned, for the precarious state of their pubescent bodies left their voices in an especially vulnerable state. From the perspective of humoral physiology, one of the dominant paradigms for understanding bodily experience in the period, boys going through puberty experience an increase in body heat and decrease in moisture. These physiological changes not only account for the development of reproductive organs—according to medical and scientific writers, all the moisture of the body is directed to the testicles, where sperm is generated—but explains why boys' voices begin to waver. As Bacon explains, "when much of the Moisture of the Body, which did before irrigate the Parts, is drawne downe to the Spermaticall vessells; it leaveth the Body more hot than it was; whence commeth the dilatation of the Pipes."[52] As the pubescent boy's body gets hotter and drier, the windpipe through which air moves to create sound enlarges, and, as a consequence, fractures. As breath motivated by the speaker's lungs courses through this breaking windpipe, the irregularities of the windpipe compromise the smoothness of the voice produced: the boy is incapable of choreographing his voice effectively, and the voice squeaks or sounds, as Hamlet phrases it, "crack'd" (*Hamlet*, 2.2.48). As with most physiological processes associated with puberty, the cracking of the wind-pipe and its effects on the movement of breath through and out the body cannot be controlled. Short of an intervention like castration, voice changes were inevitable for boys who performed on early modern English stages.[53] Given how central boys were to England's commercial theater industry, it is not surprising, as I have argued elsewhere, that boys' cracking, squeaking voices become a subject of investigation, humor, and general fascination in many of the plays written during the period.[54]

Insofar as the physiological state of the boy actor's body could compromise his capacity to move the breath that creates voice through and out of his body, the boy actor was an ideal figure for underscoring through performance the problems of vocal authority raised in the fiction of a play like *King John*. When the character Arthur thematizes voice as uncontrollable breath, he invokes the condition of the voice of the actor who plays him—a voice that, if not already cracking, carries the potential for uncontrollability. The intersection between the fictional and theatrical worlds of *King John* may help explain why the Bastard Falconbridge—who, like Arthur, is marginalized in the fiction of the play but, unlike Arthur, would have been played by an adult actor—bears little in common in terms of his use of the imagery of breath with Arthur, Constance, and Eleanor. Certainly the Bastard is more canny about vocal power than the other adult male characters in the play, for, as many critics have noted, he discovers quite quickly that the spoken word carries little authority in a world where oaths are just another "commodity" to be used at whim by wily politicians.[55] Yet unlike other marginalized characters, the Bastard does not appeal to the material form of breath when he deconstructs vocal authority. Even when his speech is referred to as breath, that speech is imagined to work more like "cannon-fire" than wind; Austria, for instance, complains that the Bastard is a "cracker [who] deafs our ears / With this abundance of superfluous breath" (2.1.147–48). Later in the play when the Bastard and Pandulph negotiate on behalf of John and Lewis, respectively, the Bastard expressly maligns breath as the authorizing force for voice. Lewis's declaration not to lay down arms is, according to the Bastard, "fury breath'd" by this "youth," whereas the Bastard's own speech is authorized by the English King whose "royalty doth speak in me" (5.2.127–29). By comparing the Bastard and Arthur, we can see that appeals to unpredictable breath as a metaphor for voice are the province of figures marginalized not only thematically, but *theatrically.*

If, as I have been suggesting, breath and its implications for agency are intimately linked to the theatrical conditions of performance, then what is the precise relationship between the movement of physical breath in a theater and a play's thematization of breath? Do the material conditions of voicing help explicate the issues of vocal agency represented in *King John*, or does the play's thematization of vocal agency reflect back on the use of voice by adult and child actors in the early modern English theater? The former, calling for a more "literary" approach, privileges the play's thematic concern with voice and authority; the latter, involving a more "theatrical" approach, privileges performance concerns, specifically the actor's vocal craft. To even frame the issue in terms of these antinomies, however, undermines the kind of performance criticism of Shakespeare I have been attempting in this essay. As W. B. Worthen argues in *Shakespeare and the Authority of Performance*, the binary of "literary" versus "theatrical," of page versus stage, has beset the discipline of performance criticism with a host of problems, preventing it "from pursuing its justifying critical agenda: to locate the space and practice of criticism in relation to the practices of performance."[56] This is not to say that we should ignore the differences between page and stage, but rather consider how the forms overlap and intersect. P. A. Skantze models such an approach in *Stillness in Motion in the Seventeenth Century Theatre*, cautioning that the binary of print versus performance will "undo the subtleties, the anxieties, the inventive crossing of forms actually at work in the creation of both plays and books."[57] Remaining open to such "inventive crossing of forms," I have tried to follow Robert Weimann's approach to *King John* and consider how the play experiments with the tension between "dramatic representations and the circumstantial world" of the theater.[58]

Weimann broadens his treatment of this tension in *Author's Pen and Actor's Voice: Playing and Writing in Shakespeare's Theatre*, which argues that "the imaginary play-world and the material world of Elizabethan playing" are equally important and interdependent "functions" of a play.[59] While Weimann is concerned primarily with explicating the relationship of "text" (which he associates with the "author's pen") and "performance" (which he associates, notably, with the "actor's voice"), his wider conceptualization of the functions of playing is useful for understanding how I have sketched the interdependent relationship between *King John*'s thematization and performance of voice as breath. On the one hand, metaphors of speech as breath call attention to the precarious process of circulating one's voice in the Elizabethan theater; Constance, Eleanor, and Arthur's successful conveyance of their voices through this unstable communication process constitutes a testament to the (tenuous) strength of the boy actor's vocal craft. At the same time, the unpredictable movement of actors' breath as they speak, particularly noticeable in the case of pubescent boy actors, can serve as the inspiration for the particular views of vocal agency that the play asserts. Indeed, the realities of playing recall, like the writings of Crooke and Bacon, the "scandalous" ways in which the agency of breath is a function of its distance from the speaker. Breath must leave the actor's body to work, but once it leaves, it becomes vulnerable to the forces of the theater air, and to the whims of audience members who receive it. Boy actors make manifest the challenges of vocal control and aural command present for all the male actors on Shakespeare's stage, indeed for anyone who communicates with the voice.

Most of all, perhaps, boy actors show the labor involved in directing windy breath. And when their voices worked successfully on the stage—as they must have for audiences to have heard Constance, Eleanor, and Arthur's powerful utterances—boy actors helped illustrate through performance a generative model of vocal agency. Performance, in Worthen's words, did "material and theoretical work."[60] Through the theatrical and thematic employment of breath, *King John* reminds its actors and the audience that listens to them that the physical performance of language sets the parameters—the limits and conditions—of vocal agency. And, as I have argued, it is the most vocally marginalized of Shakespeare's actors and characters who may have been best positioned to take advantage of these expanded parameters.

Notes

I wish to thank Bruce Smith and Valerie Traub for their insightful feedback on this work at various stages of its development. This essay has also benefited from comments offered by participants in the University of Wisconsin-Milwaukee Early Modern Reading Group; the Lawrence University Gender Studies Works in Progress series; and the Shakespeare Association of America "Historical Phenomenology" seminar, especially Carla Mazzio and Susan Zimmerman.

1. Unless otherwise noted, citations of *King John* follow L. A. Beaurline, ed., *King John*, New Cambridge Shakespeare (Cambridge: Cambridge University Press, 1990). All other citations of Shakespeare plays follow *The Riverside Shakespeare*, ed. G. Blakemore Evans, 2nd ed. (Boston: Houghton Mifflin Company, 1997), hereafter cited as Riverside.

2. The point is underscored when the pope's legate commands Philip to drop John's hand so as to destroy the symbol of their union; Philip reminds Pandulph that the bond that breath creates between two souls is less easily broken than that between two hands. Recalling the "deep-sworn faith" that was sounded by his breath, he responds, "I may disjoin my hand, but not my faith" (3.1.262).

3. Although late sixteenth-and early seventeenth-century English writers did not embark upon specific studies of sound (unlike their continental counterparts), several devote sections of their work on other topics to questions about auditory phenomena: the most significant treatments among these are Helkiah Crooke, *Microcosmographia: A Description of the Body of Man* (London, 1611) and Sir Francis Bacon, *Sylva Sylvarum: Or a Naturall Historie* (London, 1626). As noted in Penelope Gouk, "Some English Theories of Hearing in the Seventeenth Century: Before and after Descartes," in *The Second Sense: Studies in Hearing and Musical Judgment from Antiquity to the Seventeenth Century*, ed. Charles Burnett, Michael Fend, and Penelope Gouk (London: Warburg Institute, 1991), seventeenth-century English contributions to the history of acoustics are often ignored by historians of sound, since English writers do not add any new knowledge to the field. For Gouk the texts remain interesting as part of an intellectual history of English thought. For me they are useful because they help elucidate the tensions inherent in dramatic representations of the voice as a material substance.

4. Aristotle, *On the Soul*, trans. Hippocrates G. Apostle (Grinnell, Iowa: The Peripatetic Press, 1981), Book B; 8.420b.

5. Theories of matter proposed and developed by Democritus, Epicurus, Lucretius, and their followers explicitly countered Aristotle in viewing all substances, including breath, to be composed of minute, indivisible molecules, called atoms. Atomistic and "corpuscular" theories of matter experienced a revival in the sixteenth and seventeenth centuries, appearing for instance in works by Giordano Bruno, Thomas Hariot, and Francis Bacon, and in the "mechanical" philosophy of Thomas Hobbes, Renée Descartes, Pierre Gassend, among others. For an introduction to English writings concerning atomism, see Robert Hugh Kargon, *Atomism in England: From Hariot to Newton* (Oxford: Clarendon, 1966). On Bacon and atomism, see Silvia A. Manzo, "Francis Bacon and Atomism: A Reappraisal," in *Late Medieval and Early Modern Corpuscular Matter Theories*, ed. John E. Murdoch Christoph Lüthy, William R. Newman (Leiden: Brill, 2001).

6. Bruce R. Smith, *The Acoustic World of Early Modern England: Attending to the O-Factor* (Chicago: University of Chicago Press, 1999), 98–99. My discussion of early modern acoustic theory throughout this essay is much indebted to Smith's study.

7. On how characters' traditional views of oaths as "spring[ing] from the most intimate depths of a swearer's being" conflicts with their "prolix justifications" of the need to break oaths, see Jonas Barish, "*King John* and Oath Breach," in *Shakespeare: Text, Language, Criticism, Essays in Honour of Marvin Spevack*, ed. Bernhard Fabian and Kurt Tetzeli von Rosador (Hildesheim: Olms-Weidmann, 1987),

esp. 13. Barish's argument about characters' simultaneous commitment to these two understandings of oaths corroborates my findings about breath—an image that offers a similarly two-fold formulation of vocal agency. On Shakespeare's oaths and promises in the context of sixteenth and seventeenth century religious, political, and legal thought, see William Kerrigan, *Shakespeare's Promises* (Baltimore: Johns Hopkins University Press, 1999).

8. For a related view of how the metaphor of breath is associated with productive vocal failure in early modern literature, see Lynn Enterline, *The Rhetoric of the Body from Ovid to Shakespeare*, Cambridge Studies in Renaissance Literature and Culture (Cambridge: Cambridge University Press, 2000). Examining the legacy of Ovid in the Renaissance and particularly Ovid's association of poetic subjectivity with the loss of the female voice, Enterline elegantly demonstrates how tropes of air, breath, and wind enable writers to comment self-reflectively on the evanescent craft of poetry and the pressures of producing such poetry through the medium of writing. Whereas Enterline's focus is on early modern practices of writing and their relationship to ideologies of language, my emphasis is on early modern practices of speaking and their relationship to ideologies of vocal agency.

9. The set of images is articulated throughout early modern drama. For instance, in *Arden of Faversham* Alice incorporates the syllogism when she warns Mosby about swearing oaths: "Oaths are words, and words is wind, / And wind is mutable. Then I conclude / 'Tis childishness to stand upon an oath" (2.436–38). Anon., *Arden of Faversham*, ed. Martin White, New Mermaids (New York: Norton, 1995).

10. Jane Donawerth, *Shakespeare and the Sixteenth-Century Study of Language* (Urbana: University of Illinois Press, 1984), esp. 165–66.

11. On the play's critical reception through the beginning of the twentieth century, see Joseph Candido, ed., *King John, Shakespeare: The Critical Tradition* (London: Athlone Press, 1996). On modern responses and for an extensive bibliography of scholarship and performance since 1940, see Deborah T. Curren-Aquino, ed., *King John: New Perspectives* (Newark: University of Delaware Press, 1989). Introductions to both volumes offer overviews of critical dissatisfaction with the play as well as explanations for why the play has enjoyed a revival in the late twentieth century.

12. Eamon Grennan, "Shakespeare's Satirical History: A Reading of *King John*," *Shakespeare Studies* 11 (1978), esp. 32; and Donawerth, esp. 175. The seminal work on the play's depiction of language is Sigurd Burckhardt, "*King John*: The Ordering of This Present Time," *ELH* 33, no. 2 (1966): 133–52. Like Donawerth, I see the physicality of the play's speech imagery as crucial to the play's thematization of the power of speech. However, I read *King John*'s thematization of speech in terms of the play's particular conditions of production in the early modern theater and thus approach breath as a metaphor not of language more generally, but of vocal performance specifically.

13. In addition to Burckhardt, Grennan, and Donawerth, see James E. May, "Imagery of Disorderly Motion in *King John*: A Thematic Gloss," *Essays in Literature* 10, no. 1 (1983): 17–28; Barish; A. R. Braunmuller, ed., *The Life and Death of King John*, Oxford Shakespeare (New York: Oxford University Press, 1989), esp. 39–53; Edward Gieskes, "'He Is but a Bastard to the Time': Status and Service in *The Troublesome Raigne of John* and Shakespeare's *King John*," *ELH* 65, no. 4 (1998):

779–98; Dorothea Kehler, "'So Jest with Heaven': Deity in *King John*, in Curren-Aquino, 99–113; Michael Manheim, "The Four Voices of the Bastard," in Curren-Aquino, 126–35; Robert Weimann, "Mingling Vice and 'Worthiness' in *King John*," *Shakespeare Studies* 27 (1999): 109–33; Christopher Z. Hobson, "Bastard Speech: The Rhetoric of 'Commodity' in *King John*," *Shakespeare Yearbook* 2 (1991): 95–114; and Maurice Hunt, "Antimetabolic *King John*," *Style* 34, no. 3 (2000): 380–401. See also Joseph A. Porter, "Fraternal Pragmatics: Speech Acts of John and the Bastard," in Curren-Aquino, 136–43. Much critical analysis has centered on the speech of the Bastard, whose meditations on the multifarious meanings of the word "commodity" at the end of act 2 seem to index the play's figuration of "modern" ideologies of the subject's self-sufficiency. See especially Geiskes; Manheim; and Weimann, "Mingling."

14. Juliet Dusinberre, "*King John* and Embarrassing Women," *Shakespeare Survey* 42 (1990), 43. On Eleanor's intelligence and political savvy, see also Carole Levin, "'I Trust I May Not Trust Thee': Women's Visions of the World in Shakespeare's *King John*," in *Ambiguous Realities: Women in the Middle Ages and Renaissance*, ed. Carole Levin and Jeanie Watson (Detroit: Wayne State University Press, 1987): 219–34.

15. While early modern anatomists recognize an array of organs as contributing to the production of vocal sound—including, notably, the vocal chords, which had recently been anatomized—most represent the larynx as the most fundamental organ associated with speech. See, for example, Hieronymi Ab Aquapendente Fabricius, *De Visione, Voce, Auditu* (Venice, 1600), the sections of which, "De Visione," "De Voix," and "De Auditus" anatomize, respectively, the eye, the larynx, and the ear.

16. Phyllis Rackin, "Patriarchal History and Female Subversion in *King John*," in Curren-Aquino, 76–90, esp. 82. See also, Howard and Rackin, chap. 7, which expands on similar material; Levin, esp. 125; Joseph Candido, "'Women and Fools Break Off Your Conference': Pope's Degradations and the Form of *King John*," in *Shakespeare's English Histories: A Quest for Form and Genre*, ed. John W. Velz (Binghamton, NY: Medieval and Renaissance Texts and Studies, 1996): 91–110; and Dusinberre, esp. 43.

17. Rackin, "Patriarchal," 84.

18. The notion of conversation as an exchange of breath substantiates in material terms the erotic implications of "conversation," as advanced by Jeffrey Masten, *Textual Intercourse: Collaboration, Authorship, and Sexualities in Renaissance Drama*, Cambridge Studies in Renaissance Literature and Culture (Cambridge: Cambridge University Press, 1997). Some early modern writers explain that when lovers kiss, they are really conjoining their souls through the exchange of breath. Baldesar Castiglione writes that the mouth is "an issue for the wordes, that be the enterpreters of the soule, and for the inwarde breth, whiche is also called the soule: and therefore [the lover] hath a delite to joigne hys mouth with the womans beloved with a kysse: . . . bicause he feeleth that, that bonde is the openynge of an entry to the soules, whiche drawen with a coveting the one of the other, power them selves by tourn, the one into the others bodye, and be so mingled together." Baldesar Castiglione, *The Book of the Courtier*, trans. Thomas Hoby, *The Tudor Translations* (London: David Nutt, 1900), 355–56.

19. Stanley T. Williams, ed., *The Life and Death of King John*, *The Yale Shake-*

speare (New Haven: Yale University Press, 1927); Smallwood; and Riverside. Beaurline, whose edition I cite, offers a wider range of interpretations by leaving the passage unpunctuated. Beaurline, however, differs from Braunmuller and others in identifying the spokesperson for Angiers as Citizen, rather than Hubert. Given that later in the play (as I discuss below), Hubert's understanding of speech will again be contrasted with the "windy breath of soft petitions"—this time those of Constance's son—one might argue that this scene serves as a parallel to the later scene, thus supporting Braunmuller and others' contention that the speaker in this scene is, in fact, Hubert.

20. Braunmuller, *King John*, 2.1.478–80n.

21. Indeed, my reading combines Braunmuller's explanation of *windy breath* as breath belonging to Constance with other editors' interpretations of *zeal* as France's zealous commitment to Arthur's cause. Braunmuller believes the readings to be irreconcilable: "if *zeal* here were to mean the commitment to Arthur . . . the *soft petitions*, would have to be understood as Hubert's." My reading enables *melt*—which Braunmuller must take figuratively as meaning "change"—to carry its full, material significance.

22. Thomas Wright, *The Passions of the Minde in Generall*, 2nd ed. (Urbana: University of Illinois Press, 1971), 162–63. Early modern authors comment on the mysterious discovery that hot food can be cooled using the same substance, breath, that we use to produce speech. For instance, when Mistress Merrythought in Francis Beaumont and John Fletcher's *Knight of the Burning Pestle* receives a vehement lecture rather than the expected aid from Venturewell, she curses, "let him keep his wind to cool his porridge" (4.3.56–57). In David Bevington et al., eds., *English Renaissance Drama: A Norton Anthology* (New York: Norton, 2002).

23. Shoshana Felman, *The Literary Speech Act: Don Juan with J. L. Austin, or Seduction in Two Languages*, trans. Catherine Porter (Ithaca: Cornell University Press, 1983).

24. Cited in Judith Butler, *Excitable Speech: A Politics of the Performative* (New York: Routledge, 1997), 10.

25. Ibid.

26. Crooke, 691.

27. *The Compact Edition of the Oxford English Dictionary*, 2nd ed. (Oxford: Oxford University Press, 1971), s.v. "species," 5.

28. Bacon, no. 206. The prime example is a bell that, once struck, continues to ring until it is steadied. Although it would seem that the bell continues to produce one continuous sound, in fact, Bacon explains, the bell is producing a series of sounds— the "minute parts" of the bell continue to vibrate, "and so reneweth the *Percussion* of the *Aire*."

29. Jacques Derrida, "Signature Event Context," *Glyph: Johns Hopkins Textual Studies* 1 (1977): 172–97.

30. Insofar as acoustic theorists imagine vocal sound as breath that becomes disarticulated from the body that initially produces and "owns" it, their writings share common theoretical and imaginative ground with early modern descriptions of disarticulated hands and tongues. The latter have been examined by Katherine Rowe and Carla Mazzio, respectively, who note that when these expressive, but inherently itinerant, body parts are represented as disarticulated from the body to which they belong, they generate concerns about human agency. Katherine Rowe,

Dead Hands: Fictions of Agency, Renaissance to Modern (Stanford: Stanford University Press, 1999). Carla Mazzio, "Sins of the Tongue," in *The Body in Parts*: 53–79. See also, Carla Mazzio, "Staging the Vernacular: Language and Nation in Thomas Kyd's *the Spanish Tragedy*," *Studies in English Literature* 38, no. 2 (1998): 207–32.

31. Crooke, 610.

32. Bacon, no. 226.

33. Ibid., no. 290.

34. Among the environmental forces with which a vocal sound must contend is the very breath of listeners. Bacon notes that we hear best when we *"hold our Breath"* because "in all *Expiration*, the Motion is Outwards; And therefore, rather driveth away the voice, than draweth it" (no. 284). In other words, a voice approaching the senses of a listener may be weakened or altered in form by the listener's breathing because that breath pushes away the incoming air that carries the sound. Elsewhere, Bacon takes issue with ancient writers who imagine wind to be an exhalation. Bacon argues that while exhalations move the air, they are not in and of themselves winds. The "exhalations" that ancients thought made up the wind are merely helpers in its motion, not the wind's material itself: "But all impulsion of the Aire is winde; and Exhalations mixed with the aire contribute more to the motion than to the matter." Sir Francis Bacon, *The Naturall and Experimentall History of Winds*, trans. R. G. (London, 1653), 87. The distinction between breath and wind is far less stable in Shakespeare, where the terms are often substituted for and associated with each other. In addition to the examples discussed below, note, for instance, Cassio's prayer to Jove on behalf of Othello's voyage at sea: "swell his sail with thine own powerful breath" (2.1.77–78) and the description of the Cyprus coast storm as "the wind [that] hath spoke aloud at land" (2.1.5).

35. On the ways that Constance's rants have embarrassed male readers of the play—who have responded by cutting many of her lines—see Dusinberre; and Candido, "'Women and Fools.'"

36. I draw on Beaurline's glossing of this line.

37. Communication is limited insofar as Marcus, despite clearly recognizing in this scene (through his invocation of Ovid's rape story) that a rape has occurred, somehow forgets what he knows, so that he and Titus wait two acts before truly "discovering" the rape. Emily Detmer-Goebel argues that the point of this recognition and forgetting is to "tease the audience with the idea that men should know that she has been raped" thereby emphasizing, as is true about women's speech more generally in rape cases of the period, "men's ultimate reliance on Lavinia's words." Emily Detmer-Goebel, "The Need for Lavinia's Voice: *Titus Andronicus* and the Telling of Rape," *Shakespeare Studies* 29 (2001), 81. I argue that Lavinia uses her *voice* successfully in this scene, even if she does not utter "words"; that Marcus cannot retain the information she voices indicates a flaw in his listening and apprehension, not in her expression.

38. Beaurline and others have argued that Constance is one of the few characters who looks beyond the play's worldly setting toward the heavens and spiritual concerns, but, as I am suggesting, even in this speech, she lays her faith in the material world.

39. According to the Riverside gloss, "north" refers to the north winds. We

might note that Bacon's *History of Winds* explains that "Northwardly" winds are known for their stimulating effects (55).

40. Bacon, *History of Winds*, A12v.

41. Ibid., 176.

42. Rackin, *Stages*, 18; Howard and Rackin, 126; Vaughan, "Subversion," 72. See also, Janet Adelman, *Suffocating Mothers: Fantasies of Maternal Origin in Shakespeare's Plays, Hamlet to the Tempest* (New York: Routledge, 1992), 10; and Levin, 230.

43. Deborah Warner's production (Royal Shakespeare Company 1988/89), for instance, uses "the absence of women in the second half of the play to explore, through male characters aspects of the mother-child relationship." See Geraldine Cousin, *Shakespeare in Performance: King John* (Manchester: Manchester University Press, 1994), 128–29. I am grateful to Deborah Curren-Aquino for bringing this to my attention. For a key critical reading that develops this theoretical point, see Nina S. Levine, *Women's Matters: Politics, Gender, and Nation in Shakespeare's Early History Plays* (Newark: University of Delaware Press, 1998).

44. Beaurline, 3.4.19n.

45. Honnigman and the Riverside use *taste* but argue that the word is identical in meaning to *task*. Braunmuller goes further when defending his use of *test*: "Printing 'taste' would, through recourse to an archaic definition, conclude with the meaning 'test'; but the connotation of modern 'taste' would be recalled unnecessarily and distractingly" (*King John*, 3.1.148n). I argue, to the contrary, that the sensual significance of *taste* is crucial for interpreting the passage.

46. This is not the play's only reference to the relationship between tasting and hearing. When Lewis has lost all hope in France's potential for victory, he laments: "Life is as tedious as a twice-told tale, / Vexing the dull ear of a drowsy man, / And bitter shame hath spoiled the sweet word's taste" (Braunmuller, *King John*, 3.4.108–10). (I cite from Braunmuller's version, which follows the folio, rather than Beaurline's, which, as it chooses the later emendation of "world" instead of "word" elides the significance of *taste*.) Braunmuller notes that the folio *words* could also be read as plural possessive ("words' sweet taste"), which would refer to the words of the twice-told story. Additionally, when Hubert describes the way rumors of John's murder of Arthur stir through the streets, he notes one commoner "with open mouth swallowing" (4.2.195) the news. Shakespeare associates listening with the consumption of words in other plays as well. For example, Pericles describes Marina as "Another Juno, who starves the ears she feeds / And makes them hungry the more she gives them speech" (5.1.107–8). Also, Desdemona is reported to have fallen in love with Othello in the process of "devouring up" his stories with her "greedy ear" (1.3.150–51).

47. Sir Balthazar Gerbier, *The Art of Well Speaking* (London, 1650), 24.

48. Morris Palmer Tilley, *A Dictionary of the Proverbs in England in the Sixteenth and Seventeenth Centuries* (Ann Arbor: University of Michigan Press, 1950), W424. Cited in Braunmuller, *King John*, 5.2.83–87n; and Beaurline, 5.2.83–87n.

49. I derive this terminology primarily from Rowe, esp. 18–20, who argues that in "dead hand stories," the disembodied part's ability to act independently of the subject that wills it to act blurs lines between the principle (one on whose behalf an action is performed), the agent (one who or that which exerts the power to per-

form the action), the instrument (the tool that accomplishes the action), and the patient (one upon whom or which the action is performed). Rowe offers a lucid account of the history of agency as a concept and, drawing on Perry Anderson (*Arguments Within English Marxism* [London: New Left Books and Verso Editions, 1980]), she argues that the blurring of these terms can be strategically useful for making "the idea of agency both fuzzy and capacious" (18).

50. The claim regarding Hubert's compassion has been advanced most influentially by Burckhardt, 137–38.

51. Dusinberre, 49, 37n. Dusinberre assumes that the part must be played by a boy with an unbroken voice—thus the decision by directors to cast a female actor (with a high, "feminine" voice), rather than an older boy whose voice has broken. Yet, as I suggest below, a boy with a more unstable voice—for instance, a youth going through the vocal changes of puberty—would be a more apt choice in terms of highlighting the play's engagement with questions of vocal agency.

52. Bacon, *Sylva Sylvarum*, no. 180.

53. Dympna Callaghan, "The Castrator's Song: Female Impersonation on the Early Modern Stage," *Journal of Medieval and Early Modern Studies* 26, no. 2 (1996): 321–53. See also Dympna Callaghan, *Shakespeare without Women: Representing Gender and Race on the Renaissance Stage*, Accents on Shakespeare (London: Routledge, 2000).

54. Gina Bloom, "'Thy Voice Squeaks': Listening for Masculinity on the Early Modern Stage," *Renaissance Drama* 29 (2000): 39–71.

55. See, for example, Burckhardt, Donawerth, and Hobson.

56. W. B. Worthen, *Shakespeare and the Authority of Performance* (Cambridge: Cambridge University Press, 1997), esp. 152.

57. P. A. Skantze, *Stillness in Motion in the Seventeenth-Century Theatre*, Routledge Studies in Renaissance Literature and Culture (London and New York: Routledge, 2003), 27–28.

58. Weimann, "Mingling," 131.

59. Robert Weimann, *Author's Pen and Actor's Voice: Playing and Writing in Shakespeare's Theatre*, Cambridge Studies in Renaissance Literature and Culture (Cambridge: Cambridge University Press, 2000), 10–11.

60. Worthen, 180.

Shakespeare and the
Second Blackfriars Theater

Leeds Barroll

The second Blackfriars theater has drawn the attention of scholars in the last several decades either because they have been interested in the kinds of dramas that were performed in this new playing place or because they wished to determine the architecture of the playing area itself.[1] It is in some ways unfortunate that such competent and knowledgeable attention has remained focused largely on these issues because another (and admittedly speculative) area could benefit from further and more extensive questioning. The results of such questioning are likely to be of particular interest to theater historians and to biographers of Shakespeare.

The questions that I have in mind, let me hasten to say, are not for the most part original. Just when did Shakespeare and his fellows begin presenting plays in the Blackfriars playing space? And why did the King's Servants perform plays there in the first place? Inevitably caught up in ideas about the "final comedies" as a homogeneous group, and about the trajectory of Shakespeare's "final years," these issues remain unresolved. Thus it should be useful to review once more the historical documents that deal with Blackfriars, bearing in mind of course that such documents do not themselves "reveal" events. They present indications from which historians construe events, and these indications are in turn configured by the interpreter to fit the narrative he or she has espoused.

Admitting to these conceptual difficulties, I nevertheless wish to offer new observations about when the King's Servants began presenting plays at the Blackfriars location, and also about their motivation for moving there. However tentative my conclusions, they are meant to prompt a reassessment of a still frequently held critical assumption that in starting a second playing place, the King's Servants were able in 1608 to envisage the kind of theatrical situation that would characterize the London scene from, say, 1615 to 1642, when the Blackfriars and other private playhouses replaced the public theaters in prestige.

I move first to the question of when the King's Servants began playing at the Blackfriars because it is from the context of a proposed initial date that one generally speculates as to why, in fact, they began playing there at all. I would like to approach this matter by reviewing briefly the situation preceding the move, adding my own observations to what is otherwise familiar material.

It has long been known that on February 4, 1596, James Burbage had a deed executed by which he purchased space in the old Blackfriars building in the city of London.[2] Nine months later, however, the upper-class residents of the area surrounding the Blackfriars monastery petitioned the Privy Council to stop Burbage from developing this space, complaining that "the said Burbage is now altering and meaneth very shortly to convert and turn the same into a common playhouse."[3] Evidently the Privy Council supported this complaint, for in responding it "forbad the use of the said house for plays."[4] Following this episode Richard Burbage and his brother, Cuthbert (their father now being dead), extended their Blackfriars holdings by additional purchases. In fact, they launched a purchasing program, first buying interest in a property they would possess only after the death of one of the other owners.[5] They then continued to buy space in the Blackfriars structure in 1601, 1610, and 1614.

Thus it is possible that the Burbages at least initially had a long-range plan for Blackfriars that did not involve drama.[6] For it seems likely that the two brothers would be wary of continued resistance by the neighborhood to any future theater enterprise—especially since many of the residents were quite powerful and would, in fact, prevent the establishment of a new playhouse in this area in 1619.[7] Further, Privy Council orders of 1600 and 1601 stipulated the allowed number of playhouses in the city: only two theaters—those two that were already in place. And although in 1602 the acting Servants of the very influential Earl of Worcester would be allowed to open a third playhouse in seeming contravention of the orders, this was to be an exception.[8] Several years later, in 1606, an effort by Martin Slater and Aaron Holland to form a new company complete with new playhouse in London was stopped in its tracks,

Robert Cecil Earl of Salisbury and Secretary to King James acting for the Privy Council.[9]

Moreover, there is additional evidence that despite their purchasing program after 1596, the Burbages held little hope for their own theatrical future at Blackfriars. In 1600, for example, they leased the acting space they could not themselves use to a company that was presumably more acceptable to the neighborhood than an adult group: the Children of the Chapel Royal (to be renamed in 1604 the Children of the Queen's Revels). And although a twenty-one-year period was conventional in such leases, it nonetheless suggests little confidence on the part of the Burbages in the future availability of the Blackfriars to adult companies such as their own Servants of the Lord Chamberlain—especially since the Lord Chamberlain's own name had been on the petition of 1596! A similar attitude is noticeable four years later, in 1604, after the Lord Chamberlain had died, King James had acceded to the throne, and the Burbage company had become the Servants of the King. In that year, the leasees for the children's company—Henry Evans and others—approached the Burbages seeking an early termination of their lease. The fact that the Burbages declined this overture (unless perhaps they were holding out for extraordinary concessions) indicates their continuing sense of the unfeasibility of the location for their own company.

Yet after another four-year period, when the Evans group again sought to renegotiate the lease, the attitude of the Burbages seems to have changed. The troubles of the children's company, prompted when one of their plays criticized the French ambassador during the previous Lent of 1608, had reached a critical juncture. The company was closed down on March 29, 1608, and no relief from this prohibition seemed in sight as the summer began.[10] This stoppage of income forced Evans and his colleagues to re-approach the Burbages, and this time the stricken company was allowed to negotiate a surrender of their now-burdensome lease, thirteen years before its contractual expiration in 1621.

As a consequence of this transaction, as is well known, new leases of the Blackfriars space were executed on Wednesday, August 9, 1608, involving a new syndicate made up of William Shakespeare and five of his fellows among the King's Servants: Richard Burbage, Henry Condell, Thomas Evans, John Heminges, and William Sly. This syndicate became the new lease-holders of the playing space *owned* by Richard Burbage, himself the chief actor of the

King's Servants, and his brother Cuthbert.[11] And it is these transactions that configure the Blackfriars property as it is associated with Shakespeare.

It has been reasonably conjectured that the "Shakespeare group" (as I prefer to identify it) pooled their funds for the lease because the company planned to make money by presenting its plays at Blackfriars as well as at the Globe. But the key question that then arises is *when* such playing began, and further, whether productions at Blackfriars can be assumed to be the *first* productions of some plays that were performed there.

Conventional dating identifies the summer of 1608 or 1609 as the beginning of performances by the King's Servants at Blackfriars, but difficulties attend this dating. Bubonic plague, which always caused the playhouses to be closed as a precautionary safety measure, had revived in the summer of 1608: plague deaths were at fifty for the week of 28 July. Indeed, the plague death rate was to remain more than fifty per week for a year and a half—until December 14, 1609, in one of the longest plague-breaks of Shakespeare's professional career. Towards the end of December 1609, plague receded sharply for the next seven months: from December 1609 to July 1610. However, in July the disease broke out again in London, once more closing the theaters, which remained shut until December 6, 1610. These particular periods of plague thus would seem to rule out any proposed performance dates immediately following the execution of the new Blackfriars lease on August 9, 1608.[12]

Other narratives would have the King's Servants acting in Blackfriars during these plague periods because of recorded payments by the royal court to them for "private practice" (not in a particular location) during plague. John Heminges, who had annually collected the court moneys due the company from holiday performances since the beginning of James's reign, picked up payment at Whitehall on April 5, 1609, in Lent, for twelve plays presented at court during the preceding winter holidays. Then, twenty days later, Heminges was allotted an extra £40, a gratuity described as "his Majesty's reward for their private practice in the time of infection that thereby they might be enabled to perform their service before his Majesty in Christmas holidays [1608–] 1609." The reference here to "private" play would resurface a year later in a similar warrant for a royal gratuity to the King's Servants. This time Heminges picked up £30 for the King's Servants "being restrained from public playing within the City of London in the time of infection during the space of six weeks in which time they practiced privately for his Majesty's service."[13]

These remarks, however tantalizing, do not constitute proof of performances at Blackfriars since the venue for "private playing" could have been anywhere, including a Globe closed to the public, if stage space was the only desideratum. Thus some scholars have looked for further guidance in a later litigation concerning the Blackfriars in 1612. A particularly important extract from the depositions of John Heminges and Richard Burbage (responding to Edward Kirkham's litigation about the Blackfriars playing area) is dated November 2, 1612. It states in characteristically tedious—but nonetheless helpful—legal language:

> And the said John Heminges for himself further answereth and saith that he, the defendant, hath for the space of four years last past or thereabouts, [summer 1608–November 2, 1612?] had received and as yet doth receive a certain share or portion of such profits as did, or doth arise by such plays and interludes as were and are played in the said playhouse by virtue of a demise of some part of the said playhouse granted unto him by the said other defendant, Richard Burbage, sythence the surrender of the foresaid lease surrendered by the said Henry Evans, as aforesaid.[14]

The strength of this statement as chronological guide is diluted, however, not only by the relevance of theater prohibitions occasioned by plague, but also by the implications of a second (earlier) suit. This litigation (reproduced long ago by C. W. Wallace) was between Robert Keysar and the new syndicate leasing Blackfriars.[15] Entered in 1610, this action is significant not because of Keysar's own complaints and allegations—whether true or not—but because of the responses of Richard and Cuthbert Burbage. That is, they seem to accept *as given* some of Keysar's statements. The complainant sketches a background with which the respondents, counterarguing, do not disagree. Thus it is obviously in these areas of agreement that one may look for the most historically reliable account, notwithstanding other hermeneutic problems, such as the general reliance by all respondents on individual recollections.

The suit, which was begun February 8, 1610 (English N.S.), and is last heard of on June 18 of the same year, states that the Shakespeare group, since the surrender of the Evans lease, has "continued in possession for a long time and made profit thereof to themselves to the full value of fifteen hundred pounds"—a sixth of which Keysar says he is entitled to. Keysar, obviously regarding the interval between August 1608, when the syndicate took up Evans's demise, and the moment of his own complaining (February 1610) "a long time," names a sum of money that, if it accurately reflects the syndicate's profits, may be as important an indication of the starting date of performances at Blackfriars as Keysar's mere statement about duration.

Why? Because, if my figures for plague for the eighteen-month interval between August 1608 and February 1610 are accurate, it seems that playing could not have gone forward at such a rate as to garner the large amount—£1500—that Keysar stipulates. Indeed, by February 1610, playing could barely have started up again anywhere in the city.

Cold and dry weather had finally driven plague deaths down from fifty-one to twenty-eight per week for the report of December 7, 1609—below the number (thirty or forty) at which playhouses were permitted to reopen.[16] But whether the playhouses opened immediately after being closed since summer 1608 is questionable. The London Council, or the Privy Council of England, for that matter, would have seen this figure of twenty-eight plague deaths in the frightening context of seventeen consecutive, unabated months of plague—the longest continuous plague seizure of Shakespeare's professional lifetime. So the question they presumably would have asked is: "do we permit public gatherings again, right now, on December 7, solely because plague deaths are suddenly down from 51 to 28 per week?" Obviously a more prudent course would have been to wait and see what the next weekly figures might bring. What happened is that deaths declined from twenty-eight to twenty-three, held at twenty-three for the following week, then rose to thirty-nine for the week of December 28, 1609. Weekly variances after that, to the end of January 1610, were: thirty-two; nineteen; thirty-one, and twenty-five. I suggest that the playhouses were kept closed all December and perhaps through January. For as previously mentioned, the authorities knew what plague figures were typical (and undisturbing) for this time of year—five to eight plague deaths per week—not nineteen or seventeen.[17]

No doubt, as Keysar contended, the Shakespeare group had been "in possession" for eighteen months, but "possession" is not necessarily synonymous with "playing." Thus the answer of the syndicate to Keysar's contention about their profits seems important here. Agreeing that the surrender of the lease by Evans was accomplished "about the tenth of August last past" [presumably a reference to August 10, *1608*, not 1609] and that they "have entered into, occupied and enjoyed the said great hall or play house and taken the benefit and profit thereof," they "utterly deny" the series of related allegations. They deny, most importantly, that they "have made fifteen hundred pounds profit of and by the premises at any time since the said surrender made as aforesaid." In turn, Keysar, the complainant, though taking issue with many of the syndicate's denials, no longer brings up the £1500 or any claims about its earnings in Blackfriars since 1608. Again, although "possessing," "enjoying," and "occupying" (words used in the Keysar suit about the relationship of the Shakespeare group to the Blackfriars space) are words clearly pointing to ownership, it does not necessarily follow that plays were staged at Blackfriars between 1608 and 1610.

Thus in the end the most significant indicator in this suit is its date. For it coincides suspiciously with the time—January/February 1610—when London theaters may again have been permitted to open because of the recession of plague—and when money was now being made through play performance everywhere. However, since the document itself is at best ambiguous, I should like to reassess the issues it raises by taking a look at the shape of other events in the summer of 1608, when the Shakespeare group re-acquired the Blackfriars lease from Evans.

In his complaints against the Shakespeare group, Keysar had sketched a situation that they did not dispute, even elaborating upon it in the thumbnail stage history of 1608–10 that formed part of their own response. There were, they said, "but only three private playhouses in the City of London, the one of which being in the Blackfriars and in the hands of these defendants . . . one other being in the Whitefriars and in the hands of the said complainant [Keysar] himself . . . and the third near St. Paul's Church then being in the hands of one Master Pierce, but then unused for a playhouse." For, the responding document explained, "that there might be a cessation of playing and plays to be acted in the said house near St. Paul's Church," those operating the Whitefriars playhouse (including Keysar) had agreed with Pierce to pay him £20 per year to *refrain* from putting on plays at St. Paul's. But then "these defendants [the Shakespeare group] afterwards coming to play at their said house in the Blackfriars," and the Keysar group now "perceiving that the benefit of the said cessation of plays at Paul's" was likely "to turn as well to the benefit of these defendants and their company as to the benefit" of the Keysar group itself, the latter asked Burbage et al. to split with them the costs of what was called this "dead-rent." For their part, the Shakespeare group claimed that they indeed *had* assumed their share of this dead-rent, so it seems that both accounts paint an identical picture of the theatrical situation at the time that the Shakespeare syndicate took possession of the Blackfriars lease.

But the picture here requires even more contextualization. In July 1608, the Whitefriars playing place alluded to above—located in the precincts of the old Carmelite monastery, between Fleet St and the Thames, just west of Water Lane in the old monastic buildings—was occupied not by Keysar's group but by a little-understood company, the Children of the King's Revels, a group apparently activated in March 1608, several months before acquisition of Blackfriars by the Shakespeare syndicate.[18] This group, which included Martin Slater, the actor, Michael Drayton, the poet, and Lording Barry, the dramatist, would have been occupying Whitefriars at the time that the Shakespeare group took possession of their lease. Thus the syndicate would not have made agreement with Keysar about "dead-rent" paid to St. Paul's in August 1608, because at that point the Children of the King's Revels, not Keysar's boys, would have been in Whitefriars.[19]

Indeed, during this same August it appears that Keysar's boys were out of town at Leicester, playing there on August 21 as "Children of the [Queen's] Revels." They surfaced again as an entity when the group acted three plays at court in the winter of 1608–9 and were paid (Keysar being payee) as "Children of the Blackfriars,"[20] perhaps because they were subleasing from the Shakespeare group. A year later, however, the Crown would attest to the Children's new location when they were re-patented on January 4, 1610, as the Children of the Queen's Revels, with their playing place specified as "the Whitefriars in the suburbs of our City of London."[21] Indeed, in the following May of that year they would be paid (Keysar again being payee) for having presented five plays recently as "the Children of the Whitefriars."

Because Whitefriars was not a "working" location for Keysar's group (the Children of the Queen's Revels) until they could legitimately *play* there and because the company would continue, as we have seen, to style itself "the Children of Blackfriars" through the winter of 1608–9, their move *out* of the Blackfriars space must have been subsequent to the holiday season of 1608–9. Just when, it is difficult to determine. The Keysar litigation seems to describe the entrance of the Shakespeare syndicate in the midst of an ongoing situation. "These defendants" countered the syndicate, "afterwards *coming to play* [italics added] at their said house in the Blackfriars and the said Rossiter [of the Keysar group] perceiving that the benefit of the said cessation of plays at Paul's did or was likely to turn as well to the benefit of these defendants and their company as to the benefit of the said complainant [Keysar, now at Whitefriars] . . . Rossiter came unto these defendants or some of them and entreated them . . . to bear and pay one half of the charge of the said 20 pounds,"[22] to be sent to Paul's yearly as the dead-rent. The wording here obviously indicates that the King's Servants began playing subsequent to the patenting of the new Whitefriars group as Children of the Queen's Revels on January 4, 1610.[23]

To summarize thus far: although the Shakespeare group executed their lease in August 1608, it would appear that they were not playing at Blackfriars until some point after January 1610; prior to this time, Keysar's boys could have continued to use the Blackfriars name, and may also have been playing there with the syndicate's permission—we do not know when the company stopped playing at Blackfriars. Further complicating this series of events, moreover, are the plague closings during 1609, as noted above, so that the beginning of performances at Blackfriars by the King's Servants still remains a vexed question.[24] The question cannot be resolved even by the title pages of plays published subsequent to August 1608, for I find no indication of Blackfriars provenance for a play by the King's Servants until the 1625 quarto of Beaumont and Fletcher's *The Scornful Lady*, nor, to my knowledge, do any prologues mention Blackfriars during the remainder of Shakespeare's lifetime. This hardly means, of course, that the King's Servants did not perform at Blackfriars in the second decade of the seventeenth century, but the scarcity of such reference should recommend scholarly caution. Thus it is fair to say that casual conjectures about the King's Servants beginning to play at the Blackfriars in 1608–9 are not, by today's critical lights, useful. Any search for beginnings must work backwards from 1611 (N.S.), the year for which I have found the first record clearly indicating that plays were being performed in the Blackfriars space. This reference is to be found in Lionel Cranfill's cash-book: "January 10, for going to a play at Blackfriars, 7s."[25]

These remarks on date may be concluded, then, as follows.

Plague returned to London in July 1608, closing the playhouses. Then the Shakespeare group took up the Evans lease of Blackfriars on August 9, 1608.[26] However, Keysar's and Evans's group, the Children of the Queen's Revels, continued to present plays at court during Christmas 1608–9 as "the Children of Blackfriars." Then plague kept the playhouses closed through 1609, the King's Servants receiving a gratuity from Court for private practice in plague time. It began to taper off in December 1609 and certainly in January 1610. In this same month Keysar and Evans received the patent for their boys' company to play at Whitefriars. On February 8, 1610, Keysar brought suit against the Burbage group, recounting various of the foregoing events of 1609. In March 1610 the King's Servants again received a plague-gratuity from Court for practice during the previous winter for the holiday performances. The spring of 1610, after Easter on April 8, must have seen normal playing at the Globe and at the other public and private playhouses in and around London. Indeed, Prince Lewis Frederick of Wurttemberg went to the Globe (not, interestingly, to the Blackfriars) on Monday, April 30, to see *Othello*.[27]

This late estimate for the beginning of regular play performances at the Blackfriars (Christmas "practices" aside) makes problematic the idea that most of Shakespeare's final comedies were originally designed for the Blackfriars playing space. *Pericles* was probably first acted at the Globe, not Blackfriars, in the spring of 1608. *Cymbeline* and *Winter's Tale* were seen at the Globe in May 1611 by Simon Forman, while *The Tempest* was performed at court in the Christmas holidays of 1611–12,[28] a period that includes the January in which Cranfill paid to go to a play at Blackfriars. Since the Blackfriars was demonstrably available for performance only in spring 1610 when plague had ceased, future argument about the relationship of Shakespeare's final comedies to Blackfriars must pay closer attention to plays other than *The Tempest*, whose dating clearly coincides with playing at the Blackfriars.

Such future study, finally, will also need to cope with a second question to which this essay can return only briefly. What was the purpose (insofar as it may be known) of the Shakespeare syndicate in acquiring this playing space? As we have seen, there were no obvious reasons for the Burbages to believe that the residents of the area would be any more sympathetic to a new theater in their neighborhood in 1608 than they had been twelve years before; moreover, there were other ways to dispose of the Blackfriars. One recalls in this connection the systematic Burbage purchasing of *various* properties in Blackfriars that seems to conform to the usual approach of property buyers there, that is, turning spaces into apartments for wealthier residents (such as those who had signed the petition in 1596) whose in-town houses were to be found throughout this area of the city. A real estate venture is, then, one alternative mode for profiting from this property that may have interested the Burbages.

But what might have been the advantages of moving into a new playhouse at this time, despite the prospect of neighborhood resistance? Was a playhouse attractive because Blackfriars, an exclusive, expensive liberty, was exempt from City jurisdiction and thus "safer" for acting, even immune to plague closings—a common assumption in analysis about Shakespeare's professional career? This particular scenario, I would argue, is not a realistic one. For although the Blackfriars area was still connected with the Crown, this protection was soon to disappear, a fact of which Burbage and his fellows cannot have been ignorant. On September 9, 1608, barely a month after the Shakespeare syndicate acquired their lease, a new charter would formally extend the jurisdiction of the City of London to *include* Blackfriars. Thus the Blackfriars might no longer offer protection from the City authorities.[29] Further, this question of whether a Blackfriars acting place could afford exemption from plague closings would be clearly settled in the fall in a dispute involving Whitefriars.

Whitefriars, an area legally and historically comparable to Blackfriars, was yielded to the City by the Crown at the same time as was Blackfriars. During this general period, as previously observed, the public theaters remained closed by plague: on August 9, 1608, when the Burbage Blackfriars syndicate was formed, the weekly bill of mortality showed seventy deaths from plague. Several months later, on October 19, 1608, plague was still raging and Shakespeare's troupe was (significantly) playing in Coventry instead of in London at the Globe. But in this same October, some arrests were made. Those jailed were theater people, presumably members of the mysterious Children of the King's Revels who were occupying Whitefriars. The committal is dated November 17, 1608.

Item. William Pollard and Rice Gwynn were by this Court committed to the jail of Newgate there to remain during the pleasure of this Court, for that they yesterday last suffered a stage play to be publicly acted in the Whitefriars during the time of the present infection contrary to his Majesty's late proclamation.[30]

Clearly, these former liberties of Whitefriars and Blackfriars were not to be refuges for actors who wanted to perform in plague time. Nor were Shakespeare and his fellows trying to use Blackfriars in this manner. They obviously understood the situation, even if Pollard and Gwynn did not.[31]

Nevertheless, other hypotheses concerning the attraction of Blackfriars as a playing place remain. One influential factor may have been the weather. Le Roy LaDurie's well-known study of the "little ice age" in Europe has perhaps encouraged unrealistic claims about the period in which Shakespeare lived; commenting on H. H. Lamb's *Climate History and the Modern World* (1982), LaDurie observed that "around 1600, the Alpine glaciers crushed the most exposed hamlets around Chamonix, marking the start of the new seventeenth-century cold spells."[32] The worst of these glacier advances would actually occur in the 1690's, however, and thus do not affect Shakespeare's lifetime. Nevertheless, the fact is that weather had emerged as something of a problem, at least in the winter of 1607–8, before the summer in which the Blackfriars changed hands. The cold was unprecedented since the late 1590s. Thick ice covered the Thames in December and January, even causing damage to London Bridge. Thus the idea of an enclosed playhouse for winter may have come to seem attractive to Shakespeare and his fellows. Certainly James Wright's *Historia Histrionica* (1669) would later observe that

> Before the wars there were in being all these playhouses at the same time. The Blackfriars and Globe on the Bankside: a winter and summer house belonging to the same company called the "King's Servants."[33]

Distinguishing between seasons does not seem to have been necessary for Shakespeare and his fellows between 1593 and 1606, but it might well have become so as the "little ice age" began to make itself felt.

Still, in August 1608 there were no conspicuous theatrical successes for the King's Servants to emulate at Blackfriars. If the Children of the Queen's Revels had been successful there before the Crown forbad them to play in spring 1608, the authorities' tolerance of the company probably resided in the fact that the players were boys, not adults, and boy companies were generally administered less strictly. Thus the purpose behind the Blackfriars reacquisition may have been primarily preservative and speculative. For example, the group avers, in one of its responses to Keysar's litigation that Henry Evans, the lessee of the space, not only was paying £40 yearly in rent but had additionally posted a £400 bond as guarantee of regular payment and of repairs and maintenance of the building. In this connection, "the said premises lay then and had long lain void and without use for plays, whereby the same became not only burdensome and unprofitable" to Evans "but also ran far into decay for want of reparations done in and upon the premises." So the Burbages not only communicated with Evans "for the satisfaction of the bond," apparently now "forfeited" for non-payment of rent, but also "for the repairing of the premises."[34]

The decay of the premises combined with winter weather of gradually increasing severity may then have been significant factors in encouraging the syndicate to bring adult players—their own company and possibly others—to the Blackfriars space. Certainly there must have been additional motives, but they are not by any means self-evident. What is clear is that narratives that assume a straightforward linkage between the "romances" and the "new Blackfriars playing space" fail to do justice to the complexities of the historical record. They may, in fact, skew our approach to larger issues, such as the internal dynamics of the theatrical industry itself and the trajectory of Shakespeare's career within it.

Notes

1. For important studies of Blackfriars, see G. E. Bentley, *The Jacobean and Caroline Stage*, vol. 6 (Oxford: The Clarendon Press, 1968), 3–45; Herbert Berry, *Shakespeare's Playhouses* (New York: AMS Press, 1987), 45–74, and most recently his section of *English Professional Theatre, 1530–1660*, ed. Glynne Wickham, Herbert Berry, and William Ingram (Cambridge: The University Press, 2000), Part Three, Ch. 30, 501–30.

2. See James O. Hallliwell-Phillipps, *Outlines of the Life of Shakespeare*, vol. 1 (London: 1881–87), 299.

3. See Wickham, 567–68.

4. See *Malone Society Collections*, vol. 1, 90, and E. K. Chambers, *The Elizabethan Stage*, vol. 2 (Oxford: The Clarendon Press, 1923), 508ff.

5. See *MSC*, vol. 2, 70–76.

6. The assumption that the Burbages were always interested in the Blackfriars primarily because of its performance potential has been virtually unchallenged for

more than fifty years, from E. K. Chambers, *ES*, vol. 2, 508ff, to S. Schoenbaum, *William Shakespeare: A Documentary Life* (New York: Oxford University Press, 1975), 213.

7. For a description of this later opposition, see H. N. Hillebrand, *The Child Actors*, in *University of Illinois Studies in Language and Literature*, 11 (1926): 154–56.

8. See Leeds Barroll, "Defining 'Dramatic Documents,'" *Medieval and Renaissance Drama in England* 9 (1997): 112–26.

9. See Cecil Papers 197/91 [e]: *not* 199/91 (2) as per *Calendar of the MSS. of the Marquess of Salisbury* (London: HMC, 1883–1976), vol. 17, 234.

10. See Chambers, *ES*, vol. 2, 53–54.

11. Ibid., 213–14.

12. The plague figures for this time may be found in John Bells's *London's Remembrancer* (London, 1665–66), sigs. B3-B4. In printing Bell's figures for 1608–10, F.P. Wilson (*The Plague in Shakespeare's London* [Oxford: Oxford University Press, 1953], 186–87) distorts the plague configurations somewhat by omitting winter seasons. (I cite the 1963 paperback reprint of Wilson's 1927 book because the reprint has added material not in the original edition.) Other indications of plague in this period may be found in my own study (see n. 17 below).

13. For these two documents see *MSC*, vol. 6, 47–48. These gratuities seem to support the notion of plague prohibition up to December or January 1610 since both payments cover Christmas seasons for the years 1608–9 and 1609–10, but other indications may be found elsewhere. Further, since the sums are different in each case, and since £30 was mentioned in connection with six weeks, making the gratuity rate £5 per week, may one assume that the former gratuity, £40, implies payment for eight weeks?

14. See F. G. Fleay, *Chronicle History of the London Stage, 1599–1642* (London: 1890), 238.

15. See C. W. Wallace, "Shakespeare and his London Associates," *University Studies of the University of Nebraska* 10.4 (1910): 76–100.

16. See *The Calendar of the State Papers . . . of Venice* (London: HMSO, 1930), vol. 11, 401.

17. For a detailed discussion of these matters, see Leeds Barroll, *Politics, Plague, and Shakespeare's Theater* (Ithaca: Cornell University Press, 1991), esp. Ch. 6., 172–239.

18. For the Whitefriars group, see the suit: *Androwes vs. Slater*, 1609, Chancery, reproduced in J. Greenstreet, *The Whitefriars Theater in the Time of Shakespeare*, (London: 1888): 272–84. See also Chambers, *ES*, vol. 2, 64–68; and Hillebrand, 220–36.

19. See Wallace, 350–55. The Children of the King's Revels seem to have faded as a company later in 1608 and is not heard from again until 1615 when a new group bears their name. See Chambers, *ES*, vol. 2, 64–68.

20. See *MSC*, vol. 6, 47.

21. See *MSC*, vol. 1.3, 271.

22. See Wallace, 355.

23. See Wickham, 561.

24. Irwin Smith, *Shakespeare's Blackfriars Playhouse* (New York: New York University Press, 1964), 248–49, has also made this point. I first alluded to it in

"The Chronology of Shakespeare's Jacobean Plays," in *Essays on Shakespeare,* ed. Gordon Ross Smith, 115–62 (University Park: Pennsylvania State University Press, 1965).

25. See Lionel Cranfill's Cashbook, *Sackville MSS* (London: HMSO, 1940), vol. 1, 232.

26. See E. K. Chambers, *William Shakespeare: A Study of Facts and Problems* (Oxford: The Clarendon Press, 1930), vol. 2, 62–64.

27. See W. B. Rye, *England as Seen by Foreigners* (London, 1865), 61. The Prince dated English style since he placed April 30 on "Lundi."

28. See Barroll, *Politics*, 192–206.

29. See Chambers, *ES*, vol. 2, 480; 511.

30. *MSC*, vol. 2.3, 318–19.

31. Susan P. Cerasano has observed to me that the privileged status of the Blackfriars area may have been more complicated than is generally realized—even after the jurisdiction was assumed by the City.

32. See E. Le Roy LaDurie, *Times of Feast, Times of Famine*, tr. Barbara Bray and issued in paperback (New York: Doubleday & Co., 1988) with an "after word" (317ff.), 312–13.

33. However, Wright could have been referring to Caroline stage practices. He lived from 1643 to 1719.

34. See Wallace, 247.

REVIEW ARTICLE

Poets into Frenchmen: Timothy Hampton on Literature and National Sentiment in Renaissance France

Paul Cohen

Historians of France since Alexis de Tocqueville have been busily excavating the origins of the modern French nation.[1] Like scholars of other national histories, students of France have looked to the past in their efforts to make sense of the contemporary national experience. Beyond France, political scientists, sociologists, and historians have sought to understand the political characteristics of nation-states, the ideological components of nationalism, and the social histories of national communities in general. They have devoted particular attention to what we might call the cultural history of the nation, analyzing the character of national sentiment, teasing out its historical sources, and examining its role in the formation of the modern nation-state.[2]

Traditional narratives of French history recount how the state invented and in turn disseminated over many centuries a French national identity in order to unite a heterogeneous population and consolidate its own authority. Putting to use concepts like "nation-building" and "state formation," scholars of this school see the emergence of nationalism and the nation-state as a top-down process, imposed from above by an increasingly powerful state on a sometimes resistant populace over centuries in order to construct the nation-state. The gradual coalescence of France's culturally and linguistically diverse regions into a larger imagined national community was in large part the fruit of royal efforts to elaborate and disseminate a wider French sense of belonging.[3] The prominent French historian Pierre Nora summarizes eloquently this vision of French history:

Among all the old European nations, France is certainly the one for which the decisive role of the state was the most precocious, the most constant and the most constitutive, to the point of becoming almost immemorial and uninterrupted in the collective consciousness. . . . the [nation] for which the will to persist and assertion of unity came from above. . . . France is a "state-centered" nation. It has only maintained a self-consciousness through political life. . . . Hence the guiding and protective role of the State . . . were sufficient to cause a community consciousness and a national sentiment to crystallize.[4]

Over the past two decades historians have debated the history of French nationhood with renewed vigor. A number of historians have focused particular attention on the sixteenth and seventeenth centuries in order to call into question important features of such views. Traditionally, various aspects of early modern French history, like the wars of conquest of François I (reign 1515–1547) and Louis XIV (reign 1643–1715), the assertive policies of the cardinal-ministers Richelieu and Mazarin in the early decades of the seventeenth century, the imposition of an 'absolutist' monarchy under Louis XIV, the 1539 royal edict of Villers-Cotterêts that required the use of French rather than Latin in the king's law courts, and the creation of the French Academy (1635) charged with perfecting and promoting the French language were held up as evidence for a coherent, long-term centralizing project that set down the lineaments of the modern nation-state.[5] Critics of these interpretations have instead emphasized the limits on royal authority in the early modern period. Not only was the early modern French state considerably weaker than its modern counterpart, they maintain, it was fundamentally different in kind, a patchwork of dynastic imperatives, diverse local legal traditions, myriad languages and cultures, overmighty noble grandees, and assertive provincial institutions. Such approaches highlight the considerable distance that separates early modern polities from modern nation-states, in both their capacity to project authority and indeed their very nature.[6] Other critics emphasize the historical specificities that set older forms of national sentiment apart from the more recent nationalist ideologies that emerged during the nineteenth century.[7] In the French context, recent work has shown that vigorous local identities coexisted with national consciousness, that extensive linguistic diversity was accepted as a normal and even praiseworthy feature of France, and that people conceived of their political loyalties as a form of personal fidelity to the king rather than subjection to an abstract state or nation. In an important recent contribution to the historiography of French nationalism, for example, David Bell distinguishes between "national sentiment" and "nationalism." National sentiment, a feature of French culture in one form or another since the medieval period, constitutes a sense of belonging to "a group of people sharing certain important, binding qualities" that might include religious belief, language, personal loyalties to a dynastic ruler, or a shared history. Nationalism, on the other hand, represents a specifically modern ideology born of the French Revolution, "a political program which has as its goal not merely to praise, or defend, or strengthen a nation, but actively to construct one, casting its human raw material into a fundamentally new form."[8]

The study of literary sources has played an important role in the analysis of national identity in the early modern period. The significance princes themselves assigned to the world of letters, illustrated by their ample patronage of humanist erudites, poets, printers, theater companies, and literary academies, suggests that literature provided a central arena for the construction of early modern national identity. Scholars have studied various aspects of the literary history of the nation: the sociology of literary production, reconstructing the ways in which men of letters operated within patronage networks that tied them to the king or powerful figures at court; the use of literary forms as political propaganda; the emergence of national vernacular literatures conceived in self-conscious competition with rival national literatures; and the consequences of the politicization of writing for formal aspects of literary creation.[9]

Timothy Hampton's recent book, *Literature and the Nation in the Sixteenth Century: Inventing Renaissance France*, represents an ambitious contribution to the study of French national identity from a literary perspective.[10] Through close readings of texts by five French writers, François Rabelais, Marguerite de Navarre, Joachim Du Bellay, Michel de Montaigne, and Madame de Lafayette, Hampton explores how early modern French authors sought to come to terms with and write about the changing national community they inhabited. For Hampton, the emergence of new forms of nationhood during the Renaissance, as well as the successive crises provoked by the Protestant Reformation and the Wars of Religion, challenged older ways of thinking about France as well as older literary genres, and obliged writers to invent fresh genres in order to write about changing political, social, and cultural realities in new ways. In their search for new ways to represent a changing France, these authors actively contributed to the formation of new types of national sentiment. While Hampton's rich study also speaks to a series of other literary and cultural problems, including the history of literary genres, the problem of language in literary representation, and the representation of the self in literature, it is nonetheless squarely in dialogue with current interdisciplinary efforts to understand the history of national identity. I propose in this article to consider Hampton's contribution to the history of early modern French national sentiment in light of recent work on this question.

*

In *Literature and Nation*, Hampton dissects the literary consequences of political and religious crisis. For Hampton, religious conflicts, the Habsburg-Valois wars that opposed France and Spain, the threat to Christendom posed by the Ottoman Empire, and the shock of cultures provoked by the European discovery of the Americas challenged French men and women's very sense of their own identity during the sixteenth century. Faced with new political, cultural, and religious realities to which older literary genres were increasingly ill adapted—notably epic and medieval romance—, writers were forced to invent new vernacular literary forms—the novel and the essay—in order to depict their evolving universe. For Hampton, authors faced these problems most intensely when they attempted to write about France's contested political, cultural, and confessional margins. Their efforts to describe in language the physical and conceptual frontiers of a rapidly changing nation exemplify the complex relationship between politics and the process of representation. During the Renaissance, contemporaries' narrative and linguistic tools proved increasingly incapable of describing France itself, and efforts to do so generated internal tensions within literary narratives, slippages in language, and failures of the logics of genre. Indeed, for Hampton, to write coherently about a France in flux during the Renaissance was nothing less than impossible: "One cannot 'write' the French nation because, haunted as it is by discontinuity, violence, and fragmentation, it escapes representation" (xi). Renaissance French writing, then, is the fruit of a literary crisis itself born of political crisis.[11]

Hampton's book presents a series of close readings of early modern attempts to write about groups outside the national community, each illustrating how the literary encounter with the "Other" during the Renaissance generated repeated crises of genre. An introductory chapter demonstrates the problematic nature of early modern writing about France. In chapter two, Hampton examines Panurge's account of his escape from enslavement among the Ottoman Turks in Rabelais's *Pantagruel*.[12] He analyzes how Rabelais, juggling the Christian injunction to love one's neighbor with fear of the infidel, must resort (consciously or unconsciously) to "rhetorical distortion" in order to describe the Turks.[13] Chapter three turns to the Picrocholine War episode and the description of the Abbey of Theleme in Rabelais's *Gargantua*, arguing that Rabelais here displays the incompatibility of the discourse of Christian humanist charity with the martial rhetoric of sixteenth-century European warfare.[14] Chapter four compares how French territory and the changing relationships between crown and aristocracy are represented in both Marguerite de Navarre's story of Floride and Amadour in the *Heptaméron* and Madame de Lafayette's *La Princesse de Clèves*.[15] Chapter five looks at how Du Bellay invests "France" with meaning as he constructs a poetics of exile while serving his patron Jean Du Bellay in Rome.[16] The final chapter analyzes Montaigne's essay, "Of Coaches." Hampton argues that Montaigne, reflecting on the European conquest of the Americas, plays with the essay form in order to represent both the Amerindian and Spanish points of view, thus endowing himself with a distinctly French identity which in turn makes it possible to criticize the Spanish.[17] Taken together, these case studies attempt "to trace the pre-history of the relationship between secular literary culture and national identity in France" by examining the connections between "new images of the nation and new forms of secular literary representation" (x) in the early modern period.

Hampton is no newcomer to the relationship between literature and politics. In *Writing from History: The Rhetoric of Exemplarity in Renaissance Literature*, a learned and original book that has become an essential text for students of Renaissance letters, Hampton constructs a history of the philosophy of reading in sixteenth-century Europe. The humanist vision of reading as an exemplary activity, grounded in the notion that the study of the writings of Antiquity served above all to furnish reliable models for political action and personal conduct, made reading an inescapably ideological act. The very conceptual underpinnings of exemplarity depended on specific visions of history—the idea that the classical past was a golden age worthy of imitation—, of politics—the social life of an organic, consensual community united by a common vision of the good life—, and of the self—called upon to appropriate classical notions of virtue. The historical circumstances of sixteenth-century Europe challenged this model of reading: the violent confessional divisions which divided post-Reformation Europe destroyed the ideal of a society united by a common conception of virtue; Counter-Reformation Catholicism held up its own set of exemplars which competed with the pagan models drawn from ancient Greece and Rome; and the emergence of an urban commercial economy in Elizabethan England and the decline of the petty noble *hidalgo* class in Spain shook the social position of a traditional aristocracy who grounded their identity in the pursuit of such models of behavior. Humanists' study of the past also paradoxically undermined the Renaissance rhetoric of exemplarity: in their desire to acquire an ever more historicized understanding of antiquity in order to better understand and internalize its lessons, humanists grew increasingly aware of the temporal and cultural distance that separated them from their classical exemplars. Hampton analyzes how Guillaume Budé, Erasmus, Machiavelli, Tasso, Montaigne, Cervantes, and Shakespeare faced the growing problems associated with Renaissance notions of exemplarity. By century's end, exemplarity had collapsed under the weight of these external and internal pressures, and writers were forced to invent new genres like the novel to accommodate new conceptions of virtue, society and the self.[18]

The two works, then, the first on a European-wide scale, the more recent focusing specifically on France, share common concerns: to situate literary texts within wider cultural and historical contexts, to unpack the ideological implications of literary practices, and to consider the mechanisms and consequences of cultural change. And like Hampton's first book, *Literature and Nation* offers an abundance of fresh and insightful readings. His discussions of the fragmentation of language in Rabelais's writing—how Panurge's invocation of "dogs" to describe the Turks somehow materializes as real dogs who chase him upon his escape—contribute to a larger debate on the status of language in Rabelais's work.[19] Hampton's remarks on the story of Amadour and Floride in Marguerite de Navarre's *Heptaméron* show the importance of reading the canons of literary genres like chivalric romance against the collective ideologies of particular social groups like the nobility—extending an argument he initially laid out in *Writing from History* concerning Cervantes's subversion of chivalric and historic exemplarity in *Don Quixote*.[20] His study of Montaigne's shifts in moral perspective points to the urgency of inventing new ways of writing in order to apprehend Amerindian alterity. His analyses demonstrate how confrontation with different kinds of otherness placed stress on Renaissance practices of representation: language, genre, collective identity and the conception of the self.

*

But what of Hampton's larger project to show how literary language can be put to work to construct an imagined national community? Are these problems of representation truly the literary birth pangs of the modern nation-state? What is the precise nature of the political crisis that, according to Hampton, provoked a breakdown of practices of writing? Do the conclusions of recent historiography cautioning against projecting modern conceptions of nationalism and the nation-state into the early modern period support such an approach?

In developing his exploration of literary creation and national sentiment, Hampton takes pains to historicize his analytical categories in an effort to avoid the teleological problems often associated with national histories. Rather than make claims concerning the nature of nationalism itself, he defines his project as the study of an emerging vocabulary with which contemporaries increasingly represented France. This new set of words, concepts, representational techniques and myths made up a rich ideological toolbox from which, beginning in the eighteenth century, inhabitants of France would draw in order to construct French nationalism. Hampton summarizes his aims in the following terms:

> The modern notion of "nationalism" is essentially an invention of the Enlightenment. By contrast, the sense of literary "nationhood" that I explore in this study constitutes a kind of pre-history of the national. . . . the history of nationhood, as a pre-history of nationalism, might be said to involve the struggle to determine language, space, and character, and to define their interaction. My concern is the *literary* (as contrasted with the historiographical, institutional, or iconographic) construction of na-

tionhood. And in literature, this struggle may be traced by studying the representation of community. The literary sense of nationhood involves the way in which literary texts register the conflicts between the different models of community that compete in the emergence of the nation-state. (8–9)

Hampton's subject, then, is not "nationalism," but rather "nationhood"—a distinction akin to that drawn by historians careful to describe French cultural identity in the early modern as "national identity," "national sentiment," or "national consciousness" rather than "nationalism."[21] Borrowing the term "pre-history" from Terence Cave to describe this approach, Hampton adopts a perspective akin to that of scholars who have studied the ways societies construct narratives to explain themselves, and how these same narratives can be put to very different uses later in order to redefine the community.[22] Hampton argues that the elements with which writers like Rabelais, Marguerite de Navarre and Montaigne invested French nationhood should not be seen as the forebears of modern French nationalism, but rather as the cultural raw material from which French writers invented nationalism in the eighteenth and nineteenth centuries. This kind of approach to "the pre-history of nationhood" (45), grounded in careful distinctions between early modern conceptions of the national community and modern nationalism, holds considerable promise. Not only can it shed light on important features of early modern literature, it can also map the cultural materials which would later be rethought and shaped into nationalism.

Hampton, however, does not always succeed in escaping the interpretative dangers of teleology. Throughout his discussion he emphasizes the processes of state-building and territorial expansion as the fundamental structural and determining features of early modern experience. The insistence on "Francis I's attempts to centralize French politics" (11), on the "increasing emphasis on political centralization under Francis I [which] had the effect of beginning to shift power away from the traditional aristocracy and into the hands of a single ruler" (122), on "the centralization of political power attendant on the rise of the modern state" (110), and on "the absolutist state" (228) as the endpoint of his story, makes the expansion of state power and the forward march of the French "nation-state" (110) seem almost relentless. It is also striking that religion is largely absent from Hampton's narrative of the imagining of the national community. He explicitly circumscribes his subject as "secular literary culture," thus excluding works like Agrippa d'Aubigné's Protestant epic of the Wars of Religion, *Les Tragiques*, from consideration—but given the omnipresence of the religious in early modern European societies' definitions of themselves, this choice begs a more rigorous justification.[23]

Such a description oversimplifies the complex nature of the early modern French monarchy: the dizzying variety of local cultures, customs and languages within France; the equally dizzying variety of local legal, fiscal, and administrative regimes; the lack of a permanent standing army; the considerable economic, judicial, and military power of the nobility; the crown's chronic difficulties in raising sufficient taxes to pay expenses; the king's heavy dependance on local elites, provincial institutions and private financiers for everything from keeping order on the ground to covering debts to raising armies; the readiness of these very local elites and institutions to defend their liberties and privileges against the monarchy's encroachments; the imbrication of royal and ecclesiastical authority; the dynastic imperatives of royal policy that equated French interests with those of the king's house; the strength of imperial discourse in royal propaganda; the personal character of the political ties between monarch and subject; and the importance of royal patronage as a tool to win and keep the loyalty of the powerful. There is no question that at certain moments the monarchy succeeded in strengthening its authority. But the history of the crown was not a continuous, uninterrupted process of political consolidation. Rather, it was one shaped by contingency, royal policy's many failures, about-faces, and marked ruptures, and even the monarchy's near collapse during the Wars of Religion.[24] In emphasizing the monarchy's strength and centralization, in privileging the secular over the religious, and in portraying the nobility as an increasingly dominated social class subjugated by the crown, Hampton paints a portrait of French political realities at odds with recent scholarship on the nature of the early modern French polity.

This would be quibbling if such questions did not have their importance for Hampton's case. Sorting out whether it is best to characterize the early modern state as "centralized," "absolutist," a "Renaissance monarchy" as J. Russell Major would have it, a "composite monarchy" in J. H. Elliott's words, a "dynastic state" to believe Guy Rowland, and a "polyglot empire" for James Collins risks degenerating into a dull scholastic exercise in denomination for idle historians.[25] What is at stake here is not so much a question of terminology, but rather of recognizing the historical specificities of the institutions and political culture of early modern France. In certain cases these questions are central to Hampton's argument. He assigns the increase of royal authority, and the concomitant emergence of new political ideologies, the consolidation of national territory, and the decline of the aristocracy, a central causal role in his analysis. These are the very political, ideological, and social transformations that, according to Hampton, challenged early modern French writers to renew their practices of representation. These are also precisely the same processes that recent historians have called us to historicize carefully. To attribute ahistorical meanings to specific aspects of early modern political life is to run the risk of misreading particular texts.

*

Consider the role Hampton's presentation of the changing nature of kingship plays in his reading of Lafayette's *Princesse de Clèves*. For Hampton, the sixteenth century constitutes a moment of transition when the institutions and ideologies of an older medieval monarchy, steeped in feudalism and the trappings of chivalry, gave way to the cold political realities of a more centralized, rational form of government. Hampton sees the tension between these two visions of France as the key to reading the novel's account of Henri II's death in a jousting accident at court in 1559. Hampton argues that "Henry's tragic death in a tournament is an event born of the anachronistic custom of sixteenth-century monarchs playing at being romance heroes" (138), suggesting that such practices were already somewhat out of place in Henri II's time. Lafayette, writing over a century after the events she describes took place, reconstructs a past world whose values and culture are no longer those of her own time. Lafayette resolves this difficulty by inscribing "into the form of the book an ironic split between past and present, between the present of composition and the past of the events narrated" (138). The text oscillates back and forth between a voice modeled on history-writing on the one hand, and a parody of the language of chivalric romance, evoking France as "a fairyland of gentle kings and wandering knights," on the other:

> The contrast between a chivalric "kingdom" in which the king challenges all comers by posting handbills in every town square (a detail

one can assume to be pure romance in this context) and the more modern term "Etat" suggests the tension within the novel between romance cliché and novelistic observation. (139)

The political and cultural features that separate the court of Lafayette's day from that of Henri II's time, then, manifest themselves in this commingling of novelistic observation and archaic chivalric elements. This generic polysemy suspends Lafayette's story between its realistic form as seventeenth-century court memoire and its "fictions of romance"—indeed, "the novel frames images that are perceived to be exaggerated or untrue." (139)

The trouble is that it is not at all clear from Lafayette's novel that there is anything to be "perceived to be exaggerated or untrue" in her account of Henri II's last tilt. Rather than draw on *Amadis of Gaul* and the conventions of chivalric romance, as Hampton would have it, Lafayette most likely turned to an abundant historical record for her story and its discursive characteristics. There was for example nothing anachronistic about using the term "kingdom" to refer to France in either Henri II or Lafayette's day—indeed, the word was a staple of legal discourse and official royal proclamations through the eighteenth century. And far from pure romance, Henri II *did* in fact publish a handbill to announce that a tournament would be held in Paris to celebrate the recent peace between France and Spain and the marriage between Philip II of Spain and Henri's daughter Élisabeth stipulated by the Treaty of Cateau-Cambrésis. Indeed, such published announcements were far from exceptional in the sixteenth century. The announcement's language is worth reproducing at length, since it tells us much about the cultural world of the high nobility in the sixteenth century:

> After a long, cruel and violent war, during which arms were exercised and put to use in different places with effusion of human blood and the greatly pernicious acts which war produces, and after God by his holy grace, clemency and goodness desired to give peace to this afflicted [part of] Christendom, through a good, sincere and happy Peace, it is more than reasonable that all should make it their duty, with great expressions of joy, pleasure and rejoicing, to praise and celebrate such a great good, and to turn all bitterness and enmities into gentleness and perfect friendships, through the intimate bonds of consanguinity, which are established through the marriages stipulated in the aforementioned Peace agreement, . . . [the king Henri II,] considering that with the events that are planned, arms (today removed from all cruelty

and violence) can and must be put to use with pleasure and utility, by those who wish to prove and to exercise themselves in all virtuous and praiseworthy deeds and acts, makes it known to all Princes, lords, gentlemen, knights and squires following the vocation of arms and desiring to prove themselves in it, in order to incite the young to virtue, and to signal the prowess of the experienced, that in the capital city of Paris, the field is open.[26]

The text conveys the considerable importance Henri II assigned to the public display of his personal martial abilities. Warfare was so central a component of kingly and noble identity that a display of soldierly talents was a perfectly appropriate means to celebrate the coming of peace. The misfortunate Henri was also no exception. Virtually all France's sixteenth-century kings shared his taste for the hunt, the fencing hall, and the jousting list—not to mention the battlefield. Henri's father François I was famously taken prisoner on the field at the French defeat at Pavia in 1525, and Henri IV, hands-on field commander of the Huguenot armies during the Wars of Religion, was probably Europe's last monarch to personally lead cavalry charges. Indeed, when the swaggering Valois are compared with their staid fifteenth-century predecessors, it could be argued that the reputedly modernizing Renaissance monarchs made their court *more* "chivalric" than it had been a century before. The details Lafayette furnishes concerning the joust could therefore be seen as entirely consistent with novelistic description, rather than an intrusion of a chivalric literary mode.

This feature of sixteenth-century kingship does not necessarily contradict the basic outline of Hampton's argument: the coexistence of novelistic and chivalric language in the *Princesse de Clèves* might after all simply constitute literary traces of the historical transformations which had rendered chivalry anachronistic by the late seventeenth century. The differences setting Lafayette's world apart from Henri II's, however, may not have been quite as important as Hampton suggests. While it is certainly true that no French king jousted again after Henri II, and none led their horses into bloody melees after Henri IV, both Louis XIII and Louis XIV learned to ride expertly, to handle a sword, and to hunt like their predecessors, and both personally traveled to battlefields to supervise operations. More importantly, perhaps, both also continued to be represented as valorous warriors by their propagandists in paint, verse, and prose, demonstrating the persistence of traditional military values in royal ideology.[27] It is entirely unclear that Lafayette or her readers would have understood the 1559 tournament in quite the way Hampton suggests.

This aspect of early modern monarchy is developed in another text considered in *Literature and Nation*, Rabelais's recounting of the Picrocholine War in *Gargantua*. Hampton sees the contrast between this episode and the Abbey of Theleme description of an ideal humanist Christian community that concludes the work as a means both to endorse the humanist condemnation of the scandal of war between Christians and to expose this critique's limitations. Hampton reads the Picrocholine War as an allegory for the Valois-Habsburg conflicts, "an epic of 'self-defense'" in which "the themes of French patriotism are articulated through the depiction of a territory in danger" and the mobilization of "a project of national defense" (73), pitting the good Christian king of France against the evil king of Spain. For Hampton, Rabelais's allusions to François I and Charles V's rivalry focuses his text on the ideological conundrum raised by France's nascent nationhood, and the larger challenge faced by humanism as it "seeks to confront the realities of a Europe consisting of newly unified states" (76). An equally persuasive reading would be to recognize that the model of kingship presented by Rabelais looks back to more traditional conceptions of monarchy rather than forward to the exigencies of a "national community" (67) and a territorial state. Consider the quarrel which ignites the Picrocholine War: shepherds from Grandgousier's lands who are guarding the grape harvest ask to purchase bread from bakers on their way to market who hail from a nearby village in Picrochole's lands. Despite the fact that the bakers know the shepherds, and customarily sell their *fouace* (a kind of cake-bread) to them, this time they refuse, insulting the shepherds. Tempers flare, the shepherds set upon the bakers with the help of sharecroppers toiling in a nearby field, seize several loaves of *fouace* by force, and injure one baker seriously. Once the aggrieved bakers return home, they present themselves to their king Picrochole, and

recounted their grievance, showing him their broken baskets, their torn robes, their stolen *fouace*, and above all Marquet greatly injured, relating that all this was accomplished by Grandgousier's shepherds and sharecroppers, near the big crossroads by Seuillé.

[Picrochole] immediately became furiously irate, and without asking any further questions concerning how or why, ordered proclaimed across his lands his feudal levy, so that all, under penalty of hanging, should assemble armed in the great square in front of the chateau, at the hour of noon.

. . . .

Then without order or moderation they took to the fields . . . ruining and wasting all in their path, sparing neither rich nor poor, neither sacred nor profane places; taking with them cattle, cows, bulls, calves, heifers, sheep, goats and billy goats, . . . taking the walnuts, harvesting the vines, taking the mushrooms, chopping down all the fruits and trees. . . . And they found not a single person who resisted them; rather all threw themselves upon their mercy, pleading with them to be treated more humanely, considering that they had always been good and friendly neighbors, and that they had never committed any excesses or outrages towards them that might have suddenly offended them, and that God would soon punish them. To these cries they provided no answer, except that they wished to teach them how to eat *fouace*.[28]

This description seems less a struggle between great European dynasties than a petty dispute between neighboring seigneurs taking up the cause of their peasants caught up in a local quarrel. Indeed, more than anything else it resembles the countless blood feuds fought by nobles throughout France during the early modern period. Aristocrats stood ready to resort to violence to defend their own honor or that of their family, to protect or promote seigneurial privileges like hunting rights, monopolies on the grain mill, bread oven, or olive press, to stake their claims in inheritance disputes, and to defend their clients and peasants from the depredations of neighboring noblemen.[29] This *"fouace* war" is a row between peasants who know each other and who are arguing over their customary relationships. Picrochole can be seen as a local seigneur treating the defense of his bakers as a dispute in which his own honor is at stake. Grandgousier, in turn, wishes "to protect his faithful subjects and hereditary lands" from Picrochole's pillaging, although he also recognizes the justice of Picrochole's initial complaint, and in order to give satisfaction for his peasants' beating of Picrochole's bakers, offers to compensate his neighbor for the stolen bread and to cede him a tenant-farm freed of feudal obligations.[30] Rather than an "epic of self-defense" framed by considerations of nationhood, as Hampton would have it, Rabelais recounts for us what might better be called an "epic of the blood-feud," rooted instead in the prosaically local, the world of quarrelsome neighbors, seigneurs and their dependents, and the constellation of local customs and rights that regulated rural life. Hampton is right to point out that Rabelais shifts the focus to a European scope, for as the quarrel progresses Picrochole resolves to conquer the world. And as Hampton argues, this juxtaposition highlights Rabelais's central preoccupation: the challenge for Christians, whether prince or commoner, to get along with their neighbors. But this change in scale sets up a comparison between dynastic warfare opposing François I and Charles V on the one hand, and between petty noble feuds over local peasant disputes on the other. If this serves to satirize François I and Charles V's struggle, it also emphasizes that kings are nobles too—some like Gargantua's father Grandgousier hewing more closely to humanist principles of magnanimity toward one's enemies, others like the vengeful and violent Picrochole less mindful of their Christian duty toward their neighbors, but all cut from a decidedly un-modern cloth.

*

Hampton's analysis of the *Princesse de Clèves* likewise depends on interpreting the royal court as an intensely charged site for imagining the French nation as a whole. For Hampton, the fact that the duc de Nemours turns his attention away from Elizabeth I of England in order to court the Princess of Clèves represents a shift of courtly attentions toward domestic considerations, a kind of "domestication" or "nationalization" of the high nobility in tune with the novel genre. In his words, the novel

> turns the narrative away from international politics, from the intrigue with England that opens the scene, to focus on the dalliances of the French aristocracy. . . . The emergence of the novel requires a homogenous political space, free from the scandals of international relations. . . . the sense of the uniqueness of French identity emerges through the space of the novel, which limits aristocratic fiction to love intrigues among French aristocrats. Frenchness finds expression, not through the imposition of political authority, but *through literature itself*, through a narrative form that turns away from internationalism to center itself and the passion it narrates in France. (147)

Indeed, Hampton goes so far as to argue that Nemours's fascination for the home-grown Princess is a kind of symbol for the taming of the aristocracy that took place in the seventeenth century.[31]

A close reading of Lafayette's text, however, makes it possible to highlight dynastic aspects of early modern kingship which caution us against reading too much national significance into the court. It is not entirely clear, for example, how "French" the court Lafayette describes really is. For what is perhaps most interesting about the novel's depiction of the court is just how un-national it seems. It is a world of international dynastic alliances: the proposed match with Elizabeth Tudor that Nemours foregoes of course, but also the marriages between the king's daughter Élisabeth and Philip II of Spain and between the king's sister Marguerite and Emmanuel-Philibert, duc de Savoie that constitute the central historical events in the novel, and between Henri II and his Florentine queen Catherine de Médicis (herself the daughter of the duke of Florence and a noblewoman from a prominent French aristocratic house). In a European political system in which dynastic alliances were sealed by establishing kinship ties through marriage, early modern courts were necessarily international communities. This was as true in Lafayette's day as it was in Henri II's: all of the seventeenth-century Bourbons were married to foreign queens, Henri IV to Marie de Médicis of Italy, Louis XIII to Anne of Austria, and Louis XIV to Marie Theresa of Spain. This fact was, moreover, generally perceived to be a perfectly natural feature of court life.[32] It is telling that despite the prominence of Henri II's wife in the novel, who is referred to as *Reine* and *Reine mère*, not once is any mention made of the fact that Catherine de Médicis was Italian. Nor is Catherine the only foreign aristocrat to frequent both the Valois court and the pages of Lafayette's novel, and whose foreignness is passed over in indifferent silence. The *princes étrangers* (foreign princes) were sovereign princes who also possessed significant holdings within the French kingdom, were allied to the great French houses if not the royal family itself, typically served the king in war, and spent considerable time at court. The duc de Savoie (though the independent duchy of Savoy was occupied by François I in 1536 and thus came under French control, the 1559 treaty of Cateau-Cambrésis celebrated in the novel returned full sovereignty to the alpine polity in exchange for duke Emmanuel-Philibert's marriage to the king's sister), the duc de Lorraine (François de Guise, the brother of Nemours's rival in courting the Princess of Clèves), and the duc de Bouillon who was also prince de Sedan (an independent principality in Champagne)—to which we should add Antoine de Bourbon, king of Navarre—all inhabit the royal court of the *Princesse de*

Clèves.[33] Clearly, the "Frenchness" of the court is sufficiently ecumenical to encompass the dynastic Babel that was the high European aristocracy.

*

Hampton's readings of the story of Floride and Amadour in the *Heptaméron* and of the *Princesse de Clèves* also depend on a particular interpretation of the changing relationship between monarch and nobleman. For Hampton, the monarchy's centralization entailed a shift from an older set of "feudal" ties between the king and his nobles toward an impersonal link between state and subject. Rather than feel tied to their country by national sentiment, nobles in late medieval France felt part of a European-wide community of aristocrats bound together by common social and cultural values. By consolidating national borders, which limited the international circulation of nobles, and by demanding greater obedience and service from the nobility, the emergence of the central state in the early modern period profoundly transformed the aristocratic experience. The aristocracy's steady loss of autonomy also helps to explain the changing status of the chivalric romance, a genre constructed around the social ideologies of late medieval aristocracy. The shifting political conditions of the sixteenth century transformed romance from the proud literary voice of a self-assured aristocracy into the nostalgic daydreaming of a declining caste:

> From its medieval "origins" romance, as a genre of aristocratic education and socialization, projects a fantasy image of the unity of the aristocracy as an "international" class. . . . At the time of Marguerite de Navarre, the universalism that had traditionally characterized the aristocracy was beginning to be threatened by developing forms of centralized political power . . . In the face of this new threat to the internationalism of the aristocratic subject, romance began to take on a new function . . . the formidable ideological task of reaffirming, through wish fulfillment, an ideal of disappearing aristocratic independence. (116)

It is this new relationship between crown and nobility that, for Hampton, provides the key to understanding the crucial turning point in Floride and Amadour's relationship.[34] Because the valiant nobleman Amadour cannot hope to marry the object of his desire, the much higher-born Floride, he chooses instead to insinuate himself into her family's confidence, marrying her friend, providing counsel to her family, and even establishing a close friendship with her, at the same time that he serves the Spanish king with great distinction in wars in Catalonia. During a stay with Floride's family, the unexpected death of Amadour's wife suddenly robs him of the pretext that would allow him to see Floride in the future. He then receives a summons from the king to assist him in an important matter. Realizing that he may never have the occasion to meet with Floride again in private, Amadour attempts but fails to rape her. For Hampton, this moment signals the anachronistic intrusion of early modern realities into a heretofore romantic narrative, "the incursion of sixteenth-century political life into the timeless world of romance" (122). Hampton emphasizes that before the king's summons, Amadour's service to the crown has been based on aristocratic honor rather than obligation to the nation. The traditional relationships between kings and their noblemen that underpin the romance genre are undermined in the context of the centralizing monarchy of the Renaissance:

> The king's claim on Amadour comes into focus when seen in light of the situation of the French aristocracy in the early decades of the sixteenth century. The increasing emphasis on political centralization under Francis I had the effect of beginning to shift power away from the traditional aristocracy and into the hands of a single ruler. . . . This contrast between aristocratic household and centralized politics informs Marguerite's story. Throughout the tale it is made very clear that Amadour comes and goes as he pleases. His concern is for the honor of himself and his country, but he seems to have no duty, in any modern sense of the word, toward that country. Rather, political action is defined according to clan . . . [or] according to their houses.[35]

The king's request, then, constitutes a decisive political as well as narrative moment, one in which the new political realities of the sixteenth century subdue aristocratic autonomy and provoke a crisis in the relationship between Floride and Amadour, as well as a crisis in genre that recasts romance as novella: "When the king summons Amadour on an 'affair of importance,' the free-flowing circulation of desire and aristocratic male bodies that characterizes romance is suddenly channeled by an overarching authority. In an instant, Amadour becomes the subject of a state" (125).

Such a reading risks oversimplifying the history of the nobility and its relationship with the crown. Historians of the nobility have emphasized their considerable autonomy, wide local authority, independent military capacity, intense sense of their own importance, and readiness to resist the crown when they judged their interests demanded it.[36] The Wars of Religion and the Fronde, both episodes during which noble revolt brought the monarchy to its knees for sustained periods of time, are important reminders of the potential assertiveness and power of the French aristocracy. Recent scholarship has also emphasized that the growth of the state in the sixteenth and seventeenth centuries did not come at the expense of the aristocracy. Rather, the nobility were active participants in the process, finding in their service to the king, in military commissions and in royal pensions a profitable path to enrichment, promotion, and honor.[37] Above all, their relationship to the monarchy continued to be imagined in traditional terms, as a personal tie that bound the king and each nobleman together in an association of mutual obligations and privileges.[38] Consider how the spokesperson for the nobility summarized his vision of the aristocracy and the monarchy during the 1560 Estates General:

> The members of the nobility were ordained by God to give fidelity and obedience to their king, and to defend their subjects . . . And we seem to see in this the human body in which there are only two principle parts: the head which represents for us the king, and the heart which is the noble part, of which if either one or the other is injured, it is no longer possible for the man to live or to be comfortable. In the same way as in the Heavens, the Sun and the Moon represent to us the king and the nobility, in such a manner that when there is an eclipse between them, the entire earth is plunged in darkness. If the king is not in accord with his nobles, there is nothing but unrest and sedition; and when he preserves them, they defend and protect him, and are always the first to serve him.[39]

This statement, uttered at what was a high-water mark for the sixteenth-century monarchy, is an instructive reminder that the nobility did not imagine themselves as subservient subjects of an all-powerful state.

Indeed, Marguerite de Navarre and Madame de Lafayette's stories are themselves rich sources for understanding the early modern aristocracy. Both portray the personal character of the aristocracy's relationship to the crown. It is after all the king himself who personally summons Amadour, just as it is Henri II himself who calls upon Nemours to initiate marriage negotiations with Elizabeth I. It is unclear how Amadour's sense of duty to his prince, or the king's expectations concerning Nemours, differ from earlier forms of fidelity. More generally, in the social world of the court described in the *Princesse de Clèves*, it is the person of the monarch that binds its diverse members together, whether through marriage, kinship ties, ceremony, or mere proximity.

Both works also attribute considerable autonomy to the nobility. In Lafayette's novel, Nemours takes the liberty of ignoring the king's request that he open marriage negotiations with Elizabeth I. In the *Heptaméron*, one could argue that Amadour's sense of obligation to obey his king has less to do with the advancing state than it does with Amadour's own desires, ambitions, and aristocratic identity. In Navarre's story, Amadour is a minor nobleman who makes a name for himself by wielding his sword in the service of the crown. For him to choose not to answer the king's summons would not be a form of rebellion against the state, but rather a failure to sustain the honor he had won for himself with such great difficulty. His obedience is less a political than a social act.

Marguerite de Navarre herself is an excellent example of the ways in which early modern French aristocrats—particularly noble grandees—juggled the selfish interests of their own houses with the personal loyalty they owed the king. As Hampton would have it, "As sister to the king, Marguerite would have looked with favor on the processes of political centralization that I am positing as an essential, if muted, force in her text" (132). In fact, Marguerite's position and choices were considerably more complex. Her affection and devotion to her brother, François I, are beyond question. During the king's captivity after the disaster at Pavia, for example, she did not hesitate to undertake a difficult voyage to Spain in an attempt to negotiate his release. But her marriage in 1527 to Henri d'Albret, king of the independent Pyrenean kingdom of Navarre and prince of the neighboring sovereign principality of Béarn, invested her with dynastic responsibilities distinct from the interests of France: her duty to produce an heir to the throne of Navarre and to promote the interests of the house of Albret and its sovereign kingdom.

The fortunes of Béarn and Navarre in the early modern period were inextricably bound up in their fragile geopolitical situation. Throughout the fifteenth and sixteenth centuries, Béarn's sovereign princes anxiously navigated French and Spanish expansionist designs. In 1479, they capitalized on French support to acquire the

autonomous kingdom of Navarre and claim for themselves the title
of kings of Navarre. In 1512, however, Spanish soldiers marched
against Navarre's capital Pamplona and conquered Upper Navarre
south of the Pyrénées. France subsequently became Béarn and Navarre's closest ally as well as its greatest threat. On the one hand,
Béarn's rulers struggled to maintain their autonomy and privileges
and resist absorption into France. On the other hand, the principality's ruling family, the Albret, married into the French royal house,
held vast possessions in France, served the French king as royal
governor and admiral of Guyenne, sought French protection when
Spain threatened to invade, and repeatedly pestered the French
crown for military assistance to help them reconquer their lost possessions of Upper Navarre.[40]

The Albrets themselves were old hands at changing allegiances
for profit, having switched back and forth between the English and
French sides during the Hundred Years War. As recently as 1490
the Albrets had offered their support for an English invasion of
southwestern France. The Albrets did well by this strategy. Anxious to retain the loyalty of such a powerful aristocratic house an-
chored in a frontier region, the French crown showered the family
with lucrative pensions and offices.[41]

As sister to the French king and wife of the sovereign prince of
Béarn and king of Navarre, Marguerite de Navarre juggled divided
loyalties. The Marguerite of Marguerites was even willing to con-
spire secretly against the French king's policies in order to promote
her Pyrenean interests. In 1536–37, for example, at a moment when
François I was making plans to renew the war with Spain, Marguerite and Henri d'Albret opened secret negotiations with Charles V
unbeknownst to her brother. Gambling that Spain wished to avoid
war, the king and queen of Navarre offered to lobby François in
order to broker a peace between France and Spain, and in return
asked for Charles's consent for a reconstitution of Upper and Lower
Navarre under Albret control. And after François refused yet another of Henri d'Albret's supplications for troops to help retake
Pamplona, Marguerite and Albret renewed their contacts with Madrid. They went considerably further this time, proposing a marriage between their daughter, Jeanne d'Albret, and Charles V's son,
the future Philip II. The Albret house stood to benefit a great deal
from this arrangement: the hypothetical match between the Spanish heir to Upper Navarre and the French heir to Lower Navarre
would have secured for them a reunited Navarrais kingdom, and

it would have sealed their alliance with Spain. But it would also probably have meant alienating their connections with the French crown. Charles never seemed particularly interested by the Albrets' propositions, however, and after negotiations stalled, Marguerite appears to have given up on her dream to reconstitute Navarre by the fall of 1537.[42] The ways in which Marguerite navigated the dynastic responsibilities and ambitions that were part and parcel of the high aristocracy suggest that we need to be cautious when reading categories like "centralization" into such writings.

*

In *Literature and the Nation*, Hampton formulates important questions that underscore the necessity and promise of interdisciplinary approaches to the study of early modern France. His analysis of early modern writing points to the ways in which genre and representational practices both influenced and were influenced by the confrontation with confessional, political, and cultural difference, and political and social change. It suggests that specific genres carried rich political and cultural meanings that need to be unpacked in their larger historical context.

Because it relies on a reductive historical framework in order to show how political and social change altered the cultural conditions in which particular genres could be practiced, however, the book as a whole does not entirely succeed in recounting a pre-history of national consciousness. Hampton invokes an increasingly powerful and centralized monarchy, an increasingly subservient aristocracy, and an increasingly homogeneous national space as the starting points for literary change in the early modern period. At the very least, the meanings of categories like "centralization" need to be established with greater precision when they are invoked to explain what are in turn subtle features of texts in close readings. In the analysis presented in his book, these factors fail to account for the problems of writing Hampton identifies. The question of the "failure" of Ronsard's *Franciade*, for example, and the larger problem of the epic genre in a changing historical context, is an important one. But to ascribe the poem's lack of success to the crown's centralization since François I, as Hampton does, is not altogether convincing (193).

This does not imply that there was no crisis of representation or of genre in this period. Hampton demonstrates convincingly that authors wrestled with overlapping and contradictory value systems (like Christian humanism and noble violence), confessional violence, unfamiliar cultures, changing political realities, and a shifting social order. The questions Hampton raises and the textual problems he highlights with skill are indeed of considerable interest. It suggests rather that the interplay between literary construction, cultural difference, and political change were considerably more complex than presented here. The French polity that haltingly took shape in the sixteenth century, a ramshackle amalgam of imperial ideologies, dynastic interests, seigneurial principles, Roman and customary law, and an often violent nobility, governing over a multitude of local cultures and languages, resembled little the territorial state. But it no doubt shaped literary creation in important ways.

Literature and that Nation, then, suggests the importance of strengthening the dialogue between literary scholars and historians in the future. The crises of representation which Hampton identifies illustrate the political and cultural stakes in questions of genre and representation, and will provide much food for thought for historians. Likewise, a richer understanding of the complexities and vagaries of early modern political and social life will do much to advance our understanding of literary culture. Above all, Hampton's book points to the need for rigorous historicization of analytical categories and processes of change. Perhaps it is time for historians and literary scholars alike to set aside a vocabulary grounded in the teleological narrative of the rise of the nation-state that today does more to obscure than shed light on early modern history. In its stead, we might be better served by unpacking the categories historical actors themselves used, and by framing our questions around the processes of change which they perceived to be taking place.

The greatest merit of Hampton's book, perhaps, is not to have formulated a definitive description of the literary character of early modern French national sentiment, but rather to have posed big questions, advanced possible ways of thinking about genre, representation, and political life, and mapped a thought-provoking path for future research.

Notes

1. I wish to thank Sara Beam and Charles Walton for their helpful comments on earlier drafts of this paper. I owe the article's title, with apologies, to Eugen

Weber, *Peasants into Frenchmen: The Modernization of Rural France, 1879–1914* (Stanford, CA: Stanford University Press, 1976). Unless otherwise indicated, all translations are my own.

2. For important recent works on the origins of national sentiment in general, see John A. Armstrong, *Nations Before Nationalism* (Chapel Hill: University of North Carolina Press, 1982); Ernest Gellner, *Nations and Nationalism* (Oxford: Basil Blackwell, 1983); Benedict Anderson, *Imagined Communities: Reflections on the Origins of Nationalism* (1983), 2nd ed. (London: Verso, 1992); Anthony D. Smith, *The Ethnic Origins of Nations* (Oxford: Basil Blackwell, 1986); Eric J. Hobsbawm, *Nations and Nationalism since 1780: Programme, Myth, Reality* (Cambridge: Cambridge University Press, 1990); Liah Greenfeld, *Nationalism: Five Roads to Modernity* (Cambridge, MA: Harvard University Press, 1992); Adrian Hastings, *The Construction of Nationhood: Ethnicity, Religion and Nationalism* (Cambridge: Cambridge University Press, 1997).

3. For important treatments of the history of the French nation in this tradition, see Alexis de Tocqueville, *Oeuvres complètes*, 2, *L'Ancien Régime et la Révolution*, 2 vols. (Paris: Gallimard, 1952–1953; repr. 1980–1992); Ernest Lavisse, *Histoire de France depuis les origines jusques à la Révolution*, 9 vols. (Paris: Hachette, 1903–1911); Jules Michelet, *Histoire de France*, 17 vols. (Paris: Hachette, 1833–1867). On Third Republic France, see Eugen Weber's *Peasants into Frenchmen*. Concerning national identity, theoretical works that present this perspective include Smith, *The Ethnic Origins of Nations*, and *National Identity* (Reno: University of Nevada Press, 1991); Greenfeld, *Nationalism*. For overviews that adopt similar perspectives in the French context, see Marie-Madeleine Martin, *Histoire de l'unité Française. L'idée de patrie en France des origines à nos jours* (1948), 2nd ed. (Paris: Presses Universitaires de France, 1982), English translation *The Making of France: The Origins and Development of the Idea of National Unity*, trans. Barbara North and Robert North (London: Eyre and Spottiswoode, 1951); and Jean Lestocquoy, *Histoire du patriotisme français des origines à nos jours* (Paris: Albin Michel, 1968). On the medieval period, see Colette Beaune, *Naissance de la nation France* (Paris: Gallimard, 1985), English translation *The Birth of an Ideology: Myths and Symbols of Nation in Late-Medieval France*, trans. Susan Ross Huston (Berkeley: University of California Press, 1991). On the early modern period, see Myriam Yardeni, *La Conscience nationale en France pendant les guerres de religion (1559–1598)* (Louvain and Paris: B. Nauwelaerts, 1971).

4. Nora, "La Nation-Mémoire," in *Les Lieux de mémoire* (1984–1992), 3 vols. (Paris: Quarto-Gallimard, 1997), 2:2212: "la France est bien, de toutes les vieilles nations européennes, celle chez qui la détermination étatique a été le plus précoce, le plus constante et le plus constitutive, jusqu'à devenir, pour la conscience commune, presque immémoriale et ininterrompue. . . . Celle chez qui la volonté continuiste et l'affirmation unitaire sont venues d'en haut, . . . La France est une nation « stato-centrée ». Elle n'a maintenu sa conscience d'elle-même que par la politique. . . . D'où le rôle directeur et protecteur, unificateur et éducateur de l'État . . . [a] suffi à cristalliser ailleurs la conscience de la communauté et le sentiment de la nation."

5. R. J. Knecht argues that François I can be seen as the earliest architect of absolutist kingship, in *Francis I* (Cambridge: Cambridge University Press, 1982). For perspectives emphasizing the emergence of absolutism in the seventeenth

century, see for example Yves-Marie Bercé, *La Naissance dramatique de l'absolutisme (1598–1661)* (Paris: Seuil, 1992), English translation *The Birth of Absolutism: A History of France, 1598–1661*, trans. Richard Rex (New York: St. Martin's, 1996); and Emmanuel Le Roy Ladurie, *L'Ancien Régime, 1610–1770* (Paris: Hachette, 1991). Robert Muchembled has more generally argued that the state and the church succeeded during the early modern period in destroying a vibrant popular culture and replacing it with a "mass culture," in *Culture populaire et culture des élites dans la France moderne (XVᵉ–XVIIIᵉ siècle)* (Paris: Flammarion, 1978). On the invention of linguistic nationalism in early modern France, and the place of Villers-Cotterêts and the French Academy in this traditional narrative, Ferdinand Brunot's monumental linguistic history of the French language remains the foundation for this historiographical perspective, *Histoire de la langue française des origines à 1900*, 13 vols. (Paris: Armand Colin, 1905–1953); Auguste Brun's *Recherches historiques sur l'introduction du français dans les provinces du Midi* (Paris: Honoré Champion, 1923; reprint, Geneva: Slatkine, 1973) has also been influential; more recent works include Renée Balibar, *L'Institution du français. Essais sur le colinguisme des Carolingiens à la République* (Paris: Presses Universitaires de France, 1985); and Marc Fumaroli, "La Coupole," in *Les Lieux de mémoire*, 2:1923–82.

6. For one of the earliest and most influential contributions to this 'revisionist' approach, see William Beik, *Absolutism and Society in Seventeenth-Century France: State Power and Provincial Aristocracy in Languedoc* (Cambridge: Cambridge University Press, 1985). See Richard Bonney's review essay on disagreements over the nature of absolutism, "Absolutism: What's In a Name?" *French History* 1, no. 1 (March 1987): 93–117. On the weaknesses of the monarchy's fiscal system, see James B. Collins, *The Fiscal Limits of Absolutism* (Berkeley: University of California Press, 1988). See also Peter Sahlin's study of how seventeenth-century territorial expansion was a contested, two-way process, *Boundaries: The Making of France and Spain in the Pyrénées* (Berkeley and Los Angeles: University of California Press, 1989). Three recent works focusing on the royal army all demonstrate the stark limits on the monarchy's military capacities before Louis XIV's personal rule: James B. Wood, *The King's Army: Warfare, Soldiers, and Society During the Wars of Religion in France, 1562–1576* (Cambridge: Cambridge University Press, 1996); David Parrott, *Richelieu's Army: War, Government and Society in France, 1624–1642* (Cambridge: Cambridge University Press, 2001); and Guy Rowlands, *The Dynastic State and the Army Under Louis XIV: Royal Service and Private Interest, 1661–1701* (Cambridge: Cambridge University Press, 2002). I have argued that the early modern French monarchy did not possess a coherent national language-planning program in the modern sense: Cohen, "Linguistic Politics on the Periphery: Louis XIII, Béarn, and the Making of French as an Official Language in Early Modern France," in *When Languages Collide: Perspectives on Language Conflict, Language Competition, and Language Coexistence*, eds. Brian Joseph, Johanna DeStefano, Neil Jacobs, and Ilse Lehiste (Columbus: Ohio State University Press, 2003), 165–200; and "L'Imaginaire d'une langue nationale: L'État, les langues, et l'invention du mythe de l'Ordonnance de Villers-Cotterêts à l'époque moderne," *Histoire Épistémologie Langage* 25, no. 1 (2003): 19–69. For an excellent presentation of this perspective that synthesizes much recent scholarship, see James B. Collins, *The State in Early Modern France*

(Cambridge: Cambridge University Press, 1995). For a recent work that cuts against this grain and attempts to rehabilitate the concept of "absolutism" in a nuanced fashion, see John J. Hurt, *Louis XIV and the Parlements: The Assertion of Royal Authority* (Manchester: Manchester University Press, 2002).

7. For general approaches that posit the nineteenth-century as the crucible of modern European nationalism, see Gellner, *Nations and Nationalism*; Hobsbawm, *Nations and Nationalism*; Anderson, *Imagined Communities*; and Anne-Marie Thiesse, *La Création des identités nationales: Europe XVIIIe-XXe siècle* (Paris: Seuil, 1999). For an early contribution that emphasizes the Revolution as a rupture in the construction of nationalism, see Jean Lestocquoy, *Histoire du patriotisme en France*. For a review of recent literature that includes a useful overview of revisionist perspectives on French national identity, see David Bell, "Recent Works on Early Modern French National Identity," *Journal of Modern History* 68 (March 1996): 84–113. Important contributions to this scholarship include Sahlins, *Boundaries*; and David Bell, *The Cult of the Nation in France: Inventing Nationalism, 1680–1800* (Cambridge, MA: Harvard University Press, 2001). Although Alain Tallon takes issue with the theoretical claims of much of this work in the introduction to his *Conscience nationale et sentiment religieux en France au XVIe siècle* (Paris: Presses Universitaires de France, 2002), his findings concerning the intensely religious character of sixteenth-century French national sentiment are nonetheless consistent with their larger conclusions. For a criticism of Nora's *Lieux de mémoire* from this perspective, see Steven Englund, "The Ghost of Nation Past," *Journal of Modern History* 64, no. 1 (1992): 299–320. Such approaches have shaped studies of modern France as well: see for example Caroline Ford's stimulating study of cultural identity in modern Brittany, *Creating the Nation in Provincial France* (Princeton: Princeton University Press, 1993).

8. *The Cult of the Nation*, 3, 6–7, 20.

9. See David Quint's ambitious study of the politics of epic in Antiquity and in early modern Europe, *Epic and Empire: Politics and Generic Form from Virgil to Milton* (Princeton: Princeton University Press, 1993). For recent studies of the politics of literary creation in early modern France, see for example Gilbert Gadoffre, *La Révolution culturelle dans la France des humanistes. Guillaume Budé et François Ier* (Geneva: Droz, 1997); Christian Jouhaud, *Les Pouvoirs de la littérature. Histoire d'un paradoxe* (Paris: Gallimard, 2000); Hélène Merlin, "Langue et souveraineté en France au XVIIe siècle: La production autonome d'un corps de langage," *Annales HSS*, no. 2 (1994): 369–94; Merlin, *L'Absolutisme dans les lettres et la théorie des deux corps. Passions et politique* (Paris: Honoré Champion, 2000); Merlin, *L'Excentricité académique. Littérature, institution, société* (Paris: Belles Lettres, 2001). On the importance of anti-Italian sentiment in early modern French letters, see Jean Balsamo, *Les Rencontres des muses. Italianisme et anti-italianisme dans les lettres françaises de la fin du XVIe siècle* (Geneva: Slatkine, 1992); and Henry Heller, *Anti-Italianism in Sixteenth-Century France* (Toronto: University of Toronto Press, 2003). In the English context, see Richard Helgerson, *Forms of Nationhood: The Elizabethan Writing of England* (Chicago: University of Chicago Press, 1992).

10. (Ithaca: Cornell University Press, 2001).

11. Hampton writes, "what has been less noticed and analyzed by literary historians is the extent to which the emergence of secular literary culture is inter-

twined with political crisis and, in many ways, presents itself as a response to it" (9).

12. *Pantagruel*, chap. 14.

13. *Literature and the Nation*, 65. On the question of authorial intent in general, Hampton has this to say: "I will be particularly attentive to the ways in which tropes, figures, and genres distort and transform the terms of ideological discourse, often in ways that cannot be accounted for by the study of authorial intention" (xiii).

14. The Picrocholine War is in *Gargantua*, chaps. 25–51, the description of Theleme, chaps. 52–57.

15. *Heptaméron*, nouvelle 10.

16. Hampton focuses here on Du Bellay's verse collection entitled *Les Regrets*.

17. Montaigne, *Essais*, bk. 3, essay 6.

18. (Ithaca: Cornell University Press, 1990).

19. On Rabelais and the fragmentation of language, see *Literature and Nation*, chaps. 2–3. On the larger problem of language and representation in Rabelais, see for example Floyd Gray, *Rabelais et l'écriture* (Paris: A.-G. Nizet, 1974), esp. 44–45; and François Rigolot, *Les Langages de Rabelais*. Études Rabelaisiennes 20 (1972), 2nd ed. (Geneva: Droz, 1996).

20. See *Literature and Nation*, chap. 4, esp. 125–34; on romance genre and aristocratic identity in *Don Quixote*, see *Writing from History*, chap. 6.

21. On the importance of terminology, see David M. Potter, "The Historian's Use of Nationalism and Vice Versa," *American Historical Review* 67, no. 4 (July 1962): 924–50; Bell, "Recent Works" and *The Cult of the Nation in France*, esp. intro. and chap. 1. On the specific and complex character of national identity in the seventeenth and eighteenth centuries, see Sahlins, *Boundaries*, esp. 3–4.

22. See *Pré-histoires. Textes troublés au seuil de la modernité* (Geneva: Droz, 1999); and *Pré-Histoires II. Langues étrangères et troubles économiques au XVIe siècle* (Geneva: Droz, 2001). Note that Cave uses the term "pré-histoire" in a somewhat different way than Hampton. See also Armstrong, *Nations Before Nationalism*, chap. 5; Gellner identifies a similar process at work when nationalists borrow from preexisting group identities to invest their ideologies with ancient lineage, in *Nations and Nationalism*, esp. 48; Claude-Gilbert Dubois, *Celtes et gaulois au XVIe siècle. Le développement littéraire d'un mythe nationaliste* (Paris: J. Vrin, 1972), esp. 17; and Dubois, "Fonction des mythes d'origine dans le développement des idées nationalistes en France," *History of European Ideas* 16, nos. 4–6 (1993): 415–22.

23. *Literature and Nation*, 29, quote on x. On the importance of religion in defining social groups in early modern Europe, John Bossy's work is an essential starting point, see *Christianity in the West, 1400–1700* (Oxford: Oxford University Press, 1985), esp. chap. 4. On religion and social identity in sixteenth-century France, see Natalie Zemon Davis, "The Sacred and the Body Social in Sixteenth-Century Lyon," *Past and Present*, no. 90 (February 1981): 40–70; Denis Crouzet, *Les Guerriers de Dieu. La violence aux temps des troubles de religion, vers 1525-vers 1610*, 2 vols. (Seyssel: Champ Vallon, 1990); Tallon, *Conscience nationale*.

24. J. H. M. Salmon elaborates on the considerable challenges posed by the Wars of Religion, in *Society in Crisis: France in the Sixteenth Century* (London: Methuen, 1975). On the steady collapse of the monarchy's military capacity dur-

ing the Wars of Religion, see Wood, *The King's Army*. J. Russell Major argues that Henri IV and his minister the Duke of Sully attempted to put in place a radically new absolutist form of royal administration, but failed, see "Henry IV and Guyenne: A Study of Concerning Origins of Royal Absolutism," in *State and Society in Seventeenth-Century France*, ed. Raymond F. Kierstead (New York: New Viewpoints, 1975), 2–24. David Parrott documents the near-breakdown of the crown's capacity to keep its armies in the field in the decades leading up to the Fronde, in *Richelieu's Army*.

25. On the question of using the term "absolutism," see Bonney, "Absolutism: What's in a Name?" For alternatives to "absolutism," see Major, "Henri IV and Guyenne"; Elliott, "A Europe of Composite Monarchies," *Past and Present*, no. 137 (1992): 48–71; Rowlands, *The Dynastic State and the Army*, esp. 1–23, 336–62; David Parrott similarly emphasizes the dynastic aspects of royal foreign policy during the first half of the seventeenth century, in Parrott, *Richelieu's Army*; Collins, *The State in Early Modern France*, 5.

26. *La Publication Des emprises Du Tournoy Qui doibt estre faict à Paris, ville capitale du royaume de France, pour la solennité des tresheureux mariages du Roy Catholique, avec madame Elizabeth, fille aisnée du Roy Treschrestien: Et du Duc de Savoye avec madame Marguerite de France* (Lyon: Benoist Rigaud, 1559), sigs. Aii^r–Aiii^r: "Apres que par une longue guerre cruelle & violente, les armes ont esté exercées & exploictées en divers endroitz avec effusion de sang humain, & trespernicieux actes que la guerre produit, & que Dieu par sa saincte grace, clemence & bonté a voulu donner repos à ᴄᴏste affligee Chrestienté, par une bonne, sincere & heureuse Paix, Il est plus que raisonnable que chascun se mette en devoir avec toutes demonstrations de joye, plaisirs, & allegresse, de louer & celebrer un si grand bien, qu'à convertir toutes aigreurs & inimitiez en doulceurs & parfaictes amitiez, par les estroictes alliances de consanguinité, qui se font moiennant les mariages accordes par le traicté de ladicte Paix, . . . [le roi] considerant quavec les occasions qui soffrent, les armes (maintenant esloignees de toute cruaulté & violence) se peuvent & doivent employer avec plaisir & utilité, par ceux qui desirent sesprouver & exercer en tous vertueux & louables faictz & actes, Faict Assavoir à tous Princes, seigneurs, gentilz hommes, Chevaliers & Escuyers suyvans le faict des armes, & desirans faire preuve de leurs personnes en icelles, pour inciter les jeunes à vertu, & recommander la prouesse des experimentez, que en la ville capitale de Paris. 'Le pas est ouvert.'" For another such example published earlier in Henri II's reign, see *L'ordre et les articles du tournoy entrepris pour la solennité du tresheureux couronnement et triumphante entree du treschrestien Roy Henry, second de ce nom, et de la Royne son espouse* (Lyon: J. Gillet, [1548]).

27. See for example Peter Burke, *The Fabrication of Louis XIV* (New Haven: Yale University Press, 1994).

28. *Gargantua*, ed. Ruth Calder and M. A. Screech (Geneva: Droz, 1970), chap. 24, 164–65: "proposerent leur complaincte, monstrans leurs paniers rompuz, leurs robbes dessirées, leurs fouaces destroussées, et singulierement Marquet blessé enormement, disans le tout avoir esté faict par les bergiers et mestaiers de Grandgousier, auprès du grand carroy par delà Seuillé. Lequel incontinent entra en courroux furieux, et sans plus oultre se interroguer quoy ne comment, feist cryer par son pays ban et arrière ban, et que un chascun, sur peine de la hart, convint en armes en la grand place devant le chasteau, à heure de midy. . . . Adonc-

ques sans ordre et mesure prindrent les champs . . . guastans et dissipans tout par où ils passoient, sans espargner ny pouvre, ny riche, ny lieu sacré, ny prophane; emmenoient beufz, vaches, taureaux, veaulx, genisses, brebis, moutons, chevres et boucqs, . . . abastans les noix, vendangeans les vignes, emportans les seps, croullans tous les fruicts et arbres. . . . Et ne trouverent personne quelzconques leur resistast; mais un chascun se mettoit à leur mercy, les suppliant estre traictez plus humainement, en consideration de ce qu'ilz avoient de tous temps estez bons et amiables voisins, et que jamais envers eulx ne commisrent excès ne oultraige pour ainsi soubdainement estre par iceulx mal vexez, et que Dieu les en puniroit de brief. Es quelles remonstrances rien plus ne respondoient, si non qu'ilz leurs vouloient aprendre à manger de la fouace."

29. See Stuart Carroll's important forthcoming study of noble feuding in early modern France, *The Rage of the Gods.* On noble dueling, honor and violence, see Pascal Brioist, Hervé Drévillon, and Pierre Serna, *Croiser le fer. Violence et culture de l'épée dans la France moderne (XVIe–XVIIIe siècle)* (Seyssel: Champ Vallon, 2002). On the persistence of local violence and quarreling between neighbors on questions of honor through the eighteenth century, see Yves Castan, *Honnêteté et relations sociales en Languedoc (1715–1780)* (Paris: Plon, 1974).

30. *Gargantua*, chap. 27, 180: "de guarder mes feaulx subjectz et terres hereditaires"; for Grangousier's peace offering, see chap. 30, 190.

31. Hampton argues that "the erotic desire that keeps Nemours and Clèves attached to the Princess may be seen as a figure for the political submission of the French aristocracy more generally . . . The Princess stands as the imaginary center of France, as the embodiment of a centralized power that is a fiction (constructed through ceremony and ritual), but a fiction powerful enough to keep wandering aristocrats at home" (149).

32. In periods of religious and political crisis, however, the "foreignness" of queens and courtiers could prove a lightning rod for criticism: Protestants made it part of their attacks on Catherine de Médicis, and opponents of Mazarin and Anne of Austria attacked the cardinal's Italian origins and the queen's Austrian roots during the Fronde.

33. See articles on "Champagne," "Lorraine," "Navarre," and "Savoie" in Guy Cabourdin, and Georges Viard, *Lexique historique de la France d'Ancien Régime* (1978), 2nd ed. (Paris: Armand Colin, 1990); "Navarre" and "princes" in Marcel Marion, *Dictionnaire des institutions de la France aux XVIIe–XVIIIe siècles* (Paris: A. & J. Picard, 1923; repr. 1999); and "Savoie-Piémont" in Arlette Jouanna, *et al.*, *La France de la Renaissance. Histoire et dictionnaire* (Paris: Robert Laffont, 2001).

34. See *Literature and Nation*, 121–30.

35. *Literature and Nation*, quote on 122–23; see also discussion on 116–17.

36. See for example Arlette Jouanna, *L'Idée de race en France au XVIe siècle et au début du XVIIe siècle (1498–1614)*, 3 vols. (Lille and Paris: Université de Lille III-Honoré Champion, 1976), *Ordre social. Mythes et hiérarchies dans la France du XVIe siècle* (Paris: Hachette, 1977); Jouanna, *Le Devoir de révolte. La noblesse française et la gestation de l'État moderne, 1559–1661* (Paris: Fayard, 1989); Ellery Schalk, *From Valor to Pedigree: Ideas of Nobility in France in the Sixteenth and Seventeenth Centuries* (Princeton: Princeton University Press, 1986); Kristin Neuschel, *Word of Honor: Interpreting Noble Culture in Sixteenth Century France* (Ithaca: Cornell University Press, 1989); Jonathan Dewald, *Aristocratic Experience*

and the Origins of Modern Culture: France, 1570–1715 (Berkeley: University of California Press, 1993).

37. See for example Beik, *Absolutism and Society*; and Rowlands, *The Dynastic State.*

38. See Bell, *The Cult of the Nation*, intro. and chaps. 2–3.

39. Quoted in Laurent Bourquin, *La France au XVIe siècle 1483–1594* (Paris: Belin, 1996), 116: "Les nobles ont été ordonnés de Dieu pour la fidélité et obéissance à leur roi, et la défense de leurs sujets . . . Et nous semble voir le corps humain où n'y a que deux parties principales: la tête qui nous représente le roi, et le coeur qui est la partie noble, desquelles si l'une ou l'autre est blessée, il n'est pas possible que l'homme puisse plus vivre ou être à son aise. Pareillement au ciel, le Soleil et la Lune nous représentent le roi et la noblesse, tellement que, quand advient l'éclipse entre eux, toute la terre demeure obscure. Si le roi ne s'accorde avec ses nobles, ce ne sont que troubles et séditions; et quand il les maintient, ils le défendent, conservent, et sont toujours les premiers à son service."

40. On the history of Béarn and Navarre in this period, see Christian Desplat, *Peuples et élites de Béarn. Histoire d'une culture provinciale du XIVe siècle à 1789* (Pau: Hedas, 1982); Desplat, "Louis XIII and the Union of Béarn to France," in *Conquest and Coalescence: The Shaping of the State in Early Modern Europe*, ed. Mark Greengrass (London: E. Arnold, 1991), 68–83; Pierre Tucoo-Chala, *La Vicomté de Béarn et le problème de sa souveraineté des origines à 1620* (Bordeaux: Biere, 1961); Tucoo-Chala, *Histoire du Béarn* (Paris: Presses Universitaires de France, 1962); Tucoo-Chala and Desplat, *La Principauté de Béarn* (Pau: SNERD, 1980); and Clément Urrutibéhéty, *La Basse-Navarre, héritière du royaume de Navarre* (Biarritz: Atlantica, 1999).

41. David Bryson, *Queen Jeanne and the Promised Land: Dynasty, Homeland, Religion and Violence in Sixteenth-Century France* (Leiden: Brill, 1999), 44–50.

42. Pierre Jourda, *Marguerite d'Angoulême duchesse d'Alençon, reine de Navarre (1492–1549). Étude bibliographique et littéraire*, 2 vols. (Paris: Honoré Champion, 1930; repr. Geneva: Slatkine, 1978), on her marriage to Henri d'Albret, vol. 1, bk. 1, chap. 6; on 1536–37 negotiations with Spain, see vol. 1, bk. 1, chap. 8, 215–24. Lucien Febvre provides a nicely historicized presentation of the complexity of Marguerite's political loyalties and attitudes, in *Amours sacrés, amours profanes: Autour de l'*Heptaméron (1944) (Paris: Gallimard, 1996).

REVIEWS

Shakespeare's Visual Regime: Tragedy, Psychoanalysis and the Gaze
By Philip Armstrong
Houndsmills, Basingstoke, Hampshire, UK: Palgrave, 2000

Reviewer: Christopher Pye

Philip Armstrong's *Shakespeare's Visual Regime: Tragedy, Psycho-analysis and the Gaze* is a provocative, largely Lacanian, account of the visual and subjective dispensation inaugurated, he argues, during the early modern era and articulated with particular know-ingness in Shakespearean drama. The "tragedy" of the title is some-thing of a misnomer. Though the plays the book centrally engages are the tragedies—*Hamlet, Lear, Othello,* and *Macbeth*—there is lit-tle here on tragic form or philosophy. The focus is rather on larger claims concerning the necessarily fragile, even self-subverting con-solidation of a unified subject around structures of visuality during the era that saw, along with the efflorescence of the theater, the emergence of linear perspective and other mastering optical tech-nologies. The book combines literary attentiveness with a degree of topical and conceptual range: along with the plays, the book en-gages, for instance, contemporary anti-theatrical tracts, demonolog-ical treatises, and cartographic works, and the vision with which it is preoccupied is as much our own interpretive gaze as it is the exchange of looks within the plays.

This is not the first Lacanian analysis of Shakespeare, nor the first to make claims for Shakespeare's role in the history of the modern subject: one thinks of Joel Fineman's rhetorically oriented work, of course. Others have focused on the gaze in Shakespeare: Barbara Freedman, for instance, in *Staging the Gaze: Postmodernism, Psy-choanalysis and Shakespearean Comedy.* But Armstrong's intervention is notable and timely in two ways. Lacan's account of the psychoanalytic dimensions of visuality is remarkable in part for its relatively unusual historical tenor, for its willingness to speak in terms of a specifically modern scopic organization, and indeed to speak of the Cartesian horizons of the psychoanalytic project. Armstrong seizes on the possibilities opened by that intersection between psychoanalysis and the early modern historical moment, and thus the possibilities for forms of historical reading that are not simply thematic. At the same time, the dialectics of the gaze—its self-divisive, objectless, and endlessly migratory character—lets Armstrong explore in compelling ways the reflexive, implicating nature of the Shakespearean text, its systematic elision of interpretive boundaries. In Armstrong's account, for instance, the gaze of the severed head of Macbeth—sheer object—nevertheless returns upon and inscribes the royal audience that would claim its sovereignty in relation to it, and the division of the kingdom and the extravagant movement of letters within *Lear* is enacted in the divisive critical dramas played out beyond the play's bounds. The more or less unanswered question in Armstrong's analysis—the energizing question—concerns the relation between those two dimensions of its analysis, the historical and the hermeneutic: what, exactly, does it mean to write a history from which "no pure interpretive exteriority" is available (18)?

One of the strengths of *Shakespeare's Visual Regime* is the surehandedness of its account of the Lacanian gaze. Armstrong's analysis is in part corrective. The gaze, as Armstrong outlines it in his first chapter on *Hamlet*, is not equatable with the objectifying look, as critical applications of Lacan have often implied. Rather, the gaze is precisely what exceeds and at the same time enables the entire subject-object dialectic; the gaze manifests itself, but from a point that is always elsewhere, a point Lacan (and Armstrong) ambiguously associate either with castration and the intervention of symbolization or with the more radical limits of the symbolic associated with the Real. It is that strictly objectless character of the gaze that makes it difficult to align too directly with an empirical cause, as Armstrong attempts to do when, for instance, he associates it with the "actual situation" of Shakespeare's Globe, with its multiple perspective points (26). But Armstrong's larger point concerns the visual economy Lacan articulates, an economy one can fairly describe as something like a "regime." Because the unitary subject is constituted around the suppression of the gaze, the gaze returns most insistently just where the claims to scopic and subjective mastery are most decided. Thus the uncanny instabilities of *Macbeth* in Armstrong's account, a play strongly oriented around the structuring properties of the sovereign's seeing. Armstrong traces that dynamic of pressured coalescence and internal subversion as it plays out at the level of the subject in and beyond the frame of Shakespeare's plays, as well as in a range of more or less analogous registers: the political body of the sovereign, the newly consolidating nation, the textual corpus, colonial empire, the vectored, rationalized space of early modern cartography.

The chapter on *King Lear* reads the recurrent trope of blindness specifically in terms of the exorbitant dialectics of the gaze. For Armstrong, blindness in the play exposes the theatrical subject as subject to, rather than subject of, the gaze; with vision, the subject is inscribed within a function that necessarily exceeds and determines it. Such disquieting ambiguities take on a political cast in the association between the divisions of sight and the divided character of the king's "two bodies"; in a certain sense, the entire drama transpires, Armstrong suggests, within the uncanny "zone between two deaths" opened by Lear's opening dismemberment of the kingdom. In the third chapter on *Othello* Armstrong brings the logic of such inscribing reversals to bear on issues of race and gender: "Inserted—according to the visual signs of race or gender . . . —into the operations of the symbolic order, the subject is 'grasped' by the signifier—skin color, sexual anatomy—whose fixation within that syntax situates and manipulates him or her" (71). The weakness here lies in the loose and somewhat sweeping assimilation of all terms to the terms of vision. For Lacan, and elsewhere for Armstrong, the signifier can not be equated with appearances or visuality, nor, much recent criticism suggests, would race have been during the era. At the same time, the chapter offers a shrewd and surprising account of the function of the stereotype, a form Armstrong associates, not with a reduction to surfaces, but with the illusory production of depth effects, an hypostasizing of inwardness apparent even in those critics inclined to read Shakespeare's characters as self-fashioned or performative.

The most overtly invested in unbinding distinctions between primary and secondary texts, the account of *Troilus and Cressida* in chapter 4 explores the ways in which this most reflexively literary and intertextual of plays "stages the infectious, incorporative and aggressive relationship between texts, between author and source, and between player and spectator" (102). The theoretical entrée here is Derrida's analysis of the Kantian "parergon," the constitutive, ambiguously external and internal pictorial frame, and Armstrong is as interested in the contestatory dramas unfolding beyond the play in, say, Freud's relation to Jung as he is in the scenes of dismemberment, literary and otherwise, transpiring within. The summary claim that the play "demonstrates that the means by which a text seeks to establish its own identity uncannily doubles the psychoanalytic description of the formation of the ego" (133) is, of course, too summary; if this is true as an axiom, one wants an explanation for the difference between the massive agonism of the drama here and those far more playful versions of linguistic infection and erotic mediation elsewhere in Shakespeare. The chapter on the emergence of cartography—"Mapping Histories"—is the most rangy, moving as it does between a variety of literary (Shakespeare's Histories, Marlowe) and nonliterary texts. Armstrong offers an especially fine reading of the Euclidian logic of early modern mapmaking in relation to what Lacan terms the advent of the era of the ego and the accelerated imperatives of empire, as well as the inevitable anamorphic distortions haunting such rationalized spaces—the disfigurations "on the margins of [the] Elizabethan 'world picture'" revealing its radical contingencies. The book's final chapter on *Macbeth* is among its most evocative. The relations between that play, specularity, and the demonic have been well explored: the chapter owes a debt to Jonathan Goldberg's pioneering work, for instance. But Armstrong offers an innovative account of contemporary theories of vision: part of *Macbeth*'s disquieting force arises from the way it suspends itself undecidably between "extromissive" and "intromissive" versions of sight. And he brings Lacan to bear in especially telling and precise ways here, drawing out the connection between Lacan's (and Callois's) analysis of visual mimicry and the strange hollowing out of subjectivities within the play as all become inscribed within a generalized "atmosphere of treacherous masquerade" (171).

Historically minded readers may find somewhat off-putting the rapidity and ease with which Armstrong concatenates a whole series of formations—the modern (presumptively bourgeois) individual, the sovereign, the nation-state, the empire—as if they were simple analogues of one another. Indeed, it's fair to wonder whether such equivalencies amount to the kinds of imaginary identifications whose disruption Armstrong is otherwise intent on tracing. But the more intriguing questions posed by the book are, as I've suggested, the historiographic ones. To some extent, Armstrong is locating his analysis in relation to a developmental history of the subject, one oriented around the "historical foreclosure of the gaze" in theater and in the optical technologies of the era generally. Yet much of Armstrong's analysis of the elliptical, reversionary character of the gaze militates against just such a developmental account. Thus another strain of the analysis views early modernity as something like the projective horizon of our own subjective dispensation; what haunts us in Shakespeare are the limits of the visual regime that inscribes us. But, of course, horizons are themselves perspective effects, and it's hard to know which distortions in the mirror count as the measure of history, which the inevitable disturbances at the margins of the interpretive gaze, a fact perhaps made evident by Armstrong's free invocation of E. T. A. Hoffmann and Poe to clarify the workings of the uncanny in Shakespeare. To what extent will the history of the subject, even the modern subject, inevitably take the form a history of what, like the repressed, "at the moment of its occurrence, will have been"?

Trading Territories: Mapping the Early Modern World
Reaktion, 1997; Cornell University Press, 1998
and
The Renaissance Bazaar: From the Silk Road to Michelangelo
Oxford: Oxford University Press, 2003
By Jerry Brotton

Reviewer: Nabil Matar

Jerry Brotton, Senior Lecturer at Queen Mary and Director of the MA program in Renaissance Studies, has provided a vigorous interpretation of the Renaissance that challenges the nineteenth-century views by the formidable trinity of Jules Michelet, Jacob Burkhardt, and Walter Pater. In so doing, Brotton follows in the pioneering work of Walter D. Mignolo, Lisa Jardine, Deborah Howard and others who have questioned the humanistic premises from which the Renaissance is supposed to have evolved and enlarged its focus to include Islamic, Far Eastern, and sub-Saharan civilizations. Brotton takes to task the trinity for a "spiritual" and West European view of the Renaissance: although the authors had differed on the historical time frame of the Renaissance, and on its geographical locus—France or Italy—they agreed on its principal themes: "the emergence of individuality," the classical roots of the artistic and literary output, and a European/Western singularity (exclusive even of the Orthodox East). The Renaissance was a movement of genius completely isolated from world history, claiming Graeco-Roman art and the studia humanitatis as inspiration.

Trading Territories challenges this thesis by examining the background of that genius and the material conditions that allowed it to flourish. At the top of Brotton's list of material evidence and resources are maps—diagrams of the world as they started appearing, on single paper or copper sheets and in globes, soon after the "discovery" of America, and until the publication of the first atlas by Abraham Ortelius in 1570. From maps, Brotton extrapolates an alternative view of the Renaissance, one that takes into account conquest, trade, greed, commercial rivalry, and imperial desire. For the maps did not only describe the vastness of God's creation and the courage and idealism of Renaissance man who explored such vastness, but of markets and commodities, slaves and spices, commerce and plunder, battles and extermination. The production of maps, argues Brotton, hastened the development of maritime trade and technology: the sailors, and the capitalists who sent them across the unknown oceans, were not flexing intellectual muscles, nor exhibiting the "classical model of assertive, civilizing and culturally pure Renaissance Man" (49). Rather, they were developing national economies, amassing private wealth, and building empires, with all the "unpalatable" activities that accompany such development. A case in point is the rivalry between Spain and Portugal over the Moluccas, where Brotton shows how the two countries fought over maps as they did over the farthest reaches of imperial possessions. Brotton scrutinizes the Portuguese seaborne empire because it has been viewed, since the nineteenth century, as the brainchild of its truly Renaissance King, Dom Henrique. But the empire owes less to the king's humaneness and learning than to the Portuguese monopolization of the "logistical and navigational information which established precedence in the creation of commercial sea routes and specific trading points" (57). Cartography, along with the printing press that commodified maps and charts, was the key to the commercial conquests in Africa, America, and the Far East that later became the foundations of imperial wealth.

Having challenged the ideological grounding of the "Renaissance," Brotton turns to challenge its geographical parameter, arguing for the inclusion of the Ottomans in the Europe of the Renaissance. Despite conflicts and tensions between Christendom and Islamdom, there was an uninterrupted exchange of ideas and commodities that proved crucial in the making of the Renaissance. "Traditionally the Renaissance, with all its politically loaded connotations of the 'rebirth' of a selectively Aryan set of Graeco-Roman values, transmitted via a reified classical world, has been expunged of any potentially disruptive 'oriental' components or influences" (27). In this respect, Brotton brings back the Continental rather than the Atlantic view of the Renaissance, a view with which sixteenth-century Europeans were quite comfortable: when Ortelius and other cartographers determined that the eastern borders of Europe were the Urals, they did so at a moment when the Muslim Empire of the Ottomans was in possession of nearly half of the continent. Both Ortelius and later Mercator recognized that "Europe" was not just a product of the Latin legacy, but of a multiple cultural history. The chapter on "Disorienting the East: The Geography of the Ottoman Empire" shows the role of the Muslim Ottoman Empire in the making of "European" culture and "Renaissance" civilization. Brotton turns to medals, shared classics (Greek and Arabic which were later translated into Latin), painters and architects, carefully showing the influences that crossed from Christendom to Islamdom and vice versa. He examines maps, showing the role that Arabic and Turkish played in the development of navigational terms and the portolan chart; he also shows the familiarity that the greatest Ottoman cartographer, Piri Reis, had with Greek and Italian geographical material. The Renaissance extended from Antwerp to Istanbul, and from East to West—a view that seventeenth-century European writers as different as Emeric Crucé (*Le Noveau Cynée*, 1623) and William Penn (*An Essay towards the Present and Future Peace of Europe*, 1695) shared when they called for an Ottoman place at the table of European negotiations and political reconfigurations: "How is it possible, some one will say, to bring in accord peoples who are so different in wishes and affections, as the Turk and the Persian, the Frenchman and the Spaniard . . . I say that such hostilities are only political, and cannot take away the connection that is and must be between men."

The Renaissance Bazaar appeared five years after *Trading Territories*. Between the two, Brotton completed with Lisa Jardine *Global Interests: Renaissance Art between East and West* (London, 2000) that showed Christo-Islamic exchanges in Renaissance tapestry, medallions, and paintings. The book is a work of meticulous insight, with a brilliant study of tapestries that leaves little doubt about the intertwining nature of Renaissance culture. *Bazaar* is perhaps the last installment in Brotton's trilogy: it is a different kind of book in that it is written with the general reader, rather than the specialized audience, in mind: it has no notes (neither footnotes nor endnotes) although it has a general bibliography. But it maintains the rigor of investigating the global origins of the Renaissance, again showing the complexity of commercial and cultural interactions and the "dark side" of the Renaissance legacy, its "indignity of man" and its appropriation of "humanism" and the printing press by political authority.

Brotton reiterates his critique of the traditional interpretation of a Eurocentric and exclusionary Renaissance. In order to show the Renaissance "in relation to other cultures," he turns to evidence in eating and painting, architecture and mathematics: would Renaissance art and palaces and feasts have been the same, even possible, without the spices, silk, carpets, leather, textiles, horses, sugar, porcelain, coffee, currants, and the many other consumer goods that Europeans avidly sought from the Middle and the Far East? Brotton also questions the thesis that the "humanism" at the basis of the Renaissance was exclusively Latin Christian: the intellectual sources were shared by Muslims, too. Indeed, the first of the Ottoman sultans, who conquered Constantinople, owned more humanist books in his library than many of his royal counterparts in Christendom: "copies of Ptolemy's *Geography*, Avicenna's *Canones*, Aquinas's *Summa Contra Gentiles*, Homer's *Iliad*, and other texts in Greek, Hebrew, and Arabic" (51). Not only did Mehmed the Conqueror see himself as part of the humanist movement, but so did the Genoese and Venetians, too, who, soon after 1453, sent delegations to renew trading relations with the East. Within a quarter of a century, Bellini arrived in Istanbul on loan from the Doge of Venice, and within another quarter of a century, Leonardo da Vinci and Michelangelo were considering construction projects for the Grand Turk. "There were," writes Brotton, "no clear geographical or political barriers between east and west in the fifteenth century. It is a much later, nineteenth-century belief in the absolute cultural and political separation of the Islamic east and Christian west that has obscured the easy exchange of trade, art, and ideas between these two cultures" (53). Unfortunately, that separation was sustained into the twentieth century, supported by grim and darksome images about the Draculean terrors beyond Transylvania—in the "East" and the region of the "Turks." The age of European imperialism destroyed the legacy of the Renaissance bazaar.

Trading Territories, The Renaissance Bazaar, and the collaborative *Global Interests* present a forceful challenge to the nineteenth-century interpretation of the Renaissance—and the scholars who have unquestionably continued to accept, even up till the 1990s, the separation between East and West. Brotton's evidence is wide-ranging and articulately discussed—and fortunately, the publishers of all three books were willing to include reproductions of that evidence, often in color, to allow readers to see the paintings and buildings, maps and icons on which the arguments rest. It will be a long time before the intellectual breadth and the multi-disciplinary range of sources in Brotton's books will again be presented in such clarity, precision, and passion.

Note

1. *The New Cyneas,* ed. and trans. Thomas Willing Balch (Philadelphia, 1909), 84, 86.

Searching Shakespeare:
Studies in Culture and Authority
By Derek Cohen
Toronto: University of Toronto Press, 2003

Reviewer: Jonathan Baldo

Two areas of vital concern in Shakespeare scholarship over the past decade have been inwardness and the early modern subject on the one hand, and the various and conflicted uses of memory on the other. Derek Cohen's new book, *Searching Shakespeare*, joins these two areas of investigation in a fruitful partnership that offers significant and welcome contributions to both.

Cohen emphasizes "personal, private history" in the study of the plays, not because he tries to read later forms of subjectivity into early modern constructions of the subject (107). On the contrary, personal history always serves a social purpose in Shakespeare, Cohen argues, frequently by challenging the stability and authority of metanarratives. Cohen finds Shakespeare's plays to be teeming with historians, as contentious and divergent in their constructions of the past as any academic gathering: "Each individual dramatic character is shown to possess a tendency to come to terms with the present by the act of remembering and controlling the personal meaning by the use of linguistic processes not unlike those employed by professional historians writing the histories of empires and states" (107). History is alive in Shakespeare not in the banal sense that we often invoke to try to interest our more reluctant students in the past, but because the past cannot be laid to rest: "the past persists into the eternal present, a sore in the mind that worries the history being enacted and that shapes and forms the nation" (26). In a searching analysis of the relation between personal pasts and the nation's past in *King Lear*, Cohen traces the stress on personal memory to an instability of the subject. Lear's "many modes of self-construction" are linked to changing perceptions of how, whether, and to what degree his personal past is linked to the nation's past (115). The constant rethinking of these relations leads to a "radical reconsideration of the formerly stable self" (115). The

Shakespearean subject, then, is more often than not positioned in Cohen's book in a politically and socially variable role; it is far from the keystone of a bourgeois ideology that would gradually assert itself later in the early modern period.

Cohen's book reads like a collection of essays rather than a single, sustained argument driven by the engine of a powerful thesis. The author implies as much in his introduction, which begins by announcing, "The essays in this book fall into three parts, each aimed at exploring an undercurrent of the plays studied" (xi), and the book's subtitle, "Studies in Culture and Authority," reinforces that impression, giving the sense of an oversized umbrella. This is not necessarily a weakness, however, insofar as it makes each chapter a more surprising venture, and the act of reading genuinely active. It is left to the reader to connect some of the individual studies, which are linked by a number of shared concerns. This aspect of Cohen's book may derive from his healthy skepticism toward power in all its multifarious forms, a skepticism that occasionally surfaces as a direct expression of moral outrage like the following comment on the persecutions of Shylock and Caliban: "I take it personally and I am enraged at the inhumanity of the tormentors of these two definitely *not* innocent characters" (64). One could easily imagine that the absence of a controlling thesis is linked to unease with the mechanisms of control itself, and that the author's skepticism toward power extends to discursive forms as well. I do not mean at all to imply that this is a sloppily assembled book. Indeed, each essay or chapter is careful, perceptive, and attentive to the changing shapes of memory and the phantoms of subjectivity in the plays it investigates.

Still, one does get the impression that the author sometimes misses opportunities to make connections. For instance, after searching opening chapters entitled "Tragedy and the Nation" and "History and the Nation," on *Othello* and the second tetralogy respectively, the concern with history and memory unaccountably disappears for the next two chapters, which usefully differentiate the forms of slavery represented by Ariel and Caliban and investigate the scapegoat mechanism in *The Merchant of Venice*, before resurfacing in a series of chapters on *Othello*, *King Lear*, and *Macbeth*. Given Prospero's strenuous efforts to control personal and political memory, and the fragility of such control throughout *The Tempest*, it is surprising that the author does not sustain the discussion of private and public memory that he successfully launched in the first two chapters. Albert Memmi wrote in his influential study *The Colonizer and the Colonized* nearly half a century ago, the colonialist "endeavors to falsify history, he rewrites laws, he would extinguish memories—anything to succeed in transforming his usurpation into legitimacy."[1] Prospero's control of Caliban depends in part on his ability to impose his own version of history and to silence Caliban's alternative history of the island. Prospero faces repeated insurrections of personal and historical memory from multiple characters in the play, including his own daughter. Cohen unaccountably fails to connect the theme of slavery with his discussion of individualized and national memories from the first two chapters.

In addition, the author sometimes does not follow through on hints at the topical nature of the plays he discusses: for instance, when he writes of *Macbeth*, "This tendency away from the present and towards a better time is appropriate for a play so specific in its complementary references to James, the reigning monarch" (124). A line such as this opens a door onto the multitude of topical readings of the play, but no sooner does that door open than it abruptly closes shut. In the same chapter, Cohen notes, "By not providing Macbeth with a fleshed-out, substantial past, Shakespeare creates the impression of alienation: Macbeth seems not to belong to anyone; he is estranged even from the roots that personal history provides" (137). The author might have noted that King James expressed a similar sentiment: "I was alone, without father or mother, brother or sister, king of this realm and heir apparent of England. This my nakedness made me to be weak and my enemies stark. One man was as no man."[2] I wish that the multiple ideas of the past available to Jacobean England and its monarch, together with their Elizabethan counterparts, would have come into play in this book to help contextualize the otherwise rich discussion of the individual dramas.

This is an exploratory book, a careful and conscientious investigation of the variable ways in which identity in the plays is fashioned by the changing shapes of memory. It is a book with bold pronouncements and fresh insights like the following, commenting on a line from *Macbeth*: "Evident here is a clear link between tragedy and memory: the memory that produces the impulse to panic is among the most powerful stimuli of the dread by which tragedy is animated and, at the same time, that it seeks to contain" (124). As the gerund in the book's title indicates, this is a book that wears its conclusions lightly and takes pleasure in the act of searching. A like-minded reader will derive a good deal of profit from this book.

Notes

1. Albert Memmi, *The Colonizer and the Colonized*, trans. Howard Greenfeld (Boston: Beacon Press, 1967), 52.
2. *Letters of King James VI & I*, ed. G. P. V. Akrigg (Berkeley: University of California Press, 1984), 98.

The Uses of Script and Print, 1300–1700
Edited by Julia Crick and Alexandra Walsham
Cambridge: Cambridge University Press, 2004

Reviewer: Holly A. Crocker

Unsettling the boundaries between written and printed textual formations, this timely volume is as important as it is ambitious. And, since contributors variously argue that print and manuscript are mutually inflected media that similarly engage oral and aural habits of speech and hearing from the late medieval through the early modern periods, *The Uses of Script and Print, 1300–1700* is no small undertaking. Editors Julia Crick and Alexandra Walsham express studied awareness that this project shakes disciplinary distinctions, noting that methodological boundaries separating history and literature, or divides of periodization parting medieval and Renaissance studies, fall away as a consequence of these investigations.

The real danger in a volume as wide-ranging as this one, it seems, is losing one's way among a myriad of particularized readings that, taken together, add up only to the observation that print and script were partners of equal importance during this period. This collection avoids this potential problem through methodological and topical preferences that will likely be of more interest to scholars working on interfaces between orality and literacy, especially as these interchanges influence religious expression and dissent in local communities. Although my brief overview of this richly drawn collection will necessarily fail to capture the nuanced distinctions that contributors make between uses and kinds of written and print media as they are deployed in a variety of what Brian Stock elsewhere characterized as "textual communities," the organization of the volume will hopefully demonstrate that these uses of print and script focus on a specific domain.[1]

In part 1, "Script, Print, and Late Medieval Religion," contributors assess the ways that members of medieval religious communities participated in "publication." Felicity Riddy's essay, " 'Publication' before print: the case of Julian of Norwich," defines publication as "short for public conversation" (43), which allows Riddy to connect the thematic inclusiveness of *A Revelation of Love* with the emergence of her work from "the sea of talk" (48). Challenging the long-held connection between print and the Reformation, David d'Avray, in his "Printing, Mass Communication, and Religious Reformation: The Middle Ages and After," suggests that model sermon collections produced by friars comprised a type of "mass communication" that points to governmental toleration as the key to the success and longevity of religious reform movements. James G. Clark's "Print and Pre-Reformation Religion: The Benedictines and the Press, c. 1470–c. 1550" shows that the "advent of printing does not represent a break with the medieval past" (71); by cataloging the ways that monastics engaged print, institutionally through library purchases and institutional printing, and individually through monks' purchases of important or recent texts, he substantiates his contention that "older monasteries played an equally important role in the development of printing in England" (73).

Part 2 of this stimulating volume, "Script, Print, and Textual Tradition," examines the impact of writing on authoritative traditions. Anthony Musson, "Law and Text: Legal Authority and Judicial Accessibility in the Late Middle Ages," offers a rich account of the impact that the written text had on the authority of the law between the thirteenth and seventeenth centuries, arguing for the "growing power of textual law" even as he affirms the enduring power of oral proclamation within communities (97). Julia Crick's "The Art of the Unprinted: Transcription and English Antiquity in the Age of Print" is similarly interested in the ways varying textualities assume authority, performing what she calls an "experiment" by investigating the copying and reception of Latin charters of pre-Conquest England as a means for antiquarians (including Edward Coke and John Selden) to stake claims to the past that were inflected by present interests and concerns. Even as Crick's essay suggests the almost reliquary authority that manuscripts could assume, Scott Mandelbrote's detailed account of the controversies surrounding the printing and translation of the English Bible in his essay, "The Authority of the Word: Manuscript, Print and the Text of the Bible in Seventeenth-Century England," suggests that print, though acknowledged as an unstable medium, eclipsed the return to manuscript copies through the authority it gained from its relentlessly repetitive power.

The collection's third section, "Script, Print and Speech," investigates the ways that elements of speech, or what we might call "aural culture," inflect written or printed documents. Andrew Butcher's searching analysis of the ways in which medieval clerks influence the construction of urban records in his essay "The Functions of Script in the Speech Community of a Late Medieval Town, c. 1300–1500," illustrates that so-called "pragmatic literacy" expressively and imaginatively shapes the "textual construction of civic memory" (165). In his "The Sound of Print in Early Modern England: The Broadside Ballad as Song," Christopher Marsh traces the different ways that melodies inflect early modern ballads, providing ample evidence to substantiate his claim that scholars need to dedicate more critical attention to the ways in which sound created meaning in these printed texts. And, by looking at the interplay between different types of oral, written, and print media, Jonathan Barry's "Communicating with Authority: The Uses of Script, Print and Speech in Bristol 1640–1714" shows through a specific example that the contingent practices of communication urge caution about the broad assertion that a "public sphere" of print emerged during this era.

The fourth and final part of this volume, "Script, Print, and Persecution," challenges the notion that persecuted groups were invariably drawn to written and printed modes of communication. Andrea Walsham's important contribution, "Preaching Without Speaking: Script, Print, and Religious Dissent," effectively demonstrates that repressed religious groups from the fifteenth to the seventeenth centuries, Protestant and Catholic alike, used written and printed texts because such means of communication among pastoral groups were the only avenues left open to them. Similarly,

Thomas S. Freeman's essay, "Publish and Perish: The Scribal Culture of the Marian Martyrs," shows that the production and circulation of manuscripts, both treatises and letters, allowed imprisoned Protestant leaders to foster, advise, and even control their congregational members without the errors, falsehoods, and repercussions that widely disseminated printed texts might introduce into a broader community. Finally as Ann Hughes demonstrates in her "Print, Persecution, and Polemic: Thomas Edwards' *Gangraena* (1646) and Civil War Sectarianism," even a highly effective printed polemical text used non-print sources—oral report and manuscript record—to assert the authority of its portrayals.

In providing an admirable synthesis of the collection's concerns, Margaret Aston's epilogue identifies what I take to be the widely pressing question of "whether print *per se* had transformative power" (286). As she elaborates this critical issue, however, she identifies this volume's commitment to a very precise line of inquiry: "Did the Reformation succeed, where medieval heretical movements had not, through the ability of the printing press to disseminate texts in numbers and ways not possible for scribal copyists?" (286). In an acknowledgment that the specificity of this collection's focus is necessary to organize its sheer breadth, I suggest that the volume ends up illustrating the amount of work that is left to do in order to unsettle the distinctions of period and discipline that this collection identifies in relation to the interactions between script and print. That a single volume cannot address the interplay of print and script as it relates to poetic cultures (elite or popular), or as it pertains to the histories of books (pre- or post-Dissolution), speaks to the strength of its organization. Moreover, I submit that the greatest compliment one can bestow on a collection of essays is that its collective insights suggest avenues of future research: *The Uses of Script and Print, 1300–1700*, despite the limits of its focus, does just that.

Note

1. Brian Stock, *The Implications of Literacy: Written Language and Models of Interpretation in the Eleventh and Twelfth Centuries* (Princeton: Princeton University Press, 1983), 44.

Shakespeare as Literary Dramatist
By Lukas Erne
Cambridge: Cambridge University Press, 2004

Reviewer: Douglas A. Brooks

It was great while it lasted: for nearly three decades Shakespeare and Jonson constituted what—in the wake of poststructuralism— might be called a binary opposition. Struggling to extricate themselves from the stranglehold of the New Bibliography, yet also hoping to come to terms with the complex material and authorial status of plays produced in an era of burgeoning print cultures, scholars have tended to view the two playwrights as polar opposites in terms of early modern English dramatists' attitudes toward the shifting relationship between the stage and the page. We all know the mantra: Shakespeare was indifferent to print, to the publication of his plays, and, thus, to potential readers of drama; Jonson enthusiastically embraced print, fetishized the publication and authorship of his plays, and entrusted his literary posterity to his readers. Not coincidentally, perhaps, many of Shakespeare's plays were popular with theatergoers, while a number of Jonson's plays fared poorly with audiences. Moreover, Shakespeare wrote nothing about the authorship or publication of his plays; rather, the discourse of writing, books, and print chiefly offered him a ready set of metaphors with which to characterize reproduction, paternity, and legitimacy, especially in his sonnets and later plays. For Jonson, on the other hand, who wrote often and in depth about the authorship and publication of his plays, the discourse of reproduction provided him with a ready set of terms with which to characterize the material being in the world of his (and other authors') works.

The basic elements of this Shakespeare/Jonson binary are hardly new. Critics from Samuel Johnson to the New Bibliographers had found them of great use when attempting to establish the grounds of Shakespeare's singularity; but it was G. E. Bentley who gave the binary its most detailed and sustained articulation in his book, *The Profession of Dramatist in Shakespeare's Time, 1590–1642*.[1] Lis-

tening for a voice of critical reason within the theoretical cacophony sounded (in often mangled translations) by the likes of Lacan,
Derrida, and Foucault, a number of scholars embraced Bentley's
findings and sought to build on them.

Enter center stage Lukas Erne's *Shakespeare as Literary Dramatist*. Erne is having none of it. Instead, he sets out to prove that
Shakespeare intended his plays to be published and, as such, wrote
them primarily with readers—not theater audiences—in mind.
After thirty years of scholarly efforts to out the various collaborations and networks of engagements that were thought to have
enabled the coming-into-being of early modern drama in England—
even Shakespearean drama—Erne wants to send Shakespeare back
into the closet: the reading closet, that is. The "socialized text" is
dead; long live the "private text."

Despite the apparent—and self-touted—radicalism of this effort,
the reactionary position Erne argues from is itself not new, for as
W.W. Greg put it in 1942, "I do not think that Shakespeare, in his
later days at least, wrote for the stage only."[2] Some two decades
later, as Erne himself notes, Ernst Honigmann also challenged "the
modern myth of [Shakespeare's] complete indifference to the printing of his plays" (79). Furthermore, that the rise of the New Bibliography was concurrent with the institutionalization of English
literature and English departments in the academy—with the study
of Shakespeare at the epicenter—as Laurie E. Maguire has shown,[3]
should tip us off to the kind of back-to-the-futurism that intellectu-
ally funds Erne's approach to Shakespeare. Indeed, a profound
nostalgia underwrites *Shakespeare as Literary Dramatist*, an observation I will return to.

The argumentative platform Erne stands on as he sets out to demonstrate that Shakespeare's indifference to publication is "more of
a long-standing myth than a historical fact," that his literary intentions for his plays as works to be read can be known, and that, by
comparison, critical efforts to determine his intentions for the theater are "to a certain extent, doomed to failure" (177) consists of
three basic planks: 1) the Lord Chamberlain's Men actively sought
to publish Shakespeare's plays and devised a "coherent strategy"
for getting those "plays into print" (80); 2) because "about a third
of Shakespeare's plays" (135) were too long to be acted within the
early modern English norms of theatrical practice, Shakespeare
must have written them to be read, rather than performed, must
have intended them to be perceived as literature, rather than as

popular entertainment; 3) finally, because plays like *Hamlet* came to exist in at least two very different states, an inferior performance version and a vastly superior reading version, Shakespeare must have placed much greater value on the existence of his work as published "literary" texts than as non-published (or unintended-for-publication) playscripts. To restate Erne's central arguments— with a little help from Hemminge and Condell—when "His hand and mind went together," many of the plays "as he conceiued the~" spilled from Shakespeare's pen as long literary texts for the printing house, texts that he knew would have to be cut and simpli-fied for the playhouse so as to appeal to a less literary crowd. Thus perishes the Shakespeare/Jonson binary I mentioned at the outset. In fact, Erne's Shakespeare is more Jonsonian than Jonson, who made it clear in a readers' note to the very readerly/literary drama, *Sejanus, his Fall,* that the play was originally intended for the stage and had to be substantially revised for the page. Shakespeare, of course, never wrote readers' notes for any of his plays and never made any assertions as to whether a given play had been written for the theater or for a comfortable chair.

Undaunted by the conspicuous absence of Shakespeare's own statements as to his authorial intentions, Erne proceeds over an in-troduction and nine subsequent chapters to argue that Shakespeare wrote many of his plays with readers—not theatergoers—in mind. The first half of the book (five chapters) attempts to dismantle the notion that Shakespeare was indifferent to publication; the remain-ing four chapters argue for Shakespeare's embrace of publication based on the length of his plays. In the introductory chapter Erne lays out three critical foundations on which many of his later argu-ments are constructed. In the first case, he argues that Shake-speare's literary intentions for his plays can be hypothesized from the authorial self-consciousness of his poems. "No fewer than twenty-eight sonnets," Erne informs us, deal "prominently [with] the theme of poetry as immortalization" (5), then goes on to graft this thematic mind-set onto Shakespeare's plays, wherein no such comparable thematization of drama as immortalization occurs. Rather, in *Hamlet,* perhaps Shakespeare's most dramatically self-conscious play, the prince underscores the very "nowness" of drama—immediately before trying his own hand at being a play-wright by writing a "speech of some dozen or sixteen lines"—when he tells Polonius that the players "are the abstract and brief chroni-cles of the / time: after your death you were better have a bad / epitaph than their ill report while you live." The diachronic contrast here between the present and the future, between a play and an epitaph—often written in rhymed verse—seems clear, and it would be reiterated nearly forty years later when the playwright Thomas Heywood observed: "Plays have a fate in their conception lent, / Some so short liv'd, no sooner showed than spent: / But born today, tomorrow buried, and / Though taught to speak, neither to go nor stand." Nothing comparable was written about poetry in the period. Moreover, Shakespeare's "immortalizing" sonnets circulated in manuscript long after the boom of sonnet publication in the early 1590s had collapsed and were finally published for the first time in the unauthorized edition of 1609, suggesting a certain reluctance on Shakespeare's part to have them appear in print. Erne elides the distinction between poetry and drama at several key points in his argument throughout the book, despite much evidence from the period that poetry and drama were viewed as very different genres with very different printed afterlives. Thus, although—as Erne often points out—dramas were sometimes referred to as poems, the notorious uproar that greeted Jonson's decision to publish a collection of plays, epigrams, and masques together under the title of "Workes" suggests that the occasional designation of a play as a poem should be treated with some caution.

Next, Erne lays the foundation for subsequent arguments by providing examples of early modern book collections that contained published plays. He begins by dismissing Sir Thomas Bodley's oft-noted unwillingness to include printed dramas in the library he began in 1598 as being unrepresentative of contemporary attitudes. Yet, with the exception of the library of Sir John Harrington, who died in 1612, and of William Drummond, who—Erne reports—read eight plays between 1606 and 1614 (an average of one play per year!), all of the book-lists or collections he offers up as being more representative of drama's literary status date from between the 1620s and the 1660s, after the publication of the 1616 Jonson Folio, and well after "the early 1590s" in which, Erne claims, "things radically changed" (15) and the Lord Chamberlain's Men formulated a "coherent strategy" for publishing Shakespeare's plays. It is true, as Erne excitedly proclaims, that Edward 2nd Viscount Conway (1594–1665) "owned an astounding 350 English Playbooks" (14), but it is unlikely that he bought the majority of them in the first twenty or thirty years of his life. Even Bodley broke down and bought copies of the 1623 Shakespeare Folio shortly after it appeared, and an analysis of data on the publication, purchase, and authorial status of plays for the period 1565–1665 suggests that the closing of the theaters in 1642—twenty-three years before Edward 2nd Viscount Conway's death—had an enormous impact on the perceived value of printed drama. We might recall that Humphrey Moseley hoped to encourage people to purchase the Beaumont and Fletcher Folio of 1647 by reminding them that they "saw no *Playes* this Cloudy weather."

The third introductory claim grounding many of Erne's arguments is that Shakespeare's literary intentions for his plays have been profoundly obscured by what he terms "the now omnipresent performance criticism." Asserting that "performance has become a central component of Shakespeare studies" (20) since 1977, Erne repeatedly denigrates such criticism, which, for him, is exemplified chiefly by "Multi-volume editions such as the Arden (third generation), the New Cambridge or the Oxford" (20). For Erne, the main problem with these editions—and, by extension, the body of criticism to which they belong—is that they give "ample space to the theatrical dimension as evidenced not only in copious stage histories but, increasingly, throughout the introduction and annotations" (20). It's as if the New Historicism, poststructuralism, gender studies, and any number of other significant critical discourses never happened because scholars have been too busy fleshing out the "theatrical dimension" of the plays. A quick sampling of "recent studies" essays published in several journals over the past thirty years suggests that politics, race, religion, sexuality, and textual scholarship have dominated discussions of Shakespeare and early modern English drama. And a quick sampling of recent editions of plays indicates that many of these critical preoccupations receive a great deal of attention. In Stephen Greenblatt's seventy-nine-page introduction to *The Norton Shakespeare*, an edition based on the Oxford Shakespeare—which is heavily criticized by Erne for its performance-centeredness—the first thirty pages are dedicated to issues of cultural history such as politics, gender, witchcraft, and religion. By contrast, eleven pages examine what Erne might call the "theatrical dimension," while thirteen pages focus on printing and editorial issues. The critical concerns of Gordon McMullan's two-hundred-page introduction to the Arden edition (third series) of *King Henry VIII* can be broken down as follows: performance history, forty-nine pages; cultural history, ninety pages; textual history, fifty-three pages.

The critical priorities of such editions reflect closely the approaches to Shakespeare and early modern drama one finds in criticism published during the past three decades. None of these approaches, however, which attempt to locate plays within the material, social, and cultural contexts of their production, can appear in Erne's survey of the critical landscape because he needs to isolate the drama in order to produce the "private text" required by the hypothetical readers of plays for whom he so vociferously speaks. What's more, his contention that performance criticism has dominated Shakespeare studies for the past three decades is consistently belied by the extraordinary number of textual studies with which he grapples on nearly every page of the book.

It is certainly true that plays had readers, but as Zachary Lesser makes amply clear in his new book, *Renaissance Drama and the Politics of Publication: Readings in the English Book Trade*,[4] the first of these readers—after the actors—was the publisher/bookseller of a given playbook. As Lesser demonstrates, such a reader's intentions for a play, which can be determined in great detail by examining how the publisher/bookseller marketed it and what else he published, had much more to do with how and when a play was read than the kinds of authorial intentions Erne is compelled to hypothesize. In chapter 1, wherein he depicts the processes by which printed playbooks were legitimated in the last decade of the sixteenth century, Erne celebrates at great length the reader's address of the 1590 edition of *Tamburlaine,* written by the play's publisher, Richard Jones. Jones's reader address seeks to persuade potential readers that they should buy the printed text of a play they saw and enjoyed in the theatre because he has improved it by omitting "some fond and friuolous Iestures" from the playscript he acquired. For nearly a century scholars of drama, dramatic authorship, and play publication have rightly viewed this address as an important turning point in the evolution of printed drama. Calling Jones's edition, "a groundbreaking publishing venture" (52), Erne does not pursue what this venture suggests about the important role played by the marketing efforts of printers, publishers, and booksellers in the transformation of acting scripts into literary texts. Instead, like Heminge and Condell before him in their readers' address to the 1623 Folio, he moves from publication history to what Shakespeare thought and intended. This critical clairvoyance enables him to conclude that the "early publication history" of plays like *Tamburlaine* and *The Spanish Tragedy* "showed [Shakespeare] that a market for good reading material was coming into existence" (55).

Erne promises in the introduction that "chapters 1 and 2 [will] locate the primary agency for the legitimation of printed drama and the emergence of the 'Shakespeare' label in St. Paul's Churchyard" (26). This assertion turns out to be somewhat misleading because in both of these chapters Erne's underlying privileging of the "private text" seems to compel him to look beyond the unruly, social, and collaborative world of the London Book trade to the writings of individuals. In chapter 2 Erne devotes five pages—out of a total of sixteen pages of prose—to a discussion of Francis Meres's comments on Shakespeare in *Palladis Tamia* (1598) so as to substantiate his claim that Shakespeare's authorship emerged in 1598, not 1600. Nevertheless, if it is St. Paul's Churchyard where we should look for the "primary agency" of Shakespeare's authorship, then at least one fact contradicts Erne's claim for 1598. As Erne acknowledges, Shakespeare's name appears for the first time in the Stationers' Register in an entry for *Much Ado about Nothing* "dated August 23, 1600" (63). Moreover, Meres spent nearly all of his life outside of London, and to my knowledge never worked in St. Paul's Churchyard. After his reading of *Palladis Tamia*, Erne moves on to examine what can be gleaned about the literary value and authorial status of Shakespeare's plays from Edmund Bolton's "Enumeration of the best Authors for Written English" and two "literary anthologies" (71) which, like Shakespeare's name in the Stationers' Register, also appear for the first time in 1600: *England's Parnassus* and *Belvedere, or the Garden of the Muses.*

In chapter 3, according to the introduction, Erne turns from St. Paul's Churchyard "to Shakespeare himself" (26) and advances one of the book's principal arguments. Here, drawing on Peter Blayney's essay, "The Publication of Playbooks," Erne examines "the twelve plays that may have been the first written by Shakespeare for the Lord Chamberlain's Men," and argues that the "Lord Chamberlain's Men had a coherent strategy to try to get their playwright's plays into print" (80). Central to Erne's argument, that this "coherent strategy" consisted of publishing Shakespeare's plays "at an interval of roughly two years between composition and entrance" (85) into the Stationers' Register, is what he refers to as these twelve plays' "likely dates of composition" (84). Asserting that "the date of composition of several plays can be determined with relative precision" (85), here are some of the relatively precise determinations Erne offers: *Richard II* "is probably indebted to Daniel's *Civil Wars* (1595)" (85); "The topical allusion to the Spanish Vessel called the St. Andrew in the opening scene of *The Merchant of Venice* would very likely have been made soon after news of its capture reached England in July 1596" (85); "for some of the plays, such as *A Midsummer Night's Dream*, there is nothing beyond style to suggest a particular date" (85). At the conclusion of his examination of the dates of composition and entry into the Stationers' Register of Shakespeare's first twelve plays written for the Lord Chamberlain's Men, an examination that forms the basis for his claim that Shakespeare's company published them according to a "coherent strategy," Erne admits that "much of the above is necessarily conjectural" (85). Thus the "modern myth of [Shakespeare's] complete indifference to the printing of his plays" (79) is supplanted by a slightly more modern theory of Shakespeare's embrace of publication based largely on conjectures as to when he wrote his plays. The conflation of "Shakespeare himself" with the Lord Chamberlain's Men—which gets repeated by Erne throughout the book when he refers to "Shakespeare and his fellows"—in a theory aimed at revealing the dramatist's literary aspirations for his plays should cause some concern. Even if the conjectured dates that constitute this "coherent strategy" could be precisely determined (and they can't), they would not rule out the possibility that Shakespeare was indeed reluctant to have his plays published, but was compelled to defer to the financial priorities or business instincts of other sharers in the company.

Erne's admittedly conjectural basis for his argument is placed under erasure as the book proceeds. On the final page of chapter 3 Erne concludes by repeating his central claim that the publication of "what may well have been the first twelve plays Shakespeare wrote for the Lord Chamberlain's Men conform to a consistent pattern" (100). Erne may still not be completely certain about which twelve plays Shakespeare wrote first, but the "consistent pattern" of publication—based on "necessarily conjectural" evidence of when the plays were written—has by the penultimate sentence of the chapter become a pattern that "seems too regular to be accidental" (100). The evolution of speculation into certainty glimpsed here is highlighted inadvertently a page later when at the opening of chapter 4 he refers once again to his previous argument about "a recognizable pattern which bespeaks a coherent strategy" (101), then warns his readers that the "conclusions I arrive at in this chapter are altogether more tentative" (101). If "more tentative" than "necessarily conjectural" seems like a lot for a scholarly monograph to bear, it must do so because Erne is now forced to admit that by 1600 the "consistent pattern," the "coherent strategy" of publication he bestows upon "Shakespeare and his fellows" completely breaks down. Only five more plays are published before Shakespeare's death sixteen years later. It would be easy at this point in Erne's argument to counter that the "consistent pattern" he sees in 1590s may actually constitute unstrategic attempts on the part of printers/publishers to make a little profit on the Lord Chamberlain Men's plays, and that by 1600—the year in which Shakespeare's authorship is first acknowledged in the Stationers' Register—"Shakespeare and his fellows" began to have the authority they needed to honor the playwright's reluctance to publish. After all, if, as noted earlier, Erne can argue that the "early publication history" of plays like *Tamburlaine* and *The Spanish Tragedy* "showed [Shakespeare] that a market for good reading material was coming into existence," it is perhaps even more likely that it showed printers/publishers that a market for printed drama was coming into existence. Both *Tamburlaine* and *The Spanish Tragedy* went through three editions in their first seven years in print.

Faced with the inconsistent and incoherent record of Shakespeare publication in the early seventeenth century, Erne eventually moves on in the fourth chapter to new speculations derived from previous ones. The most notable of these is that Shakespeare, influenced by Jonson, had begun to think about publishing his plays in a collection. To argue for this hypothetical meeting of authorial minds on the subject of drama collections Erne begins by observing: "It seems that Jonson started to prepare the folio edition of his works as early as 1612, and may have entertained plans to do so considerably earlier, plans which Shakespeare might well have been familiar with" (110). Anticipating his reader's resistance to this line of argumentation, Erne blames this resistance on the reader's faulty beliefs: "As long as we go on believing that Shakespeare's attitude toward the publication of his plays is the very opposite of Jonson's, it will seem preposterous to assume that Shakespeare likewise came to entertain the idea of having his plays published in a collected edition" (110). Accordingly, Erne offers up an alternative belief that he states with remarkable certainty: "Once we realize, however, that he and his fellows consistently published his first dozen plays written for the Lord Chamberlain's Men unless *force majeure* prevented it, the speculation seem less implausible" (110). What began as a hypothesis based on "necessarily conjectural" evidence has become a realization; what began as "twelve plays that may have been the first written" has become "his first dozen plays written."

But Erne's discussion of Shakespeare's intentions to publish a collection of plays points to another serious problem with the book: Erne is often very selective about the scholarship he chooses to cite in support of a given argument. For example, in support of his contention that Jonson began work on his collection in 1612 and was thinking about it even earlier, Erne cites volumes 1 and 9 of Herford and Simpson's edition of Jonson's *Works*. Nowhere in the notes or list of works cited does Erne indicate an awareness of much more recent and credible bibliographical accounts of Jonson's work on the folio—published four to five years before his book—by scholars such as David L. Gants.[5] Such scholarship might have persuaded him that work on the 1616 folio did not get under way until 1615, a year before Shakespeare's death.

Chapter 5 begins with an even more confident restatement of Erne's thesis that, "Shakespeare and his fellows, far from being opposed to print publication, had a coherent strategy of trying to get Shakespeare's plays into print" (115). Having removed all doubts and hesitations from earlier versions of this formulation, he then takes on the players' "alleged opposition to print," asserting that, "Anyone who argues that the actors were opposed to the publication of playbooks must somehow account for those plays which were printed during Shakespeare's lifetime" (118). Nevertheless, as in previous chapters, rather than confront the messy, collaborative world of playing companies—a world utterly hostile to the "private text" he seeks—Erne focuses instead on the publishing intentions of two individuals, Molière and Heywood, both of whom were playwrights. In the first case, he justifies his willingness to overlook the "respective specificities of the place and time they lived in, the material conditions in which Shakespeare and Molière wrote and acted" (119) by assuring us that "[o]nly some thirty years separate the end of Shakespeare's career and the beginning of Molière's" (120). Then, noting that "a good deal more is known about the publication history of Molière's plays than about that of Shakespeare's," Erne examines the French playwright's publication record from 1658 to 1685 and reads it back onto Shakespeare's publishing intentions for his plays. Erne does acknowledge that "Molière is not Shakespeare and Paris is not London," but what he doesn't say is that in the history of dramatic authorship and publication the 1660s are certainly not the 1590s. To use Molière's attitude toward print to shed light on Shakespeare's is not unlike comparing the publication of *Titus Andronicus* with that of Dryden's *The Wild Gallant*, the first active decade of the popular theater in Elizabethan England with the first active decade of the Restoration stage: some seventy years separate these two ventures, seven decades in which the drama and dramatic authorship evolved enormously. From here, Erne takes on "the players' alleged opposition to print" by offering a reductive reading of Heywood's often tortured and nearly bipolar engagements with the London book trade. Once again the value of juxtaposing a playwright's engagements with print in the 1630s—a playwright who, it should be added, had unstable and shifting relations with a number of playing companies—with those of "Shakespeare and his fellows" in the 1590s seems anachronistic.

At the conclusion of the chapter Erne instructs us that "If we wish to discern the true attitudes toward publication of playbooks in the late sixteenth and early seventeenth centuries— Shakespeare's in particular—we must follow Peter Blayney's injunction to view such publication from the angle of London Stationers, publishers, and booksellers rather than from that of actors and dramatists primarily" (127). Appearing as it does at the end of the first half of the book devoted to drama publication, this instruction deserves attention for a number of reasons. First of all, "the angle" of only one stationer/publisher/bookseller—courtesy of one readers' address written by Richard Jones—is examined at any length in two chapters devoted ostensibly to "St. Paul's Churchyard"; those few other stationers/publishers/booksellers that are given the rare opportunity to speak much more briefly in subsequent chapters are frequently dismissed. For example, confronted with Richard Bonian and Henry Walley's reader address to the 1609 quarto edition of *Troilus and Cressida*, an address that has "been understood as referring to the King's Men withholding the play from publication" (122), Erne argues that "not much weight should be given to a preface which may well have been designed to promote sales" (123). But by this line of reasoning, then one should turn a blind eye to Jones's reader address to the published text of *Tamburlaine* as well because it too is utterly "designed to promote sales." To do so, however, is to tear up the foundation that grounds one of Erne's important early arguments—that the "early publication history" of plays like *Tamburlaine* and *The Spanish Tragedy* inspired in Shakespeare the desire to see his plays published. Ultimately, the only "angle of London Stationers, publishers, and booksellers" that Erne takes seriously and follows consistently is the one put forth in Blayney's essay on the publication of playbooks. And so Erne concludes by asserting that if we accept Blayney's central argument "that publishers in most cases had little or nothing to gain from playbooks," then "we will be open to the suggestion that players and playwrights in general and the Chamberlain's/King's Men and Shakespeare in particular had no serious objections to the publication of their plays and often actively supported it" (127–28). If one really wants to view drama publication "from the angle of London Stationers, publishers, and booksellers" rather than from the angle of one scholarly essay, the findings of which can and should be debated, then one will have to look elsewhere.

For the remaining half of the book Erne turns away from the clamor of St. Paul's Churchyard and toward the quiet world of the reading closet in order to argue what the length of published plays reports about Shakespeare's literary aspirations and our misreadings of them. Chapter 6 sets out to critique the "commonplace" assumption that "an Elizabethan play was written in order to be performed on stage, not to be read on the page" (131). Pivotal to this critique is Erne's observation that "about a dozen of Shakespeare's plays are too long to have been performed—or to have been intended to be performed—in their entirety" (172). From this observation Erne proceeds to argue that "any playtext exceeding approximately 2,800 lines would have been subject to abridgement," then claims that such "evidence has far-reaching implications for the study of Shakespeare's texts." (173). This claim, which is repeated at the outset of chapter seven, becomes the grounds for the main argument of the book's second half: "Shakespeare conceived of his plays not only as plays for the stage but also as dramas for the page" (174). For Erne "size matters," and armed with this length-based insight into Shakespeare's intentions, Erne spends the remainder of the chapter repeatedly attacking "the shift to performance-centered criticism," represented in its most reprehensible form by various recent editions of the plays, especially the Oxford Shakespeare. Quoting with approval John Kerrigan's assessment that " '[Shakespeare] becomes a self-considering artist,' a 'poet willing to engage with his own work critically, as reader and rethinker,'" (189) Erne concludes by trying to account for the shortness of *Macbeth*. The version that has come down to us, he argues—reinvigorating a distinction he elided in the introduction—"conserves what Webster called 'the play,'" that is, the text actually performed in the theater. On the other hand, "the long texts of Shakespeare's tragedies preserve 'the poem'" (190), that is, what was written for the closet. Erne understands the latter to be the true meaning of the phrase, "the true original copy."

The final two chapters of the book focus on *Romeo and Juliet*, *Henry V*, and *Hamlet* because all three plays—written for the Lord Chamberlain's Men "in the space of five years or so at the end of the sixteenth century" (194)—"survive in 'long' and 'short' versions." The first eighteen pages of chapter 8 take on much of the previous century's scholarship on the "bad" quartos, especially the theory of "memorial reconstruction." In the remaining nine pages Erne begins to argue for the merits of "bad" quartos in determining what got staged, though here once again his principal goal seems to be to challenge the notion that "memorial reconstruction" is behind any of the "bad" quartos. Indeed, his conclusion—"that the first quartos of *Romeo and Juliet*, *Henry V*, and *Hamlet* reflect, or at least dimly reflect, what Shakespeare and his fellows performed in London and elsewhere" (219)—seems uncharacteristically tentative. Erne is curiously silent about what the "bad" quarto of *King Lear* reflects, and he never does adequately account for the fact that both Q1 and F exceed the 2,800-line limit he sets for mandatory abridgement if a play were to be performed. Nor, for that matter, does he account for the existence of "bad" quartos that are truly "bad." And finally, it is impossible to reconcile his earlier arguments that plays "were printed in order to be read" (132), with his subsequent arguments that shorter printed texts reflect the "theatrical dimension," while longer ones were intended for readers. In other words, if "Shakespeare and his fellows" deliberately sought to publish his plays so that they could be read—as Erne argues throughout—and if, given Erne's repeated enthusiastic endorsements of Blayney's analysis of play-publication economics, there was little money to be made from publishing playbooks, then why did twenty of Shakespeare's short plays (all well below the 2,800 line-limit indicating "communal authorial" abridgment) ever get printed at all? Or to pose this question another way: If, as Erne contends, "the true original copy" refers to "long" poems meant to be read, then why were so many "short" plays included in a collection that advertised itself as containing plays "Published according to the True Originall copies"—"short" plays which, according to Heminge and Condell's address "To the great Variety of Readers," were clearly meant to be read.

Chapter 9 seeks to uncover the ways in which long and short versions of *Romeo and Juliet*, *Henry V*, and *Hamlet* are different, and in a critical move that might have pleased C. S. Lewis, Erne argues on largely aesthetic grounds that long texts, which fulfilled Shakespeare's literary aspirations and were meant to be read, had to be dumbed down for theater audiences. Here one can read arguments such as: "short, theatrical texts repeatedly flatten out the complex, 'life-like' characters of the long, literary texts, turning ambiguous figures, whose 'motivations' can and have been subjected to extensive analysis, into mere 'types,' the villainous king, the loyal mother Gertrude, or, in *Henry V*, the successful warrior king" (241). Erne contends that such differences between short and long, performed and read, texts of Shakespeare's plays are best understood in terms of "the respective media for which they were designed" (241), and quotes at length Walter J. Ong's outdated and oft-challenged theories on orality and literacy. Such theories, Erne observes, provide "an enabling context for an examination of the variant texts of *Hamlet* and *Henry V*" (242).

Shakespeare as Literary Dramatist is ultimately an important book, but not for what it purports to demonstrate about Shakespeare's attitude toward publication or his literary ambitions. Indeed, grounded as they are in speculations about dates of composition and authorial intentions, many of Erne's central arguments will in time—I predict—be refuted. Rather, the real significance of the book lies in what it says about Shakespeare studies at the present time. Each era, it could be argued, gets the Shakespeare and the Shakespeare criticism it needs. Not long after the splitting of the atom and the consequent fragmentation of identity that so captured the imaginations of British modernist writers such as Woolf and Joyce, Greg and the New Bibliographers set for themselves the Promethean task of restoring the corpus of Shakespeare's work (and early English drama, more generally) to its original wholeness—an effort symbolized most impressively, perhaps, by Greg's four-volume *A Bibliography of English Printed Drama*. When a range of institutions and authority systems began to be challenged during the late 1960s and early 70s, the New Historicism subsequently emerged, bringing into sharp focus a Shakespeare and a Shakespearean England that were deeply engaged with a range of cultural institutions and issues of authority. As the mass-market introduction of the personal computer began to sound—for some at least—the death knell of the epoch of print's hegemony, scholars worked to locate Shakespeare and his works in the first age of mechanical reproduction.

In this context, the rapid and largely uncritical embrace of *Shakespeare as Literary Dramatist* deserves our attention, for what it says about the kind of Shakespeare and Shakespeare criticism we currently need is troubling. How can we account for the uncritical reception of a book whose central thesis about Shakespeare's publishing intentions and literary ambitions relies on conjectures about the plays' dates of composition? A book that, despite the emphasis it places on St. Paul's Churchyard and the London Stationers, publishers, and booksellers, spends surprisingly little time exploring the printing houses or book stalls, preferring instead the testimonies of individual writers and one scholar? A book that acts as if "the death of the author" never happened?

The answer to all of these questions, it seems to me, is rather simple and obvious: *Shakespeare as Literary Dramatist* offers us a Shakespeare that is desperately needed after September 11, 2001. A post–9/11 criticism must necessarily long for the resurrection of the grand authorizing figure of the great author, a figure that, in Michael Bristol's astute characterization of Shakespeare's mythic authorship, is not unlike that of Santa Claus: nobody really believes in him but he remains a vibrant presence because he fills an important hole in our lives.[6] In a post–9/11 world, where strangers can be terrorists, where a heavy coat can be the signifier for a suicide attack or a briefcase can be a dirty bomb, where the workplace, the daily commute, the shopping center, or even the theater, can be transformed in an instant into a site of mass suffering and death, there can be little hospitality for the vagaries, the relativisms, the encounters with the Other, the collaborations (and their concomitant potential for intimacies), or the complexities and materialities of the day-to-day that so absorbed us during the previous three decades. The world is simply too unsafe for such critical liberties. The Shakespeare who emerges from Lukas Erne's book may well be the one we need in an unsafe world: the great individualized author, an author whose main ambition is to write and publish "private texts"—literary masterpieces to be read in the isolation and safety of the closet. But let's hope that such a Shakespeare will not have to accompany us into the next three decades, for there is much important work to be done.

Notes

1. (Princeton: Princeton University Press, 1971).
2. *The Editorial Problem in Shakespeare* (Oxford: Clarendon Press, 1942), viii.
3. *Shakespearean Suspect Texts: The "Bad" Quartos and their Contexts* (Cambridge: Cambridge University Press, 1996).
4. (Cambridge: Cambridge University Press, 2004),
5. For example, see Gants, "Patterns of Paper Use in *THE WORKES OF BENIAMIN JONSON* (William Stansby, 1616)," *Studies in Bibliography* 51 (1998): 127–53; and "The Printing, Proofing and Press-Correction of Ben Jonson's Folio Workes," in *Re-Presenting Jonson: Text, Performance, History* (New York: Macmillan, 1999), 39–58.
6. "Shakespeare: The Mytb," in *A Companion to Shakespeare*, ed. David Scott Kastan (Oxford: Blackwell, 1999), 489–502.

English Ethnicity and Race in Early Modern Drama
By Mary Floyd-Wilson
Cambridge: Cambridge University Press, 2003

Reviewer: Michael Schoenfeldt

This is a fine, original book that deepens our sense of the ways that earlier selves and communities were imagined. Floyd-Wilson demonstrates convincingly how notions of national character were supported by theories of what she terms geohumoralism—the idea that shared characterological traits emerge from the experience of a common climate, food, and topography. Based in the Hippocratic text, *Airs, Waters, Places*, the theory that different environments produce and explain differences in regional character derived from the ancient medical conception of the self as a porous entity subject to a variety of external influences. The concepts of geohumoralism, then, required a head-on confrontation with the central philosophical issue of environmental and genetic determinism. Most crucially, emergent fictions of both nation and race—fictions with which we are still grappling—issue from the more pernicious parameters of this doctrine.

There was much experiential evidence to support the claims of geohumoralism. Writers, for example, knew by observation that northerners could darken in southern climes, as the sun tanned their skin. But there was also much experiential evidence to challenge the doctrines of geohumoralism; writers also knew that southerners did not noticeably lighten in northern climes, and that the children of dark people in northern climes were dark. It is a measure of the suppleness, not to say incoherence, of the tenets of geohumoralism that they generally could encompass such anomalies in their various explanatory mechanisms. It is a measure of Floyd-Wilson's admirable fidelity to the material that this doctrine emerges in all its zany inconsistency.

Floyd-Wilson offers a wonderful account of the smugly self-congratulatory aspects of climate theory—particularly the ways that the first Greek and Roman theorists continually imagined Greece and Italy as the only locales where a salutary balance of mental and physical strengths was actually encouraged by the climate. It is fascinating to watch these theories migrate northward, and in the process shift their claims about what indeed constitutes the most temperate and salutary climate. It is also fascinating to see just how malleable this discourse could be—how indeed it could be used to justify the superiority of almost any climate, as long as the theorist were clever enough. The explanatory power of this paradigm is all the more impressive since it is not a particularly flattering model to the English, who are imagined to be uncivil and slow-witted compared to those from southern climates. Floyd-Wilson's book offers in part an object lesson in the strange, even perverse logic that underlies all assertions of climactic, tribal, and national superiority. One of its manifold strengths is its willingness to explore rather than ignore the radical inconsistency of these doctrines.

Throughout the book Floyd-Wilson shows herself to be an effective reader of literature, as well as a clear writer of precise, nuanced prose. In an engaging introduction, Floyd-Wilson lays out the trajectory of the history she wishes to recover—primarily, she intends to forestall concerns about the development of the ideology of white racial superiority, so that historically surprising linkages between northern whiteness and barbaric inconstancy, as well as between blackness and spiritual sagacity, can emerge. Chapter 1 traces the development of geohumoral theory from Hippocrates through the seventeenth century. Chapter 2, on British ethnology, is immensely learned, and offers fresh readings of all the usual suspects—Thomas Wright, Levinas Lemnius, Juan Huarte, Robert Burton—as well as acute analyses of figures that have not been (but soon will be) part of the scholarly conversation, such as William Rankins, Gerald of Wales, and Nathaniel Carpenter. Floyd-Wilson demonstrates how the discourse of the complexions was the source at once of a complacent superiority and of immense anxiety, particularly for residents of northern countries.

Chapter 3 focuses specifically on melancholy, particularly the curious northern European appropriation of Africa's melancholic darkness. She explores humoral discourse here as a form of early ethnology, looking closely at the various myths produced to explain the phenomenon of myriad skin colors, and making some tantalizing remarks on *Hamlet*. Chapter 4 explores Marlowe's *Tamburlaine* amid this ethnography of northern barbarity. According to Floyd-Wilson, Tamburlaine's Scythian heritage becomes a way of exploring what it means to be English, and northern. I found chapter 5, on Ben Jonson's *Masque of Blackness*, to be richly suggestive but less satisfying than the other chapters. She reads this masque performed in blackface as less about incipient racialism than as an allegory about the union of England and Scotland, and as a nervous attempt to establish whiteness as the dominant complexion amid an ideology linking the Scots with Ethiopians.

Chapter 6 offers the inevitable discussion of *Othello*, and Floyd-Wilson finds fresh things to say about this frequently discussed text by deliberately refocusing her argument from the passions concomitant with Othello's blackness to the pathological jealousy endemic to civil Italians. Floyd-Wilson shows herself less interested here in the "inchoate racial stereotype" of African barbarity that Othello is sometimes imagined to shadow than in the jealousy of Iago as a symptom of Italian "hypercivility" (132). Rather than focus on the violent outcome of Othello's jealousy, moreover, Floyd-Wilson emphasizes just how long it takes him to become jealous, and how many "proofs" he needs before he will act. This act of revisionism pays some splendid dividends, but not without some substantial costs; the chapter attends closely to the language in which Othello painstakingly describes his inner turmoil, but is less attentive to his suggestion that his blackness may be a mark of social and moral inferiority.

Floyd-Wilson concludes her book with a final chapter on *Cymbeline*, a play that "anticipates the essentialism of modern racial categories at the same time that it keeps the older geohumoral knowledge in play" (160). She contrasts the play with *Othello*, particularly in the comparative speed with which the northerner Posthumous is moved from absolute confidence in his wife to despondency over her apparent infidelity. Floyd-Wilson could do more, though, to contrast the comparatively violent and forgiving outcomes of their respective jealousies. She argues acutely that the play "prophesies a vision of Englishness that will develop into the racialized myth of Anglo-Saxon exceptionality—a myth that continues to shape the writing of British history to this day" (160).

The book suffers a bit, though, from the lack of a conclusion that would make manifest this trajectory. One could wish, moreover, for more attention throughout the book to the ways that ideas of race emerged out of this morass between the fluid hybridity of a fiction of Britishness and the progressive fixity of national identities. It is on the one hand extremely useful that Floyd-Wilson does not frame her analyses with the issue of race, since this allows her to explore the prehistory of the various prejudices and theories that would soon harden into a recognizable racial consciousness. But I think the book would have been even stronger if it had engaged more fully with the exciting work being done in early modern racial studies. We are given here a fascinating genealogy of racialism, but one that would be even more useful if its attention were firmly located on the pernicious distinctions that would soon be firmly in place. I would like to have seen more on the anxious distinctions that emerged between proximate or contiguous populations, such as the Dutch and the English, and more on the competition between regional and national identities. I wondered, moreover, why the primary literary evidence was theatrical, and what would happen to this story if its attention were directed elsewhere, such as the lyric fashion of praising "dark" mistresses. But these are the kinds of questions inevitably provoked by such a rich, learned, and stimulating book.

Increase and Multiply: Governing Cultural
Reproduction in Early Modern England
By David Glimp
Minneapolis: University of Minnesota Press, 2003

Reviewer: Paul Stevens

In this new book on population and literature in early modern England, David Glimp begins with the facts: "Sixteenth- and Seventeenth-Century England witnessed an intensified interest in registering and counting people" (xii). Because the people who actually did the counting were government officials, the representatives of parishes, cities, and the royal court, this activity signaled a new understanding of what governments could and should do. This in turn created a new urgency about social reproduction—that is, the worrisome need to make the right kind of people while foreclosing the possibility of making the wrong kind. The power to govern reproduction or "make up people" is as important as it is, Glimp feels, because it led to the development of "population" as a new theoretical and practical construct. That is, government agency led to the construction of a new discursive object that it could master, study, and manipulate. The distinctively modern meaning of this new construct or technique of power is explained by Foucault: "Governments perceived that they were not dealing simply with subjects, or even a 'people,' but with a 'population,' with its specific phenomena, and its peculiar variables: birth and death rates, life expectancy, fertility, state of health, frequency of illnesses, patterns of diet and habitation" (qtd. xv). Glimp is at pains to make it clear that he is no old fashioned new historicist— that his Foucault has been mediated through the work of philosophers and sociologists like Ian Hacking and Pierre Bourdieu. Thus, population may be a technique of power but it is not reducible to domination or oppression—"it posits [people's] agency, their ability to decide within a range of 'possibilities'" even as that range is being shaped (xvii). In its totalizing instrumentalism, however, population together with other related methods of reproduction still invites resistance.

The particular concern of Glimp's book is the role literature played in the rhetorical and actual constitution of "population" as state wealth, labor capacity, or economic growth. He feels that literature simultaneously assisted and resisted the making of "population," and that it did so directly as a reproductive practice in its own right and indirectly by representing the workings of other reproductive practices and institutions—most importantly, schools and universities, on the one hand, and domestic households, on the other. In order to demonstrate this point he sets out to analyze the work of a series of representative, canonical "authors," most importantly, Shakespeare and Milton. In Glimp's analysis, both these authors reveal highly conflicted responses, but Shakespeare's resistance to the instrumentalist state power implicit in "population" turns out to be much stronger than Milton's—the theater turns out to be more effective in assimilating and qualifying the power of "population" than theology.

Glimp begins his argument with an analysis of Sir Thomas Smith's 1581 *Discourse of the Commonweal* in order to demonstrate how verbal description in the specific form of "Commonwealth discourse" advances key terms that reshape both understanding and action. A "convenyent multitude" (qtd. 14), for instance, introduces the notion that there needs to be a balance between population and resources and that it is the responsibility of government to produce that balance. Most importantly, the emphasis on a person's proper "calling" becomes the crucial means by which real people, those whose individual aspirations contribute to the commonwealth, especially its common *wealth*, can be distinguished from unreal people, those whose aspirations don't. England's problem, according to Smith, is that it is both depopulated and overpopulated— depopulated in the sense that it has too few people with a useful, "convenient" or "treasure-increasing" calling (qtd. 22) and overpopulated in the sense that it has too many of the "rascabilite" (qtd. 27). The need to govern cultural reproduction and reduce "rascabilite" even when it appears as a superfluity of overeducated wits, "*bussardes*" and "barbarous offal" (qtd. 34), becomes imperative. No one feels this more keenly, says Glimp, than Sidney. In his *Defence of Poesie* (c. 1579), Sidney offers an extremely optimistic view of poetry's power to shape the right kind of people—but this optimism is belied by the unpredictable outcomes and failures he relates in the *Arcadia* (c. 1578–83), a specific, textual act of reproduction Sidney would have suppressed had he had his way—it was, he says, the "child I am loth to father" (qtd. 58). If Sidney's story is one of disillusionment with the power of poetry to reproduce the right kind of people, Shakespeare's story is one of the theater's triumph.

Unlike his fellow playwright Thomas Heywood, Shakespeare offers no immediate or direct response to the anti-theatrical claims that the theater not only fails to produce good men itself but also threatens to prevent the domestic household from doing so. Rather than take sides in the anti-theatrical debate, says Glimp, Shakespeare stages it in such a way as to interrogate "its basic terms" (68). In doing this, he effectively deconstructs the polar opposition between theater and household redefining the reproductive efficacy of both institutions. First, in *Love's Labors Lost* (c. 1588–94), while the reproductive power of education is satirized and that of the theater downplayed, the traditional household itself is pointedly shown to be inadequate, a place of "chilling monotony" (81). Then, in the "Henriad" (c. 1597–99), especially in the exhortations of *Henry V's* chorus, the possibilities of the theater as a model of "convenient"or balanced reproduction are dramatically reintroduced in the way the audience is required to participate in the play. The audience is required to repair excesses such as the drama's frightening representation of monstrous military reproduction and play a corrective or modifying role in the act of theatrical generation. Finally, in *Henry VIII* (c. 1612–13), especially in Cranmer's epilogue, this process is taken a critical step further. The theater effectively redefines both itself and the domestic household as more inclusive reproductive sites by explicitly extending its cooperative franchise to women in the audience: plays, so the epilogue suggests, "both construct and are constructed by the women in the audience, who in turn are able 'to conduct the conduct' of their men . . . and direct that conduct into approval of the theater's efforts" (114). The achievement evident in Shakespeare is that even in the midst of the reproductive imperatives that will eventually lead to the formation of population as a technique of state power it is possible "to define the stage as a relatively autonomous sphere of governmental practice" (114). In sharp contrast to this upbeat account of Shakespeare, Milton's story is more somber.

In an aside at the beginning of the book, Glimp laments the triumph of economics: "Indeed, our contemporary moment might be described as that in which economic modes of intelligibility have come to claim an ability to explain all human phenomena" (4).

This sad state of affairs is traced back to the seventeenth-century milieu of Milton and like-minded thinkers: *Of Education* (1644), for instance, "demonstrates the way 'oeconomy' as a mode of governmental action could serve a compelling organizing and legitimizing function." Indeed, Milton's "work participates in a crucial reconfiguration central to a genealogy of modern forms of government," a reconfiguration in which all totalities come to be understood as economies (141). As he emerges from Glimp's analysis of *Of Education*, Milton appears as a remorseless utilitarian, a Gradgrind whose apparent differences from more obvious utilitarians like Comenius or William Petty only reinforce the depth and narcissistic subtlety of his puritanical appeal to *usefulness* as the central criterion of social reproduction and principal means of distinguishing himself from the masses. This picture is qualified in Glimp's chapter on *Paradise Lost* where he detects signs of resistance. Milton's general endorsement of Petty's equivalence between people and wealth is, for instance, complicated by his sense that the latter's political arithmetic augurs "the diminishment of theology's place in national government" (164) and by his subsequent desire "to remove theological questions from the field of administrative calculation" (xxvii). But even here, unlike Shakespeare, his motives seem to be inescapably self-serving. For Milton's theological vocation itself turns out to be an elitist form of parthenogenesis, a desire to separate from ordinary people, to become one with the Angels, to take his place "among a multitude of 'Spirits Masculine' generated spontaneously by God" (177). As Lawrence Lipking recently observed, Milton "was not a nice person."

As the argument of *Increase and Multiply* unfolds, it becomes more and more difficult to take it at face value. This is not to say that the book is not a stimulating and sometimes fascinating piece of work. Glimp is clearly a talented critic; he writes with great self-assurance and his analyses of literary texts are routinely forceful and ingenious. He is unusually well informed and his foregrounding of social thinkers like Thomas Smith and William Petty is especially suggestive. The impression remains, however, that the book is more a bravura performance than a substantial contribution to knowledge. Two problems immediately come to mind—one to do with methodology and the other with the definition of terms.

First, *Increase and Multiply* announces itself as a contribution to the sociology of literature, but it is largely a thematic reading of a few literary texts in the light of certain sociological concerns. Important as these concerns are, it seems unlikely that reading a random selection of plays and poems drawn from the traditional canon of English literature will necessarily do that much to illuminate those concerns. That is, literary criticism in the specific sense of interpreting famous plays and poems may not be the discipline best suited to the study of issues like the relation between literary practice and "the development of population as a theoretical and practical construct." Such a study should surely concentrate on the details of material practice, on conditions of textual production, on systems of dissemination, on evidence of reception and response, and on verifiable outcomes. This seems especially important when one wants to make the kind of large claims that Glimp does for Shakespeare—that the playwright effectively redefined the theater as a reproductive site.

This problem is compounded by the overly generous definition of cultural reproduction as "any activity" as long as "it is described as making persons" (xxi). Since almost any activity may be so described, Glimp allows himself enormous latitude in what he chooses to discuss as reproduction. What he gains in suggestiveness, he loses in precision. His overall argument is then too undisciplined, and while it does so much less than expected in terms of explaining how literature contributed to the constitution of "population," it inadvertently reveals a powerful, secondary agenda—the revision and correction of the work of first-generation new historicists. Thus, his account of Shakespeare seems to be driven by the need to revise the old subversion-containment debate. Over and again, one hears him lecturing the ghosts of 1981: "This is to argue not that the stage subverted the monarchy or any other form of authority (though it certainly may, under certain circumstances) but that the Chorus specifies the relative autonomy of theatrical practice" (99). The locus of authority is now the theater itself—it contains subversion and reinforces its reproductive power by allowing "a limited form of unruly conduct" (114). The need to correct old new historicists is even more evident in his account of Milton. Having dispatched antique "Miltonolatric" scholars like Parker and Sirluck, Glimp directs his energy toward negotiating a path between those who see Milton entirely in the grip of nascent modernity (Armstrong and Tennenhouse in 1992) and those who see him standing heroically in opposition to the onset of Foucault's carceral society (Quint in 1988). Veering closer to Armstrong and Tennenhouse, what Glimp produces is the strange caricature Milton described above—the egotist whose religious convictions Glimp dismisses almost as impatiently as Petty might have done. The cultivation of a garden resonant with echoes of the Song of Songs becomes a matter of "waste management" (158). Milton clearly was influenced, constrained, interpellated by innumerable ideological imperatives, but had Glimp allowed himself to be better disciplined by definition and the less selective use of evidence, he might have given us a clearer and more just idea of the changing arrangement and interplay of those imperatives. It is not clear to me, for instance, how anyone can insist on Milton's unreflective subjection to "usefulness" as the principal criterion for reproduction when over and again Milton looks into himself and articulates the agonized sentiments of sonnet 19—in a way that would alarm Thomas Smith, the intensely introspective Milton casts aside his calling and identifies himself with the most useless of Petty's despised servants, those who "only stand and wait."

The Ottoman Empire and Early Modern Europe
By Daniel Goffman
Cambridge: Cambridge University Press, 2003

Reviewer: Palmira Brummett

The nature of the Ottoman empire and its intersections with the states and peoples of the lands comprising Europe are currently the subject of considerable reflection in the fields of history and English literature. This particular work is not so much a study of Ottoman-European relations as an attempt to present a clarified Ottoman world against which various notions of Ottoman-European relations can be assessed. Goffman's primary objective is not to explore the intricacies of diplomatic relations (or, for that matter, the narration of "turning Turk"), but rather to set out the ways in which the empire functioned and the ways in which it dealt with European states and merchants in what one might call the "long sixteenth century." The primary focus of the work is that period from the Ottoman conquest of Constantinople in 1453 to the end of the sixteenth century. Its final, substantive chapter shifts focus to the seventeenth century and what the author calls the "integration" of the empire into Europe.

Daniel Goffman is an Ottomanist historian whose earlier work has assessed the commerce of Izmir and the question of Britons in the Ottoman empire. He notes in the preface that this book is addressed to both general and student audiences. As such it works well, in large part due to the author's flowing prose, although it often presumes certain knowledge of the general framework of contemporary Euro-Asian and Mediterranean history (e.g., the identity of "the Mamluks" and the significance of claiming "the caliphal title"). Goffman provides a scholarly apparatus that makes his history accessible to the nonspecialist reader. The book includes chronological and dynastic tables, a glossary, an index, useful suggestions for further reading, and a set of visual aids including thirty black and white illustrations and seven maps. The illustrations (mostly European engravings of the sultan, his soldiers, and other Ottomans in quasi-real or imagined costumes) are generally well placed and lend themselves to classroom discussion of cross-cultural representation. Their captions, however, range from thoughtful and thought-provoking, to superficial and careless. The maps provide critical support for an audience that may be striving to envision the location of Aleppo or the spatial relationship of Venice to the Morea.

Beyond these enhancements, Goffman has employed several narrative devices to draw the reader into the Ottoman world that he presents. He begins each chapter with an extended quote, designed in most cases to provide a European description of Ottoman rule. These quotes enliven the narrative and provide the opportunity for a knowledgeable instructor to comment further. Unfortunately, some (e.g., 55, 59) contain caricatures lacking explanation or direct connections to the surrounding text, and hence their efficacy is diminished. Such quotes are a typical narrative device, but the author also ventures into the realm of fictional biography to enliven the reader's vision of Ottoman space. He begins each chapter with one segment of the story of an Ottoman personality named Kubad. The title character is an Ottoman *çavus* (messenger), the sultan's official emissary to the Venetian republic. Kubad was apparently a historical figure, but Goffman supplements the sketchy details available on his life and mission with imagined thoughts and dialogues, drawing what he believes to be likely scenarios. At its best, this approach can appeal to students, humanize the Ottomans (by showing them, for example, carousing and conversing with their Venetian counterparts), and enhance the text with the sights and sounds of Istanbul or Venice. At its worst, the tale of Kubad may become a bit tiresome, its vignettes lacking sufficient resonance with surrounding content. It is also worth noting that in the opening tale of Kubad's youth the date for the 1534 Ottoman campaign against Baghdad is misprinted as 1634 (23).

Goffman does an excellent job of synthesizing information from a variety of secondary sources, interspersing that information with insights from his previous work and allusions to primary source materials from the Ottoman archives. He routinely includes comparisons of events and processes in the Ottoman empire to those in Europe. These comparisons are sometimes forced (e.g., 64 on imperial and European marriage habits) but they are always thought-provoking, prompting the reader to avoid assumptions about the necessarily distinctive nature of Ottoman and European societies. As a teaching tool, *The Ottoman Empire and Early Modern Europe* could be paired with Donald Quataert's *The Ottoman Empire 1700–1922*, which is part of the same series.[1] Scholars and teachers requiring more expansive or detailed treatments of the Ottomans in this era should consult other sources beginning with Goffman's suggestions for further reading.[2]

The book suffers from the gaps and interpretative errors common to this type of short introductory work. For example: the reader must wait until the second chapter to find a history of the emergence and coming to prominence of the Ottoman state; the characterization of Ottoman elite cadres as "owned" men may confuse readers unfamiliar with the scope of their power; and the discussion of the roles of Muslim merchants in enhancing cross-cultural contacts could be more developed. Nonetheless, the reader is left with a coherent, unbiased vision of the workings of the empire in this era, and a set of insights on Muslim relations with non-Muslims that serve as a corrective to standard textbook fare and to contemporary notions of unbreachable communal divides.

Goffman's introduction begins by addressing the common stereotype of the Early Modern Ottoman empire as relentlessly and somehow uniquely militaristic. He highlights nonmilitary relations and commerce, arguing, quite correctly, that the empire must be viewed as an integral part of the European world. Edirne and Constantinople were, after all, "European" capitals; and Rumelia, in the Balkans, was (along with Anatolia) the central core of the empire and the source of much of its wealth and many of its officials. In drawing the essential connection between the empire and Europe, the author emphasizes the role of Jews and Christians as the conduits of cross-cultural exchange. This is an important point, although it can be overemphasized. The introduction concludes with an argument about periodization, suggesting that by 1700 "Europe" no longer feared "the Turk." While it is certainly the case that the Ottoman empire did not intimidate its European rivals in 1700 in the same ways that it had in 1600, it remained a potent military power that retained a prominent place in the European imagination. Tracts, travel narratives, and geographic literatures preserved the rhetorics of the Ottoman threat, even as political philosophers debated the utility of Ottoman absolutism.

Chapter 2, entitled "Fabricating the Ottoman State," invokes the historiography of Ottoman origins and clearly delineates the evolution of the Ottoman slave-based janissary corps and the "fief" (*timar*) system that supported its free Muslim cavalry. This is a strong chapter that deftly addresses the roles of race, religion, and gender in the Ottoman state system. The author makes the critical point that the "privileged class had no basis in ethnicity, race, or religion" (51), emphasizing the heterodox nature of the early Ottoman state and its accommodation of newly conquered Christian territories. Ottoman flexibility, in policy and in law, was a key element in the success of Ottoman expansion and in the overall longevity of the state. That theme of accommodation is repeated in chapter 6, which provides a nuanced and vibrant treatment of eastern Mediterranean commercial relations. Brief case studies on Florence, Dubrovnik, and Ottoman communities of Jews and Armenians illustrate the flexibility and variety inherent in the ways that the Ottoman empire treated both foreigners and its *dhimmi* (non-Muslim subject) populations.

Chapter 3 is another strong chapter elaborating on Ottoman institutions that were "neither comprehensive nor static by the 16th century" (60). Goffman explains the imperial household and the roles of religious and military-administrative elites, and non-elites. He employs a nuanced presentation of ethno-religious identities, illustrating, for example, the religiously mixed nature of the urban workforce. The Ottoman development of an elite slave culture (the *kul* system) is well outlined, demonstrating the ways in which a levy on boys from the empire's non-Muslim population produced a talented ruling class and a formidable infantry. The author's conclusion to this section, however, is rather extravagant. It was certainly much more than "happenstance" that a "pseudo-aristocracy" rather than "a system of plantation-style slavery" developed in the sixteenth-century Ottomans state (69). Further, while "pseudo-aristocracy" suggests both an approximation to European systems and some of the ways in which Ottoman pashas employed and retained power, in general it conveys a sense of lineage-linked privilege that does not suit the Ottoman hierarchy.

In Chapter 4, the author focuses on Ottoman themes in the context of the Protestant Reformation. He employs the reign of Süleiman the Magnificent (1520–1566) as an illustration of Ottoman ceremonial and claims to world power, pointing out the sultan's "attentiveness to personal glory" in the forms of lawmaking, display, and patronage. In the course of this discussion, the author's characterizations of the empire as dependent upon the abilities of a single man, and of the Protestant-Catholic divide, are rather too sweeping. Long before Süleiman, the sultan was dependent upon extensive delegation of power to manage his troops and to cement control over conquered provinces. And while Luther may have viewed the Ottoman sultan as "the arch-enemy of his own arch-enemies" (110), sixteenth-century German woodcuts commonly depicted pope and sultan as compatriots, Anti-Christ variants, both leading "Christendom" into the abyss.

Chapter 5, on the Ottoman-Venetian association, is weaker than the preceeding chapters. A vignette on Kubad in Venice concludes with the protagonist expressing indignation at Venice's supposedly overbearing Catholic communalism, a characterization that would have surprised many sixteenth-century Venetians. Despite an initial assertion that war was the exception in Ottoman-Venetian relations of the era, the bulk of the chapter is devoted to a recitation of the Ottoman-Venetian wars. While Goffman rightly points out the potential that Ottoman-Venetian relations provided for "cultural chameleons," he exaggerates the extent to which influential Venetian notables had spent, or wanted to spend, time in Istanbul. Indeed, Venetian notables tapped for service in the empire often tried to dodge those assignments because of the burdens such service placed on finances and health. The author also exaggerates the scope of seapower in the sixteenth-century Mediterranean and preserves the distorted notion of a radical shift in Mediterranean affairs in the aftermath of Lepanto. Ottoman fleets could not control the seas; and Venice's appearance in the Eastern Mediterranean after 1539 did not "hinge upon the indulgence of the rival Ottoman state" (149). Nor did the infamous battle of Lepanto in 1571 at once end an era of Ottoman naval dominance and launch a new one of piratic activity. After 1571, Goffman argues, "the very nature of warfare on the Mediterranean changed . . . No longer did large and treasury-depleting armadas cruise open waters" (161). In fact, the change was more gradual, and although the Ottomans did mobilize formidable naval power in the sixteenth century, it never consisted of large armadas cruising open water. Rather the norm was smaller fleets that spent a majority of their time in harbor or attempting, with little success, to quell corsairing raids against Ottoman coasts and merchant shipping.

The final substantive chapter, chapter 7, is juxtaposed to the rest of the book, because it focuses on the seventeenth century and on the rise of the trading nations of France, England, and the Netherlands. In 1575, shortly before the queen authorized the formation of the English Levant Company, the Ottoman Porte "granted Edward Osborne and Richard Staper permission to trade in its domains, and three years later William Harborne settled in Istanbul as their envoy" (195). These men were soon followed by other traders, entrepreneurs, and clergymen from England. Goffman uses the stories of two such clergymen, Isaac Basire de Preaumont and Robert Frampton, to explore the legal status of foreigners in Ottoman lands and the limits of Ottoman tolerance for proselytizing. Basire, once a chaplain extraordinaire to Charles I, spent the greater part of fifteen years, beginning in 1651, traveling in the empire. During that time he preached in Ottoman Greece, presented an Arabic version of the Anglican catechism to the Patriarch of Antioch, and enjoyed the protection of the Ottoman regime. Frampton, an evangelist appointed as chaplain to the English factory in Aleppo in 1655, spent twelve years in that city, becoming fluent in Arabic and numbering among his friends the Orthodox patriarch and the chief Muslim judge. Goffman argues that the Ottoman world made such fraternization possible, although it certainly did not encourage Christian proselytizing. The Ottoman empire, he concludes, was more a part of Europe in the seventeenth century than in the sixteenth, in part because the empire no longer posed a significant military threat and in part because "cliched understandings of the 'Terrible Turk' in northern Europe began to break down" (222–24). Nonetheless, older modes of representing Ottoman sovereignty, society, and territory remained very resilient. Even in the seventeenth century, the Ottoman conquest of Constantinople could still be recounted as "temporary," and Ottoman lands continued to be depicted (and named) as the sites of classical and Church history, without regard for the events or occupiers of the fifteenth and sixteenth centuries. The varying ways in which the Ottomans were mapped onto Early Modern European consciousness thus remains a subject for more scholarly investigation.

Notes

1. Donald Quataert, *The Ottoman Empire, 1700–1922* (Cambridge: Cambridge University Press, 2000).

2. For example, Halil Inalcık, *The Ottoman Empire: The Classical Age 1300–1600* (rpt. ed. Phoenix Press, 2001); Stanford Shaw, *History of the Ottoman Empire and Modern Turkey*, vol. *1, Empire of the Gazis: The Rise and Decline of the Ottoman Empire 1280–1808* (Cambridge: Cambridge University Press, 1976); Colin Imber, *The Ottoman Empire* (London: Palgrave, 2002); Metin Kunt and Christine Woodhead, eds., *Süleyman the Magnificent and His Age: The Ottoman Empire in the Early Modern World* (London: Longman, 1995); Halil Inalcık and Cemal Kafadar, eds. *Süleyman the Second and His Time* (Istanbul: Isis Press, 1993); Leslie Peirce, *The Imperial Harem: Women and Sovereignty in the Ottoman Empire* (New York: Oxford University Press, 1993); Rhoads Murphey, *Ottoman Warfare 1500–1700* (New Brunswick: Rutgers University Press, 1999); and Palmira Brummett, *Ottoman Seapower and Levantine Diplomacy in the Age of Discovery* (Albany: State University of New York Press, 1994).

Tempest in the Caribbean
By Jonathan Goldberg
Minneapolis and London:
University of Minnesota Press, 2004

Reviewer: Peter Hulme

The "tempest" of Jonathan Goldberg's title refers both to Shake-speare's play and to the flurry of twentieth-century Caribbean texts that have engaged with the play, often using it for anticolonial pur-poses. Goldberg's founding assumptions might be described as con-servatively radical, grounded as they are in the New Historicist and cultural materialist accounts of the play that see it as a colonialist document intricately related to the development of English imperi-alism in the Americas. He is therefore briefly dismissive of the more recent emphases on the Mediterranean and Old World contexts of the play, which are in any case less relevant to the Caribbean appro-priations that provide his main subject matter.

The book's center of gravity is very much the Caribbean. Gold-berg immerses himself in the writings of some of its leading figures—Frantz Fanon, George Lamming, Aimé Césaire, Sylvia Wynter, Roberto Fernández Retamar, Kamau Brathwaite, and Mi-chelle Cliff—and is primarily concerned with the possibilities their work might offer toward a new social future: he notes in the preface that the inspiring force behind the book lay with the "living possi-bilities" inherent "in these diaporic texts" (xi). Goldberg offers a particularly compelling account of Wynter's work: indeed, the whole book is in a sense a dialogue with and sympathetic extension of Wynter's ideas. The particular issue which Goldberg wants to highlight in his rereading of the revisionary texts by Caribbean writers is that of sexuality. Caliban remains the central figure of analysis, but Sycorax and Miranda are also constant reference points, whereas other characters, even Prospero, feature hardly at all.

One of the most attractive features of *Tempest in the Caribbean* is therefore its full engagement with the region's writers. Caribbean readings and reinscriptions of *The Tempest* have increasingly been granted some small recognition by Shakespearean scholarship (as in Jonathan Bate's *The Genius of Shakespeare* [1997]), but have hardly even taken center stage, while analysts of Caribbean writing have paid little attention to the light such texts might actually throw on Shakespeare's play. Goldberg offers Lamming and Wynter and Cliff the compliment of reading their texts with the care and attention he uses in reading Shakespeare. His respect always illuminates the material he discusses.

When *Tempest in the Caribbean* returns to Europe, it engages with Hegel, Locke, and Kant more directly than with Shakespeare. Nevertheless, *The Tempest* and its characters are present on almost every page and, since the play's appropriations have so often developed out of what Goldberg calls "moments of textual trouble" (4), his analyses often take him back to the Shakespearean text, indeed to a consideration of intricate editorial matters. The formidable intelligence of Goldberg's writing about *The Tempest* and about the issues surrounding the play ensures that *Tempest in the Caribbean* will be seen as a major contribution to Shakespeare studies as well as to Caribbean studies.

*

The book's three long chapters (one very long) of thirty-seven, seventy-five, and thirty-two pages offer only a rough organization of its materials. The first chapter begins by discussing the way in which the figure of Caliban can become—especially in the work of C. L. R. James, Fernández Retamar, Sylvia Wynter, and David Scott—an emblem for the "new man" dreamed of by the region's intellectuals such as José Martí and Che Guevara. Yet, as such formulations often indicate in their very language, the invention of novelty is often itself founded on further unexamined exclusions: of North America in the case of Fernández Retamar's essay "Caliban," of homosexuals in the case of Martí. Goldberg's technique here—as elsewhere—is to offer dialectical readings of texts such as Retamar's essay, questioning it "precisely in the spirit of the inclusiveness heralded as 'our *mestizo* America'" (9). Retamar is therefore pressed hard—but with generosity of spirit—on the language of his essay and on his creative misreadings of both Shakespeare and Martí. Drawing on excellent recent work by Sylvia Molloy, Goldberg brings Martí's essays on Wilde and Whitman into play, complicating Retamar's initial severance of Martí (Caliban) from his Uruguayan contemporary José Enrique Rodó (Ariel).

Retamar's somewhat gnomic references to George Lamming are scrutinized as the opening chapter moves to the other significant first-generation figure of Caribbean *Tempest* reinscription. Lamming's views in his essay from *The Pleasures of Exile* are carefully positioned with respect to those of Octave Mannoni and of Frantz Fanon. This first generation—Retamar, Lamming, Césaire, and Fanon—can easily be criticized for its masculinism, with Caliban its ready crucible, but Goldberg is always alert to other strands in their thinking, signs of more complexly gendered positions, however conflicted and unresolved these may be. A dozen pages are accorded to acute observations on Lamming's novels, focusing on the female characters such as Fola (in *Season of Adventure*), Penelope (in *Of Age and Innocence*), and Mrs Gore-Brittain (in *Water with Berries*. Particularly brilliant readings are given of an entry from Penelope's diary that connects it with the speech that Lamming gave at the First International Congress of Black Writers and Artists in Paris in 1956, on a podium he shared with Fanon; and of the sexual accusation at the climax of the conversation between Teeton and Jeremy in *Water with Berries*, one of the most powerful but opaque scenes in modern Caribbean writing.

Issues of sexuality become unavoidable here. They are of course fundamental to *The Tempest* itself—constantly raised by Prospero in his attention to Ferdinand's courtship of Miranda and by Miranda herself in the accusation of rape against Caliban. They are also at least implicit in the central role that cultural *mestizaje* plays for both Retamar and Lamming, and are brought into play by Fanon's psychoanalytical model—in which Goldberg sees the characters of *The Tempest* at work even though Fanon rarely mentions them directly. In this context Goldberg probes and prods the different versions of the family romance that *The Tempest*'s readers and reinscribers have produced, either as dream or nightmare. The paradigmatic couple of Prospero and Caliban can be readily dismissed because of its occlusion of women, and Goldberg is intrigued later in his book by the attempts to give both the marginal figure of Caliban's mother, Sycorax, and the completely absent figure of "Caliban's woman" a role in new Caribbean stories. But he doesn't rush to dismiss Prospero and Caliban quite so quickly, not least because that strange pair "cannot in any simple way produce normatively gendered figures" (25), a distinct advantage in Goldberg's eyes.

Goldberg's interest in Caribbean writing results from its powerful intimation of a utopic futurity, as sexual as it is political—if those two adjectives can be fully distinguished. Standing at the end of Utopia's central avenue is the monument that Fanon conjures toward the end of *Black Skin, White Masks*:

> On the field of battle, its four corners marked by the scores of Negroes hanged by their testicles, a monument is slowly being built that promises to be majestic.
> And, at the top of the monument, I can already see a white man and a black man *hand in hand*. (quoted 25)

As Goldberg points out, these sentences of Fanon's are almost impossible to read: "Is this the terrifying vision of the complicity of the white-masked black man, the abhorrent spectacle (for Fanon) of male-male intimacy that is the coupling of two castrated males, one black, one homosexual? Or is it the vision of a desired future, beyond difference and alienation, of mutual recognition?" (25). Goldberg suggests that such a vision can be found in Lamming's essay too, at least as "the unspeakable desire toward which Lamming points" (24), even if he never names it as such.

The central part of *Tempest in the Caribbean* maps what Goldberg calls "the 'monstruous' possibilities of nonnormative sexualities" found in the work of a number of more recent Caribbean writers and theorists, the most important of whom are Sylvia Wynter and Michelle Cliff. The title of this central chapter is "Caliban's 'Woman,'" which Goldberg adopts from Wynter's 1990 essay, "Beyond Miranda's Meanings: Un/Silencing the 'Demonic Ground' of Caliban's 'Woman.'" Wynter's argument is directed against any assumption of a universal category of "woman"—especially one that might be represented by Miranda. She also deliberately reaches beyond the category of the play's named but absent women—Sycorax, Claribel, and Prospero's wife—to a woman who is not even imagined within the play, let alone put onto stage. Here Goldberg is especially alert to the places in Wynter or Cliff where they engage with *The Tempest* only to imagine *beyond* its limits, limits that carry the name Caliban.

Although in some general sense Wynter's "beyond" moves Goldberg away from *The Tempest* itself, this long central chapter is actually built on the foundation of a detailed textual discussion of *The Tempest*'s two most famous editorial cruxes: Nicholas Rowe's emendation of the Folio reference to Sycorax as "he" to "she" ("Then was this Island / (Save for the Son that [s]he did littour heere, / A frekelld whelpe hag-borne) not honour'd with / A humane shape") and the now frequent modern emendation of "So rare a wondered father, and a wise" to "and a wife."

In the first case Goldberg is intrigued that the supposedly "mistaken" reading (he)—commonplace throughout the early editions of the play—should be so appropriate since, by turning Caliban's mother into a man, Sycorax's "lack of a humane shape," or at least the appropriate one for giving birth, is underscored. Caliban's humanity is further called into question: he is not a man born of woman and therefore, on at least one biblical definition, not human.

Goldberg points to the peculiarity of the three seventeenth-century editions of the play which, while correcting other clear misprints, were perfectly happy to leave the Folio's "he" to do the littering of Caliban. He speculates that these editors were perhaps swayed by the propriety of the monstruous offspring being "prodigiously and unnaturally mothered" (44), but he also points to Prospero's elaborate birthing metaphor in his account to Miranda in act 1, scene 2 of their preservation and to Prospero's utterance in act 5, scene 1 of lines taken from Ovid's Medea—other examples of what has traditionally been seen as a female realm being appropriated by the male, in a plot which Goldberg identifies as "masculinist." He concludes:

> If one were to treat the Folio's "mistake" as not mistaken, it would be with the aim of preserving and exploring what is monstruous in this moment rather than seeing it as part of the way Prospero's seamless power overrides all opposition, including gendered difference. Such a critical gesture would be congruent with an anticolonialist seizure of the territory of denigration as a site of reclamation. (46)

Goldberg's argument is intriguing but ultimately unconvincing. For a start, Goldberg misreads the lines that follow "Then was this island . . ." Sycorax is not excluded from humanity by Prospero's words since she has already died before his arrival on the island; in fact Prospero's "then" can be taken as meaning "after Sycorax (the other human being) had died." But more crucially for Goldberg's overall argument, Sycorax needs her humanity in order for Caliban to be precisely the *mixed* body that Goldberg analyzes so well, since Prospero has insisted on the diabolical nature of Caliban's father.

Interestingly, of course, the best-known textual crux in *The Tempest* also involves matters of gender: the relatively recent reappearance of the possibility of reading Ferdinand's lines during the masque, "So rare a wondered father, and a wise, / Makes this place paradise" as "So rare a wondered father, and a wife," a reading adopted in Stephen Orgel's Oxford edition of the play. Via Orgel, Goldberg summarizes Jeanne Addison Roberts's now well-known argument that early in the Folio print run, the cross-bar of the f broke off, transforming "wife" to "wise," an argument that—as Goldberg acknowledges—has now been challenged on technical grounds by Peter Blayney. But Goldberg is less interested in the typographical issue itself—which he suggests is irresolvable—than he is in the nature of the arguments that are used to support particular readings. Here, again, he follows the implications of Orgel's remark that what makes for the "rightness" of a reading is never simply the facts but the climate in which they become available and visible. He has great fun at the expense of editors justifying their retention of "wise" on spurious ideological grounds which they try to pass off as technical (and therefore merely "factual"). And he concludes by pointing out—as Orgel himself has also done—that if "wife" is a reading whose time had seemed to come in the 1980s, it may now be a reading whose time has passed, with the new Arden and Pelican editions restoring "wise."

To explain this turn of events Goldberg comments sardonically on renewed editorial awe "at the male mastery and at the secrets he guards" (61). But this seems like wanting to have his cake and eat it, inasmuch as he himself has just made out a powerful case for the limitations of the gains that might be imagined for enlightened gender relations if Ferdinand's "wife" was allowed to share his imagined paradise along with her husband and father: "Putting 'wife' in the line . . . hardly ensures her independence or her existence outside the patriarchal arrangements being celebrated here as Prospero hands her over to his chosen son-in-law" (57). Indeed, the implicit contrast between a feminist interest in Miranda and a Caribbean interest in "Caliban's woman," which motivates what Goldberg clearly regards as the inspiring force behind his book, would suggest that he wants to pass beyond a time when it mattered that Shakespeare should be seen to have included Miranda in Ferdinand's cozy arrangements.

The third and final chapter takes off from the only other major textual crux in *The Tempest*, the frequent reassignment of Miranda's "Abhorred slave" speech to Prospero, lines that are crucial to Wynter's analysis of (in Goldberg's summary and quotation of her words) "the seismic displacement which allowed 'Woman' to join the regimes of 'Man' as 'a co-participant, if to a lesser *derived* extent'" (119). Following Wynter, Goldberg examines the resonance of Miranda's phrase describing Caliban—"thy vile race"—with its suggestion of somebody nominally human but nonetheless incapable of achieving full humanity (120). There follows a fresh look at Shakespeare's various uses of the word "race," with the conclusion: "'Race' in Miranda's lines pushes in the direction of modern racism as it ontologizes the divide between human and savage" (121), a distinction indissolubly social and natural.

For Miranda, the clearest mark of Caliban's vileness is his resistance to "any print of goodness." He may, in other words, be human but he is irrevocably a "natural man," an "untutored man" (as Meredith's translation of Kant's *Critique of Judgment* has it), "a raw man" (as Gayatri Spivak translates the same Kantian term), or a "bare" man (in Giorgio Agamben's more recent terminology). These references indicate the field into which Goldberg inserts his discussion of just what Miranda means. To simplify: the kinds of distinction that Miranda makes in order to place Caliban discursively are the same ones that are found in Enlightenment racial science and, therefore, if we accept our modernity as a product of the Enlightenment, we must recognize the direct relevance of Miranda's language to contemporary thought. Caribbean writers, suggests Goldberg, have tended to understand this rather better than European critics.

Especially in its later stages the book's argument lacks some discipline as it moves from one topic to another almost at times it seems by free association. "This connects to . . ." is a frequent link, often imaginative and intriguing, but still speculative and ungrounded. A stronger editorial hand might have helped here, and would certainly have varied "stunning" as the main term of praise: no fewer than three "stunning moments" in Michelle Cliff's novel, *Abeng*, are referred to within the space of a few pages—three more than many readers have found, it has to be said. The book's argument often bounces critically off Rob Nixon's 1987 essay, "Caribbean and African Appropriations of *The Tempest*," giving no recognition to the breakthrough that essay offered at the time.

These caveats are minor. Even a relatively lengthy review cannot do justice to Goldberg's consistent subtlety and insight. Beautifully produced by the University of Minnesota Press, the book's only noticeable misprint turns the Cuban poet Heberto Padilla into Padillo, a masculinization whose significance it would need a critic of Goldberg's own ingenuity to disentangle.

Staging Slander and Gender in Early Modern England
By Ina Habermann
Aldershot and Burlington: Ashgate, 2003

Reviewer: Rosemary Kegl

In her introduction to *Staging Slander and Gender in Early Modern England*, Ina Habermann recalls the questions that governed her project in its earliest stages: "How is slander defined? What is its linguistic basis? What is the nature of its threat? How does the community deal with it? Who talks about it, how, and why? How does it affect the sense of selfhood of those involved in it?" (1–2). She soon discovered that answering those questions required sorting through a number of methodological difficulties. Like other forms of oral communication, slander is a speech act whose "actual moment of enunciation is elusive"—an elusiveness compounded by the various "interests and perspectives of the writers" who provide slander's textual traces (2). Unlike other forms of oral communication, slander is particularly clandestine and contentious: "really successful slander by definition is not detected and therefore not recognized as a distinctive exercise in bad faith" and "quite apart from the difficulties of placing a verbal injury in the appropriate context and assessing damage, the malicious intent which is usually taken to be a crucial ingredient of slander is notoriously difficult to prove" (2). Habermann responds to the methodological pressures of her project with an interdisciplinary analysis—viewing "slander from various perspectives, highlighting different sections of the discursive field in quest of a bigger picture," following "several pathways, as if exploring some forest, looking for slander in language, rhetoric, the law, communal interaction, literature and authorship, the body, and religion," and conceiving her book as a "chapter in the history of culture" that draws on "legal history, social history and legal anthropology, philosophy, theology, literary criticism and gender studies" (2–3).

Habermann's interdisciplinary scholarship produces a rich and learned account of English Renaissance slander and its negotiation in Mary Sidney's translation of the Psalms and in the drama of Elizabeth Cary, Giovanni Guarini, Ben Jonson, Thomas Rowley, William Shakespeare, John Webster, and Mary Wroth. The book's first four chapters are organized around slander as a linguistic, rhetorical, and juridical phenomenon. The first chapter outlines the Renaissance preoccupation with the gap between words and things that enables and haunts tropes and figures in the linguistic sphere, and the gap between saying and meaning that enables and haunts persuasive speech in the social sphere. Slander is an opportunistic phenomenon that "insinuates itself into," "exploits," and "makes use of" those gaps (25). The second chapter specifies slander as a form of deviant speech that relies on "persuasion rather than manipulation because it must be believed to develop its harmful power. To foster belief, the slanderer employs a rhetorical strategy suggesting an intrinsic, functional relation between language, materiality and agency expressed in the two most powerful metaphors for slander—poison and witchcraft" (30). By emphasizing slander's idiosyncratic communicative and rhetorical traits and by analyzing *Othello*'s depiction of slander as an essentially theatrical practice, this chapter demonstrates convincingly the interpretive advantage of insisting on slander as a inherently dramatic "triangular constellation which I label the 'slander triangle'—regardless of the number of people actually involved, there are three positions, namely those of slanderer, listener, and victim" (2). The chapter ends with what Habermann terms her "most striking discovery at an early stage of the project": the gendering of good and bad eloquence, and the "increasingly strong historical and symbolic link . . . between femininity and slander" (2–3). The third and fourth chapters locate slander in a juridical context—the third chapter tracing the "importance of the discourse of slander for the development of juridical thought and procedure in early modern England," the fourth chapter exploring "women's position in the legal discourse of slander" (43, 59). Both chapters elaborate on the "concept of equity, or fair judgment in view of the special circumstances of a case" (49). The third chapter considers equity's increasing importance and application in legal theory and practice. Given slander's association with linguistic and communicative instability, slander law offers a particularly resonant instance of the juridical changes, including a reliance on equity, that follow from humanism's "new and different attention to the flexibility of language as a medium of communication as well as the hermeneutic inquiry into historical detail" (49). The fourth chapter extends this discussion by exploring the juridical link between women and slander that disproportionately identifies cases involving women as special instances that require the application of equity.

The fourth chapter's discussion of Shakespeare's *The Merry Wives of Windsor,* Webster's *The Devil's Law Case,* and Webster and Rowley's *A Cure for a Cuckold* assumes that drama is a form of equity, a "means of exploring particular cases which cannot adequately be dealt with in either legal theory or practice" (59). This chapter inaugurates a series of nuanced and persuasive analyses of how English Renaissance plays negotiate among slander, gender, and equity at the level of genre, plot, and characterization. The fifth chapter, "Femininity between Praise and Slander," considers the professional motivations for and gendered consequences of the tension between epideictic rhetoric and equitable inquiry in Guarini's *Il Pastor Fido,* Jonson's *The Devil is an Ass,* and Wroth's *Love's Victory.* The eighth and final chapter, "The Slandered Heroine," asks what Shakespeare's *Othello* and Cary's *The Tragedy of Mariam* might tell us about Renaissance constructions of female subjectivity and women's agency. This final analysis draws on Habermann's work on the unruly female tongue in the two preceding chapters. The sixth chapter had investigated the unruly female tongue in Renaissance treatises on defamation with an eye to analyzing slander's shifting and unstable physiological qualities. Slander's characteristic oscillation between the figurative and the literal at times draws on its medieval roots among the "sins of the tongue" and thus is "conceived as a direct physical injury . . . in an increasingly pragmatic and rational environment," and at times draws on an emerging distinction between mind and body that acknowledges the flexibility of slander and allows it to "be deployed as a modern technology of power" (113). The seventh chapter had asked how women's religious writings—including Mary Sidney's translation of the Psalms—carve out a niche for women's authority and women's authorship in their responses to pastoral writing on the sins of the tongue. When Habermann turns to the slandered heroine in her final chapter, she argues that Shakespeare and Cary share a Renaissance conviction that slander provides a fertile resource for drama both in its characteristic oscillation between the figurative and the literal and in its highly theatrical and inevitably gendered slander triangle. Even so, the playwrights diverge in their depiction of the psychic and the social, of what is internal to and extrinsic to the body, as they place their tragic heroines in the service of the plays' very different generic requirements and their very different visions of women's agency in Renaissance England.

This is an altogether impressive book—original in its claims about the intersections among slander, gender, equity, and Renaissance drama; persuasive in its detailed arguments about slander as a linguistic, rhetorical, and juridical phenomenon; generous and yet exacting in its relation to previous scholarship (including Joel Altman's argument about Renaissance dramatic appropriations of "rhetorical instruments of deliberation like the *controversia,* the *suasoria* and the *argumentum in utramque partem*" [6], Lorna Hutson's assessment of equity, and John Hamilton Baker's and Ian Maclean's underestimation of the impact of humanism on the law); and enormously compelling in its analyses of the slander triangle, and in particular the slandered heroine, in Renaissance drama.

I did find *Staging Slander and Gender in Early Modern England* particularly fascinating when Habermann offered extended analyses of the plays in the book's fourth, fifth, and eighth chapters. Initially, I attributed this impression to my critical preoccupations and to Habermann's style. She tends to introduce several of her chapters with general and fairly uncontentious claims (for instance, that "eloquence was considered precarious in the early modern period" and that " 'good' eloquence was distinguished from 'bad' through a process of gendering" or that the "tongue as an unruly body member is seen to be responsible for transgressive speech, and due to the culturally ingrained connection between embodiment and femininity, transgressive speech is feminized") and then to work carefully to her more precise formulations about how slander helps us to reevaluate equity, humanism and the law, or medieval and early modern conceptions of the "relationship between substance and thought" (27, 99, 113). All of which is to say that, given the structure of these chapters, her original claims are often a bit buried. When she turns to more conventionally literary materials (Mary Sidney's translation of the Psalms and the drama of Cary, Guarini, Jonson, Rowley, Shakespeare, Webster, and Wroth) she is more likely to frame her analyses in terms of "how plays such as Webster's *The Devil's Law Case* and *A Cure for a Cuckold* as well as Shakespeare's *The Merry Wives of Windsor* imagine—in a predominantly comic mode—women's use of and active responses to slander"; how women's religious writing negotiates the "issue of the unruly tongue"; how, unlike her male counterparts, "Wroth is not concerned with the construction of femininity between praise and slander, but transforms [pastoral tragicomedy] in search of a more comprehensive, or equitable, negotiation of gender relations"; and how, unlike Shakespeare, Cary uses the convention of the slandered heroine to "vindicate the character of her assertive heroine," drawing on the "discourse of slander for a strongly political vision of human agency" (59, 115, 77, 135). Given the structure of these chapters, the originality of Habermann's study is always apparent. The "how" chapters that focus on drama offer striking insights about the intersection of slander and gender in comedy, tragedy, and tragicomedy and the very particular ways that each play works within and between these genres—most perceptively, in analyses of the relative weight of the comic and the tragic in Wroth's *Love's Victory*, the production of tragic affect in *Othello*, and the tragicomic elements in *The Tragedy of Mariam*.

It is worth noting that my impression—my preference for the extended analyses of the plays—also might be attributed to the disciplinary character of Habermann's interdisciplinary scholarship, a formulation that strangely enough, over the last few decades, has come to feel less and less like an oxymoron as interdisciplinarity has taken hold in the imaginary of English literary studies. In Renaissance literary studies this sort of interdisciplinarity often involves focusing on objects of analysis that had been associated with work in disciplines such as anthropology, economics, linguistics, history, philosophy, and psychoanalysis; relying on the insights of those disciplines; or (although this is less common) incorporating their analytical techniques. It is continuous with a long history of disciplinary borrowing in literary studies and with a long history

of literary criticism whose historical contextualizing, at its best, il-
luminated the plays, poems, and prose that tended to be the focus
of most research and teaching in our discipline. It distinguishes itself from most of that earlier work in a number of ways, including
the kinds of abstract questions that motivate its scholarship—"How
is slander defined? What is its linguistic basis? What is the nature
of its threat? How does the community deal with it? Who talks
about it, how, and why? How does it affect the sense of selfhood of
those involved in it?" (1–2). And yet, at least in Renaissance literary studies, professional training and professional exigency tend to
privilege the explanatory power of literary objects of analysis.
"This study is conceived as a chapter in the history of culture, and
must therefore necessarily be interdisciplinary, drawing on legal
history, social history and legal anthropology, philosophy, theology, literary criticism and gender studies," Habermann explains.
"But comparing a range of materials—perhaps in line with my
training as a literary critic—I have found drama to offer the most
comprehensive contemporary negotiation of slander and have accordingly made it the principal scene of this book" (3). I offer this
assessment not as a criticism of Habermann's scholarship but as an
effort to locate it within contemporary literary studies. Whatever
might be lost for a purer notion of interdisciplinarity, our understanding of English Renaissance drama is certainly richer for the
publication of *Staging Slander and Gender in Early Modern England.*

Figuring Sex between Men from Shakespeare to Rochester
By Paul Hammond
Oxford: Oxford University Press, 2002

Reviewer: Alan Stewart

Figuring Sex between Men from Shakespeare to Rochester is a return to territory that Paul Hammond previously studied in his 1996

Love between Men in English Literature. As the titles suggest, Hammond has now narrowed his field of vision to the seventeenth century (the earlier book continued through to the 1950s); but, with that slip from "Love" to "Sex," he has also brought into play more blatantly sexual material. The seventeenth century has of course been a key period for scholars of male homosexuality in England since the publication of Alan Bray's seminal work *Homosexuality in Renaissance England* in 1982. Bray pointed out how, in the sixteenth and early seventeenth centuries, "sodomy," in Hammond's rendering, "was more of an ideological category than an erotic preference: sodomites were bracketed with Jesuits, Spanish spies, and werewolves as agents of social and moral subversion," a "way of thinking" that "provided no resources for self-definition" (9). By the early eighteenth century, however, London at least had a burgeoning subculture, centered on the so-called molly houses, where men met for company and sex, and developed "the private and collective exploration of sexual role-playing, cross-dressing, parodic rituals, and specialized slang" (11). Hammond's interest is in how poetic endeavors might be read against this historical backdrop. Around 1600, when supposedly there were "no resources for self-definition," he argues, "one finds poetry explicitly articulating homoerotic desire, along with plays in which homoerotic possibilities are teasingly explored." Conversely, and equally mysteriously, by 1700, "it is hard to find any literature which celebrates the male body homoerotically," although there is a "self-confident, self-defining subculture" (1).

While there is much that Bray's paradigm leaves unanswered, Hammond adopts it uncritically, and to good effect, showing that it is with this paradox in mind that literary criticism can truly come into its own. Following the lead of Bruce Smith (whose *Homosexual Desire in Shakespeare's England: A Cultural Poetics* [1991] remains an invaluable survey), Hammond studies the strategies by which authors throughout the period negotiated the constraints and potentialities afforded by poetic expression—either by the appropriation of coded genres, such as classical pastoral, or the exploration of charged relationships, such as master and servant, brothers in arms, poet, and patron. This literature, according to Hammond, "offered a world of free play, with the possibility of discontinuous identity, resources for temporary and shifting modes of self-definition," without inviting the reader to "label himself as a man with exclusive or unusual sexual preferences" (11).

Hammond's critical technique is thus to examine "the rhetoric of sex between men, exploring how literature creates an imagined world in which homosexual relations can be figured, and how readers responded to those creations by adapting, rewriting, and censoring those texts" (4). He declares his intention to avoid new historicist and cultural materialist approaches (although Foucault is a constant companion through the book)—and some readers may find the approach strangely old-fashioned, given the subject matter, usually on the cutting edge of theoretical inquiry. But the joy of Hammond's book is in its raw materials: thoroughly at ease with Latin texts and manuscript sources, Hammond provides copious quotation of hitherto little-known works that will widen the (usually distressingly limited) repertoire available to scholars of every ilk. His opening chapter, for example, gives us Thomas Hobbes on Socrates' interest in Alcibiades; a wonderful array of travel writings involving sodomy not only in the usual suspects (Italy, Spain, Turkey), but also Siam and the island of Capul; and a variety of writings concerning Sir John Finch and Sir Thomas Baines, who share a monument in Christ's College chapel in Cambridge (although Alan Bray's last book, *The Friend*, published more recently, extends this inquiry much further). Hammond introduces us to the passionate poetry of Nicholas Oldisworth, much of it obsessed with his friend Richard Bacon; the sodomitical pope in Barnabe Barnes's intriguing 1607 play *The Divils Charter*; and a whole host of highly anxious translations of classical writers, especially Theocritus. A long chapter on "Politics and 'Sodomy' " investigates various renderings of the notorious sodomy of Edward II and Piers Gaveston (though not the Marlowe play), James I and the duke of Buckingham (including a remarkable 1655 play by Francis Osborne entitled *The True Tragicomedy*), and, more unusually, the later seventeenth-century sodomites *du jour* Titus Oates and William III. Finally, two shorter case studies examine the charges of impotence and sexual ambiguity against Andrew Marvell, of all people; and the more predictable libertine circles of the earl of Rochester.

Readers of this journal will probably be most interested in Hammond's second chapter, on "Shakespearian Figures" (62–116). Building again on work done in his earlier book (*Love Between Men*, 58–87), Hammond explores "the kinds of imagined space which Shakespeare creates for the presentation of strong male bonds," analyzes the way he adapts his sources, and examines the ways in which later Shakespeare editors and adaptors sought to "close down the possibilities and erase homosexual meanings from his texts" (62). Starting with the *Sonnets*, Hammond argues that Shakespeare "seems addicted to multiple definitions which by their sheer proliferation over-delineate, perpetually redescribing the young man, the poet, and their relationship" (63), through the use of *correctio* or *epanorthosis*, and *paradiastole* (redescription). Hammond's technique is to toy fiercely with keywords such as "self," "will," and "love," puns, figures of possession and dispossession, or even a simple verb, such as "have." But this dogged close reading sometimes produces a real insight, as when he notes, almost in passing, that "the most important word in the *Sonnets* is 'but'" (64). He also revisits the familiar territory of the Antonios of *The Merchant of Venice* and *Twelfth Night*, through their source materials (respectively Ser Giovanni's novella *Il Pecorone* and the Sienese play *Gl'Ingannati*) showing how Shakespeare used "his imagined Italy [as] a space where homosexual desire might be given voice, if not satisfaction" (100). Given his use of Bray's model in which the seventeenth century sees the (unexplained) rise of a gay subculture and a concomitant unwillingness to explore homoeroticism in literature (except scurrilously and pornographically), it isn't surprising to read Hammond finds that century's editors and adapters of Shakespeare quietly eviscerating the works of their homoerotic potential: he suggests cautiously that "there is a sufficiently coherent pattern here to suggest that these Restoration adaptations were motivated partly by a concern to protect male friendship from the suspicion of homosexual desire" (116).

More controversial, perhaps, will be Hammond's strongly voiced argument that Shakespeare was indebted to a writer of clearly homoerotic sonnets, Richard Barnfield. While some of his comparisons convince—as Victorian editor A. B. Grosart long ago noted, Shakespeare's sonnet 20 clearly echoes Barnfield's "The Teares of an Affectionate Shepherd" ("I love thee for thy gifts, She for hir pleasure; / I for thy Vertue, She for Beauties treasure")—others may simply point to a shared pool of ideas, familiar from classical and humanist literature; for example, both men's interest in how the boy's beauty will fade with age. The jury remains out on this one, although Hammond's argument will give teachers plenty of guidance for classroom comparisons of Barnfield and Shakespeare— allowing us to conclude, as Hammond notes, that the two poets diverge wildly in their treatment: "[w]here Barnfield's poetry speaks of the desire of an older man to possess a younger man, erot-

icizing his body and multiplying images of physical consummation, Shakespeare's poetry moves inward, analysing various kinds
of possession and dispossession" (84).

There are only a couple of points of fact that might be challenged
in Hammond's book: the *Corona Regia*, although credited to Isaac
Casaubon, is thought not to be his work (not least because he was
dead by 1615) (138); and the possibility that a reference to burning
in a satire against James may invoke a convicted sodomite burning
at the stake (146) seems improbable, given that (unlike countries
such as France) England had not burned sodomites for well over
a century. But these are isolated incidents. Throughout this study,
Hammond's scholarship is employed to great effect. This is a thoroughly enjoyable, thoughtful, and generous book that gives us all
plenty of meat to chew on, and will find admirers even among
those whose critical approaches differ widely from those of its author.

*Sick Economies: Drama, Mercantilism, and Disease
in Shakespeare's England*
By Jonathan Gil Harris
Philadelphia: University of Pennsylvania Press,
2004

Reviewer: Katherine Rowe

Sick Economies focuses on an aspect of early English economic
thought, mercantilism, which has remained offstage during the
past decade of lively conversation about theater and economic
practice. Approaching mercantilism as an ongoing debate about the
virtues of transnational finance and trade (rather than a defined period or commercial policy), Harris shows how deeply that debate
engaged contemporary theories of disease. Infection in particular,
he argues, was a hybrid set of concepts that drew equally on late
humoralism and emergent ideas about invasion by "foreign bod-

ies" articulated in early mercantilist writings. Figures of infection linked a "double helix of medical and mercantile signification" in which the foreign was reimagined as pathological (2–3). In fact the study resembles a triple helix. Successive chapters braid the work of six economic theorists with medical discussions of contagion. A third strand of analysis explores mercantilist drama by Shakespeare, Jonson, Middelton, and Dekker.

Tracking the way metaphors of disease cross-pollinate drama, economy, and medicine, *Sick Economies* offers marvelously unprogrammatic readings focused on the terms shared by mercantile and medical writings. The topics are a mix of familiar and strange: syphilis, taint, gangrene, canker, plague, hepatitis, castration, and consumption. Harris brings significant new insights into even the most familiar of these topoi. Chapter 3, for example, offers an utterly fresh, page-turning reading of the *Merchant of Venice,* theories of contamination, and usury. In contemporary mercantilist writings usury appears less as a sinful way to grow capital than as a transnational mode of commerce that corrupts and confuses categories the way taint or gangrene comingles dead and live tissue. The itinerary of these metaphors links the figure of the English Jew to a proliferation of dangerously hybrid identities, from Venetians to Marrano immigrants from the Netherlands.

Figures of health and disease migrate in both directions, giving us early modern theories of medical protectionism (Timothy Bright) and neo-Galenic scenes of consumption as a nutritive intake of goods (*The Roaring Girl*). As Harris tracks these migrations across different discourses what emerges is an extended itinerary of medico-economic tropes in the mode of Raymond Williams. These tropes become the site for a categorical division between salubrious ("global") and pathological or dangerous ("foreign") kinds of transnationalism. The kinds of transnationalism were no more stable and consistent in the late sixteenth century, Harris reminds us, than they are now. But the division itself, emerging at the intersection of early medical and economic theory, has remained remarkably stable. And it has a persistent hold on the way Westerners think about the economic health of the nation.

In the largest sense, then. *Sick Economies* is invested in historical epistemology: why Western culture understands economic life—an individual's or a state's—in terms of health and disease. In answering this question, Harris's readings outpace the model of historical change, derived from Williams, that frames them. When describing larger patterns of change, the study is strongly attached to homologies. Changes in economy neatly parallel changes in medicine, with exogeny playing the emergent role in both discourses. For the role of vestige or residue in this drama, *Sick Economies* presents a stock version of late humoralism, which it describes as primarily concerned with the balance of internal fluids.

Yet as recent scholarship has emphasized, humoralism was a transactional system in its own right, equally concerned with the environmental regulation of intake and output. And like mercantilism, it is better understood as a field of debate, shot through with diverse and sometimes conflicting sources, rather than a neatly defined program or episteme. Thus, whereas Harris reads the salutary view of consumption explored in *The Roaring Girl* as foreshadowing Adam Smith's idea of healthy consumption, it seems rather that the play is applying earlier neo-Stoic principles of controlled intake to commodities. The play seems to be testing the claim that purchasing habits could be a kind of "non-natural": an external that the civil gentleman should partake of judiciously, along with diet, sleep, air, exercise, emotion, and elimination.

Moreover, humoral writers have their own preoccupations with transnationalism. Andrew Boorde's *Breviary*, for example, glosses illness in humoral terms but its remedies and preventives were collected from his travels across Europe and the Middle East. The *Breviary* would seem to model—rather than serve as the anti-type of—the kind of "controlled encounter with foreignness" that "safeguards the health of the body politic" in Middleton and Dekker's play (27). If this example complicates a tidy narrative of emergent transnationalist thinking, it supports what I take to be the subtler core of *Sick Economies*: that cross-pollination with economic debates helps recolor the normative humoral exchanges between external and internal *as* pathological.

Among the most important aspects of this thought-provoking study may be that it demonstrates the limits of a terminology and model of historical change that has been foundational, compelling, and deeply satisfying for many literary critics (including this one). Raymond Williams's work helped free us from the search for definitive historical origins and a Whiggish progressivism. But emergent/residual retains a temporal progressivism that may not suit the lateral career of social tropes. "Career" is the term Harris invokes from Arjun Appadurai's discussion of the commodity: "constituted within and by a diachronic trajectory of exchange . . . objects do not simply acquire meaning or value by virtue of their present social contexts. Rather, they impart significance to those contexts as a result of the paths they have traced through time and space" (119). *Sick Economies* seems to be on the brink of theorizing the movement of disease metaphors in similar terms. But it does not pursue this.

What if we took such lateral movement—wheeling, unpredictable movement, as the etymology of *career* implies—as a model for the circulation of metaphors? Among other things, we'd need to remember that the same metaphor may be doing different, even opposite conceptual work in the different fields that it passes through. In this view, both discursive fields, humoral and mercantile, would look more like what they are—heterogenous sites for the convergence and conflict of different ideas drawn from multiple periods— than the framework of this study permits. *Sick Economies* tracks the social metaphors as they move among different fields of knowledge and experience. What we need now is to frame this incisive reading practice with a theory that suits it.

The Actor as Playwright in Early Modern England
By Nora Johnson
Cambridge: Cambridge University Press, 2003

Reviewer: A. R. Braunmuller

As Imogen Stubbs, Stephen Fry, or Steve Martin among current actors demonstrate, actors often write for the stage. So, too, long ago. In a note to their invaluable volume concerning theatrical wills, Ernst Honigmann and Susan Brock remark on the large number of early modern English actor-playwrights—"Tarlton, Christopher Beeston, Nathan Field, John Honyman, William Bird, John Shank senior, William Rowley.[1] They might have added, among the still greater, Jonson and Shakespeare, however poor or limited each of them seems to have been as actors.[2]

Nora Johnson has been inspired to write a book about early modern English actor-playwrights and playwright-actors.[3] Her choices are Armin, Field, Munday, and Heywood, and she later (152–53) adds Robert Wilson and William Rowley and possibly Richard Brome as others she might have studied. John Webster and Wil Barksted are more distant possibilities (191–92n.9), though it is phantasmagorical for me to imagine crabbed Websterio on the boards. None of the chosen four is now especially famous, or taught, or written about. Nor is there much surviving information—archival or anecdotal or textual—to ease a critic's way. Through Johnson's thoughtful criticism, all become remarkable, and she turns evidential fragments into gold. In each of her four main chapters, Nora Johnson approaches authorship-as-acting/acting-as-authorship from different tangents: it is important to realize that the first two nouns of her title could have appeared in either order or, were English syntax a trifle more flexible, in both. Her goals throughout are calmly revisionary: "to read early modern theater as a realm without authors—or to see the construction of authorship only in the exclusive gestures of Jonson and his peers—is unnecessarily to surrender the institution of authorship to its later and more elitist incarnations" (125). Or as the index entry for "Foucault, Michel" puts it—between "theories of authorship" and "summarized"— "shortcomings of."

This book asks other scholars to think hard about small moments of hard-to-interpret matters like Armin's stand-up comedy and audience-inspired jokes (chapter 1): textual survivals give later readers almost nothing to understand or revivify when they attempt to reimagine what went on when Armin spoke and acted, or Tarlton appeared behind whatever the "Tapistrie" was from behind which he so famously is said (again, the textual evidence snarls in our later faces) to have peeped.[4] To say it another way, "At the moment that Tarlton becomes most himself in print, that is, he becomes most emphatically the possession of others" (27): the comedian, the actor, is his audience's hostage both on stage as he lived and, later to us, a hostage or manipulated and manipulable figure, as he is entombed in print.

Manipulation and actors manipulated are Johnson's next topic when she turns to the critically evergreen episode of the *Hero and Leander* puppets and Jonson's apparent reference (*Bartholomew Fair*, act 5) to Nathan Field's apparent presence as actor (as Cokes? as Littlewit? [see 62]) and Nathan Field as the possible butt of Jonson's jokes. Nora Johnson does some wonderful things with the possibilities, even likelihoods, that this episode alludes to Nathan Field's Puritan minister-father, John (though naming him "virtually martyred" [62] is rhetorical excess).[5] As she teases out the complexities of the Jonson-Field relation and its father-son/king-subject intricacies, she offers a significant and, for me, convincing revision of some current verities—Ben Jonson, the first-modern author; Ben Jonson, the anti-theatrical man of the theater; and Ben Jonson, the absolutist artist-king. Those views have dominated criticism for decades, but Johnson sees their inherent paradoxicality, if not their mere incoherence. For example:

> What *Bartholomew Fair* may ultimately establish through its vivid contests of representation is not so much the serene authority of the author or the sovereign, but the intermingling of those roles with actors and audiences. In the last analysis, what may matter most is not that authors model themselves upon monarchs but that self-representation per se is fundamentally dominated by the work of the player, by the puppet who speaks from the mouth of another. (79)

Or more succinctly: "to establish himself as anti-spectacle, Jonson had to make himself a spectacle" (78).

Along with the persuasive challenge to many current claims about Jonson and the invention of authorship, Johnson offers some excellently independent criticism of Nathan Field's own plays; she is especially cogent on his apparently contradictory relation with the women in his audiences: "Field emphasizes the potential power of his writing to control women, but the power that *Amends* [*for Ladies*] exercises over Lady Perfect seems to imply a sharp critique of Field's own comic project" (76).

As popular and admired as Field was among contemporaries, Anthony Munday, coauthor of *Sir Thomas More*, seems to have been the very reverse, noted especially for his ethical duplicity. Johnson frames her discussion of that play with considerations of Munday's writings—pro and con—about Roman Catholic martyrs and martyrdom and the place of the stage in early modern England. By successively defending contradictory moral positions, "Munday is suspected of playing rather than being, of performing for reward the forms of integrity for which he wants to be known. Because his conscience seems so utterly driven by the authorial marketplace, Munday embodies for his readers a set of connections between acting and authorship that render the author at once a powerful figure and a duplicitous one" (86).

Given her interests, it is no surprise that Johnson concentrates on the scene in *More* where More himself speaks about the scaffold as if it were a stage (act 5, scene 4 in the Gabrieli-Melchiori Revels edition) and on the episode concerning the performance of *The Marriage of Wit and Wisdom*. In both she finds "players" deeply dependent upon their audiences, "authors" who are also players and, in multiple ways for More, players who are authors who are audiences—"the forms of agency attributable to theater are riven by the sense that theatrical performance and theatrical writing alike are forms of self-division" (94–95). As Edmund Tilney's well-known marginalia on the manuscript attest, no less than the play's failure to be licensed for performance, the authors of *More* failed to walk a fine line between admiration for More (and hence at least a form of crypto-Catholicism) and criticism of Henry VIII (and hence of later Tudor policies more generally). Johnson links those difficulties with Munday's *English Roman Lyfe* and his "vicious campaign of pamphlet writing against [Edmund] Campion" (99). At stake in all these writings "is the prevailing sense of fraud, of reversible identity, of sham performance . . . [t]he epistemological uncertainties of martyrdom and authorship alike" (98, 105). The martyr, or accounts of martyrdom, measures "[t]he author on stage and the author in print . . . against the standards of the autonomous conscience" (105). The chapter on Munday concludes with a fine treatment of *The Downfall* and *The Death of Robert Earl of Huntingdon*, paying (again as one would expect) special attention to the authorial status of Skelton, who also plays Tuck and serves as narrator, and to the concluding scenes of Mathilda's martyrdom (110–21).

Just as bringing new light into the arena of authorship long in Jonson's enormous shadow was a theme of the author's treatment in chapter 2 of Nathan Field's different, but Jonsonianly inflected form of authorship, chapter 4 turns to Thomas Heywood's court masque, *Love's Mistress* (1634), the *Age* plays (*Golden, Silver, Brazen,* and *Iron* in two parts, 1611–32), and *The Rape of Lucrece* (1608) and finds an anti-Jonsonian form of "the staging of humanist authority" (122). Heywood's letter to the reader before *Love's Mistress* actively praises "that admirable artist, Master Inigo Jones . . . who to every act . . . gave such an extraordinary lustre . . . it was above my apprehension to conceive" (quoted 127). As Johnson astutely concludes:

> For critics accustomed to assuming [with Ben Jonson] that theatrical spectacle competes with authorship, that it introduces unwelcome collaboration and distracts audiences from the excellence of an author's composition, Heywood's masque opens up less obvious possibilities: that spectacle could be seen to legitimate authorship, that a writer could brag about keeping company with an elite designer, that the relation between print and performance could be mutually reinforcing. (129)

The *Age* plays and *Lucrece* appear here as "forms of authorship . . . marked by a distinctly early modern encounter between actors and classical authority" (134). Moving from Homer as author and authority in *The Golden Age* through forms of paternity dramatized in the *Age* plays, Johnson eventually reaches a view of Heywood (and a view of Heywood's view of himself) as "property and owner, sovereign and subject, [Foucauldian] principle of thrift and point of entry for material and social constraint" (143).

Specialist readers of this monograph and of this journal will have found only glancing references to William Shakespeare, but to ignore Johnson's work would be perilous. She opens a spacious area for Shakespeareans' study, and she makes abundantly clear that there is much more to be thought about Shakespeare as well as about his texts' relation to others' and the performance of his texts and theirs. Ben Jonson and his modern expositors have been an overt obstacle to uncovering some of the critical treasures here. With "Coda: the Shakespearean silence," Johnson considers claims for "a growing [i.e., through the career] anti-histrionic bias in Shakespeare's writing" (154), claims that would make him Jonson's historical and critical ally. Much turns on how we interpret the supposed replacement of Kemp (? = the first Falstaff?) by Armin (? = the first Feste) in Shakespeare's company, and in a close reading of *Twelfth Night*, Johnson makes a case that at the play's end Feste "may . . . be consolidating a form of comic authority that has relied upon adversity from its first moments in" the play (159). That is, Shakespeare has not reined in Kemp's unruly clowning so much as leaving a different actor with different comic skills a different kind of theatrical and actorly space. The "Shakespearean silence" is of course his textual silence on such topics as authorship, his career, and fame, and Johnson has consciously and successfully "determined to look elsewhere for . . . information about theatrical authorship in Renaissance England" (162). Unlike the examples that fill her book, Shakespeare offers "abstractions of theatrical production: vices and plotters, Gower, Prospero, choruses, mechanicals, the idea of the play, the thematization of writing" (162–63), and the silence or emptiness invites subjective responses. Johnson speculates, further, on how that silence has "exert[ed] an undue influence upon our thinking about dramatic authorship. . . . Shakespeare's silence on the subject of his own career seems to have prompted, or at very least been particularly friendly to, the development of essentialist notions of authorial subjectivity" (163). That is well observed, and the chapters that precede the observation uncover some very different possibilities and argue a very different case.

The scholarship in this book and the attention to earlier scholarship are meticulous and admirable. Where work from the nineteenth or early or mid or late twentieth centuries serves to support or advance the argument, it receives full due. That's unusual, alas. Johnson treats a centuries-long scholarly and critical conversation and its many topics with respect, or skepticism, or simply as information to be recorded, where each of those responses is warranted. The notes are comprehensive, largely impeccable (though Madeleine Doran and Nicholas Brooke do lose their respective terminal *es*), and unfailingly considerate, not dismissive. I caught a mistranscription and a typo. Sometimes, the author has been let down by the typesetters, whose computers acknowledge the "smart-quote," but occasionally fail to distinguish between ['] and [']—the latter error appears in, for example, a line quoted from *Sir Thomas More*, "And elevate my better part 'bove sight" where one would hope for "And elevate my better part 'bove sight" (92).[6] Unless one is an editor of early modern play-texts, why bother with such typographic minutiae? The answer is simply that this book deserves the very best possible presentation because its arguments are very good, and one hopes for the fewest humanly possibly glitches in those arguments' presentation.

Nora Johnson's *Actor as Playwright* merits thorough reading: its writing is lucid, its spirit generous, its argument innovative. And who could resist a book in which Tarlton and Shakespeare, assisted by Armin, become quince pie (17–18, 26)?

Notes

1. *Playhouse Wills 1556–1642* (Manchester: Manchester University Press, 1993), 26 n. 9.

2. Thomas Dekker in *Satiromastix* offers the principal evidence for Jonson as actor, and his
funny, satirical claims may be doubted; the Shakespeare first folio mentions Jonson as an actor.

3. Declaration of an interest: Nora Johnson was an exceptional undergraduate student in one of my classes and later attended, happily for me, an NEH seminar we shared at the Folger Shakespeare Library.

4. See 19.

5. Johnson honorably, as everywhere else, cites the scholarly tradition and appropriately credits Keith Sturgess for his splendid discovery of Jonson's sources for his vitriol here (Johnson, 58 n 15 and 63 n 31).

6. As my intrusive square brackets might imply, the designer for this volume has also intruded them in the endnotes in a rather odd fashion.

Gender and Jewish Difference from Paul to Shakespeare
By Lisa Lampert
Philadelphia: University of Pennsylvania Press, 2004

Reviewer: M. Lindsay Kaplan

Lisa Lampert's *Gender and Jewish Difference from Shakespeare* interrogates the production of Christian identity in terms of its relationship to gender and Judaism, demonstrating that this identity is neither static nor fixed. Arguing in her introductory chapter that the "Christian" is just as constructed a term as the "Jew," Lampert seeks to de-center Christianity from its normative position in explaining medieval texts and release "the study of . . . representations of Jews and Judaism from a restricted economy of particularism." Jews in these depictions do not merely represent the "Other," "but are implicated in the fundamental understand-

ings of reading, interpretation, and identity that these texts engage"
(1). The exploration of a mutable Christian self-definition is extended to include gender because of the parallels between Jews and
women in the exegetical tradition that align the spiritual and masculine with the Christian in opposition to the carnal, feminine, and
Jewish. In seeking to explore the ways in which Jewish difference
and gender are mutually constituted in medieval English texts,
Lampert is influenced by the theoretical project of "intersectionality" that argues for the necessary study of race and gender in terms
of each other. She also demonstrates how her investigation contributes to contemporary arguments about "identity politics" and recent attempts by Laclau and others "to recuperate the universal for
radical political ends" (170). Lampert argues for the need to study
the supersessionist medieval/early modern religious roots of the
universal and consider its influence on current universalist-partic-
ularist debates. Jeremy Cohen's concept of the "hermeneutical
Jew," an "ideological construction created not as a reflection of actual reality but as a tool of Christian theology" and self-definition
(9), provides Lampert with a model to discuss both Jewish difference and gender—in the concept of the "hermeneutical woman"—
within the Christian exegetical tradition. These figures are doubly
hermeneutic insofar as their particular representations are structured in terms of reading or misreading in relation to a supersessionist "true" reading. This notion of a failed interpretive approach
extends beyond representations of Jews—and can be formulated in
the absence of actual Jews—to fuel accusations of "judaizing" in
charges of heresy and conflicts between Christians. Lampert points
out that supersessionist views extend to symbolic representations
of the body "as hermeneutical paradigms are 'made flesh'" (11); the
Incarnation, which establishes the Christian hierarchy of the spirit
over the letter, takes place, as she argues, "through the body of a
woman who is both virgin and mother, Christian and Jew" (11).

Another aim of Lampert's book is to challenge tendencies to peri-
odize and dichotomize medieval and early modern culture. She extends her consideration of Christian exegesis to include the
Merchant of Venice's engagement with this tradition in its representation of Jews and gender in relation to questions of Christian
identity. This broader chronology also enables her to argue that just
as there is continuity in representations of gender from the Middle
Ages to the early modern era, so too medieval ideas about race and
religious difference contribute to early modern formulations of the

concept. Lampert makes a carefully argued case for the consideration of medieval constructions of Jewish racial identity. She cites the work of Robert Stacey, who identifies in thirteenth-century English Christian thought "an irreducible element to Jewish identity . . . , which no amount of baptismal water could entirely eradicate," as well as the scholarship of Robert Bartlett, who argues that race is more synonymous with ethnicity, with its emphasis on social and cultural, rather than somatic markers of difference (17).

In her second chapter, "The Hermeneutics of Difference," Lampert draws on the work of Daniel Boyarin and Carolyn Dinshaw to develop parallels between women and Jews in Christian exegesis. In Paul's metaphor of the olive tree in Romans 11:16–24, he defines Christians both in terms of and in opposition to Jews; this bifurcated view of the Jews results in a polarized representation of them: "good" Jews who are willing to convert to Christianity and "bad" ones who resist it. Women are similarly depicted in binary terms as either virgin or whore. Her argument, however, could be refined here, since she does not demonstrate how women are as central as Jews to the questions of religious identity; furthermore, the theological problems that gender poses for Christianity go beyond hermeneutics. Nevertheless, in the context of Christian hermeneutics, women and Jews both become associated with carnality and faulty reading. They are "good" only insofar as they can suppress their respective difference—femininity or Jewishness—and become like male Christians. And, as established by Augustine, the way to become a true Christian is to read rightly: according to the spirit, not the flesh. Exegetical views of women and Jews converge, as Lampert argues, in the figure of Mary, a Jewish woman who literally embodies the Incarnation, the crucial moment of supersession.

> Polarized representations of women, the division in representation of pre- and post-Crucifixion Jews, the dichotomy between letter and spirit, and the Incarnation—each play a role in medieval representations of Mary, a figure at the center of multiple paradoxes. At the moment of the Incarnation, the Word is made Flesh, and Christian understanding is seen as freed from the tyranny of the letter, making the dawn of a new era of Christian spiritual understanding. The Incarnation itself, therefore, stands as a central premise of Christian understanding of the relation between letter and spirit. (49)

Lampert includes a discussion of Jewish polemic against the Incarnation which focuses on Mary's corporeal pollution and sinfulness,

and by extension Jesus' as well. Christians responding to these attacks are forced to insist on the goodness of the human body in general and the particular holiness of Jesus and Mary's bodies. This
conflict provides another paradigm for considering Christian self-
definition in relation to Jews and women. Judith Butler's development of Kristeva's concept of abjection, "that site of dreaded identification against which—and by virtue of which—the domain of the
subject will circumscribe its own claim to autonomy and to life"
supplies an apt account of Christian response to Jewish and female
others (55). However, Lampert needs to explore fully the paradox
of Christian theology significant for her argument: that the advent
of God in a carnal, human body provides a spiritual freedom from
the tyranny of the letter. This contradiction that Jewish critics ex-
ploited threatens the distinction between spirit and letter crucial to
Christian identity. While Lampert claims that Jewish and feminine
particularity are part of a Christian universal that can never be fully
subsumed, it seems more precise to argue that Jesus' carnality
poses the central problem to Christian exegesis and its disturbing
ramifications are displaced and projected onto the hermeneutical
Jew and/or woman in order to attenuate its threat.

In chapter 3, Lollardy and the debate that it represents for medieval Christian belief and identity is the context for examining the
negotiation of that identity with Jews and women in Chaucer's
work. Lampert demonstrates, with reference to the work of Ruth
Nissé, ways in which Lollards and the orthodox clergy both associate their opponents with Jews. This controversy informs Lampert's
consideration of Fragments VII and VIII of the *Canterbury Tales*,
specifically the *Shipman's Tale,* the *Prioress's Tale,* the *Second
Nun's Tale* and the *Parson's Tale*. In her reading, the *Prioress's Tale*
serves as a response to the disturbing sexual and financial circula-
tions represented in the usury and adultery of the *Shipman's Tale*.
Her tale reorders the "moral chaos" (72) of the previous tale; her
demonizing representation of Jews calms anxieties within the
Christian community over gender transgression, in the polarized
threat of the unfaithful wife or the powerful Mary, and the blurring
of religious boundaries, in the Christian practice of "Jewish" usury.
The *Second Nun's Tale*, like that of the Prioress, also sets up a religious Other against which to define a true Christian identity. While
the Others in this tale are pagans, not Jews, Lampert argues that the
Prioress's formulation of "Jewish particularity" shapes the Second
Nun's account of the Roman Gentiles, and that both representations

offer a contrast to a Christian identity "linked to ideas of fulfilled understanding, spirituality and holiness" (89). However, since pagans are, by definition, *not* Jews, Lampert needs to argue this point more rigorously, especially in the light of the important role Gentiles play in the construction of Christian identity in the passages from Romans considered before. Her consideration of the *Second Nun's Tale* collapses categories that the exegetical tradition would have seen as opposed. Lampert then turns to a consideration of the topos of childhood in *Thopas/Melibee* sequence, delineated in the work of Lee Patterson, and associates it with the supersessionary idea of the younger Christian taking precedence over the elder Jew, which, without further evidence, lacks persuasive power. Finally, in her discussion of the *Parson's Tale*, she focuses on the significance of the Passion, and its association with the Jews, in Chaucer's delineation of Penitence. All of these examples are adduced to make the argument that views of Jews need to be considered even when they are not explicitly present in the text because "it is in relation to Jews and Judaism that Christians continually negotiate what it means to be Christian" (100). But this claim threatens to transform all alterity into Jewish difference, and calls into question the status of gender for her argument.

Furthermore, the concept of Christian self-definition could be given greater nuance in this chapter by a more consistent attention to the text. In the example from the *Parson's Tale*, penitence is achieved in part through a consideration of the Passion. While Jews are often associated with this event, not all mentions of the Passion, or even Jewish complicity in the crucifixion, are necessarily a supersessionist move made to establish a superior Christian identity. Lampert quotes X.598, which asserts that swearing is in effect to despise the body of Jesus, "moore booldely than dide the cursede Jewes or elles the devel" (99). However, here the sinning Christian is *worse* than the Jew or the devil himself; penitence requires the acknowledgment of one's own sin, even or especially if it is worse than that of the abject other, and the renunciation of one's transgression. I would argue that this is precisely a counter-supersessionist moment, when the Christian is required to abase him or herself before God and not condemn the Other.

Chapter 4 considers the fifteenth-century Croxton *Play of the Sacrament* and the "Nativity" and "Assumption" segments of the N-Town cycle. Each represent a doubter, one Jewish male, one Christian female, who are linked through the "topos of the stricken hand," a sign of their carnality and faithlessness (102). The plays interrogate Christian identity not only in terms of these "Others" but also in the representation of other "bad" Christians in the play; members of the plays' audience could explore their own commitment to the faith by identifying with or condemning the plays' malefactors (105). As in the earlier chapters, Lampert is interested in demonstrating the fragile and constructed nature of Christian self-definition: "The representations of paradigmatic doubters, Jew and woman, are particular identities through and against which a vision of Christian identity is created" (101). Interestingly, while the Jews of the Croxton play are converted at its conclusion, they are not integrated into the Christian community as the other transgressing and repentant Christians are. Lampert notes that the "universalist closure of Christian comedy cannot fully accommodate Jewish particularity," but does not explain the significance of this point for her argument (122). The construction of medieval concepts of racial identity would be a logical issue to consider at this point, since the play is set, as Lampert emphasizes, in Spain, includes characters of other national origin and represents Jews in terms of Muslims, when Jonathas prays to "Machomet" as his god. Engaging with race here would strengthen Lampert's claims to intersectional analysis as well as her challenge to periodizing ideas of race.

Her consideration of women and Jews in terms of each other is not so successful in this chapter; once the stricken hand topos has been established, the two "Others" are discussed somewhat separately. The woman, like the Jew, represents a source of origin, as Lampert asserts early in her argument (2). However, the threat of the female midwife in the N-Town cycle is mitigated by the fact that there are two midwives who try to examine the postpartum Mary, Zelome, who does so without consequence, and Salome, who expresses doubt more than concern for Mary's condition and is therefore punished. This point needs explanation in order to make the rest of Lampert's claims about midwives' transgressive power more convincing. Furthermore, while Lampert links the midwife's name to that of the treacherous step-daughter of Herod, she fails to identify this Salome as a Jew hostile to Jesus' teachings. This oversight highlights a larger one in the project: the decision not to consider the few medieval representations of female Jews. The discussion of "Jews" in relation to the separate category of "women" in the first four chapters has the unfortunate effect of reinforcing the notion that "Jews" are not comprised of both genders, notwithstanding the passing mention of Mary's Jewishness. Lampert thereby weakens her theoretical model and reinforces a periodizing split between these earlier chapters and the final chapter on *The Merchant of Venice.*

Lampert's analysis of the *Merchant of Venice* seeks to demonstrate the continuity of patristic and medieval hermeneutics in this early modern play's engagement with the analogy of the letter and the spirit (139). She combines Christian allegorical, Jewish cultural studies and feminist approaches to the play to continue the discussion of Christian interpretation and identity developed in the preceding chapters. Lampert sees the figure of Jessica as posing a threat to the distinctions between letter and spirit, appearance and inner worth; the confusion over her religious identity—is she a Jew or is she a Christian?—calls into question the stability of Christian self-definition. Portia's inability to determine "which is the Merchant here? and which the Jew?" (141) becomes symptomatic, for Lampert, of the difficulty the Venetian Christians have in determining and maintaining important hermeneutic distinctions. The play's sustained interrogation of ideas of race are at the root of this interpretive dilemma. The repeated consideration of the indelibility of racial difference in its representations of Morocco, Aragon, Launcelot's Moorish mistress, and the "Indian" beauty, helps reinforce the idea of an essential Jewish difference for both Jessica and Shylock. But both Morocco's and Shylock's pleas to be considered on the basis of a shared internal humanity, not judged by their racial/religious exteriors, draw precisely on the exegetical analogy of preferring the spirit to the letter. The logic of race espoused by the play's Christians is subverted by their own hermeneutic tradition. Even more troubling is the fact that Jessica possesses a racial difference that cannot be perceived nor erased by conversion, which creates a crisis for the doctrine of supersession. This investigation of the play's exploration of the medieval Christian tradition offers a persuasive and insightful perspective on the play.

However, in her goal to fit the play into the analogy of letter versus spirit and challenge periodizing distinctions, she does not always supply convincing interpretations of the text. For example, Lampert argues that Antonio's speech condemning Shylock's use of scripture—ending in "O what a goodly outside falsehood hath!" (I.i.97)—contrasts a "Jewish" way of reading and valuing the exterior, to a spiritual Christian reading of the interior truth. However,

the interior referred to here is not Christian truth, but a lie dis-
guised as truth; Jews are not represented as carnally misinterpret-
ing the text but in using the goodly outside of scripture to hide a
lie. This same attempt to make the text fit the letter/spirit analogy
provides an unconvincing interpretation of Bassanio's speech in
III.i condemning the falseness of fair "outward shows" that hide
evil beneath. Furthermore, she ignores some important shifts in
early modern attitudes toward commerce and religion, which results in a misreading of the play. Lampert argues that the "discourses of commerce and exploration can be seen [as] corroding
religious discourse throughout" the *Merchant of Venice*, as she similarly contended in her discussion of the Croxton play (141). However, by the late sixteenth century, commerce and Christianity were
seen less as competing than cooperative values to further European
imperialism. Missionary motives were increasingly used to justify
financial and territorial ventures in the New World. The merchant's
commercial ventures came to be seen as so compatible with Christian values that Daniel Price, an early seventeenth-century
preacher, could deliver a sermon on "The Merchant," extolling
him as the ideal Christian, using Matthew 13:45–46 as his proof-
text: "The kingdom of heaven is like unto a merchant man."

Gender and Jewish Difference from Paul to Shakespeare engages
with an ambitious range of important issues: the medieval exegetical construction of Christian identity in terms of Jewish and female hermeneutics; current theoretical debates on the universal-
particular; intersectionality and the mutual construction of race
and gender; periodization; and articulating Jewish particularity beyond representations of actual Jews. The wide scope of this book
somewhat weakens the impact of its collective ideas; Lampert
makes a great case for interrogating these points, but she does not
seek to synthesize them into a powerful single argument. Furthermore, in considering so many issues, and covering so much material in this richly researched book, Lampert is not able to attend to
some important textual and analytic details that could have refined
and strengthened her argument. Still, Lampert's book puts an overlooked area of study on the map—the intersection of gender and
Jewish difference in Christian culture—and establishes a critical
conversation that all who follow in her footsteps must engage and
grapple with.

*London Civic Theatre: City Drama and Pageantry
from Roman Times to 1558*
By Anne Lancashire
Cambridge: Cambridge University Press, 2002

Reviewer: Lukas Erne

As Anne Lancashire points out in the introduction to her study, the history of English theater usually takes a U-turn somewhere in the course of the sixteenth century. The history of late medieval English theater is essentially a matter of the provinces, chiefly because manuscripts of the great Corpus Christi cycles from York, Chester, Wakefield, and N-Town but no dramatic manuscripts of similar importance from London have survived. Yet the stage of Elizabethan and Jacobean theater is firmly set in London and at the nearby court. The way the history of English theater has been scripted has resulted in two big holes, that of early modern provincial theater and that of earlier London-based theater. Thanks to the Records of Early English Drama (REED), a large-scale research project based at the University of Toronto, the former is about to be filled by the more than twenty already published and over thirty projected volumes. As for the latter, Anne Lancashire's monograph, clearly an early offspring of her projected REED volume on "London Corporation and Guilds," which raises the fascinating question of what "can be said about the theater . . . that eventually gave rise . . . to Shakespeare and his contemporaries," provides what she modestly calls "the beginning, not the end, of the building of a new theater history for early civic London and for early London more broadly as well" (15).

In her introduction, Lancashire provides a useful guide both to previous scholarship and to her own study. She defines *civic* theater as "theater sponsored, wholly or in part, by the city of London itself or by the London craft guilds or livery companies" (7). What this excludes, at least in theory, is court theatrical activities, though as Lancashire herself is acutely aware, a central aspect of late medieval London life is "an easy mixing of court and city for social and entertainment purposes" (40), making a neat separation impossible. The rest of her study is divided into two parts, part 1 covering the period from Roman times to 1410 and part 2 that from 1410 to 1558. The first chapter deals with Roman London in which various kinds of entertainment must have been provided in a public amphitheater—found in excavations in 1987–88—and mimes and pantomimes may have been presented in a public open-air theater—none has been discovered to date. Chapter 2 covers the period from 410 to 1200, roughly what historians of earlier generations used to refer to as the "Dark Ages." Inadequate though the label may be in other ways, it does justice to the scarcity of extant evidence. As Lancashire stresses, this does not mean, however, that there was not "some general continuing theatrical activity" (28), at least until the Viking raids in the ninth century. Slightly more is known about the period covered in the third chapter, 1200–1410, allowing for a survey of the various kinds of civic theater or pageantry that must or is likely to have existed, including mummings, royal and other formal entries into the city, and the Clerkenwell play, an outdoor religious play performed up to roughly 1410, providing the chronological endpoint of the first part of this study.

While part 1 is organized chronologically, the chapters in part 2 function thematically, with chapters devoted to various types of London civic theater in the period from 1410 to 1558. Chapter 4 discusses craft guild records that show that the Drapers, Blacksmiths, Cutlers, Brewers, and other companies hired professional (though not necessarily full-time) players to perform in halls on certain feastive occasions, both serving as entertainment and displaying the companies' wealth and status. The following chapter investigates "what kind of plays were performed at livery feasts from the fifteenth century on to 1558" (95) and, in the absence of direct evidence, speculates based on what we know was performed elsewhere and for different auspices: "plays on biblical subject matter" (104), "saint/miracle plays" (105), "morality plays" (106), "classically influenced texts" (107), "folk-type entertainment" (107), "mummings" (108), or early sixteenth-century plays such as *Mundus et Infans* or John Heywood's *The Four PP*. Chapter 6 is devoted to John Lydgate, author of the only extant texts, written in the early fifteenth century, known to have been performed in civic halls in pre-Elizabethan London. The three mummings—*A Mumming at Bishopswood*, *A Mumming for the Mercers of London*, and *A Mumming for the Goldsmiths of London*—basically consist of "verses written to be recited by a presenter of a costumed spectacle" (118), which are variously classical, biblical, or allegorical in nature.

The four remaining chapters deal with various forms of London civic pageantry. Chapter 7 argues for the importance of formal entries into the city of English and foreign royalty as well as of emissaries from abroad "as a constant, continuing part of London civic theater" (131) in pre-Elizabethan London, an argument that is backed up by a long list of "Royal and Other Entries 1400–1558" provided in an appendix. Chapter 8 deals with civic water pageantry, a subject that has received little attention to date. Lancashire shows that the Thames was a space "of continuing importance to London as an entertainment location and political display space" (141) and discusses various forms of water shows, notably "entry water shows" (143) and "civic oath-takings by water" (145). The Midsummer Watch, the "largest and most important annual or near-annual civic spectacle in London" (153) in the early sixteenth century, is the subject of the following chapter. It consisted of a procession on the eves of the feast days of St. John Baptist (June 24) and of Sts. Peter and Paul (June 29), "of men in armour, musicians, cresset-bearers, giants, wildmen, morris dancers, swordsmen, and a varying number of 'pageants,' i.e., of wood and canvas constructions, carried through the streets by porters, depicting characters and events largely from the Bible, much less frequently from English history, and from classical mythology and allegory" (153). Finally, chapter 10 discusses the beginnings of the Lord Mayor's Show, which became London's major annual pageant spectacle around the middle of the sixteenth century, after the Midsummer Watch had come to an end for reasons which remain obscure.

There are obvious reasons why we have had to wait for a long time for a comprehensive study of London theater prior to the reign of Queen Elizabeth. Firstly, there are hardly any extant theatrical texts we can study. While Lancashire is at no pains to show that it is eminently worthwhile studying what other sources we have access to, the shortage of primary material has obviously not been conducive to sustained study. Lancashire calls this "the general prejudice, until very recently, of theater scholars against pageantry and in favour of play texts" (3), and her shift in emphasis is clearly spelled out by the presence of the word "pageantry" in the subtitle.

A rather different reason why Lancashire's study fills such a conspicuous hole is that the scholarly skills and effort required for a full investigation of the topic are such that few would have dared or have been equipped to undertake it. Many of us rarely recall how much of our scholarship ultimately depends on earlier Herculean scholarly labors—say E. K. Chambers's *Elizabethan Stage* and G. E. Bentley's *Jacobean and Caroline Stage* for a later period—so it may be important to remember that there was no Chambers and no Bentley for Lancashire to build upon. The number of thick manuscript volumes and manuscript rolls Lancashire has studied and the paleographical skills required to read them may in themselves be solid ground for respect. Lancashire's introduction is preceded by a seven-page list of abbreviations, conveying a sense of the breadth of her scholarship, and it is a tribute to the grasp she has of her material that her writing is nonetheless uncluttered and clear.

There is one more scholarly skill Lancashire displays throughout her study. In the absence of fuller documentation, all the evidence allows for is often speculative extrapolation. There are several dangers beleaguering speculative historical research, including the temptation to push one case as far as possible while neglecting possible alternative accounts, or the erroneous belief that absence of evidence is necessarily evidence of absence. Yet Lancashire successfully refrains from stretching her points, pondering probabilities and alternatives (as in the case of the reasons for the disappearance of the Midsummer Watch in London in the mid-sixteenth century) or asking the right questions instead of fishing in the dark for non-available answers. To admit that we can safely infer little or nothing from the scant extant evidence, as Lancashire repeatedly does, may not be a sexy thing to do, but her ability to handle evidence responsibly adds a further strength to what is in many ways an important and impressive scholarly achievement.

Dreams of the Burning Child: Sacrificial Sons and the Father's Witness
By David Lee Miller
Ithaca: Cornell University Press, 2003

Reviewer: Suzanne Verderber

In *Dreams of the Burning Child: Sacrificial Sons and the Father's Witness*, David Lee Miller seeks to interpret the motif named in the book's title. Why, he asks, does the sacrifice of sons, performed before the eyes of their fathers, permeate canonical texts of Western literature? What can explain the persistence of this fantasy in texts that include Genesis, the Gospels, the *Aeneid* and its Homeric precursors, Shakespeare's *Hamlet* and *The Winter's Tale*, Dickens's *Dombey and Son*, writings by Jonson, Freud, and Lacan, and finally Achebe's *Things Fall Apart*? This compelling question provokes Miller to improvise an interpretive approach that seeks to compensate for the limits of archetypal criticism and historicism, for the failure of these interpretive models to account for a fantasy that persists across millenia. Archetypal criticism, most famously espoused by Northrop Frye in the *Anatomy of Criticism*, fails because it resorts to, as Miller nicely puts it, "discredited notions of a universal human imagination" (209), while historicism fails due to its unrelenting synchronic perspective, its incapacity or unwillingness to seek answers beyond immediate historical context, "contemporary material interests and social practices" (209), in what sometimes seems to be a paranoid effort to avoid the charge of essentialism.

Guided by the specificity of the question itself, Miller engages in a form of historicism that takes the unconscious and desire into account, an approach that heeds recalcitrant, unconscious structural formations that persist beneath empirically observable reality. Indeed, how else can the endurance of a shared cultural fantasy be explained? Though interestingly he does not discuss Lacan in depth until chapter 5, I believe he nonetheless bases his answer upon the Lacanian conceptualization of the subject as split by language and other sociosymbolic systems. Economic and material conditions may change, as the historicists point out, but in Western culture one structure in particular has persisted and continued to function as the basis of the logic upon which the social order, including language, is predicated: patriarchy. Miller wisely points out that in Western patriarchal systems the assumption of a gendered identity is predicated on a double perception of lack: the boy's perception that the mother lacks a penis, and, most crucial for the present argument, the father's lack of a body. Implicitly adapting a Lacanian framework, Miller reminds us that paternal authority in Western culture is based on the invisibility of his body, so that the father appears purely as a symbolic function and is thus able to guarantee the truth and sense of the Law.

This absence of a paternal body opens a breach that can only, he argues, spur endless efforts of representation that attempt to seal it over. It is precisely because the relationship between a father and son is not corporeal that this relationship must be subject to unending symbolic representation. Among the many compelling hypotheses Miller offers, a principal one is that the sacrifice of a son before his father's gaze guarantees, in horrifically destructive fashion, the otherwise invisible tie that binds them. "If the fatherly body existed," he writes, "it would join the male progenitor to his heirs; since it does not, they can be joined only disjunctively, through the testimony of the mother-wife and in the abstract, corporate 'body' of the lineage-group . . . But if blood sacrifice in some mysterious way substantiates the otherwise merely notional patriline, displaying its reality in the opened body of the victim, then filial sacrfice goes to the heart of this mystery, forcing its paradox to the breaking point by offering up, in the firstborn son, the very body that creates fatherhood in the full patriarchal and patrilineal sense" (5). Because patrilineal descent is a social rather than a biological relation, it must be represented in the form of ritual.

I found it striking that while Miller painstakingly examines multitudes of examples of filial sacrifice in the Western canon, and numerous texts by Freud, he neglects to discuss the latter's *Totem and Taboo* (1913). This is an interesting omission because here Freud develops what he considered to be the founding myth of Western culture, the banding together of sons to kill the primal father, their subsequent development of laws against incest and murder, and their erection of patriarchal religions spurred by a sense of ambivalent love toward the murdered father and collective guilt. The text is also crucial to Miller's argument because it is here that Freud first develops, without being as explicit as Lacan will later be, the notion of paternity as a symbolic function. Perhaps the reason for the omission is that in this text Freud locates the origins of civilization in the sons' collective destruction of their father, while Miller is arguing that the image of fathers' destruction of their sons serves a similar purpose. Miller's argument may have benefited from a fuller and more overt exposition of its psychoanalytic framework, but such an approach would have probably undercut one of the most admirable aspects of the book, its joyful and productive disrespect for the boundaries, the taboos, that structure traditional historicism as well as the distinction between "theory" and "literature." Rather than "theory" being applied to "literature," all texts concerned are subject to rigorous and elegant close readings; unprocessed, obsessive mourning for sacrificed sons appears in Freud as well as Dickens, in Lacan as well as Shakespeare. Just he examines the tortured relations and identifications between fathers and sons, a confusion crystallized in the figure of the *puer senex*, he does the same in the relation between theory and literature, freeing texts from their generic appellations and clearing space for the creation of new significations and relations between texts through close reading. This book is as important for its argument—its content—as it is for the novelty and freshness of its approach.

The argument takes as its point of departure an examination of the reversals that take place in the spectacle of filial sacrifice between the Old and New Testaments. The father's perspective in Genesis is transformed into that of the son in the Gospels. God's command to Abraham to sacrifice Isaac, Abraham's acquiescence, and God's last-minute reprieve, Miller argues, confer that status of paternity upon Abraham that would otherwise remain unsymbolized. In the "postmodern" texts that constitute the Gospels, the human father withdraws and the stories are told from the perspective of the son to be sacrificed, Jesus Christ. God's absence at the spectacle of his son's sacrifice (Miller notes that God is rarely shown in depictions of the Crucifixion), which effectively tries to conceal the horrific nature of His command, is compensated for in representation by the presence of the grieving mother, in particular in Michelangelo's transcendent depiction of Mary in his version of the *pietà*. Miller effectively uses depictions of the *pietà* and the Nativity to demonstrate the tortured temporality relating Christ's birth and death, that he is essentially born to die, a theme that is picked up in chapter 2, an exploration of the theme of filial sacrifice in the *Aeneid*.

In this chapter, a *tour de force* of close textual analysis, Miller demonstrates how Virgil, through an intricate web of textual allusions, draws upon the Homeric corpus to embed the trauma of filial sacrifice in his own text, and to suggest its original and essential place in the founding of Rome. Miller suggests that Virgil's account of the founding of Rome should be read as Freud would an analysand, as a subject beset by a trauma that, destined to remain repressed, is condemned to be repeated, accounting for the poem's maddeningly complex temporality:

> Virgil apprehends the question of Rome's being as the question of its ability through history to redeem a polluted origin that persists within each failed attempt to rebuild the fallen Troy. The poem demonstrates exhaustively that empire carries this origin forward within itself as an irreducible contradiction, one it can neither overcome nor leave behind ... does Roman history progress, or does it end where it began, trapped in a pattern of compulsive repetition, endlessly reversed but never undone? (61)

Miller views the epic genre as primarily a work of mourning for the sons who had to be sacrificed, before the eyes of their fathers, in order for the empire to be established. The complex identification of fathers to their sons is expressed in the figure of the *puer senex*, and in temporal schizophrenia manifested in the poem's frequently unfathomable syntax and confusion of tenses. The Minotaur's labyrinth comes to figure the tortured, wayward temporality Miller argues underlies Virgil's recounting of the history of Rome.

Shakespeare's *The Winter's Tale* perhaps most explicitly of all the texts discussed reveals that the motive behind filial sacrifice lies in the compensation for the missing body of patriarchy. Leontes' madness is seemingly brought on by the sight of his wife's heavily pregnant body, which emphasizes his lack of bodily connection to his own son, Mamillius, in whom he desperately searches for signs of physical likeness. In order to guarantee his position as father, he must, in turn sacrifice his entire family, a loss that, true to the romance genre, is redeemed and restored at the play's end. Miller brilliantly concludes this chapter by reading *The Winter's Tale* as an intentional mirror image of *Hamlet* through the deployment of a structuralist analysis focusing on the transformation of narrative functions between the two plays, and the presentation of textual allusions that indicate that the two plays were, indeed, meant to be seen as related.

The next chapter, on Dickens, focuses on *Dombey and Son*, in which the father's gaze produces his son as the quintessential *puer senex*. Blind to his son as a child, he can only see him as the grown-up who will eventually take over the family business, obliterating the son's identity. The argument recalls Lacan's concept of the jouissance of the Other: the child must build up a fantasy against the overwhelming investment of the Other (the parents) in him or herself, a process essential to the construction of subjectivity. This chapter opens onto a discussion of authorship as a form of fatherhood, Dickens' seeming fascination with, and ability to benefit from, sacrificing children in his novels. The question of fatherhood and authorship will be explored in even greater depth in the succeeding chapter, which examines the dream of the burning child in texts by Ben Jonson, Freud, and Lacan. Miller questions why the dream of the burning child, which introduces the seventh chapter of the *Interpretation of Dreams*, should evoke the collective fascination that it does; it is dreamt and redreamt, by a woman who heard it recounted at a lecture and brought to Freud as her own dream, by Freud, by Lacan, and, in a slightly modified version, by Ben Jonson as well.

Here the urgency of Miller's central question reaches a pitch of intensity: what is it about the image of the burning son, returning from the dead to repudiate his father, that endures and continues to exert its fascination in Western culture? At this point, he reiterates in greater theoretical detail the answer he has elaborated thoughout the book: "My argument in this book has been that although the body of fatherhood remains an impossible concept, produced only in the moment of its negation, it nevertheless belongs to what Lacan describes as 'the real,' and it exercises considerable force" (192). If what we are witnessing is a seemingly endless mourning process for the lost body of patriarchy, as Miller ultimately argues, how, he asks, will this process ever end? In the context of his final reading of Achebe's *Things Fall Apart* he asks, "What might a post-patriarchal self look like? A self in which the sacrificial cross and the Oedipal crossroads have been reconceived as a scene not of filial agony or patricidal rage, but of un-fathered convergence and exchange?" (217–18). By the end of this compelling book, the stakes of his question come to seem huge. If the sacrifice of sons before the eyes of their fathers is the form taken by the return of the patriarchal repressed, a way of attributing reality to the invisible relation between fathers and their sons, I found myself asking how Miller would interpret the Iraq War were he to add yet another chapter to his book. Could the sacrifice of sons in a war of choice be read as an attempt to legitimize a presidency that is, to the eyes of many, illegitimate?

The Anonymous Renaissance: Cultures of Discretion in Tudor-Stuart England
By Marcy L. North
Chicago: University of Chicago Press, 2003

Reviewer: Evelyn B. Tribble

Marcy L. North's *The Anonymous Renaissance* makes an extremely important contribution to studies of early modern print culture, authorship, and canon formation. Carefully argued and readable throughout, North's book challenges teleological arguments about anonymity through a meticulous examination of the evidence for attribution practices in the Renaissance.

North argues that histories of the book have tended to equate the advent of printing with the decline of anonymity, with the latter mode consigned to medieval practices prior to the emergence of a concept of possessive authorship. Such assumptions also inform the highly influential theoretical work of Roland Barthes and Michel Foucault, whose arguments about authorship, according to North, "perpetuated another questionable but very popular assumption, that anonymity is the original state and natural characteristic of all writing" (38). Throughout the book, North argues against what she terms "a binary history of early authorship" (3), claiming instead that "early modern authors and book producers utilized anonymity as an alternative source of authority, privilege, control, text presentation, and even identity" (33). Rather, "print opened up new possibilities for anonymity" (29). This is a provocative claim, but one that North buttresses with a plethora of evidence taken from texts ranging from printed miscellanies, to religious controversies, to manuscript commonplace books. North stresses throughout the "functionality" (5) of anonymity. Far from a mere "bibliographic inconvenience" (5), anonymity was a flexible and useful mode that was employed in a wide variety of settings in the Renaissance.

North surveys these contexts throughout seven chapters. Chapter 1, "Medieval Anonymity and the 'Modern Author,'" follows upon the introduction in establishing the historical and methodological parameters of the study. North challenges the common tendency of scholars of the early modern period to posit the medieval period as a convenient other, a backdrop against which the early unfolding of modernity plays out. Indeed, medieval anonymity is itself a convention, often used knowingly, and it not simply a point of departure for the early modern period. Sometimes anonymity is an accident, but at other times it is a deliberate practice, a "conscious gesture" (52).

Chapters 2 and 3 treat "Ignoto and the Book Industry" and "Printed Anonymity and its Readers." The first is a discussion of the variety of agents who used print to construct anonymity through "conventionality" and "ambiguity" (58). Arguing that both attribution and anonymity are collaborative choices made by a variety of agents involved in book production, North here examines the evidence of title pages and other paratextual markers of authorship. She argues that title pages provide new modes for anonymity as well as new modes for attribution. Following this section is an entertaining and instructive section on the use of initials as attribution, a common practice that should not be read transparently. In the printed miscellany *The Phoenix Nest* (1593), initials are social rather than individuating markers; they "combine the best of identity and discretion" (72). Similarly the use of pointedly anonymous signing conventions such as "Ignoto" have their own complex significations and demonstrate how the title page can be used for a variety of rhetorical functions. Certainly the name of the author became increasingly common on the title page, particularly in circumstances in which the name could sell the book. This point is well known, but North's contribution here is to stress that anonymity could be just as marketable as signed authorship, and that many attribution practices in fact existed between attribution and naming: anagrams, initials, Latin names, and pseudonyms are all examples.

Yet this device was not without its detractors, and these are taken up in the next chapter. North identifies three types of such detractors: those who viewed anonymity as a "dangerous new convention"; those who justified "elite and courtly conventions of anonymity," and, finally, the example of Andrew Maunsell, who attempted a full catalog of English books and thus was faced with practical difficulties of attribution. The first set of examples is taken from religious controversy, where anonymity is equated with cowardice, and the second from literary productions, including Spenser's *The Shepheardes Calendar* and Puttenham's *The Arte of English Poesie* (published, it must be noted, anonymously). These latter texts provide examples of what North nicely calls "ambitious anonymity" (108), the use of anonymity to both conceal and reveal the complex social affiliations of the text. These arguments are convincing, if not strikingly original. The real payoff of this chapter comes in the original and exciting examination of Andrew Maunsell's 1595 *Catalogue of English Printed Books*. Maunsell's catalog is an alphabetical listing of all books, old and new, save for recent books written by "fugitive Papistes" (110). "Books which are without authors" are cataloged either by title or by "matter" or by both (110). Where initials only are available, the printer provides blank spaces for filling in the full names, should they become known. North notes Maunsell does not equate "old" books with anonymity, in part because so many of the "new" books are also anonymous. Anonymity is not treated as a particular problem and Maunsell "gives us a sense of the ease with which anonymity conventions fit in with those of naming" (115). As North admits, the evidence from Maunsell could be marshaled *against* her argument, since the blank spaces do seem to construct anonymity as a lack, to be remedied as possible. Taken together, however, the three sections of this chapter demonstrate the ubiquity of anonymity, and its diverse functions within a complex system of attribution.

Chapters 4 and 5 discuss the uses of anonymity in religious controversies, Catholic and Protestant. It must be said that the brief chapter 4 seems somewhat repetitive of the material in the first section of chapter 3 about the moral valence of anonymity, although the point is here expanded to include a discussion of the awareness of the usefulness of the complexity and ambiguity of anonymity. Chapter 5 extends this discussion into Puritan controversies, particularly the infamous Martin Marprelate controversy. The Marprelate controversy is a special case because of sharply delineated voice of the pseudonymous Martin. As North argues, "Along with Piers, Colin, and Pasquil, Martin came to symbolize a distinct authorial personality that functioned independent of an actual author's name" (134). She concludes that "in this case, anonymity *is* an identity" (157). I found the distinctions between anonymity and pseudonymity a bit hard to grasp here. North argues that the Marprelate tracts are distinct "because they authored anonymity with such flair, humor, and self-consciousness" (158), but surely this is a description of the effect of *pseudo*nomity, the taking of a distinctive name for satiric purposes. While I admire North's determination not to create a taxonomy of anonymity, the practice of pseudonmity seems to me enough of a special case to merit more sustained treatment than it receives in the book.

The last two chapters are particularly valuable and make extremely important contributions to the study of canon formation, particularly around the lyric and issues of gender. North deliberately leaves the discussion of manuscript anonymity for the latter sections of the book, in an effort to "dispel any myths that anonymity always originates in manuscript and sneaks into print as an unwelcome guest" (159). As North demonstrates, anonymity and attribution existed in fluid modes of exchange, with compilers of manuscript collections sometimes omitting attributions from named printed works. North focuses on the "conventions of anonymity" (160) that structured literary coterie culture, arguing that the dialogue between "identification and discretion" (161) was essential to its construction. This chapter poses a "theoretical conundrum" (162) in that it is necessary to attribute in order to fully understand anonymity. This conundrum is in my view more apparent than real. Thankfully North does not dismiss the importance of the scholarship of attribution, but she uses this work in the service of understanding the "social dynamic" of attribution practices rather than identifying particular authors. Accordingly, North focuses her attention on the attribution practices of compilers rather than on authorial identification.

A similar strategy marks the final, and most original, chapter: "Reading the Anonymous Female Voice." If, as the popular saying goes, "Anonymous was a woman," how does one determine *which* "anons" are gendered female? As North points out, much work on this question has been structured by somewhat dubious assumptions, most notably the idea that one can determine with precision a "female voice." North thus identifies a kind of theoretical impasse "whereby the identities that enable us to analyze the function of anonymity partly distort our view of that function" (220). Her solution is elegant: she poses instead the question of the relationship between anonymity and gender and asks how anonymity "creates the illusion of female authorship." This method produces some interesting results and allows North to examine a number of genres that have been ruled out of court by anthologies seeking so-called authentic female voices. These include the anonymous lament, the seductress poem, the rebuff/reply poem, and the defense of women poem. These have often been excluded from the emerging canon of female-authored poems because of "commonsense" judgments that such poems are likely to be male ventriloquism of the female voice, a suspicion particularly strong for seductress poems that seem to play to male fantasies. Similarly, there has been a reluctance to accept "anonymous poems that are gendered paratextually" (249). North concludes this important chapter by positing a new methodology that extends Margaret Ferguson's argument about interpreting in the absence of clear gender identification: "we must learn to interpret without knowing for certain that the author is a woman, but also, I would add, without assuming that the author of a less feminine voice is male" (255). To do so, it is necessary to question internal markers of the feminine and repudiate the assumption that "all women authors will speak for and as women" (255). North thus attempts to disarticulate the female voice from female authorship. Anonymity, then, should be seen not as an "obstacle between the voice and the author but as a function of both conventions" (256).

North's work will be highly influential in the field of early modern print culture, but it also makes important contributions to studies of periodization, early modern religious discourse, authorship studies, canon formation, and gender studies. She combines strong writing and argumentation, clear methodology, fine close reading, and impressive archival work, and the reader of *The Anonymous Renaissance* comes away with a radically altered sense of the significance of "anon."

Shakespeare and the Victorians
By Adrian Poole
London: Thomson Learning, 2004

Reviewer: Julia Thomas

The Victorians were haunted by Shakespeare. According to Adrian Poole, Shakespeare was "the most powerful of ghosts" (2), present in the Victorians' very utterances, their way of accounting for themselves and their relation to the world. *Shakespeare and the Victorians* forms part of a growing critical interest in how Shakespeare and his works were appropriated in the Victorian period. If, as Michael Dobson has argued, Shakespeare was constructed as a national poet in the late seventeenth and eighteenth centuries, this status was both consolidated and problematized in the nineteenth century.[1] Poole's other major contribution to this topic, the two-volume *Victorian Shakespeare*, coedited with Gail Marshall and published by Palgrave in 2003, suggests the complexities of Shakespeare's place in Victorian culture, not least in its own division between theater, drama and performance (volume 1) and literature and culture (volume 2). *Shakespeare and the Victorians* attempts to bring these subject areas together, even if the theater, visual arts, novels, and poetry are discussed in separate chapters. These chapter divisions are in some ways limiting, especially considering Poole's indebtedness to the brilliant, but much overlooked, *Realizations* by Martin Meisel, which argues that the narrative arts in the nineteenth century cannot be so easily dismantled.[2] However, within this format Poole offers some remarkably fresh insights into how Shakespeare was represented in performances, paintings, and texts of the period. With his witty, engaging, and lucid style, he manages successfully to address the specialist and nonspecialist reader alike.

The first chapter is a lively and informative discussion of the Victorian theater and the great Shakespearean actors and actresses who trod the boards in London. The chapter, like the book as a whole, offers numerous signposts to the reader in the subsections into which it is arranged, a device that makes the book particularly useful for undergraduate courses. The chapter is a little light on critical analysis, on why certain plays were more popular, or the possible reasons why scenes were modified or performed in particular ways, but the material discussed is fascinating, Poole bombarding the reader with anecdotes and revelations about how Shakespeare appeared on the stage. In one of the more unsavory London theaters, for example, Shakespeare's plays were performed on horseback as a way of luring in the crowds. Even the more illustrious theaters attempted to make watching Shakespeare more entertaining, whether this was in the form of the spectacular sets and costumes for which the Victorians are famous, or the inclusion of other plays alongside Shakespeare's. Contemporary playbills show that performances could be as long as five or six hours, with Shakespeare sandwiched between juggling acts, farces, and Christmas pantomimes. What effect did this have on the meanings of *King Lear* or *Macbeth*, one wonders?

Poole has a gift for setting the scene. His anecdote of a besotted Henry James listening to the acerbic remarks of the elderly Fanny Kemble is a gem ("Good heavens, she's touching him!" exclaimed a horrified Kemble when Ellen Terry's Portia got a little too close to her Bassanio in the closet scene). Poole's fascination for the subject shines through on every page and leads him to focus on aspects of Victorian performances of Shakespeare that have largely been neglected, such as the acting techniques favored by Henry Irving and William Macready. Macready was so desperate to control the passionate intensity of his performances that he would rehearse alone without moving his body and with his arms bandaged up. He was also desperate, as Poole points out, to control his leading ladies and some attention is devoted to the often fraught relationships between actresses and their actor-managers. In this context, Sargent's famous painting of Ellen Terry as Lady Macbeth is read by Poole both as a celebration of an independence she never achieved onstage and a turning toward madness and death.

The appeal of this discussion of the theater, and in many ways of the book as a whole, lies in the richness of the material and the obvious enthusiasm with which the author engages with it. This comes to the fore in an imaginative list of the top eleven performances that Poole would have liked to have attended (coming in at number two is Macready's Macbeth at Drury Lane in 1843, preferably sat next to Charles Dickens on June 14). This enthusiasm permeates the second chapter on the visual arts. Shakespeare was the most popular literary source for paintings in this period and Poole does justice to such a substantial field by focusing on a variety of visual genres, from fairy paintings, keepsake annuals, and Pre-Raphaelite paintings, to book illustrations. His analysis encompasses iconic images like John Everett Millais's *Ophelia* and the less familiar pen and ink drawing of Ophelia and Hamlet by Dante Gabriel Rossetti. There are also innovative points of entry to the material—the hairiness, for example, of Shakespearean patriarchs in these pictures.

Like an accomplished Victorian critic, Poole recounts the stories embedded in the images. Suggesting that the difference of pictorial representation lies in its ability to arrest a moment in time, the author focuses on the often erotically charged moments that Victorian artists pick out from Shakespeare's plays. His analysis is enlightening but at times it does not go far enough in indicating why these particular moments might have been so significant. What was it about these specific scenes that the Victorians found seductive or repellent (according to Poole, George Eliot was disgusted by William Holman Hunt's painting, *Valentine Rescuing Sylvia from Proteus*)?

This question is intimately related to Victorian values and ideologies and Poole does come close to providing an answer in his analysis of visual representations of Jacques's speech on "The Seven Ages of Man." Victorian artists, it seems, could not get pictures of this scene quite right. No doubt this failure had something to do with the generic distinction between temporal texts and spatial images, the fact that pictures cannot progress in time. The Victorians, after all, were great admirers of Gotthold Ephraim Lessing, the exponent of this artistic division. But, as Poole convincingly argues, there is another idea of progress at stake here. Artists found it hard to reconcile Jacques's bleak vision with nineteenth-century notions of the progress of civilization. For this reason, visual images of the scene in this period tend to differ from the play in their emphasis not on death and decay but on regeneration and renewal.

Poole's evocative descriptions of Victorian paintings animate the images. He dramatically recreates the events leading up to and succeeding the pregnant moments shown in the pictures: the recrimination that will follow Isabella's appeal to Claudio in Hunt's painting of *Measure for Measure*, or the subsequent collapse of Julia into the withered leaves at her feet in *Valentine Rescuing Sylvia from Proteus*. It is, of course, precisely this response that narrative pictures encourage. Victorian artists painted their figures to give the impression that they were thinking and breathing, that they had a life beyond the canvas.

It is the apparent "life" of Shakespeare's protagonists that is emphasized in chapter 3. Taking character, story, and plot as its subject matter, this chapter seems out of place alongside others that discuss the use of Shakespeare in specific genres. Poole here identifies a variety of Victorian texts and images that rework Shakespearean characters and plots, focusing, in particular, on how *Othello*, with its story of marriage and murder, is central to the novels of Mary Elizabeth Braddon, William Makepeace Thackeray, and Charlotte Brontë.

The chapter is an illuminating one, not least for its clear account of how Victorian writers including Anna Jameson and Mary Cowden Clarke, produced imaginative tales based on the lives of Shakespeare's heroines. As Poole writes, too many critics have never read these texts but are ready to dismiss them. Poole clearly *has* read them and obviously delights in their storytelling. What is not clear from this chapter, however, is why the Victorians were compelled to construct these lives in the first place. There is some uncertainty here about the status of Shakespeare's characters *as* characters. While Poole seems keen to avoid regarding Shakespeare himself as a God-like creator of these figures, he also steers clear of the idea that this very notion of character, of seeing Shakespeare's figures as psychologically real, might be culturally motivated. The result is an impasse in which the "characters" either emit their own energy, or the readers (a transhistorical "we") naturally see them in this way. Falstaff, then, "tries to escape from plot into myth" (83), Shakespeare's heroines "yearn for more presence than their plays allow, and hence for more 'story'" (89) and, as readers, "there is so much more we want to know or more fully imagine about many of Shakespeare's characters" (93). Such comments, which imply that Shakespeare's protagonists are always already characters, are problematic in a discussion that sets out to locate these figures in a historical context. Indeed, the realist novels analyzed in the chapter's conclusion suggest another possibility: that the very emphasis on these figures' lives and the construction of their characters might be the product of this particular cultural moment.

Poole's account of how Victorian novelists interacted with Shakespeare continues into chapter 4 with a discussion of Dickens, Eliot, and Hardy. Although the texts discussed are well known,

Poole's reading of them is innovative and convincing. He not only points to intertextual allusions, but also demonstrates the complexity with which they are woven into Victorian narratives. In Dickens's novels, for example, it is the difference from Shakespearean analogues that generates meanings. This dependence on and difference from Shakespeare is similarly emphasized in Eliot's novels with their chapter mottoes often taken from Shakespearean sources. For Eliot, Poole argues, the Forest of Arden turns into a prison. In Hardy too the dialogue with Shakespeare is ambivalent. Figures who quote from Shakespeare are usually those who are not to be trusted, while competing Shakespearean voices permeate the texts, whether Hamlet's in the graveyard, Macbeth's last speech, or those of the kindly and loyal fools who populate the plays.

As Poole is keen to point out, however, it was not just Shakespeare's drama that held a significant place in Victorian culture. This was also a period in which his poetry was given a new status, incorporated alongside extracts from the plays in anthologies and other marketable publications like "birthday books." Again, the reaction to Shakespeare's texts is far from monolithic or transparent. The sonnets were taken up by the Victorians with "nervous relish" (161). Editors attempted to neutralize their content, some arguing that a relationship between men of different ages was acceptable, others that the poems were an example of a Platonic pursuit of Beauty and Truth. Henry Hallam, the father of Tennyson's close friend Arthur, wrote that he wished Shakespeare had never written the sonnets. Yet, for all their anxieties about these poems, the Victorians were drawn toward them. It is no wonder that in his trial Oscar Wilde revealed the sonnets as the literary source that inspired Basil Hallward's worship of Dorian Gray.

Poole's discussion of how Victorian poetry was itself influenced by Shakespeare hits on something vital about the Victorians' complex relation to the bard:

> When Shakespeare helped the Victorians to distinctive poetic achievements it was by forcing them to think what they owed to their present no less than to their past. The best of them sought not directly to emulate but rather to gauge their distance from the old Shakespearean models of language and literary form. This meant asking themselves what made modern love *modern*. (156)

By "distancing" themselves from Shakespeare, the Victorians used him to define themselves and their specific historical moment. In this sense, the Victorians did not so much construct a notion of Shakespeare as Shakespeare constructed a notion of the Victorians.

Poole's case that the dialogue with Shakespeare is a plural one in which Shakespeare and his works are simultaneously revered and rejected becomes more apparent toward the end of the nineteenth century with George Bernard Shaw's denouncement of Bardolatry. However, even Ruskin and Carlyle, those great mid-Victorian critics, had a tense relationship with Shakespeare, Ruskin finding it especially hard to deal with the fact that the good and the righteous die in the tragedies. With characteristic wit, Poole manages perfectly to capture the contradictory reactions to Shakespeare in the closing decades of the century: whereas "Wilde would have been happy to drink champagne with Shakespeare," he remarks, "Shaw would have thrown it in his face" (235–36).

The last section of the book, which analyzes Shakespeare's reception in Germany, America, and Ireland (where *The Tempest* and the figure of Caliban were especially significant), is indicative of the text as a whole. *Shakespeare and the Victorians* is a comprehensive analysis, packed full of interesting and entertaining facts, which sweeps with ease across the course of the Victorian period, while never losing sight of the different historical moments that make up this century. Poole's address to the general as well as scholarly reader means that he justifiably keeps secondary criticism to a minimum in the body of the text, although the select bibliography, neatly divided into the subject areas covered by each chapter, will be especially useful for students. In some ways, the book's extraordinary breadth of knowledge and range of references can be a weakness. The discussion at times lacks critical rigor and fails to engage with some of the wider cultural issues at stake in the Victorians' dialogue with Shakespeare. However, the fact that it raises more questions than it answers is much in its favor. What makes this book so appealing is the lively way in which Poole discusses his material. From beginning to end, *Shakespeare and the Victorians* is a stimulating read that, despite its focus on familiar texts and modes of representation, offers new insights into what "Shakespeare" meant to the Victorians.

Notes

1. Michael Dobson, *The Making of the National Poet: Shakespeare, Adaptation and Authorship, 1660–1769* (Oxford: Oxford University Press, 1992).

2. Martin Meisel, *Realizations: Narrative, Pictorial, and Theatrical Arts in Nineteenth-Century England* (Princeton: Princeton University Press, 1983).

Beggary and Theatre in Early Modern England
By Paola Pugliatti
Aldershot, Hants., and Burlington, VT:
Ashgate, 2003

Reviewer: Lars Engle

The "theatre" in the title of Paola Pugliatti's *Beggary and Theatre in Early Modern England* should be taken in a general rather than a specific sense, as should "early modern England." Her very interesting and instructive book in fact treats beggary, deception, and theatrical self-presentation in early modern Europe, with considerable detailed discussion of German and Italian examples as well as English ones. It largely eschews particular discussions of early modern English plays or of English theatrical practice, though there is some interesting commentary on the relations between Italian theatre and the quasi-theatrical activities of the piazza. One gathers from her introduction that her avoidance of play interpretation is partly a matter of deference to the excellent discussion of dramatizations of beggary in William Carroll's *Fat King, Lean Beggar*, which came out in 1996 when Pugliatti's study was already underway, and partly a result of her discovery that she had a great deal to say about the Elizabethan pamphlet literature concerning beggars, rogues, and conny-catchers. The national specificity of her title is partly justified by Pugliatti's focus on continental materials that are related to or feed into the literature, law, and theory on beggary in England that she describes.

Her book offers a rich array of interesting materials, analyzed with consistent intelligence. Pugliatti goes back over ground mapped by earlier scholars and frequently finds ways to supplement and correct their arguments, both by supplying continental

contexts and by enriching their account of English texts and attitudes. This is true both in her treatment of the legislative history of
her topic and in her treatment of the homiletic and literary traditions.

Thus she demonstrates that there were English statutes outlawing various forms of dramatic performance as early as 1284, and
that the famous act of 1572 penalizing unlicensed actors along with
other rogues and vagabonds had a rich background in earlier sixteenth-century legislation, including an astonishing, soon-repealed
statute from Edward VI's reign that authorized any citizen who
brought an able-bodied beggar before two J.P.s to own the beggar
(now branded with a V for "vagabond" on his breast) for two years
as a slave. Repeat offenders could become slaves for life and be
branded with an S on forehead or cheek. Pugliatti sees Elizabeth's
statute of 1572 as the confluence of three legislative streams: one
outlawing sturdy begging, one criminalizing various wicked kinds
of disguise, and a third forbidding unlicensed theatrical activity. In
documenting all three legislative traditions, and taking them into
the seventeenth century, she makes an interesting history clearer.
You may know that the sumptuary laws in England were dropped
in 1604, but I did not until Pugliatti informed me of this. She also
points out intelligently that the emphases in legislation about begging and disguise were not entirely in harmony with the comments
in the homilies, which condemned anyone who was ostentatious
for vanity rather than specifically damning those who wore clothes
above their station.

Pugliatti does much the same sort of thing with respect to the literary traditions of representation of beggars, vagabonds, conny-
catchers, and the like. Basically she makes a sharp distinction between the literature on deceptive begging and the literature on
conny-catching, seeing the first as a fairly rural form of writing in
which the authors are not professionals, and the second as over-
whelmingly an urban literature engaged in by professional writers
(especially playwrights like Robert Greene and Thomas Dekker).
She sees the picaresque, in which begging, deception, and other
countercultural activities are romanticized, as involving a contamination of these two traditions, and she gives an interesting historical account of both traditions, culminating in two very fine
chapters on English prose treatments of beggars and of conny-
catchers, respectively.

As I have said, this is a valuable presentation of interesting material, intelligently framed. Pugliatti's overall argument remains somewhat elusive through most of the book, however. Her modes of analysis, moreover, differ rather noticeably from chapter to chapter. The rhetorical, linguistic, and narratological analysis in terms taken from Mikhail Bakhtin, Gerard Genette, Roman Jakobson, and others in the final chapter on Gilbert Walker's *A Manifest Declaration of Diceplay* and pamphlets by Greene and Dekker is, for instance, entirely confined to that chapter and not used in discussing Thomas Harman's *A Caveat for Common Cursitors*, nor are Bakthin's very pregnant analytical terms mobilized in discussions of the general social phenomenon of beggary earlier in the book. Pugliatti begins by saying that she will discuss beggary as a "philosophical threat" (1)—a term she borrows from Carroll—, and she makes some valuable suggestions as to why, for early modern authorities, "disguising is bad . . . in a very complex, almost total way" (65). But she does not in fact move on from this to argue that deceptive disguise, theatrical representations, rejection of the social order that has apparently denied one a sufficient living, and the conviction that there's a sucker lurking within every well-heeled citizen cohere philosophically: they are all aspects of a sophistical, relativizing challenge to the prevailing Renaissance Christian-Platonic view that stable reality underlies appearance and that truth awaits the earnest seeker after it. This surely explains why moralistic anti-theatricality, which is a species of philosophical discomfort with sophistry and pragmatism, flows together with official condemnation of idle poverty, deceptive begging, and confidence trickery in the period.

In her epilogue, Pugliatti takes up the prevailing contemporary view that the poor, no longer sharply divided between the genuinely impotent to be helped and the idly able-bodied to be condemned, count as failures in the social order that point to the incoherence or immorality of that order: "anxiety about mendicity has now become part of the guilty conscience which involves all of us as regards the great dichotomies which dominate the world and about which we are unable, or unwilling, to envisage effective remedies" (191). Pugliatti regards this anxiety as distinctively modern. But a lot of her evidence suggests otherwise. After all both the early modern law and the early modern literature she analyzes display a combination of fear and hope with respect to beggars and the poor: a fear of beggars, a fear of being deceived by beggars, a hope that beggars are not a real symptom of the failure of the social order, and a fear that one's actions toward beggars are not reaching the right people. Much of the law and literature she treats displace the fear, anger, and shame associated with beggary onto those who would exploit it, especially beggars themselves. This is a nexus of discomfort, and a way of dealing with it, that goes with inequality and thus seems almost transhistorical: think of the myth of the welfare queen in our own recent national debates on poverty, for instance. One aspect of this nexus that is, as Pugliatti shows, fairly specific to early modern England is its interconnection with specific hostility to plays and players.

Word Against Word: Shakespearean Utterance
By James R. Siemon
Amherst and Boston: University of Massachusetts
Press, 2002.

Reviewer: Michael D. Bristol

Evidently James Siemon has not been told that no one will publish a full-length scholarly monograph about a single play by Shakespeare. If he had been given more sensible guidance at the start he might have devoted his time and energy to a project with more obvious market appeal. What he has done in the absence of such advice is to produce a real book. *Word Against Word* is a work of genuine originality and distinction, something that will challenge and inspire even the most blasé of Shakespeare scholars. Arthur Kinney and the editorial board for the University of Massachusetts Press' *Massachusetts Studies in Early Modern Culture* deserve some credit for recognizing the importance of Siemon's project. I will say something more about the credit James Siemon deserves in just a moment. But first a word of caution. *Word Against Word* is going to shake things up. It's going to unsettle your complacencies if you read it but you'll be having too much fun to put up much resistance.

Siemon's idea is to orchestrate a dialogue between two major thinkers about human utterance—William Shakespeare and Mikhail Bakhtin. This is not quite the same thing as "A Bakhtinian approach" to Shakespeare, since the two writers are understood to be mutually answerable to each other as well as to the readers of *Word Against Word*. The basic method is called "listening around," a phrase that nicely captures the playfulness and the promiscuity of Siemon's orientation to criticism. The importance of listening for Shakespeare scholarship is beginning to be articulated in, for example, Wes Folkerth's *The Sound of Shakespeare* or in John Madden's *Shakespeare in Love*. Siemon conceptualizes "listening around" in relation to the rhetorical figure of *enthymeme*, a type of informal reasoning that either omits crucial steps in an argument or bases conclusions on the truth of a contrary proposition. In practice this means paying a lot of attention to what isn't said and to the inevitably of conflict or dissent already embedded in every utterance. Siemon is interested in listening to "other voices" as he attends to the Shakespearean or the Bakhtinian text—the voices resonating in those texts along with all kinds of other voices Siemon happens to like hearing. The idea is based on V. N. Voloinov's discussion of poetic utterance as an extension of the speech of everyday life. This seemingly harmless suggestion that Shakespeare's poetry is a form of vernacular speech turns out to be powerfully explosive in the way it sets up a second methodological principle, namely dialogue.

For Bakhtin and for Siemon dialogue is not simply what happens when two people talk to each other in the immediacy of a face to face situation. Meaning is always tied to the context of the utterance but that context is not limited to the situation of co-present interlocutors. Every word is "already dialogized," saturated with conflicted evaluations that will be activated only at the moment of their deployment in a specific verbal interaction. This turns out to mean that we're always going to read Shakespeare and also Bakhtin for and by ourselves. What gets exploded here is the distinction between "presentism" and "historicism," along with the claim so often repeated by historicizers from Hardin Craig to E. M. W. Tillyard to David Kastan that we're not really reading Shakespeare unless we're reading him in the historical context of early modern society and culture. This is not wrong, so much as it is basically meaningless. James Siemon is much too nice to put it so bluntly. What he says instead is that his "book fosters no illusion that our themes are, in any simple sense, Shakespeare's themes (or Bakh-

tin's themes). I do believe that there are meaningful proportionalities and overlaps, sites and interests that continue to tie us socially
and ideologically" to Shakespeare's writing and to Bakhtin's (31).

One of the most brilliant and impressive elements in *Word
Against Word* is Siemon's ability to cash out the idea of reading
Shakespeare in historical context. The scope of Siemon's reading
in what are called primary sources is daunting and I can think of
no one who discusses this historical evidence more creatively. His
treatment of Richard's description of Bolingbroke's "courtship to
the common people" is only one example of many that illustrates
how rich Siemon's approach can be. He begins by noting that his
American students often have trouble understanding the evaluative
intonation of the speech as well as their own response to Richard's
attitude to ideas of political "popularity." Siemon then cites a number of early modern texts to show that the notion of "popularity"
that Richard describes is extremely complex. Courting the com-
mons can be interpreted as evil and Machiavellian, or as demean-
ing, or as admirable, or as merely expedient. The passages Siemon
quotes suggest that Shakespeare may have been listening to a wide
range of contending voices in his own historical situation. But even
if Shakespeare wasn't listening to all that stuff, the singular persons
who made up his audience would have been able to assign many
different evaluative assessments to the "humility" of powerful men
who want people with very different interests to think of them as
"regular guys." The "meaningful proportionalities and overlaps"
with contemporary American politics are too depressing to think
about.

Word Against Word takes on a range of significant topics in contemporary interpretations of *Richard II*, including the socioeco-
nomic context of agrarian change, issues of character and
subjectivity, the play's "tonality of elegy and lamentation," and an
excellent concluding chapter on carnival and the carnivalesque.
Carnival is perhaps the best-known of Bakhtin's ideas, at least for
scholars of early modern literature. The earliest treatments of this
idea in relation to Shakespeare described the plays with some success as a carnivalesque or plebeian resistance to the culture of the
dominant classes. But other scholars have always been skeptical of
this kind of interpretation, maintaining instead that Shakespeare is
aligned primarily with the court and that he includes elements of
carnival only to mock the popular culture from which they originate. *Richard II* presents an interesting challenge to conventional

theories of carnivalesque uncrowning, since its focus is more on the face than on the "lower bodily stratum." Unlike *I Henry IV*, where the carnival elements have an obvious and palpable shape in the figure of Falstaff, *Richard II* seems gloomy, depressing, and basically conservative in its orientation towards early modern popular culture. Siemon's discussion of this topic is, not surprisingly, much more complex and detailed than anything attempted in the previous scholarship. He focuses on Bakhtin's category of "reduced laughter" to account for the carnival elements in the plays, "a laughter that arises where pathos and mockery, commitment and gay relativity meet in a more evenly matched contest" (219). On this view both the robust, celebratory elements of carnival and its relationship with persecution, intolerance and summary popular justice are held in tension with each other. Carnival is scary and often violently hostile not only to a patrician culture that it sees as oppressive but also to all sorts of outsiders and innocent bystanders. Siemon is particularly effective in bringing out the multilingual aspect of this tradition through his consideration of ballads, and other forms of popular literature.

For this reader the pivotal essay in *Word Against Word* is not the discussion of carnival, but an earlier chapter which brings out the larger theoretical—or should I say ethical—implications of Siemon's book. "Word Itself Against the Word: Close Reading after Voloinov" argues for the value of close reading skills in examining "nonaesthetic textual material" (36). Siemon's argument develops out of Voloinov's claim that "the work of art is a 'powerful condenser of unarticulated social evaluations'" (8). Close reading skills on this account do not figure as an elite practice. To the contrary, close reading is fundamental to the vernacular forms of utterance and communication, whether we're reading a Shakespearean tragedy, or listening to mortifying sexual confessions on Oprah, or having an argument with a lover. Siemon describes critical writing, his own as well as everyone else's as " the encounter of utterance with utterance, with the aim of embedding the text's words in its contemporary counterwords *as well as in our own paraphrases and indirect locutions*" (93, emphasis supplied). Siemon's work gives qualified assent to the idea that we're not really reading Shakespeare unless we're reading historically. But it adds to that the complementary maxim that we're not really reading Shakespeare unless we're reading closely. What *Word Against Word* really

shows, however, is that you can't do either of these two things
without putting yourself squarely and honestly in the picture.

Leonard Cohen once described the experience of enlightenment
as achieving the ability to lighten up. I think James Siemon has
abundantly demonstrated that ability in *Word Against Word*, and
its what I admire the most about his achievement here. You might
think it strange to describe a book of more than three hundred
pages with so many big words in it as having the quality of light-
ness. And to be sure, his scholarly monograph on a single work of
Shakespeare's is magisterial in its learning and its critical intelligence. But somehow the designation of magisterial strikes a false
note to describe a writer so sure of himself and at the same time so
free of pretension and self-importance. Siemon's prose style is not
calibrated to be "accessible"—this is not the sort of book one gives
to a high school student who's interested in studying Shakespeare.
It is, nevertheless, very well written and it conscientiously avoids
the note of grievance and denunciation that gets into a lot of recent
work on Shakespeare. Listen around while you're reading and
you'll hear what I mean by light. There are extensive notes and a
serviceable index, but no comprehensive bibliography. The volume
has been well designed and beautifully produced by the University
of Massachusetts Press. The binding appears to be very sturdy,
which is a good thing because your copy or the one in your library
is going to get a lot of use. *Word Against Word* is a challenging work
of critical scholarship that no one in the field of literary studies will
be able to overlook. It takes on the big questions about reading and
about writing and about teaching. It's not a quick read; you really
have to think hard about what Siemon has to say. Fortunately the
payoffs are considerable.

Subordinate Subjects: Gender, the Political Nation, and Literary Form in England, 1588–1688
By Mihoko Suzuki
Aldershot: Ashgate, 2003.

Reviewer: Carole Levin

Mihoko Suzuki carefully puts together class and gender in her study, *Subordinate Subjects: Gender, the Political Nation, and Literary Form in England, 1588–1688*, by showing the similarities and linkages as well as the differences between apprentices and women in their desire to be part of the political nation in early modern England. At the time their attempts to gain power and autonomy were ultimately unsuccessful but they did have important ramifications later. Historians and political theorists have traditionally seen the French revolution as the beginning of the ideal of equality, what Suzuki calls "the political imaginary of equality" (2). Yet more than a century before 1789, English women and apprentices gave expression to the value of the rights of all citizens. The careful way Suzuki demonstrates the interconnections of early modern English class and gender provides the reader with an important lesson on the necessity of not separating gender from other considerations.

Over the course of the hundred years under consideration, Suzuki describes the ways apprentices and women developed as political agents, eventually refusing to accept subordinate status either in the family or the larger political social structure. Though some scholars see the clash between Parliament and monarchy as a political conflict rather than revolutionary change, Suzuki disagrees, and indeed refers to it not as the English civil war but the "English Revolution." After the 1650s, England would never be the same. Suzuki argues that even with the restoration of Charles II and the Stuart monarchy, the political desires of women and apprentices were not dissipated but rather evolved in different ways.

Suzuki begins her study in 1588, the year of the Spanish Armada, one of the most challenging events for England's sixteenth-century queen, Elizabeth I. She describes it as the beginning of the "long seventeenth century," but however one puts Elizabeth chronologically she certainly belongs in the discussion of rising political consciousness. Even if the queen was not herself specifically interested in bringing women into the political nation, Elizabeth was a valuable model and precedent for women in the generations after.

Suzuki's discussion of Renaissance drama and audience response to it is especially enlightening. For example, she shows how in Elizabethan domestic drama such as *Arden of Feversham* and *A Warning for Fair Women*, there are not only unhappy wives but men of subaltern status eager to rebel against their subordinate position within the social order. Particularly thoughtful is her analysis of *Measure for Measure*, a play she finds poised between comedy and tragedy. In the play Shakespeare explored what could happen when an ordinary woman finds it necessary to intervene politically; uniquely for the time, Shakespeare does not render Isabella monstrous or punish her for seeking a public role. Powerfully, in the final act, Isabella demands "Justice, Justice, Justice!" However, while Isabella is rhetorically powerful throughout the play, Shakespeare seems deliberately not to provide her with an answer to the Duke's proposal at the end, suggesting perhaps that while the Duke wants to domesticate her as wife and subject, her silence is demonstrating her resistance.

Suzuki is equally comfortable discussing the poetry of Aemilia Lanyer and such prose texts as the pamphlet wars over women's capabilities. Her thorough discussion of Rachel Speght is especially interesting when she demonstrates how Speght drew on the earlier work of Christine de Pizan. She is also valuable in her discussion of the role of apprentices during the English Revolution, showing their activity in rioting and petitioning in 1641 and 1647. Apprentices were strongly critical of Parliament in 1649, throwing their support to the Levelers. A decade later, apprentices were calling for a "free parliament," opposing the tyrannical rule of the army.

Suzuki demonstrates her far-reaching scholarship by her use of literary, popular, and political texts for which she provides significant cultural contexts. Her wide-ranging scholarship asks important questions, and also provides answers to large-scale social, political, and cultural concerns. This is not an easy book to read but the work is more than repaid by the insights Suzuki provides. Scholars interested in literature and drama, in politics, in gender and class, and in cultural development will all find much of value in this book.

Theaters and Encyclopedias in Early Modern Europe
By William N. West
Cambridge: Cambridge University Press, 2002

Reviewer: Julian Yates

One of the strengths of this history of the conjoined ideas of the encyclopedia and theater in early modern Europe is the author's ability to combine rigorous intellectual history with a sensitive and frequently illuminating account of performance. Readers will find here both an account of the origins and development of the concepts of "encyclopedia" and "theater" and an intriguing, if incomplete, rearticulation of the works of Shakespeare, Jonson, and Bacon that parses out the interrelations between early modern philosophical and moral treatises, the public theater, the masque, and the theater of scientific experiment. Add to this a deft ability to make great sense of stage business as it relates to larger social and cultural movements, and West's book begins to offer something as important as it is unusual in Renaissance studies, an approach that, rather than treating dramatic texts as cultural symptoms, demonstrates how they participate in the culture that produced them.

The book begins deceptively simply by asking what it means that "the culture of early modern Europe was [both] a theater culture ... and an encyclopedia culture," "fascinated," on the one hand, "by ostentation, performance, pretence, and pretentiousness of all kinds" and yet obsessed, on the other, "with collecting and sorting information, diligently reducing knowledge to the possession of discrete facts [and] driven by the desire to map the world's order and to construct a universal theory of everything"? (1) As readers quickly discover, the apparent opposition between "theater" and encyclopedia" turns out to be a good deal more complex than modern eyes will allow. In their origins as metaphors for particular ways of organizing knowledge, the encyclopedia and the theater shared "a conception of knowledge as the ordered representation of everything" (1). In the encyclopedia, a reader found the world separated into its elements, inventoried, ordered, rendered still for consideration or contemplation. In the textual theater that was the

Humanist ideal, one rediscovered them on display, in a mode of "performance" that "mimick[ed] the static visual order of the encyclopedia" (2). As the metaphorical theaters of Humanist learning became features worth remarking and even attending in early modern cities, their rationale changed and the theater of actuality "revealed itself as a space of duplicity and equivocation, where word and spectacle . . . could be placed in uneasy conjunction" (2) violating the strict demarcations and stability envisaged by Humanist educators. It would be incorrect, however, to understand West's argument as necessarily valorizing the theater's pull to apparent independence. On the contrary, the key to his approach lies in how the set of practices we understand by "encyclopedia" and "theater" represent not antithetical impulses but different, complementary logics of representing the world, and of posing the question of what it means to represent things by words. "During the Renaissance," West observes, "the likeness of theatre and encyclopedia became visible precisely because for the first time it was being called into question" (9)—a latency or potentiality in their relationship became knowable as each pressed more insistently on the other. The two forms collided to produce texts that were at once "serious" and "playful" in their treatment of the world.

While West's focus is squarely on the sixteenth and seventeenth centuries, he casts a long look forward to remark that our current turn to things, to objects of all kinds (both as a culture and as a discipline), marks another "event" in the narrative he offers. "We are currently undergoing a similar shift from the concept of objectified knowledge as a commodity," he argues "to one that incorporates many of the ideas of knowledge as performance banished by the thinkers of the Enlightenment" (9). Whether or not we agree with this account of our particular moment, his gesture toward the present signals that the motor of this account of early modernity is not the encyclopedia-theater phenomenon as cipher for some absent cause (such as the rise of the individual or the commodity form) but rather as index to a particular set of problems in representation—problems that remain insistently with us.

The book falls roughly into two parts. The first two chapters offer parallel word-histories, "explain[ing] what significance the ideas of encyclopedia and theater possessed before their realizations in the sixteenth century, posing the twin ideals of vision and space they share" (12). The following four chapters are all, in some sense, case studies—readings of texts or the works of a particular writer, humanist pedagogue, encyclopedist or polymath, providing an analysis of how the different impulses in the conjoined idea of the theater and encyclopedia were canalized by different genres or mediums.

Chapter 1, "The Space of the Encyclopedia," describes the evolution of the form, charting within that story an essential doubleness epitomized by Rabelais's allegory of encyclopedism in *Pantraguel* (1535), which captures the way the encyclopedia appears as "alternately, and often in the same form, a spring of truth and a pit of error because one of [its] . . . functions . . . is to combine different fields of analysis and coordinate them—theory and practice, active and passive, subject and object, any number of apparently contradictory categories" (15). As the ideology of encyclopedism develops, what permits and stabilizes this perilous doubleness is its separation from the world, enabling readers to "contemplate" or scrutinize "possibilities . . . without their ill effects spilling into the world" (23–24). The encyclopedia serves as a parallel world, then, a space for experiment and counterfactual imagining. The danger derives from the potential paralysis that may ensue from a failure to set limits "to the pure reverie in the marvels of nature [that a reader may experience] and in moving from wonder to action" (35). And this peril West observes is Western culture's "unwitting joke on itself, as it continually reforgets what it knew about the limits of knowing and the irony of trying to take the task seriously" (41). West's key proposition is that this irony is part of the figure of encyclopedism during the early modern period—belief in the form's sufficiency to its task is only a post-Enlightenment "naiveté."

Chapter 2, "The idea of a theatre," describes the impact that the appearance of purpose-built theaters in London during the sixteenth century had on the script of encyclopedism. "To its humanist analysts," observes West, "the 'theatre' they read about in ancient accounts seemed to have nothing to do with contemporary popular performances that they had seen" (44). These performances departed from the humanist ideal in that they were not "unabashedly didactic and ideological" (44). With the building of actual theaters we witness the inherent possibilities in the word *theatrum* play out as the metaphor gets away from its authors, revealing the latent content to the original definition. West makes a good case for the purpose-building of theaters in England as the realization of this sense of separation, elaborating Steven Mullaney's justly famous statement that "popular theaters in England got under way by occupying or taking up a place in the landscape that was not quite proper to it."[1] As the theatrical metaphor material-ized in cities so also did the body of the actor and all the possibili-ties for error, deviation, and pleasure that might lead audiences awry or, in less pathologized terms, to the theater as an end in it-self.

Chapter 3, "Tricks of Vision, Truths of Discourse" focuses on dif-ferent strategies within the *ars combinatoria* or combinatory method of codifying knowledge that is the founding logic of the en-cyclopedia in Camillo's *L'Idea del Theatro* (1550), which serves as the exemplar of the method that aims to produce a combinative guide or metalanguage for phenomena; and Conrad Gessner's *Hist-oriae Animalium* (1551), which offers a different, complementary strategy, producing a lexicon that "provides only the elements that must be combined in a grammar of animals . . . [something akin to a] dictionary" (97). Where Camillo's combinatory method derives a common code by performing its object, Gessner offers an inventory of elements "that one could use to complete a specular project of one's own" (98). While West passes no judgments here, there is a clear preference for the productivity of Gessner's "open system" over the "closed system" of Camillo. Both attempt to regulate the "heteroglossia" or cacophony threatened always by attending to every aspect of a phenomenon, but Gessner's is susceptible to its object—allows it to speak, as it were, and change the scales of what it means to know something.

Chapter 4, "Holding the mirror up to nature?" traces the drift from the humanist conception of physical theater as something "very similar to those set out in the textual theatres" (111) of Ges-sner and Camillo to the deformed spaces of revenge tragedy imag-ined in the *Spanish Tragedy* and *Hamlet*. Here West comes close to articulating the ontological status of drama in performance, and so to providing a potential answer to the problems that haunted New Historicism and Cultural Materialism in their ambiguous placing of the stage as a liminal presence within the representational econ-omy of early modern England. While the implications are not fully explored, West offers this intriguing possibility—that the errancy that both haunts and enables physical theater "forces the theatre into a realm that is neither fully fact nor fiction, neither poesy nor something else, but which levels all distinctions through second-guessing and always demands at least a second corrective reading to rework a first reading that is recognized as insufficient" (142).

West folds this point back into the story he tells and so announces this "indeterminacy . . . [as] the death blow to the humanist idea of the encyclopedia" (142) but the stakes seem much larger here; he provides us with the close analysis of the origins of a rational discourse that inaugurates what is routinely described over a century later as the "public sphere." Furthermore, it seems important for readers to notice the potential here for enlarging our understanding of the way different articulatory spaces (such as the scaffold, theater, encyclopedia, coffeehouse, and pulpit), despite their chronological distance from one another, serve as compeers in a common story.

Chapter 5, "The show of learning and the performance of knowledge," rereads the works of Ben Jonson as an engagement with the very legacy of the encyclopedia that West delivers. Jonson appears here as a hybridizer or experimental dramatist, who produces plays which, like *Every Man in His Humor* (1598) and *Every Man Out of His Humor* (1599), directly address the problem of mechanical repetition and the gap between words and sense. While West makes an interesting case for Jonson responding directly to the idea of encyclopedism, the true payoff comes in the rereadings of the plays themselves—which center characters such as Clove and Orange in *Every Man Out of His Humor* who respond the same way regardless of their situation, dramatizing the limitations of encyclopedic characters, and leading an audience to ask hard questions about interiority, humoral psychology, the alchemy of exchange. Jonson's plays are read as a type of pedagogical program, writing him into the tradition of the "*prudential* or *ethical* encyclopedia" (157) that takes not the library but postprandial table talk as its ideal and conversation or the performance of knowledge as its end. West's reading of the *Alchemist* as a play that produces a "performative knowledge" that reveals "that individuals are not in themselves centered or humorous, but that a social network produces both sorts through the exchange of money and the investment of desire" (192) offers a useful alternative to recent uses of Jonson as a cipher for humoral theory and also to the Jonson we receive from too exclusive a focus on the masque.

Chapter 6 "Francis Bacon's Theatre of Orpheus," completes the arc of the book as the encyclopedia dovetails with experimental science. Though not cast in terms of tropes, the Baconian emphasis on *katabasis*, "sermo rerum" (the discourse of things) (194) or *prosopopeia* and the evidentiary economies each attempts to balance, records an experimental rhetoric that runs through all of his works. West reads the results of Bacon's experiments with the genres of knowledge in the passage from a theater of representation to the scientific laboratory (then and now) where things seem to speak for themselves. The difference, and it is a difference that West would find articulated also in the reading of Bacon that begins Adorno and Horkheimer's *The Dialectic of Enlightenment*,[2] trades heavily on the fact that the Enlightenment rearticulation of the encyclopedia will "forget the second half of Bacon's task—of revealing the technologies through which his science hid its human origins and made itself into pure fact" (196). It is this fracture, this forgetting that produces the two cultures model of the sciences and the humanities as well as the critique of scientific practice from the field known as "science studies," and whose prehistory West describes in this book. Finally, as with Gessner's "open systems," Bacon's radical empiricism that ventures "there is no ground for dismissing any of the meanings in things themselves; Bacon's nature knows no 'no'" (208) and his sense that when things do speak "they must do so with many tongues" (208), marks a positive model of experimental knowledge and receives West's (and I confess my) approval. Again, it is the fact that we are currently living with the legacies of a science that forgets its own rhetoricity that lends West's rereading of Bacon as something other than an avatar of modernity its urgency and critical purchase.

If I were to level one criticism at this otherwise excellent book it would be that West tends to hold his theoretical cards very much to his chest, effectively encrypting his methodology. The effect is ironically that "theatres" and "encyclopedias" actually appear to speak for themselves, even if they speak with many tongues. And to apply West's own terms, he runs the risk that readers more accustomed to the protocols of historicist recovery projects will simply miss the grander scheme of his story and the subtlety of his method in favor of the "wondrous" objects he recovers. Perhaps I am reading too much into the repetition of terms such as "open" and "closed systems" (110), the casual reference to Michel Serres (225), to "inputs" and "outputs" (154–55), a nod here to Foucault or the casual cameo provided by Frederic Jameson in the guise of a Jonsonian character (174–75), but if not, I think West misses a crucial opportunity to establish the usefulness of chaos theory / cybernetics in an historical inquiry, and here in shaping his own reading of "theater" and "encyclopedia" as terms in a self-organizing system that produces local phenomena, which take on their own life, in this case objects familiar to readers of *Shakespeare Studies*, as Renaissance drama and "Shakespeare" him/itself. Whether this omission is merely my projection or stems from modesty, the exigencies of the editorial process, or from a sense that these theoretical investments were somehow secondary to the historical trajectory of the book, it is a real shame that they are not more prominently displayed, for much of that is truly original in this book is conducted in the way texts are read and those readings relate to a larger story. In the final analysis, my misgivings should be judged ungenerous. It is perhaps not itself quite the prudential encyclopedia that West credits to Jonson, but this book certainly repays its reader page for page. Who can ask for more?

Notes

1. Steven Mullaney, *The Place of the Stage* (Ann Arbor: University of Michigan Press, 1988), 8.
2. Max Horkheimer and Theodor W. Adorno, *The Dialectic of Enlightenment*, trans. John Cumming (New York: Continuum, 1990), 3–4.

Index